PUTIN'S HYBRID WAR AND THE JEWS
ANTISEMITISM, PROPAGANDA, AND THE
DISPLACEMENT OF UKRAINIAN JEWRY

Praise for *Putin's Hybrid War and the Jews*

"Sokol's extensive range of interviews with Jewish refugees, fighters, presidents and victims [is] seamlessly woven into the wider context to create a book that is broad in scope but always returns to individual people. The story is tragic and complex, and the book is impossible to put down."
The Moscow Times

"The chosen style may vaguely resemble Elie Wiesel's *The Jews of Silence* on multiple occasions, and while Sam Sokol does not have the poetic artistic style of the Nobel Prize laureate, his book provides a no less important insight into the contemporary Eastern European situation in way that makes it accessible to a very wide audience, Jewish and non-Jewish alike."
Journal of Contemporary Antisemitism

"*Putin's Hybrid War and the Jews* is the most complete account [of] how Ukrainian Jews fared in post-Maidan Ukraine to date. ... While Sokol carefully examines the unfolding events and activities of various agencies and institutions, he never loses focus on the human cost. His book ... brings to light the tragedy of the last few years of the conflict in eastern Ukraine."
New Eastern Europe

"Sokol's book is an important contribution to our knowledge about what happened in Ukraine in 2014 and provides lessons for the way discussions about 'Jews' become part of ... weaponized media propaganda."
The Jerusalem Post

"... does a great job illustrating how Russian propaganda used, and in some cases invented, anti-Semitism for its needs."

Jewish Telegraphic Agency

"The final product is a work well worth reading. *Putin's Hybrid War and the Jews* is full of gripping personal vignettes, important insights, and eyewitness accounts. ... Anyone with a serious interest in Russia and Ukraine, or in Jews in the former Soviet Union, will find this a truly worthwhile read."
Israel Journal of Foreign Affairs

"Sokol handles the political complexities of his subject matter well, presenting the reader with a subtler and more accurate picture than can be found elsewhere."
Mosaic

"… an indispensable book on the response of Ukraine's Jewish community to Russia's invasion of eastern Ukraine. … Sokol has performed a masterful feat in bringing together the strands that make the ongoing Russian-Ukrainian [conflict] understandable, and shedding light on the political background of the present."
Jewish Book Council

"With antisemitism on the ascent around the world and a particularly xenophobic form growing in Eastern Europe, Sam Sokol's *Putin's Hybrid War and the Jews* is especially timely. There has been relatively little reporting on the threats to the Jewish community in Ukraine, and what has been reported on is often misleading. This book pushes back on the propaganda and reports in great detail about the facts on the ground and how Putin's war in Ukraine plays into the larger narrative of Eastern European antisemitism."
Ira Forman, Former US Special Envoy
to Monitor and Combat Antisemitism

"The story of Ukraine's war battered Jews, as told in this timely and important book by Sam Sokol, transcends narrow ethnic interest and provides wider lessons that shed light on both Russia's hybrid war strategy and the politics of memory in the countries of the former Warsaw Pact. He has succeeded in telling an engaging and fluent story of sweeping impact through the eyes of the everyday people who bore witness to Europe's latest conflagration. It is an invaluable contribution."
David Patrikarakos, Author of
War in 140 Characters

"Sam Sokol's *Putin's Hybrid War and the Jews* provides remarkable detail on the dynamics of historical memory in revolutionary Ukraine, and how these dynamics affected the lives of thousands of Ukrainian Jews. The stories of the everyday people who were caught in the grips of a remarkable historical moment, and the ways that moment reflected both changes to and the reestablishment of historical prejudices in Ukrainian society, will serve as an important basis for future work. More important, they offer us a glimpse into the contemporary challenges of addressing and minimizing the social and political roles played today by antisemitism and historical memory of the past."
Robert Williams, former Chair of the IHRA Committee
on Antisemitism and Holocaust Denial

"Sam Sokol takes us on a journey that is both historical in scope and personal in nature, and *Putin's Hybrid War and the Jews* is a page turner, uncovering a poignant and important chapter in Jewish history."

Sarah Tuttle-Singer, Times of Israel

"From personal experience as well as from extensive reading, Samuel Sokol knows the situation in Ukraine intimately. His reports are clearly and engagingly set forth and will be eye-opening for readers interested in learning about the challenges to Jewish life in that country."

Alvin Rosenfeld, Institute for the Study of Contemporary Antisemitism at Indiana University

"Sokol has written an intelligent and well-informed first-hand account of the current conflict in Ukraine, with particular attention to the situation of its Jewish minority. Based upon years of extensive reporting from the region, this is as much an inquiry into the present conflict as a commentary on the complex history of Ukrainian-Jewish relations. At a time and in a region where history is legislated and government agencies are tasked with rehabilitation of the legacies of ultranationalist groups, including those with a brutal legacy of anti-Jewish violence, Sokol's dispassionate and even-handed inquiry of the current conflict is essential reading."

Per A. Rudling, Lund University

"Sam Sokol has distinguished himself as an expert on the impact that the Ukraine revolution and subsequent war have had on the country's Jewish community. This book is borne of years of research and reporting, combined with elegant prose, making it informative and enjoyable to read. I recommend it to anyone concerned about the rise of antisemitism and interested in learning about its contemporary geopolitical context."

Lahav Harkov, Jerusalem Post

"Samuel Sokol has written a timely and deeply reported study, adding nuance to our understanding of Jewish life during Ukraine's Maidan revolution and conflict with Putin's Russia, and debunking in a number of cases false narratives that emerged in the public discussion of these events."

David Loyd Stern
Ukraine-based independent journalist

Sam Sokol

PUTIN'S HYBRID WAR AND THE JEWS

ANTISEMITISM, PROPAGANDA, AND THE DISPLACEMENT OF UKRAINIAN JEWRY

Published by ISGAP
Oxford • Cambridge • New York • Jerusalem • Toronto • Rome
www.isgap.org
info@isgap.org

ISBN 979-8-807402-48-6

*Putin's Hybrid War and the Jews: Antisemitism, Propaganda,
and the Displacement of Ukrainian Jewry*

First edition 2019
Second edition 2022
© Sam Sokol and ISGAP 2019, 2022

The Institute for the Study of Global Antisemitism and Policy (ISGAP) is dedicated to the academic study of antisemitism and others forms of prejudice. The opinions expressed in this work are those of the author and do not necessarily reflect the views of ISGAP, its officers, or the members of its boards.

The ISGAP monograph series is edited by Charles Asher Small.

Cover design and layout by AETS
Cover image courtesy of Larisa Lavrenchuk and Svoboda: Ukrainian ultranationalists from the Svoboda party march with torches in Kyiv

For dad,
Who taught me to love the written word

Contents

Preface

On Thursday, February 24, 2022, Russian forces, which had been massing on the border for months, invaded Ukraine in order to, in President Vladimir Putin's words, "demilitarize and denazify" the former Soviet republic.

Putin's unwarranted attack on a peaceful neighbor, which he justified on the grounds of "protect[ing] people who, for eight years now, have been facing humiliation and genocide," was greeted with disdain by Ukrainian Jews, who had suffered greatly from Russian aggression over the preceding eight years.

As I write these words, thousands of Ukrainian Jews have joined their Ukrainian countrymen in streaming over the border to Poland and Moldova, with many others hunkered down as the Russian army ravages their land. I can't know what will happen in the days ahead, but I do know that the story of how we got to this point is a critical one that must be told in order to refute Russia's malicious and cynical propaganda.

This is a work inspired and shaped by guilt. While I was born into a life of middle class comfort in New York City in the early 1980s, my mother had come into the world in a displaced persons (DP) camp in Germany following the Second World War. Born to Polish Holocaust survivors, she arrived in the United States not speaking a word of English and her early years were ones of struggle. As I grew up, she would recount how her parents' tales of the Holocaust gave her nightmares, and I, in turn, began dreaming of the Gestapo marching down West End Avenue. As the years passed, I learned in school about the endless parade of pogroms, expulsions, and inquisitions that were inflicted upon my time-battered people since the destruction of the Temple in Jerusalem by the Romans in the first century CE.

When I was assigned the Jewish World beat at the *Jerusalem Post* in early 2013, it was a period of rising antisemitism. Jews in Continental Europe were extremely anxious regarding the future. Buffeted by the twin threats of Muslim Judeophobia and antisemitic right-wing populism, they were suffering from increasing threats against both their physical safety and religious liberties. Efforts to ban kosher slaughter in Poland and circumcision in Germany were accompanied by the rise of antisemitic parties such as Jobbik in Hungary and Golden Dawn in Greece. At the time, it almost felt as if a day didn't pass without news of a new antisemitic incident in Paris or Brussels, purportedly the safe centers of our progressive western civilization.

In late 2013, when hundreds of thousands of angry Ukrainians took to the streets to protest their country's corrupt post-Soviet government, many of my colleagues turned their eyes to Kyiv. After all, among the most prominent (and violent) of the anti-government demonstrators were members of Svoboda, a vocally antisemitic ultra-nationalist party. I was far from the only journalist who covered the protests and subsequent war from a Jewish perspective, but as the conflict dragged on and increasing numbers of Jews were displaced the number of my colleagues continuing to travel to Ukraine rapidly decreased. I, however, felt compelled to continue covering the conflict, seeing my mother and grandparents in the miserable refugees who had lost everything to a war in which both sides used the specter of antisemitism as a propaganda weapon but could not really care less about the Jews.

Two trends quickly emerged. The first was the use of anti-semitic leitmotifs in Russia's hybrid-war strategy, in which the Kremlin used the threat of Ukrainian action against the Jews as a justification for its revanchism. Jews and other national minorities, the propaganda line went, were in danger from the xenophobia of Ukraine's newly installed "fascist junta." Of course, this was pure agitprop, but that didn't stop Russia's state-controlled media from unleashing a torrent of fake news asserting that Ukraine's Jews were being harassed and displaced by a hostile administration. Ironically, the biggest displacement of Jewish life was caused by the takeover of Ukraine's industrial Donbas region by Russian-backed separatists who were ostensibly there for their protection. In a matter of months, communities which had been painstakingly rebuilt after decades of communism were scattered to the winds. The second trend was an intensification of Ukrainian nationalism in the face of Moscow's land grab. In response to outside aggression, the Ukrainian government began constructing an alternate national historiography honoring those who fought against the Soviet Union, rehabilitating virulently racist Nazi collaborators such as Stepan Bandera and Roman Shukhevych. Meanwhile, the blatant hate-mongering of contemporary far-right militias fighting the Russians was tolerated as senior administration officials forged ties with vigilantes and militants, who would eventually violently turn against members of their country's Roma and LGBT communities.

Caught between the torments of the dead, who have been denied the minimal dignity of accurate remembrance, and the suffering of the living, cursed with the burden of exile, there was simply no way that I could turn away and remain sane. In his seminal novel *Babi Yar*, the Ukrainian writer Anatoli Kuznetsov described the reasons which impelled him to risk his life and freedom to write truthfully in the face of communist censorship. I think that his words, printed during the height of the Cold War, ring true today in our age of hybrid conflict and perfectly capture my own emotions, all these decades later.

"I did not write this book simply to recall the past: I am writing today about the occupation of Kiev, which I happened to witness and which is well documented; because the same sort of thing is happening now; and there is no guarantee whatever that even more sinister events will not occur tomorrow. Not the slightest guarantee … The world has learnt nothing. It has become only a more gloomy place. It is crammed with misguided puppets and unthinking blockheads who, with the light of fanatical conviction in their eyes, are ready to shoot at any target their leaders may command, and trample underfoot any country they are sent to; and it is frightful to think of the weapons they have in their hands today. If you tell them out loud, to their faces, that they are being deceived and that they are no more than cannon fodder and tools in the hands of scoundrels, they won't listen. They will say it is only a malicious slander. And if you produce facts, they just won't believe you. They will say: 'Such things never happened.'"[1]

Someone has to bear witness so that one day we can look back and recall that these events did, in fact, occur.

I would not have been able to tell these stories without the support of many extraordinary individuals, starting with Dr. Charles Asher Small of the *Institute for the Study of Global Antisemitism and Policy* (ISGAP). I owe him my undying gratitude for all of his encouragement and support. Ilan Evyatar and Steve Linde, respectively the News Editor and Editor-in-Chief of the *Jerusalem Post* during my tenure there, provided me with the latitude to continue reporting on Ukraine even when many at the paper thought my interest had turned into an unhealthy obsession. I could not have organized all of my material without the help of my intern Daniel Ofman, who helped me create timelines, conduct interviews and translate material. Tanya Olevsky assisted me in transcribing and translating more than 60 hours of recorded interviews in Hebrew and Russian, and without her this project would never have gotten off the ground.

After leaving the *Post,* I continued reporting on Ukrainian Jews for a number of publications, both in Israel and abroad. In writing this revised and expanded edition of *Putin's Hybrid War and the Jews*, I have adapted reporting previously published by the *Forward*, the *Times of Israel*, *Kyiv Post*, the *Jewish Chronicle*, and the Jewish Telegraphic Agency. I would like to thank all of my editors at these august publications for permitting me to reproduce parts of my reporting in expanding this book. I would especially like to thank the *Times of Israel*'s David Horovitz, who sent me on my final reporting trip to Ukraine in January 2020, immediately prior to the outbreak of the Covid-19 pandemic and the concomitant global aviation shutdown.

In May 2021, I joined the team at the English edition of Israel's storied *Haaretz* daily. As of the writing of this revised preface, around a quarter of Ukraine's overall population has been displaced by the Russian invasion. Thousands more have been killed, with both Kyiv and Washington accusing Russian forces, which have targeted civilian neighborhoods and besieged the city of Mariupol, of war crimes. Since the first Russian troops crossed the Ukrainian border, I have spent nearly all of my time in the *Haaretz* newsroom covering Israel's response to the emerging crisis under the leadership of excellent editors such as Avi Scharf, Amir Tibon, Yishai Halper, Jillian Jones, and Jonathan Gorodischer.

I am a reporter, not an academic and cannot thank enough Dr. Per Anders Rudling of Lund University, Dr. Jared McBride of UCLA, and Dr. Tarik Cyril Amar of Koç University for reviewing my work, providing me with copious amounts of background material, and exhibiting almost superhuman patience with my constant questions. I have cited them all at length in this book. Dr. Kiril Feferman of Ariel University and Chabad.org's Dovid Margolin provided invaluable explanations of Chabad Hasidic politics. I am also indebted to Dr. Dovid Katz of Vilnius Gediminas Technical University, a scholar and activist whose work on Double Genocide Theory is key to understanding contemporary memory politics in the FSU. Izabella Tabarovsky of the Wilson Center, Josh Cohen, and Lev Golinkin have been incredible resources, and I thank them for their feedback. Avi Woolf read and critiqued portions of the book, improving its flow immensely. Vladislav Davidzon of *Tablet Magazine* was a friendly sounding board who challenged my ideas. Dr. Laurence Weinbaum of the Israel Council on Foreign Relations has both encouraged me and published some of my writings on the issue of national memory in the *Israel Journal of Foreign Affairs*, providing me with an opportunity to see how my approach was received by the scholarly community, for which I am deeply grateful. None of this would have been possible without the help of Ukrainian-Israeli journalists Shimon Briman and Alex Kogan, who sent me links, provided me with contacts, and schooled me on Ukrainian Jewry.

Finally, I must thank my mother and father for inculcating in me a deep and abiding love of reading that eventually led me to journalism. More than any other person, I have to thank my lovely wife Chava, who took upon herself to run things during my frequent absences, encourage me when I was down, and show me love when I was distracted and irritable. She is truly a woman of valor. And above all, I give thanks to G-d who gave me life, sustained me, and allowed me to reach this day.

I pray that further bloodshed can be avoided and that peace will once again return to Ukraine.

Sam Sokol
Beit Shemesh
March 27, 2022

CHAPTER ONE

ARRIVAL IN KYIV

Kyiv
December 12, 2013

The freezing wind cut through my thin leather jacket and tattered Yankees cap as I ducked my head low between my shoulders and hugged my arms for warmth. My sneakers crunched through Kyiv's December snow as I made my way through the Ukrainian capital, intent on reaching the city's central square, known as the Maidan. Ahead of me a line of minibuses stretched perpendicular to the street, blocking off access. I continued my slow march through the frigid conditions, placing one numb foot in front of the other, intent only on skirting the blockade, when an armored member of the Berkut, Ukraine's riot police, yelled something in unintelligible Russian and motioned for me to head back.

"What the hell am I doing here," I wondered as I turned away, searching for a clear path between my hotel and the site of Ukraine's second popular revolt in less than a decade.

At the time I was the Diaspora Correspondent for the *Jerusalem Post*—with a beat that encompassed Jewish communal, religious, and political life on several continents—and I had been lured (or, more accurately, had lured myself) to this former Soviet republic's capital by the promise of a story involving antisemitism, neo-Nazis, and a violent revolution that had many of the country's approximately 70,000 Jews[1] in the grips of existential fear. I would soon learn that things are rarely that simple.

I soon found myself walking down Khreshchatyk Street—a wide boulevard that serves as downtown Kyiv's main shopping district—and coming across another set of barricades. Rather than being made of buses and backed by masked and armed police, however, this barrier belonged to the protesters and was a slapdash affair put together from aluminum siding, park benches, wooden beams, bags of snow, and any other detritus that its builders had been able to scrounge within the confines of the territory they has staked out.

Before entering the Maidan proper, however, I was determined to enter the belly of the beast (as I grandiosely thought of it at the time), the Kyiv City Council building, which had recently been taken by fighters loyal to the far-right nationalist Svoboda party and turned into a makeshift protest headquarters.

It was primarily my interest in Svoboda that had brought me to Kyiv. How, I wondered, was the local Jewish community faring during a revolution in which radical antisemites were playing such a prominent role?

Blocking the doors of the imposing Soviet era municipal building were several masked men wearing Svoboda armbands and orange construction helmets, one of which was emblazoned with the Wolfsangel, a Germanic symbol popular among neo-Nazis. I joined a line of protesters and we moved forward as, one by one, the helmeted nationalists allowed us through the wooden and glass doors into the building's lobby. Barely breathing as I walked past Svoboda propaganda plastered across the foyer's walls, I made my way through the crowd and up a grand marble stairway to the second floor where helmeted men were rolling up fire hoses on the slick tiles next to the windows overlooking the street below.

At one in the morning, only hours before my arrival from Tel Aviv, the police had stormed the barricades and attempted to enter the building, only to be driven back by protesters firing high-pressure jets of water. Perversely, distress that I had missed the fighting mingled with relief that I had not been present when the fighting had broken out.

Entering the building's two-story tall main chamber, my heart pounded as I gazed at the Svoboda banners hanging limply from the gallery, each with its yellow hand against a blue field flashing an eternal victory sign. Standing in the center of the grand plenum chamber of Kyiv's Stalinist Gothic city council building, young men in combat boots and army helmets jostling around me, I felt intensely alone. Alongside the Svoboda flags were suspended the black and red standard of the Ukrainian Insurgent Army, an extreme nationalist militia which had carried out an infamous "campaign of ethnic cleansing of Poles, Jews, and other minorities" during the Second World War.[2] Protesters sleeping on floor mats filled much of the floor space around the edge of the hall, many with gas masks and helmets kept on the cold marble within easy reach. Several men draped in Ukraine's blue and yellow flags slept upright in velvet upholstered wooden chairs in the center of the room, while a party leader standing on a stage harangued the mob over a public address system.

Unnerved by my surroundings, I struck up a conversation with a young man, a linguist by trade, who sought to reassure me that, despite the fears of many in the Jewish community, there was no real danger of an outbreak of antisemitism, even with the active participation of Svoboda in the protests. "I've been teased and called a Jew by friends for standing up against antisemitism, and I support Svoboda here," he said, adding that he believed that the opposition must be supported as an alternative to an inept and corrupt ruling elite. It wasn't very comforting.

Turning to leave I ran into a small table near the stage manned by a diminutive and elderly woman with a doughy face and red knit cap. The table held a number of items sporting the Svoboda logo. When she looked away I quickly pocketed a small flag and made my way back down the stairs and into the street. Suddenly, I was able to breath again.

In the city council chamber, I had hooked up with a local television crew. After we left they brought me through the barricades and into a building housing the revolutionaries' media center, where I was given my press credentials. Thus armed with as much protection as a small piece of paper issued by anti-government forces could provide, I set out to meet with a representative of the Jewish community. As I made my way back out of the Maidan and away from the hub of the conflict, the streets became progressively calmer and quieter. I was trying to find the address of the Ukrainian Jewish Committee (UJC), an advocacy group funded by Aleksandr Feldman, a Jewish oligarch and member of parliament who had been outspoken in his criticism of the protesters.

Only meters from the UJC's offices, I stopped, transfixed by a swastika scrawled outside a small restaurant. "This can't be real," I thought. By that time, frozen both in spirit and in body, I had wrapped myself up as tightly as possible, my face hidden between the upturned collar of my jacket and the lowered brim of my hat, making me unidentifiable at a glance. I had forgotten that I was carrying the Svoboda flag. Glancing up as I entered, the secretary took one look at me and began to scream.

But let's back up. How did I get here?

THE GROWING THREAT

"The enemy came … but they were not afraid; likewise we must not be afraid. [Our people] hung their machine guns on their necks and went into the woods. They fought against the Russians, Germans, Jews, and other scum who wanted to take away our Ukrainian state! And therefore our task—for every one of you, the young, the old, the gray-headed and the youthful—is to defend our native land!"

—Oleh Tiahnybok[3]

Budapest, Hungary
May 5, 2013

It was a chilly evening in the Hungarian capital of Budapest seven months earlier when Ronald Lauder ascended the podium at the World Jewish Congress's fourteenth plenary assembly. As President of the Congress, Lauder was about to issue a dire warning regarding the political resurgence of the far right in Europe on behalf of the collective Jewish communities of the world. Addressing Hungary's conservative president Viktor Orban in front of hundreds of delegates, Lauder recalled the rise of totalitarian parties and states in the early years of the twentieth century and asserted that "today we are seeing, once again, growing ignorance, growing intolerance [and] growing hatred."

Expressing the growing concerns of his constituents, he remarked that not only was the growth of the neo-Nazi Jobbik party in Hungary a source of worry but so were similar developments in "Greece, in Ukraine and elsewhere," an obvious reference to the Golden Dawn and Svoboda parties. All three factions had broken into the political mainstream within a few years of each other, and their rhetoric was extreme enough that two days after Lauder's speech the WJC passed a resolution calling for them to be banned.[4]

Founded as the Social National Party of Ukraine shortly after Ukrainian independence in the early 1990s, the party that would later come to be known as Svoboda early on positioned itself as the heir of the Organization of Ukrainian Nationalists—also known as the OUN—a brutally violent and authoritarian Ukrainian ultra-nationalist organization that collaborated with the Nazis. Due to its adoption of the Wolfsangel as its symbol and its recruitment of skinheads, the party was such an unpalatable option for Ukrainian voters that few would have regarded it as an eventual contender for political power.[5]

In fact, as recently as 2011, Anton Shekhovtsov, a Ukrainian expert on the far right,[6] could state that Ukraine was unique in that "there has been no overtly nationalist group in the parliament (Verkhovna Rada) since independence, and no Ukrainian radical right-wing political party as such has ever been elected" to the legislature.[7] However, despite only garnering less than one percent support in parliamentary elections in 2006, the party made steady gains in local races until, in 2012, it managed to obtain eight percent of the national vote. Suddenly Svoboda had 37 out of 450 seats in the Rada. Although the party was most popular in western Ukraine, where the legacies of the OUN and its offshoot the Ukrainian Insurgent Army (UPA) were still celebrated, it is believed that this breakout beyond its natural base of support had less to do with Svoboda's ideology and more with its decision to position itself as an alternative to a political class widely regarded as corrupt.[8]

Ironically, the success of Svoboda may have been, in some ways, directly attributable to Viktor Yanukovych and his pro-Russian Party of Regions. Secret party ledgers released in 2016 by government investigators purported to show a cash payment of 200,000 dollars to Svoboda, adding weight to previously unproven allegations[9] that the President was supporting extremists in order to delegitimize his opponents as racists. Whatever Yanukovych's role in Svoboda's rise, efforts by the group's leadership to shake off their image as a gathering of hooligans certainly played a crucial role in legitimizing the party as a mainstream actor. As soon as he ascended to the leadership in 2004, current party head Oleh Tiahnybok began a vigorous rebranding campaign, which included swapping out its Nazi-tainted logo and changing his organization's name to Svoboda, which means freedom in Ukrainian. Despite such superficial changes, however, the antisemitic nature of Svoboda under Tiahnybok was obvious to even the most casual observer.

In 2004, shortly after the rebranding began, Tiahnybok gave a speech in which he praised the OUN and UPA for fighting "against the Muscovite, Germans, Jews, and other scum who wanted to take away our Ukrainian state." Turning to the present day, he further alleged that a "Jewish-Russian mafia" had taken over the country. The connection was hard to miss. The following year he went even further, writing to then-President Viktor Yushchenko to demand that Kyiv "stop the criminal activity of organized Jewry." This activity, he asserted, included a plan for a genocide[10] of ethnic Ukrainians. As the years went by, the Svoboda leader's rhetoric continued to escalate, and in 2008 he gave a speech alleging that Jews and Russians had "seized power," necessitating "a tough, merciless purge." He would later call to close down all Jewish organizations in the country and lobby to block the annual influx of Jewish pilgrims to the grave of the Hasidic Rabbi Nachman of Breslov in Uman. Needless to say, such rhetoric, especially after the 2012 elections, did nothing to calm the fears of Ukrainian Jewry. But while Ukrainian Jews were united in their opposition to Svoboda, they diverged radically in how they proposed to deal with the perceived threat.

Kyiv
April 23, 2013

A month before flying to Hungary to cover Lauder's speech, I was in Ukraine for the 2013 Kyiv Interfaith Forum, an annual conference organized by Aleksandr Feldman. I had come in order to see for myself how members of Ukrainian civil society were responding to the major changes wracking their country. On the first evening of the conference, I was walking down the street with an acquaintance from Israel when we stumbled upon a statue of a Jewish moneychanger located outside a theme restaurant. The figure was hunched over, his long beaked nose aimed, together with his intense gaze, at the piles of ersatz coins on the table before him. A large neon sign in the shape of a bearded Hasid illuminated the storefront, while in a corridor leading inside I found frescos of Jews gracing the walls, including a caricature of a confused looking orthodox man with long side-curls and a gigantic hook nose.

Turning and hurrying away, I immediately, and shamefully, took off my kippa, worried about the imagined dangers of walking the nighttime streets of a city where such an eatery would make enough money to stay in business. Images of Gil Shefler, my predecessor at the *Post*, beaten and bloodied in Athens, flashed through my head as I scuttled furtively back to my hotel. Just a year earlier, Gil had been on a similar assign-ment, attempting to make contact with the Golden Dawn party when he was beaten by a mob wielding bats and clubs.[11] Street violence against Jews was not, and still isn't, a common occur-rence in Ukraine,[12] but the prevalence of antisemitic rhetoric in the political discourse, coupled with the sight of images that could have come straight out of *Der Stürmer*, was extremely disturbing, especially to a grandchild of Holocaust survivors.

Testifying before the House Foreign Affairs Subcommittee on Human Rights two months earlier, Ukraine's US-born Chief Rabbi Yaakov Dov Bleich,[13] co-founder of the Jewish Confedera-tion of Ukraine, had warned against "overstating" the problem of hate, given that independent manifestations of antisemitism in popular culture had declined and antisemitic attacks were rare.[14] Others, however, were less sanguine about the dangers posed by Svoboda. Only weeks after Bleich's remarks, a number of Ukrainian Jewish and non-Jewish civil society figures[15] sent a letter to Jewish Agency Chairman Natan Sharansky arguing against the quasi-governmental organization holding its upcom-ing board of governors meeting in Kyiv.[16] Like Sharansky, Josef Zissels, the letter's primary driver, was a former Soviet dissident. Now, in his role as the chairman of the Association of Jewish

Organizations and Communities (Vaad) of Ukraine, Zissels was calling on his fellow refusenik to refrain from any moves which would "provoke an increase in antisemitic attitudes."

Zissels and his colleagues' call was rebuffed by Sharansky, as well as by other prominent local communal figures, who argued that they did not represent Ukrainian Jewry. Among those protesting Zissels's call was Aleksandr Feldman (at the time affiliated with Yanukovych's Party of Regions), who asserted that most of the letter's signatories were "not Jews, but active Ukrainian opposition [politicians]." His objections to the kind of rhetoric employed by figures such as Zissels, however, did not prevent him from opining on the dangers of Svoboda during my visit. The Jewish MP accused Svoboda of engaging in cynical economic populism to court the disadvantaged, alleging that the nationalists viewed the Jews as a "useful and convenient target." And while a significant amount of the party's support was apparently the result of Ukrainians casting protest votes, their support for Svoboda had the unintended side effect of eroding an already weak cultural stigma against public displays of antisemitism. "What used to be shameful and hidden is getting pretty obvious," he complained.

✶✶✶

The evening after my encounter with the moneylender, I sat sipping a vodka in a dim bar with Eduard Dolinsky.[17] A youthful looking man in his mid-forties with a broad face and receding light brown hair, Eduard was the director of the Ukrainian Jewish Committee. He would, in the years to come, become known as one of the most outspoken and caustic Jewish figures in Kyiv. Nursing his drink, his trademark jeweled Menorah pin sparkling in the low light, Eduard confirmed that the Jewish community was somewhat in disarray since the last elections. "No one expected Svoboda to gain so many seats. Every Jewish community in Ukraine, every Jewish organization, is actually on alert. [They] do not yet have a solution and a plan."

But, he announced grimly, "we are ready to fight."[18]

CHAPTER TWO

RUN-UP TO REVOLUTION

"Piss off, you Jewish garbage!"

—Euromaidan protesters to oligarch Petro Poroshenko

Kyiv
November 21, 2013

It was a freezing winter day in Kyiv when Prime Minister Mykola Azarov made the last-minute announcement that Ukraine had decided not to sign an association agreement with the European Union. Such issues, seemingly dull and esoteric, are generally of little import to most people, and Azarov likely thought that there would be little, if any, domestic response. Certainly, if Yanukovych had known that it would spark a revolution that would sweep him out of power, he would probably have made a different decision.

Following Azarov's announcement, opposition politicians and angry students began calling for a gathering on the Maidan Nezalezhnosti, or Independence Square, the sprawling plaza in central Kyiv that had served as the epicenter of massive anti-Yanukovych protests a decade earlier. By the next evening some two thousand souls had congregated in the Maidan. Violent crackdowns by the Berkut riot police galvanized the public, causing the protests to swell in size as even those with no emotional investment in closer European integration grew angered over the televised images of governmental brutality. Within days, the crowd had grown to several hundred thousand people. Over the coming days, barricades went up in the center of Kyiv, surrounding an impromptu protest camp in which a festive and colorful, almost gay atmosphere prevailed. The wide boulevards between the imposing stone government buildings filled up with so many people that just crossing the street became nearly impossible. And as the protests grew, so did the far right's presence in the square.

Shortly after the beginning of the protests, the Svoboda party joined forces with boxer-turned-politician Vitaliy Klitschko's Ukrainian Democratic Alliance for Reform and Yulia Tymoshenko's Fatherland faction (then lead by Arseniy Yatsenyuk) to form the Action Committee of National Resistance, an umbrella organization intended to attempt to coordinate the largely decentralized anti-government protests. Alongside Svoboda, the far right was represented by Right Sector (Pravy Sektor), a coalition formed out of a variety of "radical and openly anti-Semitic"[1] groups for the purpose of serving as the defensive arm of the revolution. Among the groups represented in Right Sector were Patriot of Ukraine, a paramilitary group previously affiliated with Svoboda, and the Social-National Assembly, a union of neo-Nazi organizations. Right Sector, which only had several hundred members, played a disproportionate role in defending the barricades against the Berkut and Titushky (hired thugs used by the government).[2]

The sight of Ukrainian protesters brandishing antisemitic symbols such as the Wolfsangel and the Celtic Cross was immensely disturbing to many in the organized Jewish community. As the days went by, more and more black and red UPA banners appeared alongside the blue and yellow Ukrainian national flag throughout the square. Accompanying the signs were several cartoons pinned up on walls depicting antisemitic themes, including one portraying Jewish oligarch Ihor Kolomoisky devouring Ukraine.[3] In an incident demonstrating the anti-semitism of some of the protesters, chocolate magnate (and future president) Petro Poroshenko was verbally assaulted while visiting the Maidan. While not Jewish himself, Poroshenko was subjected to jeers, with some protesters screaming "piss off, you Jewish garbage,"[4] a reference to the conspiracy theory that he was secretly a Jew named Valtzman. Only days later, standing on a stage in the Maidan, a speaker exhorted the crowd "to protect the white race"[5] and "not to give in to the Jews."

In mid-December, when I arrived in the Maidan, there was evidence of alcohol consumption throughout the square. Garbage cans and gutters in the surrounding streets were filled with vodka and beer bottles. Chatting with the cashier of a kosher grocery located next to the Brodsky Choral Synagogue—an imposing late nineteenth century Romanesque structure located less than two kilometers from the protests—I heard of the community's fear. Drunk protesters posed a danger should they decide to turn against the Jews, the bearded Hasid sitting behind the counter in the narrow and dark shop fretted, citing as support for his concerns several local websites which he said were keeping a running tally of the political views of prominent Jewish figures. While antisemitism had not been an issue the last time Ukrainians had come out into the streets en masse a decade earlier, Jews have long memories and Ukraine has a history of violence. Between 1905 and 1919, tens of thousands of Ukrainian Jews had been murdered in pogroms connected to the political upheaval then engulfing the Russian Empire. There was certainly ample precedent for the shopkeeper's worries.

The first days of the protests coincided with the holiday of Hanukkah, a synchronicity which posed a conundrum for the leaders of Kyiv's Jewish communities who were used to celebrating the holiday in public. Two distinct approaches would soon emerge.[6]

Rabbi Moshe Azman, a member of the Chabad Hasidic sect and the Rabbi of the Brodsky Synagogue, expressed serious concerns about safety.[7] After lighting the Menorah in the capital's Central Synagogue, he "announced the cancellation of all the events and performances" due to fear of Svoboda and "hooligans."[8] Rabbi Jonathan Markovitch, the leader of a competing Chabad community in Kyiv, took a radically different approach. In his eyes, there was no connection between the protests and the Jewish community, and his community continued to hold public events, including Menorah lightings, in honor of the holiday.[9]

Kyiv
December 15, 2013

Markovitch was not the only one to ignore Azman's warning for Jews to keep their heads down. Josef Zissels, the outspoken head of the Vaad of Ukraine, had come out strongly in favor of the Euromaidan movement. The Vaad claimed to speak for 265 local organizations throughout Ukraine, although Azman countered that many of them were defunct and that Zissels was largely irrelevant. Regardless of his communal leadership role, or lack thereof, Zissels's involvement was a real coup for a protest movement dogged by accusations of antisemitism.

Short and thin with a neat gray beard and unruly hair, Zissels[10] has proven to be a divisive figure among Ukrainian Jews, due in part to his early initial embrace of the Euromaidan. It was 30 degrees Fahrenheit, below freezing, on the day that Zissels strode out onto the large stage erected by the protesters on Khreshchatyk Street directly across from Kyiv's Independence Monument—a bronze statue of the mythical Berehynia atop a tall, slender marble column. Wearing a thick green coat atop a dark sweater, his black hood thrown back over his shoulders, Zissels stood beside opposition leader and future Prime Minister Arseniy Yatsenyuk, his speech firmly clutched in his hands.

According to Zissels—who told the crowd he was speaking specifically in his capacity as a Jew—the Yanukovych government was attempting to divide Ukrainian citizens by demonizing the opposition as fascists and racists.[11] Rejecting the objections of other prominent Jews, who had endorsed a policy of communal neutrality, Zissels called for his coreligionists to participate in the revolution en masse. The Jews, he said, had always "followed an instinct of self-preservation available to communities living in a diaspora" and, by necessity, tended to be government loyalists. However, such a policy was not suited to contemporary Ukraine, and the Jewish community, as a collective, faced a binary choice between endorsing the protesters or siding with an "authoritarian regime" dedicated to "thievery and corruption."

"Three thousand years ago my people took forty years to walk from slavery to freedom," he declared. "We—the people of Ukraine—have already gone halfway. There is not much longer to go!"[12]

The aging anti-communist wasn't the only Jewish figure to ascend the stage in the Maidan that December. Sporting a bushy beard just beginning to go gray under a broad-brimmed black hat, Hillel Cohen looked like a Hasid out of central casting. A member of the Breslover sect who had immigrated from Israel, he was best known as the director of Hatzalah Ukraina, a small emergency services organization and couldn't legitimately speak for any of Kyiv's organized Jewish communities. He was nevertheless asked by Zissels to address the crowd during an interfaith prayer for peace, most likely, Cohen later mused, because he "had the appearance of a rabbi."

Staring down at the rostrum, Cohen spoke slowly and monotonously, making small gestures with his hands and describing Ukraine's "need for peace."[13]

While Cohen later praised himself for his "courageous" actions, communal leaders were unimpressed. "None of the rabbis agreed to go," recalled Zvika Klein, who covered the protests for the Israeli daily *Maariv*. "Everybody was talking about this. It was a big disgrace for the Jewish community, especially since the Jewish community was very cautious about not taking any sides … they wanted to be neutral … for once they actually spoke [with] one voice." One such leader who declined to speak at the Maidan was Alexander Dukhovny, Ukraine's Chief Reform Rabbi, who believed that addressing the crowd could be dangerous for both himself personally and for his congregants.[14] However, as we shall soon see, while the leadership of the organized synagogue communities were mostly opposed to taking sides or getting involved, many of their less strongly affiliated coreligionists would take the opportunity to become intensely political.

ON THE BARRICADES

"I really don't want to walk next to the people walking with the Svoboda flags and I don't think it's the right thing to do. … Most of my friends are very hesitant to walk around those people, and we really do not tolerate when people say that Jews should not be here. But generally, it's more on Facebook; but once you're at Maidan and you are there in the atmosphere it's kind of [different] they don't care about it that much."

—Alexandra Oleynikova

Kyiv
December 29, 2013

Only days after Cohen's address calling for inter-religious comity, the Maidan stage hosted a show inciting the exact opposite when actor turned Svoboda MP Bogdan Benyuk took to the boards in a play widely seen as deeply antisemitic.[15] Affecting a mock Yiddish accent and wearing a black hat, ersatz side-curls, and a wide white scarf meant to look like a prayer shawl, Benyuk played a Jewish character dubbed *zhyd*, a deeply offensive term for Jews synonymous with the English slur kike.[16] In an op-ed for the *Huffington Post* condemning the protests, Aleksandr

Feldman described the play, which he saw as a metaphor for the Maidan, in stark and disturbing terms.

> "Benyuk ... play[ed] a stereotypical Orthodox Jewish wheeler-dealer character ... who creates obstacles for the new-born Jesus from behind the scenes, and contemplates taking a bribe from a character evoking both King Herod and President Yanukovych to help him crush the protestors. Explaining to the crowd that he is involved in various occupations, including banking, stock market speculation, loan sharking, and hosting a talk show, the Jewish oligarch character sings gleefully, 'East and West belong to me; our people are everywhere.' Fascinatingly, however, the Jew switches sides and joins the opposition when he learns that on orders from Herod/Yanukovych, the regime's special forces are preparing to kill the first-born. Nevertheless, the audience is given to understand, the character apparently changes course not necessarily due to a belated outburst of conscience but rather because, in the last analysis, 'There is no greater fighter than a frightened Jew.'"[17]

Kyiv
January 1, 2014

Two days later, on New Year's Eve, Kyiv's nationalists marched along Khreshchatyk Street shouting jingoistic slogans and carrying red and black UPA flags in honor of the birthday of Stepan Bandera, the wartime leader of the Organization of Ukrainian Nationalists.[18] Organized by Svoboda and attended by around fifteen thousand people,[19] the march was a paean to a figure reviled by many for his racism and authoritarianism.

Despite its initial collaboration, the Bandera faction of the OUN broke with the Germans after declaring an independent Ukrainian state in 1941. Bandera himself ended the war incarcerated in a German concentration camp. And while the relationship between Ukrainian nationalists and Nazis may have been complex, their views on Jews and other minorities were decidedly less so: the OUN(b)'s 1941 manifesto called on its members to "liquidate undesirable Poles, Muscovites, and Jews."[20]

Among the slogans being shouted by the marchers was "glory to the nation, death to its enemies." This was a chilling phrase with disturbing connotations for those who understood its significance. Not everybody did. Denying that it had any anti-semitic subtext when used by the protesters, Igor, a Ukrainian expat who returned home from Germany to join the Maidan, told me in mid-December that those screaming it had nothing against Jews or other minorities. Holding aloft a banner urging Yanukovych to resign, he asserted that many people chanted nationalist slogans without understanding their meaning. Not everybody agreed. Eduard Dolinsky recalled how one Orthodox Israeli of his acquaintance was rebuffed when he attempting to take part in the demonstrations. The protesters told him that they did "not need Jews or Russians to look over us any more."

Local Jews' experiences and perspectives on the Maidan varied greatly depending on their age, education, and level of religious observance. Many young Jews, acting as Ukrainian citizens rather than as members of a specific religious subculture, did indeed take part in the Euromaidan and testified to a broad acceptance by the other protesters. According to activist Alexandra Oleynikova, while many Jews had stayed away out of fear, others had flocked to the Maidan and "were on the front lines of the fighting." However, she added, nobody went out of their way to advertise their religion. Alexander Iudashkin, another Jewish protester, agreed, saying that "nobody runs and screams 'I hate Jews' or anything like that, but you can hear it between the words sometimes."[21]

Anna Beskorovaynaya, a resident of Kyiv's Moishe House, the local branch of a global network of Jewish co-living spaces, had a more upbeat view of the protesters. While her roommates stayed home out of anxiety,[22] she went out to bring them supplies and described the Jewish community as being "full of volunteers." Like other young Jewish Maidan activists interviewed for this book, Beskorovaynaya seemed unconcerned about the possibility of antisemitism. Citing persistent rumors regarding Petro Poroshenko's supposed Jewish roots, she asserted that such talk was actually indicative of a positive trend in Ukrainian society. "People are talking about his Jewish roots because he is part Jewish. ... Now Jewish culture is a trend. So you have to understand that being Jewish is super cool right now." However, despite the optimism of Beskorovaynaya and many of her fellow Maidan supporters, as January wore on and the demonstrations escalated, so too did attacks on the Jews.

HUNTING SEASON

"Our home was full of people ... frightened [and] bewildered. ... There is a nasty Russian saying 'when there is no water in the taps it means that Jews drank it all.' ... That's the first thing that occurred to [us]. Where people are hungry they are looking for someone to blame. [Especially] when Putin is too strong and too far away and we are here. It was frightening."
—Elka Markovitch

Podil District, Kyiv
January 11, 2014

It was a Saturday evening when Hillel Wertheimer walked out of the Great Choral Synagogue in the quiet residential neighborhood of Podil. The Sabbath had just concluded, and he and his friend and boss Binyamin Gutfarb were on their way home following the evening prayer service.[23] The 26-year-old Israeli was a teacher at the Hebrew school adjacent to the synagogue and certainly looked the part. Wearing the typical Hasidic outfit of dark suit, white shirt, and black fur hat, Wertheimer would have been an obvious target for someone looking to attack a Jew.

Security camera footage would later show that, as they made their way home, the pair were followed by four young men who had been loitering outside the synagogue gate. The two friends went their separate ways at Gutfarb's building, and several minutes later Wertheimer arrived at his home, only to be jumped and beaten as he entered the lobby. As the young men rained blows down upon him, he screamed, drawing the attention of a neighbor. Suddenly confronted with a witness, the attackers fled, leaving Wertheimer bruised and scared on the floor. Soon after, Gutfarb, who lived only a block away, received a call from Wertheimer's wife informing him of the attack.

"We left the synagogue together. After that I heard what had happened to him. I was home and I went into a panic," Gutfarb later recalled. Until that point the Podil neighborhood had been relatively quiet despite the disturbances three kilometers away in the city center. Attacks on Jews in "our ghetto," even verbal harassment, were unheard of, he explained. Despite a growing sense of panic, Gutfarb and many others thought that the incident was a one-off occurrence perpetrated by "a bunch of drunks."

But within days it would happen again.

Before the revolution's violence engulfed Podil, however, its erstwhile leader, Yaakov Dov Bleich, still held out hope for a peaceful conclusion to the crisis. Outspoken and gregarious with a heavy New York accent, the stocky and bearded middle-aged Karlin-Stolin Hasid had come to Ukraine from his native Brooklyn in the late 1980s as part of the wave of ultra-orthodox rabbis looking to revitalize Jewish life in the former Soviet Union.[24] While he had left the Podil community and moved back to United States not long before the Maidan, Bleich still regularly commuted to Kyiv to take part in various events in his role as Kyiv's officially recognized chief rabbi.[25] Only weeks before Wertheimer's beating, Bleich had taken part in a government-sponsored roundtable bringing together government officials with civil society and opposition leaders in a last ditch effort to avoid a crisis. But despite his best efforts, the protests continued and his community was forced to bear the consequences.

✳✳✳

The next victim was Dov Ber Glickman, a Russian Talmudic scholar in his early thirties. Walking home following synagogue services the Friday evening after Wertheimer was attacked, the young man had no idea that he would soon face the same fate as his coreligionist. Having tarried until most of the other worshippers had already left before leaving the synagogue, Glickman was all alone. Within a few feet of the synagogue he noticed three men loitering at a nearby crossroads. Remembering Wertheimer and noting with alarm that the men's faces were covered, Glickman turned around and started walking the other way. It didn't help.

"They waited for me to get to a dark street and ran after me," he recalled during a bedside interview with an Israeli journalist in the hospital several days later.[26] "They yelled at me, beat me with their fists, they kicked me in the legs, apparently with nails [on their shoes]. … My glasses fell, I lost consciousness and they kept kicking me in the legs." Like Wertheimer the week before, Glickman screamed for help, attracting the attention of residents who came out onto their balconies to see what was happening. Those looking down at the scene began to yell at the assailants, who jumped into a nearby car and sped off. Bleeding profusely, Glickman managed to drag himself back to the synagogue compound, leaving trails of blood across the white floor as he made his way into the changing area of the ritual bath, where he collapsed. "Everything was black, I was bleeding a lot and only when I arrived at the hospital and they stitched up my cuts did I realize that they had beaten and stabbed me only out of anti-semitism."[27]

The next day, an incident occurred which went a long way toward convincing Kyiv's Jews that the attacks had been linked.

Members of the community out on an ad hoc patrol of the neighborhood came across an apparent skinhead with "a short haircut, high combat boots, and a short jacket"[28] following a yeshiva student. The man had been "writing down every street the yeshiva students walked on." When confronted, he "started stuttering"[29] and was unable to adequately explain what he was doing there. After being questioned by the police, the suspect was allowed to walk free, leaving the community in an even greater state of panic.

Bleich was "astonished by the lack of [official] reaction" to what he described as a series of "planned attacks"[30] that had generated "tremendous fear" and forced him to strengthen security at his community's institutions at enormous cost. "People were afraid to leave their homes and go to the synagogue, people were afraid to leave the synagogue and go to their homes," he recalled. "We had guards walking people."

Parents of students in the Hebrew school were terrified. According to Zvika Klein, who visited Podil immediately after the attacks, the violence prompted a number of families to stop sending their children, and new rules were implemented for the older yeshiva students, including a ban on walking alone at night. Community leaders also recommended that women and children not venture outside without an escort.

In the weeks to come, although the synagogue's newly strengthened security had to contend with several minor trespassing incidents, things appeared to have calmed down somewhat. But the situation would get worse before it got better. On January 16, the same day that Glickman was sent to the hospital, the Rada passed the so-called dictatorship laws, a series of regulations banning public gatherings and curtailing freedom of speech and assembly. Those violating the new rules were threatened by the regime with a "tough response."[31]

Almost immediately Kyiv went up in flames, with fierce fighting on Hrushevskoho Street as thousands of protesters attempted to force their way into the Rada. Firebomb-throwing Maidanistas squared off in the smoke-shrouded city center against Berkut officers carrying riot shields. Soon the protests turned lethal as one rioter fell to his death from an arch near Dynamo Stadium and two others were shot by government forces. And while in December the protesters had broken up the ice covering the Maidan in order to build barricades, now they were pulling up the paving stones in order to use them as weapons.[32] In his diary, Andrei Kurkov, a novelist who lived near the square, recorded a striking scene. January 19 marked the commemoration of Jesus' baptism, and on that day in 2014 "Hrushevskoho Street was also baptized. There were more than 10,000 protesters there but also more Berkutovsky and soldiers than there had been the day before. The police fired water cannons at protesters to chase them from the barricades. Outside, it is 7°C. But the Maidanistas, soaked to the skin, chanted: 'Vodokhreshcha! Vodokhreshcha!' ('Baptism! Baptism!')."[33]

The Jewish community, already shaken by the recent attacks in Podil, hunkered down and waited for the storm to pass. Fearful, community leaders canceled a Holocaust commemoration that had been slated to be held in downtown Kyiv's Brodsky Synagogue, less than two kilometers from the deadly clashes.[34] Bleich's wasn't the only community to go into lockdown mode. Elka Markovitch, the wife of Rabbi Jonathan Markovitch, recalled how the fear of the protests spread like wildfire among her constituents. As the fighting ramped up, the subways stopped working and panicked residents began raiding supermarkets. A number of local businesses stopped functioning. As a result, many members of her community suddenly found themselves without livelihoods.

Everyone "went to the supermarkets and bought basic foods. Flour, oil, eggs, whatever. We did it also. We bought [a] truck of food because rumor said the supermarkets would be closed soon and nobody knew what was going to happen. There was a total emotional chaos because people understood it was the beginning of something," she remembered. "We have a yeshiva here so first of all when the shooting started we sent them home. We couldn't be responsible for the children. We stayed here and a lot of people turned to my husband [for] emotional support. Our home was full of people, not necessarily hungry but frightened [and] bewildered. ... There is a nasty Russian saying that 'when there is no water in the taps it means that Jews drank it all'. ... That's the first thing that occurred to [us]. Where people are hungry they are looking for someone to blame. [Especially] when Putin is too strong and too far away and we are here. It was frightening." Markovitch's community—like those of Azman and Bleich—was forced to hire armed guards as a precaution against the chaos that had engulfed the city.

While there had been an unanimous call for increased security following the Wertheimer and Glickman incidents, there was also a stark divergence of views regarding their causes. The World Jewish Congress blamed the attacks on Svoboda's "anti-semitic incitement and extremist activities," while Zissels and the Vaad accused the government of orchestrating them as provocations meant to delegitimize the Euromaidan.[35] The fact that the Podil attacks had come around the same time as the promulgation of the dictatorship laws, following a period in which the government had consistently warned of "a possible threat to national minorities from national radicals," led EAJC anti-semitism researcher Vyacheslav Likhachev, a close Zissels ally, to the same conclusion.[36] In a subsequent report on antisemitism in Ukraine, Likhachev elaborated on his theory, explaining that when Glickman was attacked "the Euromaidan was preparing for a crackdown, and particularly then [sic] even the protesting national-radicals had absolutely no time for the Jews."[37] Moreover, he supposed, if the attackers had come from the ranks of the opposition, a more tempting, and closer, target would have been the Brodsky Synagogue.

Whatever the source of the sudden aggression, the hate was not exclusively directed toward the Jews of Kyiv. Over the course of the month, two Holocaust memorials, in Poltava and Oleksandriia respectively, would be defaced with graffiti reading "death to kikes." And as January faded into February, and the battles in the Maidan grew in size, the rising violence would give the Jewish community, along with the rest of Kyiv, new reasons to worry.

UNCERTAIN TIMES

"At the moment Jews are not [being] specifically targeted, but if general violence erupts, [we] can become an easy target."

—Eduard Dolinsky

Maidan Nezalezhnosti, Kyiv
February 20, 2014

The violence in central Kyiv had reached a crescendo. The pop and whine of bullets mixed with the harsh screams of the wounded and the crackling of fires. Masked by the smoke from burning tires, men in drab green Soviet-style helmets and camouflage outfits huddled together behind makeshift riot shields as live rounds ricocheted off the sidewalk around them. Lying prone on the edges of the Maidan, policemen in balaclavas methodically squeezed the triggers of sniper rifles and fired off rounds from Kalashnikovs. As protesters were struck down by the policemen's fire, others would run to them, hunched over to present as small a target as possible, and drag their comrades to whatever safety could be found. By the end of the day, dozens of bodies were strewn across the city center. The final count, including sixteen policemen who fell in the square, would be well over a hundred.[38] Added to the thousands wounded over the past several months, the human cost was staggering.[39]

Less than two weeks earlier, on February 9, opposition leaders had called on the demonstrators to "grab baseball bats and helmets" and form self-defense teams to protect the now sprawling tent encampment.[40] By February 18 things began to come to a head, when a large mob approached the Rada. The protesters demanded that lawmakers restore the 2004 constitution.[41] That document had contained a number of provisions limiting presidential power which had been subsequently purged by the judiciary. As the Maidanistas confronted the police outside the imposing white structure with its distinctive pillars and flag-topped dome "the jostling began, degenerating into fighting, and soon after that the first three protesters had been killed."[42]

Following clashes described as "open warfare" by the *Kyiv Post* (at least four people were reported killed), the protesters retreated to the Maidan, where they prepared for a fresh assault. During that fighting retreat, police used "clubs, tear gas and flash grenades" against the marchers, who responded with "sticks, stones, metal bars, fireworks and Molotov cocktails and other explosives."[43]

"The Berkut, mounting a counter-attack, took the barricades in Hrushevskoho Street, and seized Ukraine House and the October Palace," Kurkov wrote in his diary. "At the same time, its men began moving on Institutskaya Street, forcing the Maidanistas back. The retreating protesters gathered in the Maidan, about eight thousand of them. They set fire to anything they could find in order to create a barricade of flames."

Anticipating the worst, Vitaliy Klitschko issued an appeal for women and children to leave the Maidan.[44] The government, meanwhile, gave the opposition until six o'clock that evening to clear the city center. Shortly before the deadline they began their assault, sending in the Berkut, supported by truck-mounted water cannons.[45] What followed was a mash-up between a medieval battle, a rave, and the Fourth of July, with men clashing shield-to-shield as multicolored fireworks exploded around them and flashing strobes illuminated the inferno that used to be a European capital.

Some in the Jewish community began expressing renewed concern over the possibility that the violence could spill over into antisemitic attacks against them.[46] Rabbi Azman issued a call for his congregation to flee the city, citing "constant warnings concerning intentions to attack Jewish institutions."[47] The city's Hebrew schools were closed down for the duration, and many Orthodox Jews began avoiding public places.[48] Fearful of further attacks, Binyamin Gutfarb and the other Israeli expatriates living in Podil got together for an emergency meeting to discuss the possibility of fleeing the country. Citing the Talmudic dictum that one who is on his way to do a *mitzvah* (a Biblical commandment) is protected from harm, Gutfarb argued that he and the other Israeli teachers were on a mission to serve the community. "There is a danger to Jews here and we're going to leave them here and flee? What kind of example are we setting for them," he recalled asking. Such a course would be tantamount to abandoning the city's Jews to their fate, he argued. "So we decided that we needed to stay with them no matter what. ... And really, that's what helped us through this ordeal."

Like Gutfarb, Alena Druzhynina refused to abandon her fellow Jews. On February 21, the Maidan was a wreck. Acrid smoke wafted through the air from the previous days' fighting as the protesters prepared for the next round of clashes. As the tensions ratcheted up, Druzhynina made her way through the barricades, her long brown hair topped with a white construction helmet, a small brown rucksack slung over her back. Several elderly Jews living in flats within the confines of the protest camp had been unable to go outside for days and were running low on food and medication. Alena, together with several friends, was on a resupply mission.

"Because of the barricades and shooting and fire and Molotov cocktails and burning tires and other things, these elderly people couldn't go outside. They stayed there for several days without medication or food," she later recalled. Living just beyond the barricades on Hrushevskoho Street was Mikhail Solomonovich, an 82-year-old pensioner in dire need of assistance. Thin and frail, with a seamed face, a gray fringe of hair, and a prominent nose, he had sat alone throughout the upheaval of the revolution, the sounds of explosions and gunshots rattling his small flat.

As she approached the barricades on Hrushevskoho Street, the protesters called to Druzhynina that the square was too dangerous and ordered her to turn around. Implacable, she refused, telling them she would be getting in come hell or high water. Offering a compromise, the protesters offered to deliver her relief supplies for her but again she demurred, insisting that they would have to let her and her friends in. Eventually, the protesters gave in and let them through. Handing them helmets, the protesters accompanied the aid workers on their short journey. Passing a "lot of tense, tired people," the group ran until they reached Solomonovich's courtyard. As they walked inside their anxiety began to dissipate.

"Are you crazy? What are you doing here," Solomonovich demanded, incredulously, as he opened the door to his small flat. As the visitors entered his living room, its walls plastered with handwritten motivational quotes and its furnishings permeated with the smell of burning tires, the old man told Druzhynina that he believed there was a sniper on the roof of the building. While the Maidanistas counted their dead and shored up their defenses, the group spent several hours with Solomonovich, listening to stories of his childhood as explosions sounded in the distance.[49] As the group sat and socialized amid the wreckage, Yanukovych and the opposition were coming to their own agreement to bring the fighting to a close. And while the deal—which would have meant early elections, a return to the old constitution, and a national unity government[50]—was met with objections by some elements on the Maidan,[51] these reservations quickly became irrelevant. By the next day, the president had fled the capital and the police began pulling back from the square. The Maidanistas had won. Kyiv was in their hands.

Ukraine's Chief Reform Rabbi was ecstatic. Writing in the *Forward*, Alexander Dukhovny asserted that, while there were some "marginal groups" with antisemitic views, most Ukrainians had fought for a European future free from corruption. And while the country's Jewish communities were "confronting the uncertainty over [the] political future," they also "look[ed] forward to Ukraine's journey back to Europe."[52] Others were also optimistic, if a bit more guarded in terms of rhetoric.

As the revolutionaries went about taking over government buildings and opposition lawmakers voted to strip Yanukovych of his position, Rabbi Moshe Azman recanted his earlier warnings, informing his flock that while woman and children should avoid walking the streets for a couple of weeks until things returned to normal, there was no need to flee. The Jews of Kyiv, he said, had been miraculously saved. He hoped that "from now on, only brotherhood and love will develop between the different camps in Ukraine."[53]

The day after his comments, a synagogue in Zaporizhia was targeted with Molotov cocktails.[54]

CHAPTER THREE

HYBRID WAR

Simferopol, Crimea
February 28, 2014

It was a cold, overcast Friday morning when Misha Kapustin stood on the sidewalk gazing up at the defaced facade of the Ner Tamid Synagogue. With mounting horror, he read the simple slogan, flanked by two swastikas and a Wolfsangel, scrawled in black paint across the door. "Death to the Jews," he muttered to himself.

The 34-year-old Reform rabbi, who had grown up the son of a Soviet naval officer, was once again getting a taste of life under Russian rule. Only two days before, things had seemed relatively normal. He had been on a business trip to Kerch, a small city on the far eastern coast of the Crimean peninsula, when he heard the news: the opposition had established an interim government and clashes had erupted between pro and anti-Russia demonstrators in the regional capital of Simferopol. Rattling down the highway on his way home, Kapustin pulled out his cell phone and called his wife, instructing her to add their children's names to her passport, just in case.

By the morning after Kapustin's return, soldiers in unmarked uniforms had taken the Crimean parliament and raised the Russian flag. Throughout the day, the "little green men," as they came to be known, fanned out across the city, capturing government buildings. Soon, behind closed doors and under Russian guns, the autonomous region's parliament voted to request Russian security assistance. Walking around his adopted city, Kapustin was enraged. Was this really twenty-first century Europe, he asked himself.

Around four o'clock in the morning on Friday, as the Russians went about their ostensibly covert operations, the synagogue's video camera captured footage of a solitary man removing a can of spray paint from his rucksack and going to work on the door.[1] Several hours later, Kapustin received a call from Anatoly Gendin, the elderly, staunchly pro-Russian chairman of the community, instructing him to come as fast as he could. As they stood before the peeling paint of the building's gray double doors, surrounded by journalists and police, Kapustin couldn't help but feel a nagging sense of unease. Something about the graffiti just wasn't right.

"I saw an interesting symbol I [had] never seen … before," he later recalled. "I checked it out and I realized it was a mirror projection of the symbol of the Right Sector. … That's a little bit strange. If somebody is a Nazi he knows how to draw a swastika. It's clear. It's logical. If someone belongs to Right Sector he knows how to draw his symbol. It's also logical."

The Wolfsangel, adopted as the symbol of the Social-National Assembly, a neo-Nazi group whose members were among the founders of Right Sector, was indeed scribbled on the wall. However, as Kapustin had noticed, if it had been painted by a member of that group, it would have been facing the opposite direction. Kapustin was also surprised that such an incident had occurred in Simferopol, where both Right Sector and ultra-nationalism had a marginal presence, leading him to suspect that maybe the antisemitic vandalism wasn't motivated by racism at all.

Gendin wasn't so sure. In a statement distributed through the World Union for Progressive Judaism, he took a different tack, stating that it had been "important for the antisemites to commit this crime." Linking the incident to rising prices in the wake of the revolution, Gendin said that "as usual, Jews are blamed [for] these disasters and Jews are held responsible." Despite their differences, both men were afraid to see what would come next.

The Crimean Jewish community was largely assimilated, and that evening even fewer people than usual showed up for Shabbat prayers in the synagogue. Addressing the handful of congregants who had braved the streets to attend, Kapustin said he would be leading an abbreviated service and asked them to remain home come morning. "I cannot guarantee your safety," he told them.

The next morning the young rabbi prayed by himself in Ner Tamid's empty sanctuary. He was a lonely figure, standing before the wooden ark and surrounded by the empty hard-backed chairs usually filled by singing congregants. Beseeching the Almighty for peace, he felt "unstable, without a clue" and wondered what would come next. When he checked the news online that evening, he discovered that the Duma, Russia's rubber-stamp parliament, had unanimously given President Vladimir Putin the go-ahead to use armed force in Ukraine, effectively turning a de facto situation de jure.[2] Kapustin was livid. "I had to do something. I was a religious leader for many people and I was often on TV, in the news and so on, and people kept asking me what to do and how to react."

While requesting that his congregants remain silent, the rabbi felt compelled to speak out. Several days later, on March 2, he penned an open letter intended for distribution to Jewish communities around the globe. It was only three sentences long, but it was highly significant in that it marked the beginning of a rabbinic conflict over Ukraine—fought alongside, and in parallel to, the Russian propaganda campaign which would make the Jewish question an inextricable part of Moscow's hybrid war. "Our town, Simferopol, is occupied by the Russians," he wrote.

"Help us, save our country, save Ukraine! Ask your government for help!"[3] This statement was out of step with public sentiment in the Crimean Jewish community. Many held deep reservations about the Maidan and were heavily influenced by Russian television.[4] As many Jewish leaders in Kyiv were coming around to Zissels's outspoken patriotism in the face of Russian aggression, many of those in the Crimean community were unhappy with their rabbi's very public stance and let him know it. To do so, they turned to Anatoly Gendin.

The pair were alone in the synagogue, each working in his own office, when the white haired, bespectacled community chief approached Kapustin and told him that several influential Jews insisted that he keep his mouth shut. "I spoke on my own behalf and mostly to foreign journalists," Kapustin fired back, noting that he was more circumspect when speaking with local media.

He was very much aware of the potential consequences should he say the wrong thing on Crimean television, he later explained, noting that he had already begun planning his escape from the Russian-occupied peninsula.

✶✶✶

Already on the evening of February 22, as Putin ally Yanukovych was fleeing Kyiv, the Russian president was working on a strategy for his invasion. Calling senior military and defense officials to the Kremlin, he assigned them the task of saving Yanukovych, whom he claimed was in danger of being "liquidated."[5] The next morning, after a full night's discussion, Putin's officials were getting up and preparing to leave when the president called for their attention. He had one last instruction: "we are forced to begin the work to bring Crimea back into Russia." As Putin was planning to violate Ukrainian sovereignty, the country's new leaders were busy forming an interim government that would hold the reins of power until new elections could be organized. Intended as a temporary placeholder, the new "Kamikaze Cabinet" included four Svoboda members, among them Rear Admiral Ihor Tenyukh and party ideologist and history professor Oleksandr Sych, who were installed as Minister of Defense and Vice Prime Minister respectively.[6]

On the same day that interim leader Oleksandr Turchynov announced the formation of the new cabinet, Duma Chairman Sergey Naryshkin told reporters at a press conference in Jerusalem that Russia was concerned about Ukrainian antisemitism.[7] His comments at that point were more or less in line with statements by both Israel[8] and the United States[9] calling for all parties to refrain from antisemitism and for the government to investigate antisemitic incidents. Turchynov was likely aware of these demands when, the evening before Naryshkin's comments, he met with Bleich and promised to safeguard the Jewish community.[10] Whatever assurances had been made, though, Svoboda's newfound control of the country's defense apparatus, on top of its sizable representation in parliament, certainly appeared to be cause for worry. And while Naryshkin's statement was relatively restrained, Russia would soon escalate its rhetoric.

✳✳✳

During the Euromaidan, the organized Jewish communities of Ukraine had for the most part stayed out of politics, having no desire to get in the middle of an internecine squabble. Faced with outside aggression, however, such a position quickly became untenable. The Russian media was engaged in a full-throated campaign of delegitimization predicated on the idea that the new government in Kyiv was a "fascist junta" controlled by Nazis and Banderites. In fact, the propaganda got so bad that one reporter on RT America, the US affiliate of the Kremlin controlled Russia Today network, quit on air immediately following a segment making such claims.[11]

Meanwhile, as the little green men continued to cement their control over Crimea, the Kremlin was working to drum up support for separatism. Billboards presenting two maps of Ukraine, one superimposed with a swastika and another with the colors of the Russian flag, began to go up across the peninsula. The Crimeans were being presented with a stark choice: live with Russia or suffer under Nazism.[12]

Back in New York, Bleich decided to hold a press conference and address the issue head on. Speaking in his thick Brooklyn accent, the rabbi was blunt, accusing Russia of borrowing tactics from the Third Reich, which in 1938 fabricated stories of rioting in Austria in order to justify the annexation of its neighbor. It was a classic example of the sort of hybrid war that Russia would later perfect. "Things may be done by Russians dressing up as Ukrainian nationalists … the same way the Nazis did when they wanted to go into Austria and created provocations," Bleich said, intimating that the attacks on Wertheimer and Glickman had been orchestrated by Moscow.[13] "The Russians are blowing [Ukrainian antisemitism] way, way out of proportion. There were many differences of opinion throughout the revolution, but today all that is gone. We're faced by an outside threat called Russia. It's brought everyone together."

This was more than Russia's Jewish leaders could tolerate. During his rise to power, Putin had worked hard to bind Russia's organized Jewish community to his regime, sidelining the more independently-minded Russian Jewish Congress and positioning the Chabad-aligned Federation of Jewish Communities of Russia (FEOR) as the dominant force in Russian Judaism.[14] In exchange, Berel Lazar, the Italian-born, New York-educated chief rabbi, became a staunch Kremlin ally, calling on Jewish organizations to stop criticizing the president and his controversial policies, such as a 2013 bill prohibiting positive media coverage of homosexual relationships.[15] Some have even gone so far as to call him Putin's Court Jew, a term with intensely negative connotations.[16]

Now, responding to the Ukrainian Jews' harsh words, Russia's Kremlin-aligned rabbinic leadership came to Putin's defense. As the clock ticked down on a Russian deadline for Ukrainian forces in Crimea to surrender,[17] Alexander Boroda, the president of the Federation of Jewish Communities of Russia, urged his Ukrainian coreligionists to remain silent. "Jews and rabbis should stay away from politics," he flatly stated, asserting that the Russo-Ukrainian conflict was "not connected to the Jews." And while the current climate was not one of rampant antisemitism, he said, the future was still uncertain. "We feel like one family, the Jews in Ukraine and Russia, like one community, and we worry for the Ukrainian Jews."[18]

That same afternoon Vladimir Putin held a press conference in Moscow in which he both denied that the little green men were Russian troops and stated that any Russia military action would, in fact, be totally legal, as he had received a "direct appeal" from Viktor Yanukovych, the "legitimate" president of Ukraine, for him to use Russia's armed forces "to protect the lives, freedom and health of the citizens of Ukraine."

"What is our biggest concern," he asked rhetorically. "We see the rampage of reactionary forces, nationalist and antisemitic forces going on in certain parts of Ukraine, including Kiev." Reciting a litany of alleged Ukrainian abuses, Putin asserted that Russia retained the right "to use all available means to protect those people."[19,20]

The heads of a number of Jewish organizations, including the leaders of the Ukrainian branches of the Reform and Conservative movements, were livid. In a joint letter to Putin, they accused the Russian ruler of propagating "lies and slander." Putin may have gotten "Ukraine confused with Russia, where Jewish organizations have noticed growth in antisemitic tendencies last year," they declared sardonically. "Our very few nationalists are well controlled by civil society and the new Ukrainian government—which is more than can be said for the Russian neo-Nazis, who are encouraged by your security services."[21] Moreover, they continued, minorities were also well represented in the cabinet, with Volodymyr Groysman, the Jewish mayor of Vinnytsia, having been appointed as a Vice Prime Minister. Stating that the main threat to Ukraine was Putin himself, the Jewish leaders emphatically concluded they did "not wish to be 'defended' by sundering Ukraine and annexing its territory."

Meanwhile, in the eastern Ukrainian city of Dnipropetrovsk, Rabbi Shmuel Kaminezki was also preparing to bring his congregation into the fray. A regional capital of one million residents and a major industrial/commercial center, the city was just beginning to feel the first stirrings of separatism that were blowing through the districts bordering Russia. Since the fall of communism, Dnipropetrovsk's Jewish life had exploded and it was now home to Hebrew schools, kosher restaurants, synagogues, a Holocaust museum, and other institutions. Many of them were housed in the recently constructed Menorah Center, a marble-lined complex consisting of seven interlinked towers billed as the world's largest consolidated Jewish community center.

Since the end of the Euromaidan, the organized community had become increasingly patriotic. Describing the immediate post-Maidan period, Zelig Brez—the round-faced, bearded, and perpetually friendly director of the Dnipropetrovsk Jewish community—said that he believed a new political Ukrainian nation had been born in the fires of the conflict, one in which the historic mistrust between the various ethnic groups in the country had begun to disappear. Jews, he said, were "feeling proud to be the citizens of Ukraine," and are no longer "a very isolated group that was ... not so involved in the general community."[22]

Part of this may have been due to the influence of Ihor Kolomoisky. Within days of the end of the revolution, the new government in Kyiv had appointed the foul-mouthed Jewish oligarch to the position of regional governor in the Dnipropetrovsk Oblast (province). He immediately announced that he would nip separatism in the bud.[23]

This sentiment was ostentatiously on display when Kaminezki ascended the stage during a Purim celebration at the Menorah Center on March 16, the same day as the Russian-backed Crimean referendum. Addressing his flock, who had gathered to celebrate the Jewish people's victory over their enemies in ancient Persia, Kaminezki lashed out at their neighbor to the east by comparing Vladimir Putin to a genocidal Biblical villain. "We have lived together with the Ukrainians for a thousand years and Ukraine is our homeland," the rabbi declared. "Today we will read from the scroll of Esther, as we have for thousands of years on Purim. And today that reading if of particular importance. Today, a new Haman, our common enemy with the Ukrainians, is very near…." The room exploded in applause.[24]

Berel Lazar was quick to respond. Kaminezki, like the Russian chief rabbi, was a member of the Chabad-Lubavitch Hasidic movement, and it must have been galling to see him take the Ukrainian side. On the March 18, the same day that he stood and applauded as President Putin announced the annexation of Crimea[25] (denouncing Ukrainian "nationalists, neo-Nazis, Russophobes and antisemites" in the process[26]), Lazar published an open letter decrying Ukrainian rabbinical protests. "We, the rabbis in Russia and Ukraine, see our duty to urge all parties, and first of all our coreligionists, to peace and search for mutual understanding at this difficult time. We understand that there are political problems, but believe people, especially spiritual leaders and community leaders, should not interfere in the sphere of activity of politicians. We must not forget that any rash word can lead to dangerous consequences for many people," he wrote.

Co-signed by 54 other Chabad rabbis, both in Russia and Ukraine, the letter[27] somewhat undercut the simple narrative that there was a clear demarcation between Ukrainian and Russian religious leaders, with each taking his own country's side. And while it is reasonable to assume that Lazar, as close as he was to President Putin, was engaging in politics (something he denied[28]), it is not necessarily a valid assumption that the Ukrainian rabbis were doing the same. As we shall see during the course of this book, many of those affiliated with Chabad earnestly believed in keeping their heads down and staying out of trouble, not out of any loyalty to the Russian Federation but rather out of deep-seated religious conviction.

Dr. Kiril Feferman, a fellow at the USC Shoah Foundation Center for Advanced Genocide Research, has advanced a theory positing a dichotomy between contemporary and pre-modern approaches to government-Jewish community relations which I feel explains both the Ukrainian-Russian rabbinic divide and the decision by many Ukrainian rabbis to call for communal silence, even in the face of outright aggression. "It seems that the attitudes of the Russian and Ukrainian rabbis vis-à-vis the Ukrainian crisis mirror to no small extent the line pursued by their governments. The Ukrainian government repeatedly claimed that Ukraine was at war with Russia; therefore, the Ukrainian rabbis acted in accordance with this position by calling upon their coreligionists to unequivocally support Ukraine in this struggle," Feferman explained.[29]

> "The Kremlin persists in claiming that Russia is not at war with Ukraine, but rather that Ukraine is embroiled in a civil war. This enables the Russian rabbis to steer away from the conflict and call upon Ukrainian Jews to follow their example by not getting entangled in a war that has nothing to do with them. In fact, the Russian rabbis' position is reminiscent of a Jewish pre-

modern communal policy of refraining from getting involved in state affairs, especially the wars waged by Gentiles. It seems that as long as the Kremlin does not ask all political, ethnic, and religious groups to fully commit to supporting Russian policies in Ukraine, the Russian rabbis are able to remain noncommittal."

Feferman contrasted the Russian example with that of Ukraine, "a young nation-state in the process of state building" which felt threatened and whose "government expects all ethnic and religious groups to support its policies unequivocally. In such a setting, the Ukrainian rabbis do not have the same leeway as do their Russian counterparts, and have no choice but to fully identify with the policies of their government. In fact, the Ukrainian rabbis' stance is in keeping with the modern Jewish behavior pattern of unequivocally aligning with the nation-state of which one is a citizen."[30] Taking Feferman's hypothesis into account, the behavior of the rabbis aligned with Lazar can be explained by their distance from the centers of power in Ukraine and their ideological alignment with Chabad. Many of those who did speak out—such as Bleich, Dukhovny, and Stamov—were either close to the Ukrainian authorities or members of more progressive, socially integrated denominations. Lazar appeared to have been banking on this natural reticence to engage in politics to bring his fellow "Chabadniks" in Ukraine around in opposition to their more outspoken colleagues.

✳✳✳

Outside of Crimea, life slowly began to return to normal, but like many other Ukrainians the Jews were still plagued by feelings of anxiety and uncertainty. Ongoing economic problems, exacerbated by political instability, had severely impacted the financial health of many Jewish institutions. "The middle class has almost disappeared, and that's where we got most of the money from locally," Bleich lamented. "We lost most of our local donors."[31]

The crisis also created a need for larger security budgets. In Kyiv, Jewish institutions, including the local offices of the Joint Distribution Committee (JDC), invested heavily in beefing up their security, which often proved to be a hefty and unsustainable burden, with fees reaching up to a thousand dollars a day.[32] Most local organizations ceased activities which required their members to congregate in one place and "simply [went] into hibernation," threatening "to undo the fabric of the community."[33]

One of the primary issues was financial stability, not just for institutions but also for the individuals they served. In Elka Markovitch's community, as in Bleich's, donors who had previously given generously found that they had nothing left to give, and those who had hitherto stood on their own two feet found themselves reluctantly turning to the rabbi for a handout. "They just came to my husband and hugged him and started crying," she recalled, describing how she and her husband had been forced to scale back vital programs in the community, including one providing food for needy schoolchildren. "There were months with no meat ... and for these children it's crucial because many of them don't get [real food] at home. ... We have a professor now in Kyiv University who has not been paid in eight months so we give him food parcels. He cries [because] he's ashamed. ... It's total depression."

One of the Markovitchs' primary foreign donors was Rabbi Yechiel Eckstein, the late president of the International Fellowship of Christians and Jews (IFCJ). An international charitable network well known for soliciting donations from American evangelicals, the IFCJ served as a major source of funding for both Chabad and the JDC's programs in Ukraine. Shortly after the Maidan, Eckstein told me that he was distributing around 2,500 food packages a month but that he believed they were "needed by literally twenty thousand families." Whether or not this was an exaggeration (he provided no evidence to back up his claim), the economic crisis was very real. Inflation, rising food and medical costs, and a stagnant economy had caused problems not only for the elderly and the poor but also for many in the middle class.

These problems were by no means limited to the capital. Refael Kruskal, CEO of the Tikva organization, which runs a network of schools and orphanages in the southern port city of Odessa, told me that he felt extremely frustrated by the response of Jewish organizations, describing efforts to obtain outside help as "talking to a brick wall." Writing in the *Times of Israel*, he described the problems faced by his community in a heartbreaking plea for help from the wider Diaspora.

> "The Jewish community in Ukraine is one of the poorest in the world. Years of shifting economic, political and social boundaries have taken their toll. Even at our most stable, Ukraine still has problems with how to support people and as a society we often rely on the generosity of others to give vulnerable children, older people and people with disabilities the life chances they deserve. That said, we're also a vibrant community—we have strong religious and community leaders and are fully active in Ukrainian society. When I look down the street of my local synagogue, I usually see a flurry of activity as people come and go to worship, socialize and do business.
>
> That's all changed now, and there's one thing that the Jewish community here always dreads: change. It's during times of change that the Jewish community, which lives very peacefully, becomes especially vulnerable to anti-Semitism, anger, blame and attack. When an area becomes lawless, those who usually hide in the shadows feel confident to emerge and we become a target.
>
> The street with my synagogue is now surrounded by riot police after the arrest of a Pro-Russian leader. The Jewish Agency has been inundated with enquiries about making Aliyah and moving to Israel and there is constant speculation about our uncertain future. People are stockpiling food and hiding in their homes, expecting the worse—we're all scared, and we're right to be."[34]

In Kyiv, worries over security led Alexander Levin, the head of the World Forum of Russian-Speaking Jewry, to bring in three Israeli veterans to instruct members of the community in self-defense.[35]

However, despite all of the precautions being taken, those in leadership roles consistently reinforced the message that the worst had passed. "We only had four cases of antisemitism during three months of revolution—and we think they have been provoked by Russia so that President Putin can say he is fighting antisemitism," commented Dukhovny. "In Kiev, we are fine. It has settled down since the revolution, and we are carrying on with full services in our synagogues as normal."[36]

Responding to a report in the Israeli daily *Maariv* which claimed that Ukrainian yeshiva students were planning to flee the country in order to avoid being drafted to fight Russia, Bleich likewise contended that things were calming down.[37] Despite the recent antisemitic attacks, he was optimistic, describing the situation as "critical but stable." While not feeling as secure as they had before the revolution, Kyiv's Jews certainly felt safer than they had during the chaos of the revolution, and, while he took the attacks against his congregants very seriously, the rabbi didn't believe that they portended a rise in antisemitism.

Part of the reason for that may have been self-restraint on the part of the far right, especially in the wake of increased international attention to their activities. Since the end of the revolution, Right Sector had gone out of its way to dissociate itself from the taint of xenophobia regardless of its members' actual views.

In early March, only days after the end of the revolution, Israeli ambassador Reuven Din El and Right Sector leader Dmytro Yarosh sat down in a bid to "prevent provocations."[38] Afterward, the two sides announced that they had opened up a "hotline" to facilitate coordination, with the embassy stating that Yarosh had assured them that his movement would "oppose all phenomena, especially antisemitism, with all legitimate means." Yarosh also declared that he adhered to Bandera's principles, which required him to respect national minorities. Over the coming, months this message would be repeated on numerous occasions, including by Boreslav Bereza, one of the movement's spokesmen … and a Jew.

A big bruiser of a man with a receding hairline and a single earring in his left ear, Bereza has been described as looking "more like a sophisticated metrosexual than a hardliner"[39] and as "a cross between a drinking buddy, an Israeli paratrooper, and the aggressively militant Jewish partisan played by Liev Schreiber in *Defiance*."[40] He explained Bandera's ostensible minority policy in an interview with *Tablet*'s Vladislav Davidzon in late 2014.

> "[Bandera] said: 'If you help me, reach out your hand to help me create a free Ukraine, you are my brother.' He also added, 'However, if you don't help me, do not reach out your hand to help me, but neither do you hinder me, you can live here. There is enough room here and you can live here.' That was his classic phrase, 'There is room here.' But, the conclusion: 'If you hinder the process, stick spokes in the wheel, then you are an enemy and you need to be destroyed.' So, it is all very simple.
>
> For my ideological brothers in the movement I am much more Ukrainian than an ethnic Ukrainian like [Ukrainian Communist Party leader Petro] Symonenko. When we speak, for example about Bandera, I was too once one of those who thought, having imbibed Soviet propaganda, that he was a fascist. But I was able to read many books and to think and figure out the truth: that this was a man who spent much of the war inside of a German internment camp. That he was liquidated by Soviet, rather than Nazi, intelligence agents."[41]

Such an outlook was, of course, about as far from Bandera's true feelings as can be. Under his leadership the OUN had issued a resolution stating that it opposed Jews as "supporters of the Russian Bolshevik regime" and intended to engage in the "cleansing of [such] hostile elements."[42] Bereza was not the only Jewish figure involved in the Maidan who promoted a revisionist view of Bandera. I would not be surprised if Right Sector's leaders encouraged Bereza to make such pronouncements in order to capitalize on his outspoken Jewish pride as a cover for their own intolerance and extremism. What is certain is that following Yanukovych's ouster Right Sector actively promoted itself as a philo-Semitic organization. Speaking at a press conference organized by the Ukraine Crisis Media Center the day after his meeting with Din El, Yarosh reiterated this message, stating that the group's activities were the "best proof" that it stood "against xenophobia and antisemitism."[43] Highly aware of the optics of the situation, especially in light of Russian propaganda, Right Sector actually did make an effort to reach out to the Jewish community, although its motives were highly suspect.[44]

In early April, as tensions rose across southern and eastern Ukraine amid a wave of separatist sentiment, graffiti calling for the death of Jews began appearing in Odessa. Accompanied by Right Sector's name, the violent slogans were found sprayed on buildings across the city, including on private houses, the local headquarters of the Security Service of Ukraine (SBU), and a Jewish cemetery. Avraham Wolf, the city's Chabad rabbi, was quick to call the incident a provocation by "forces that have come to Ukraine from the outside to incite unrest."[45] In what was likely an attempt to undo the public relations damage caused by the vandalism, Yarosh hurried to Odessa where he met with Wolf and staged a photo-op in the rabbi's study. Standing against the backdrop of heavy shelves filled with oversized volumes of the Talmud, the militant Ukrainian nationalist, dressed in camouflage fatigues and a black beret, had an appearance that contrasted sharply with that of the graying rabbi, who was garbed in a Hasidic Jew's dark suit and velvet kippa. Posturing for the cameras, Yarosh vowed that his men would track down and "punish" those behind the graffiti. It was, he explained, a matter of honor. Shortly thereafter, the pair made their way to one of the vandalized sites and painted over one of the hateful slogans together.

Kyiv
March 13, 2014

Since the beginning of the protests three and a half months earlier, Hillel Cohen had shrugged off concerns about anti-semitism. Despite living through the same terrors as the rest of Kyiv's Jews, the Hatzalah director never believed that a major wave of hate would sweep through the city. He strongly disapproved of Azman's call for an evacuation.

Prior to the Euromaidan there had been the occasional anti-semitic catcall, but all in all he had felt secure.[46] To Cohen, the greatest threat to the community was the anarchy accompanying the breakdown of government, which had turned the capital into "a kind of Wild West." He later described the feel of the period as "frightening and hallucinatory." While he didn't think that the demonstrations themselves would motivate Kyivans to attack their Jewish neighbors, he did worry that the lack of law enforcement would allow antisemites greater opportunities for indulging their violent whims. Despite his calm, on March 13, Cohen, who was used to saving lives, suddenly found his own as risk in the first violent antisemitic incident in the new Ukraine.

It was the evening of the Fast of Esther when Cohen stepped out onto the dark street after visiting a Jewish patient at a local hospital.[47] As he walked down the sidewalk, he suddenly felt something slam into him from behind and knock him to the ground. He almost blacked out from the pain as two men, dressed in black and bearing clubs, screamed antisemitic epithets in Russian and beat him mercilessly.

> "I fell on the floor, they stabbed me in the legs with something … apparently they had nailed shoes, and I felt very unpleasant. I woke up and realized that I had to get up to survive. They ran and entered a car. No doubt they followed me. It was something

premeditated, the same thing happened to all of the preceding [victims]. These happened all within a month, two months, all of these incidents, and then it got quiet. They caught me, stabbed me, said a few words and fled and there was no opportunity to identify them, there was nothing … no cameras."

For his part, Cohen was unsure just who had attacked him and was unwilling to rule out "pro-Russian [provocateurs] who wanted to say that there is antisemitism in Ukraine."[48] That was certainly how Zissels interpreted it. Following the attack he engaged in another round of anti-Russian pronouncements, accusing Moscow of trying to discredit the new government. "I have never claimed that the Russian government or Yanukovych administration were antisemitic," he said. "It is much worse—they are cynically willing to play the Jewish card in the implementation of their objectives, and are therefore [shown to be] willing to sacrifice Jews."[49]

Despite the temporary resurgence in antisemitic violence, however, it would be simplistic to portray this period as one of unrelieved fear. There were also many young Jews who were ecstatic at the overthrow of the Yanukovych regime and had busied themselves with activism on behalf of a country with which they increasingly identified. Following the revolution, a number of Jewish activists engaged in an effort to airlift as many of the injured protesters as possible to Israel, where they could receive medical care of a level generally unavailable in Ukraine. Tzvi Arieli, one of the organizers, explained that those taking part in the initiative were bound together by their "Jewish identity and [a] deep desire to do something to alleviate the suffering of those who have been injured during recent events."[50] Another Jewish activist who was optimistic about the future was 48-year-old Valerii Pekar. An entrepreneur and instructor at Kyiv-Mohyla University's business school, he had helped run the Open University of Maidan, an educational initiative aimed at providing the demonstrators with lessons on important political and social issues. Following Yanukovych's ouster, he also helped establish (but was not a member of) the Maidan Circle of Trust, a coalition of disparate protest leaders who continued to press their demands for reform with the new government.[51] Jewish Maidan activists such as Pekar went out of their way to minimize the fear felt by their coreligionists, instead preferring to promote a narrative of heroic collective action that had unified their country's disparate ethnic, linguistic, and religious groups. "I spoke [with] many people from the Jewish community," he recalled. "There were no worries and no fear. … I never heard this kind of fear or worry."

Following the revolution, Ukraine's Jewish leaders, who obviously disagreed with Pekar's description of their communal experiences, began lobbying the new government to step up its fight against antisemitism. In early March, Zissels met with Valentyn Nalyvaichenko, the newly appointed head of the SBU, to press for the reestablishment of the intelligence agency's anti-discrimination, xenophobia, and antisemitism unit.[52] Within days of the attack on Hillel Cohen, Rabbi Bleich held a similar meeting with newly appointed Prime Minister Arseniy Yatsenyuk and extracted a promise—similar to Turchynov's—that the government would protect Ukrainian Jewry.[53]

As hope clashed with fear and the Ukrainian nation sought to rebuild itself from the ashes, Russia took advantage of the renewal in antisemitic attacks to escalate its propaganda campaign.

Simferopol
March 14–17, 2014

Misha Kapustin slowly made his way around the synagogue's office, picking books off the shelves and packing them neatly into cardboard boxes. A camera crew from Russia Today followed closely behind. Neither Kapustin nor his wife, a native of the Crimean peninsula, were particularly enthusiastic about living under Russian occupation, and they had decided to flee. The rabbi had initially pushed for his wife to go immediately after the first appearance of the little green men, but she had refused, telling him she would not leave him behind. Between the hateful messages that were pouring in as a result of his outspoken pro-Ukrainian stance and the armed men on the streets near the synagogue, the rabbi was scared for his family's safety.

A week and a half after the crisis began, the couple made their decision. Kapustin sent a letter to his rabbinical colleagues announcing his resignation. He explained that he no longer believed that he could serve as an effective spiritual leader and that his continued presence would only politicize the community. The rabbi and his family left on March 16, the day after Purim, which just so happened to coincide with the Crimean referendum. It seemed appropriate. One of the major themes of the holiday is the concept of *v'nahafochu*, the world turned upside down. That was certainly the case in Simferopol as Kapustin celebrated a miraculous salvation one day and became a refugee the next. "It was really hard," he recalled. "I read the Megillah [scroll of Esther], spoke to people, drank a lot. I remember I wanted to be drunk. Usually I don't drink. It was a very hard decision for me to leave. I was very moved by saying goodbye to people for an uncertain period of time because I didn't know for how long I was leaving."

The next day he and his wife "took everything we could carry, the stroller, the kids," and boarded a train to Kyiv.[54] Those watching Russia Today got an entirely different perspective on Kapustin's exit, however. On March 15, as Kapustin busied himself with preparations for his last communal celebration in the Crimean capital, his segment went live. Following a deluge of confused and worried phone calls from friends, Kapustin sat down at his computer, opened YouTube, and played the clip of his interview. Entitled "Rabbi in Crimea urges Jews to leave

Ukraine, fears neo-Nazi attacks,"[55] it juxtaposed his story with the attack on Hillel Cohen and led viewers to believe that he was fleeing out of fear of Ukrainian antisemitism.

As he finished watching the video, Kapustin was rocked by a feeling of betrayal. "I needed a psychologist, [I was] a rabbi who needed a psychologist," he recalled. "I felt terrible … I thought that I was set up … I did not expect anything to be done like that. They just misused my words … they just perverted my words, you know. In fact it was me, my voice, my words, it was me all the time there, and I must admit they did it professionally, they professionally changed the context so nicely."

Like all good propaganda, Russia Today had taken real events and re-contextualized them, twisted the truth so as to portray a narrative far removed from reality. The network summed up the message that the Kremlin wanted its viewers to walk away with when it wrote, in an article accompanying the segment, that "many from the Jewish minority [have said that] they feel they will be forced to leave the country."[56]

This claim was as far from reality as possible. In the coming years, as war gripped the country and the economy sunk deeper into recession, tens of thousands of Jews would end up fleeing, but not one out of the dozens interviewed for this book indicated that he or she left because of antisemitism. The question is why the Kremlin would have an interest in Ukrainian Jews. The truth is, it didn't. It would be incorrect to assert that the media reports of Ukrainian antisemitism were particularly useful in and of themselves in rallying Russian domestic support for action in Ukraine. I would contend, however, that the use of Nazi imagery did serve two distinct purposes.[57]

The instrumentalization of the Jewish issue was key to Vladimir Putin's goal of awakening Russian national memory related to the Second World War. Known to former Soviet citizens as the Great Patriotic War, the memory of the millions of lives lost in the struggle against Nazism and fascism still resonates in Russia today. By packaging the war as a fight against the modern-day successors of the Nazis, Putin was able to tap into a reservoir of emotion, which is incredibly useful in any attempt to mobilize popular support.[58]

Accusations of antisemitism also provided Putin with a (flimsy) pretext for interfering in his neighbor's affairs while supplying a ready-made propaganda weapon for the delegitimization of the new administration in Kyiv. Antisemitism is one of the more pressing issues in contemporary Europe, and by linking Ukraine to problems in France, England, and elsewhere the Russian leadership likely hoped to influence public opinion abroad to at least some degree.

There was certainly a precedent for such a delegitimization campaign, especially when it came to the use of Nazi imagery. In his book *Russia and the Western Far Right*, Anton Shekhovtsov describes how the Soviet Union, wary of the Federal Republic of Germany's imminent accession to NATO in the late 1950s, instructed its agents within the former Reich to "goad [neo-Nazi groups] into extremist activities" so that Moscow could then turn around and condemn the "alleged resurgence of Nazism" as part of a campaign to "discredit West Germany."

As part of this effort, the Kremlin initiated the "Swastika graffiti operation" in which "KGB agents painted swastikas and anti-Semitic slogans on synagogues, tombstones and Jewish-owned shops" in West Germany which would hopefully (from the point of view of the Russians) "produce a snowball effect where troublemakers would carry out anti-Semitic activities on their own." The damage to Germany was so severe that as a result "its diplomats were ostracized, West German products were boycotted, Bonn assailed for the alleged inability to deal with Nazism and questions raised about the credibility of the country as a member of NATO."[59]

✦✦✦

There was another, parallel theme in Russian propaganda in early 2014, also centered on the role of Jews in the conflict. This one, however, was designed for domestic audiences and had a distinctly less sympathetic tone. Apparently in order to garner support for its war aims among members of the Russian ultra-nationalist camp (some of whom would end up fighting in eastern Ukraine), the state-controlled media began trafficking in more traditional antisemitic stereotypes to complement the ersatz philo-Semitism it had thus far been disseminating.

One of the first such broadcasts aired on March 23, when a discussion about the Ukraine crisis between Russia-24 TV anchor Evelina Zakamskaya and ultra-nationalist author Aleksandr Prokhanov spiraled into Holocaust revisionism.[60] "It's strange that these Jewish organizations—European and our Russian ones—support the Maidan," Prokhanov mused. "What are they doing? Don't they understand that with their own hands they're bringing a second Holocaust?" "They did it the first time too," Zakamskaya replied, looking into the camera and grinning. "It's an amazing blindness that is being repeated again," Prokhanov continued, adding the claim that "until 1933 many liberal European organizations fed the Führer."

Blaming Jews manifested itself in two ways. The first (as we saw in the case of Prokhanov) consisted of seeking to play up the role of the Jews in bringing disaster upon themselves, transforming them from victims into collaborators.

Another example of this was a television segment aired in late February in which Dmitry Kiselyov, the head of the Rossiya Segodnya television network, condemned liberal Jewish journalist Yevgenia Albats for her support of the Euromaidan. Displayed on screen next to Albats' picture was the question "what kind of Jew are you" written in Hebrew.[61]

The Russian state media was not content with merely presenting the Jews as complicit in their own destruction, however. In late March, two separate television documentaries purported to prove that both former Ukrainian President Yulia Tymoshenko and interim Prime Minister Yatsenyuk were secret Jews. "One must take into consideration his Jewish origin. He is a Jew on his mother's side, and is one of the fifty most famous Zionists in Ukraine," the program said of Yatsenyuk.[62] Ironically, this campaign actually had the effect of fostering fear of domestic antisemitism among Russian Jews, with the Russian Jewish Congress (RJC) decrying the "growth of anti-Semitism in [Russian] society" in the form of "public anti-Semitic statements, the number of which has increased dramatically."[63]

In a contemporaneous report, the BBC detailed how the government-aligned *Komsomolskaya Pravda* newspaper had listed Jewish-sounding participants in a Moscow peace march and described them as "Russia's 'true shame.'"[64] Incidents like this marked a "shift in Russian public national politics towards openly anti-Semitic rhetoric," the British broadcaster quoted a local Jewish website as saying. And in an earlier incident in mid-February, the RJC slammed Kiselyov for a segment in which he emphasized the Jewish patronymic of an opponent. In a statement, the organization recalled how such tactics were employed by Josef Stalin "to stir up an anti-Semitic campaign, the continuation of which was the notorious 'doctors' affair' … which almost led to a new catastrophe on the territory of the Soviet Union."[65]

✳✳✳

As the Kremlin went about disseminating antisemitism (and causing concern among Russian Jews), Berel Lazar continued defending Putin from the criticisms of his Ukrainian counterparts. Only a day after the Prokhanov/Zakamskaya interview, the rabbi told reporters that he believed it was inappropriate for Jewish communities to send messages to President Barack Obama, Putin, or "any other leader." The desire to get involved in issues not directly impacting on Jewish concerns demonstrated the "wrong attitude," he continued, adding that he was unsure of what to make of accusations that antisemitic incidents were really premeditated provocations.[66]

Despite his stated opposition to mixing politics and religion, Lazar appeared to wade into the political fray, reaching out to the Simon Wiesenthal Center in order to enlist its aid in condemning the new Ukrainian government. On March 28, Dr. Efraim Zuroff, the director of the Center's Jerusalem office, received a letter from Lazar calling on him to "publicly express its position on the development of the situation in Ukraine."[67] Citing the Center's inclusion of two of Svoboda's leaders in its 2012 "Top Ten Anti-Semitic/Anti-Israel Slurs" list,[68] Lazar asserted that it was "necessary to use the authority of your organization to clearly warn the [sic] official Kiev and the entire world community about the impermissibility of a conciliatory attitude toward ultranationalists and antisemites."

"The special status of the Simon Wiesenthal Center as the guardian of memory of Nazi crimes and the Holocaust of the European Jewry gives you the moral right and moral duty to declare that any attempt to install professed antisemites in the political establishment will cause irreparable damage not only to the prestige of the new Ukrainian authorities but to the Ukrainian state as a whole," Lazar wrote.

The letter, which was accompanied by several phone calls pressing for a public statement, was firmly rejected by the Center's leadership in Los Angeles.

"He wanted the Wiesenthal Center to come out against the revival of fascism in Ukraine. [The Wiesenthal Center] doesn't need Berel Lazar to tell us about the fight against the revival of fascism. We're the experts and we've been doing it long before anyone else was doing it ... consistently and at great cost to our public standing in these countries," Zuroff declared, accusing Lazar of "trying to help Putin."

Asked about Zuroff's accusations, Lazar replied that he had been worried about the presence of openly antisemitic groups in Ukraine and had thought that it was "a situation where the Jewish community actually [did] have to get involved. Sadly, we see that other political issues are in the way and the response wasn't as we expected."

Within days, Jews around the world, including Zuroff, would indeed be speaking up as the specter of antisemitism cast a shadow over the Ukrainian east.

UNREST IN THE DONBAS

"Due to the fact that the leaders of the Jewish community of Ukraine supported the Banderite Junta and oppose the pro-Slavic People's Republic of Donetsk [it has been] decided that all citizens of Jewish descent over 16 years of age and residing within the republic's territory are required to report to the Commissioner for Nationalities in the Donetsk Regional Administration building and register."

—"Separatist" ultimatum to the Donetsk Jewish community

Donetsk
April 14, 2014

It was the second night of the Passover holiday and there was a crowd outside the Donetsk synagogue, a low-slung red-brick structure on a downward sloping hill lined with decrepit houses. As the congregants milled around, chatting, three masked men carrying a Russian flag approached and began handing out flyers in the name of the Donetsk People's Republic (DNR), the Russian-backed separatist government that had taken over the city.

Addressed to "Ukrainian citizens of Jewish nationality," the letter stated that "due to the fact that the leaders of the Jewish community of Ukraine supported the Banderite Junta and oppose the pro-Slavic People's Republic of Donetsk [it has been] decided that all citizens of Jewish descent over 16 years of age and residing within the republic's territory are required to report to the Commissioner for Nationalities in the Donetsk Regional Administration building and register."

In addition, all registrants would be required to pay a 50-dollar fee and report all motor vehicles and real estate in their possession. Failure to comply would result the revocation of citizenship, the confiscation of property, and, finally, deportation.[69] The new orders were unpleasantly similar to measures enacted during the Nazi occupation, when thousands of the city's Jews had been registered, confined to a ghetto, and murdered.[70]

Something about the signs seemed off to Pinchas Vishedski, the diminutive Israeli Chabad Hasid who had arrived in Donetsk soon after the fall of the Soviet Union to reestablish communal life among the city's 10,000-11,000 Jews.[71] He believed that the flyers were likely a provocation. They seemed out of character for the leadership of the DNR. Concerned, he sent a representative to the address provided on the flyer but found that "there was nobody there."[72] As a result, he became convinced that the flyers had been planted by "someone trying to use the Jewish community in Donetsk as an instrument in this conflict."[73]

DNR leader Denis Pushilin quickly disavowed the letters, stating that they had been distributed by "freaks" who did not represent his movement.[74] He laid the blame squarely on Kyiv.[75] For its part, the Ukrainian response was swift and unambiguous. Prime Minister Yatsenyuk called upon Ukraine's security services to "find these bastards and to bring them to justice."[76] Even Svoboda got in on the act, issuing its own condemnation of the ultimatum.[77]

Theories abounded as to the identity of the masked men. At the time, the city was crawling with agents of Russian influence—including members of the Black Hundreds, the reincarnation of a turn-of-the-century Russian ultra-nationalist movement notable for its involvement in pogroms against the Empire's

Jews[78]—and some members of the community were worried about a possible uptick in antisemitic activity.

Anastasia Morzak, a 28-year-old English teacher, believed that Ukrainian nationalists belonging to Pravy Sektor were behind the flyers. She recalled a Shabbat dinner at Vishedski's home shortly after the incident during which he attempted to calm his congregants' concerns that they were living in an "antisemitic state" and assured them that a representative of the DNR had "personally come to confirm that is not their doing and that they had nothing to do with it."

"Everybody was really outraged, really outraged at that because everybody knew that this was somebody trying to set up the government of the DNR," Morzak said. And while the initial fear quickly dissipated, the incident left residual tension and anger among many.

Reports of incidents of antisemitic vandalism in Mykolayiv and Sevastopol around this time would certainly have done little to improve the general atmosphere.[79]

✳✳✳

As the Crimean crisis raged in early March, the first stirrings of separatist sentiment began stirring in Ukraine's Russian-speaking east, especially in the cities of the heavily industrialized Donbas region. The country has always been split ideologically and linguistically between the more nationalist, Ukrainian-speaking west and the Russophone east. Many living along the border with Russia saw the overthrow of Viktor Yanukovych, once the governor of the Donetsk Oblast, as a direct assault against their regional interests, and some, fed on a diet of Russian media, even saw the new government as a "fascist junta."[80]

As one protester in Donetsk, an industrial city of some one million people, told the *Guardian* in mid-April, there was a real need to "fight for our rights and protect the Donbas from Bandera supporters."[81] Certainly, the new Ukrainian authorities, brought to power with the help of nationalists whose base of support was in the far west, at first did little to ameliorate the worries of their eastern neighbors. In late February, the Rada sought to overturn a 2012 law that established Russian as an official language in certain regions. While acting-President Oleksandr Turchynov and Prime Minister Arseniy Yatsenyuk quickly walked the move back, pledging to decentralize power and "strengthen the special status of the Russian language,"[82] many remained unconvinced. Prior to the move to repeal the language law, a full 33 percent of regional residents had indicated that they supported joining Russia.[83]

With Russian troops massing along the border, fighting began breaking out between pro-Russian and pro-Ukrainian activists, and by early March large anti-Kyiv demonstrations were taking place across the east. Government buildings from Donetsk to Kharkiv were occupied and quickly retaken by Ukrainian security services, but the clashes continued, with the country spiraling toward civil war.

One of the worst outbreaks of fratricidal violence occurred on May 2 in the Black Sea port of Odessa when, after hours of armed clashes between pro-Russian and pro-Kyiv demonstrators, a group of pro-Russian activists retreated to the city's Trade Union Building. Shortly after the sun set that evening, they were under siege, with both sides throwing firebombs at each other against a backdrop of gunfire. The supporters of Ukrainian unity soon stormed the building, which went up in flames. Forty-two people were killed in the blaze, and almost 250 were treated for injuries ranging from burns to stab and gunshot wounds.[84]

Following the violence, several leaders of the city's Jewish community expressed concern over the deteriorating security situation, which, while not directed against Jews, could potentially spill over to affect their constituents. In an interview with this author in the *Jerusalem Post*,[85] Refael Kruskal, a rabbi who runs a local network of orphanages and schools, recounted the steps that had been taken to secure the community, including temporarily closing the synagogue and sending text messages urging local Jews to stay indoors. The Jewish community, he explained, was hunkered down and trying to ride out the storm.

"When there is shooting in the streets, the first plan is to take [the children] out of the center of the city," Kruskal said. "If it gets worse, then we'll take them out of the city. We have plans to take them both out of the city and even to a different country if necessary, plans which we prefer not to talk about which we have in place." Fearful of further violence, he said that he was considering renting a holiday camp to house 600 Jews, adding that in his estimation the coming weekend, marking the anniversary of the Soviet victory over Nazi Germany, was "going to be very violent."

Rabbi Avraham Wolf, the local Chabad emissary sounded a similar note, citing the presence of beefed-up security at communal institutions and noting that contingency plans were in place for a mass evacuation. The Jewish community, together with the International Fellowship of Christians and Jews, had prepared a fleet of 70 buses, fueled and ready to go "if, God forbid, we have to evacuate" the community's children and any adults who want to leave, he said, adding that during the clashes twenty buses had been parked outside of Chabad's school as a precaution. There were a number of options available, ranging from relocation within the city to an evacuation to Kishinev, two-and-a-half hours away in neighboring Moldova.

"We are doing everything to strengthen the Jewish community in its normal life. We are responsible for [the children of the community] and we will do everything not to leave and not to evacuate and give them the best life possible. We really hope [that] it doesn't get to that and that all will be okay," he said.

The Russian media was quick to pick up on this story, with multiple state-aligned outlets running stories that made it seem as if an evacuation was imminent. *Pravda*, Russia Today, Interfax, *Komsomolskaya Pravda* and Vesti all ran articles citing the *Jerusalem Post*.[86] Other outlets took the reports further, claiming that the community was anticipating a pogrom.[87] This wall-to-wall coverage prompted a flood of worried calls to local community leaders, compelling them to issue a denial of their earlier statements. In a post on its website, Chabad of Odessa stated unequivocally that "no such plans exist."[88]

A representative of the local Bet Grand community center likewise pushed back, stating that "the reports about evacuation are baseless rumors" and that, while Jews in Odessa were worried about the violence, they had "no special plans to leave as a community."[89] And when a Radio Free Europe/Radio Liberty (RFE/RL) correspondent visited the city a week after the fire, he reported that he saw no buses and only one security guard at the synagogue.[90]

In response to the brouhaha, a spokesman for the Russian Jewish Congress, which had also disavowed the evacuation report, explained that he believed the Russian media had exaggerated the *Post*'s story. They "changed this information a bit. Some of them wrote that Ukrainian Jews were going to be evacuated right now."[91] It was a textbook example of the kind of media strategy that had caused so much anguish for Misha Kapustin as he was preparing to leave his beloved Crimea.

Luhansk
April 6, 2014

A week before the incident with the flyers, the situation in Ukraine had degenerated sharply. Separatist fighters had taken over government buildings in cities including Kharkiv, Donetsk, and Luhansk, capturing weapons and, in the case of Donetsk, declaring an independent People's Republic.[92] And just as in Donetsk, antisemitism was present in separatist Luhansk. Gathered in a park near the Luhansk Regional State Administration building at the end of March, hundreds of pro-Russian protesters standing in the chilly winter air cheered as a speaker loudly called for the expulsion of the Jews who had supposedly orchestrated the Euromaidan revolution.[93]

"Today the Maidanistas say: 'We have had a national liberation revolution.' I say—and which nation? … Yes this is a real bandit gathering! Or, speaking more scientifically, this is a coup, it's a putsch—and a putsch that the Zionists have committed! And this must be said directly," he declared to the crowd's raucous approval.[94]

The local Jewish community had bolstered its security following the revolution, hiring armed guards for its institutions. Nevertheless, recalled Shalom Gopin, the local rabbi, there was not much of a sense that there was any particular problem with antisemitism in Luhansk. Nevertheless, the proximity of the city's synagogue to the separatist-occupied regional headquarters of the SBU was worrying. The two buildings were a matter of minutes from each other, making the walk to the synagogue particularly harrowing.

Chana Gopin, the rabbi's wife, described that period in a lengthy essay published online.

> "The day before the rebellion, the separatists put roadblocks on all the main roads of [the] city. It wouldn't have been a problem if not for their strategic location—100 meters from the synagogue. Why there? Perhaps they knew that there's a blessing around a synagogue, though more likely because of the police station in the area. This was the turning point; all of the downturns in the situation started then. In one night, they took control of the police station and hunkered down in it with thousands of weapons that they'd captured."[95]

A year earlier, one of the members of the community had decided to commission the writing of a Torah scroll in honor of Rabbi Gopin. Such an undertaking is a major expense, as new scrolls go for at least 24,000 dollars. As the date for the dedication ceremony approached, the members of the Luhansk Jewish community held an emergency meeting to decide if it was "right to celebrate the writing of a new Torah scroll" when the city seemed on the edge of armed conflict. The discussion went back and forth and finally it was decided that while there would be a celebration, it would be one of a relatively modest nature. When April 28 rolled around, preparations were underway, but things did not work out the way the Chana Gopin had hoped.

> "There was a lot of tension on the day of the event. I got to the synagogue to check on how things were coming along and to see what I could do to help. And then it happened. A motley crew of vicious rabble tried to get past the wall surrounding the synagogue. A few years ago, thank G-d, we moved to a new building, which shone like a lighthouse of Judaism in Luhansk. But the building wasn't finished, and there was only a temporary wall around it. For a few seconds, I stood mesmerized. A situation that had seemed like child's play had just become dangerous. The building's supervisor, Isana Razinkova, who is very devoted to the activities of the community, tried to scare away the rabble, but they soon toppled the fence and Isana fell on the ground. We called in our security company for backup, and they managed to scatter the hooligans. How did it end? Isana was lightly wounded; one of the community's supporters decided that the community needed and deserved more robust security; and another community supporter, who is a contractor, decided that the time had come to build a more permanent wall. And they did."

No walls could protect the synagogue from what happened next though. In Dnipropetrovsk, regional governor Ihor Kolomoisky had taken to his new job with gusto, cracking down on separatist sentiment and putting millions of dollars of his own money into raising and equipping a private militia to supplement the over-whelmed and under-equipped Ukrainian army.[96] Along with Volodymyr Groysman, Kolomoisky was one of the most visible Jewish faces in the Ukrainian government.[97]

It was Kolomoisky's outspoken Jewishness and fierce opposition to separatism that made him so dangerous in the eyes of the Luhansk Jewish community, Gopin would later recall, describing how many in Luhansk were genuinely worried that the role of such a prominent Jew in the government's counter-insurgency would provoke antisemitic sentiments among the separatists. "In Kyiv there were people who honored him but [in the Donbas] everybody hated him, also the Jews. They spoke rudely about him, about his politics, which were not harmless. I suffered from it," he said, describing how this antipathy spilled over onto his congregation.

Gopin was utterly shocked when, on Friday, May 2, a group of ten men, armed with Kalashnikov assault rifles, raided his synagogue. They had received a tip that a truckload of food delivered to the Jewish community the day before was really a shipment of weapons sent by Kolomoisky, who was allegedly slowly building up his forces in the synagogue in preparation for an offensive.[98] At first the rabbi remained in his office, preferring to allow his secretary to deal with the intruders, but he was soon compelled to confront the issue head-on.

He demanded to know why they thought they had the authority to search the synagogue. Brandishing their Kalashnikovs, the separatists declared that their weapons were their authority. Gopin felt that he had no choice but to comply.

"They went room to room over the course of two hours, searching … until I went and opened the warehouse for them to see what there really was," he recalled. "They checked the boxes, and when they saw everything there they relaxed. I wasn't afraid, but it was unpleasant. They behaved well." Despite its peaceful conclusion, the raid left many in the community "shaken and distressed." Afterwards, Gopin removed two of the synagogue's three Torah scrolls to protect them from being looted.

"That Shabbat, as we read the weekly portion from our old, small Torah, the atmosphere was bitter," his wife later wrote.

"Until that day, synagogues had been neutral territory, disconnected from political conflict. One felt the holiness when entering the synagogue and forgot the strife in the streets. Because of this, even more Jews than usual flocked to the synagogue, as if they were running away from the turmoil outside."

Not long thereafter, Gopin penned an open letter disavowing Kolomoisky and all but calling him a traitor to the Jewish people. The letter, which was partially motivated by the raid, was released on the same day that Russian media outlets published what they claimed was a recording of a telephone conversation in which the Dnipropetrovsk governor informed pro-Russian politician Oleg Tsaryov that he had placed a one-million-dollar bounty on his head.

Kolomoisky:	Listen, there was as bad mess here. A Jew from the Dnepropetrovsk community was killed.
Tsaryov:	What's up there?
Kolomoisky:	A Jew was killed from the Dnepropetrovsk community. I'm in the synagogue now.
Tsaryov:	What did he do there?
Kolomoisky:	Never mind what he did. They say [profanity] big bucks are promised for your head now.
Tsaryov:	My head?
Kolomoisky:	Yeah. One million bucks. They say they will hunt you down anywhere. I've let you know. Stay in Moscow, don't go anywhere.
Tsaryov:	I want to tell you something. In Africa there are some…
Kolomoisky:	Your associates will be hunted down too.
Tsaryov:	In Africa there is such a … such a poison…
Kolomoisky:	Listen, bollocks to what is in Africa. Stop spinning yarns to me. I tell you there was a prayer in the synagogue on the eve of Shabbat. Pray for that man, comrade Shlemkevitch, the Jew who was killed in Mariupol [profanity].[99]

Apart from the recording, which Kolomoisky confirmed was real,[100] there was no evidence that Shlemkevitch was actually

Jewish. In fact, according to multiple Ukrainian media outlets, the young soldier had studied for the priesthood at the Volyn Orthodox Theological Academy, a decidedly non-Jewish undertaking.[101]

The recording, real or not, certainly elicited a strong response from a community already wary of being too closely identified with Kolomoisky's aggressive nationalism. After writing that Luhansk's Jews mourned the "innocent victims of the hideous massacre organized by the radicals in Odessa" and all others who had died in Ukraine's "other hotbeds of the fratricidal war," Gopin asserted that the spirit of Judaism was one of "love for mankind, tolerance, respect for other people and nations."

> "Today Mr. Kolomoisky's appeal has been made public, and no normal person, no G-d fearing Jew can believe it! The special cynicism of what he said is that someone arrogated to himself the right to say that on behalf of the Jewish people from the place of redemption and prayer—the synagogue! We would like to expressly claim that anti-human people's killings, peaceful citizens' executions, paying money for a murder have no relation to the Jewish people's traditions and way of living, but solely characterize Mr. Kolomoisky's personality, his business regulation methods and political activities. The man, having murdered an innocent, having paid for a murder, will be cursed for ages along with his descendants!"[102]

The rabbi concluded by demanding that Kolomoisky "never and nowhere again relate his activities with the Jewish people, nor speak on their behalf." The oligarch, he said, must not "disgrace the memory of millions of those who were murdered, burnt, and tortured to death, but did not betray their fathers' faith."

✶✶✶

Kolomoisky and Gopin were not the only people speaking in the name of the Jewish community. During a radio interview, Bleich made the surprising assertion that, while Ukrainian Jews were "quite optimistic," most Jews were "preparing documents so that if they want to make Aliyah there will be nothing to hold them up."[103] This was likely an exaggeration. Subsequent interviews with refugees and Jewish Agency employees showed that for many there was a great reluctance to flee and that many only left after considerable hardship. Despite that, his rhetoric was indicative of the elevated level of tension following the recent breakdown in civic order.[104]

One manifestation of this tension was the formation of a small self-defense group in Kyiv, led by Tzvi Arieli, a Latvian veteran of the Israeli army. Intended as a rapid reaction force to protect local Jews from the kind of antisemitic attacks that had rocked the capital during the Maidan, the group was composed of eight young men armed with baseball bats donated by an American benefactor. It was, Bleich explained at the time, akin to the ultra-orthodox Shomrim neighborhood watch organizations active in Jewish communities from Brooklyn to London. During a period when the police were overloaded, it was a "no-brainer" to form a community group that worked "along with police and the local authorities to strengthen the protection of communal buildings and the local community."[105]

Back in Odessa, the location of the Trade Union fire, the Jews were likewise taking steps to protect themselves, with the local Jewish community center, located a short walk away from one of the flashpoints of the recent riots, curtailing its activities as a security measure. "It's not safe to have people gather in one place right now," the local head of the JDC said in an interview with the Jewish Telegraphic Agency (JTA).[106]

Luhansk
June 2, 2014

On the evening of the Torah dedication ceremony, a number of members of the Luhansk Jewish community gathered in the synagogue to take a group photo. "This is a picture of before the war," one of the congregants told Gopin. "The last picture before the war." It was a prophetic statement. "It's like today when you visit elderly people in Luhansk it is certain that they will show you a picture ('dovoennye photographii' we call it) of them and their families from before the war," Gopin explained.[107] "This was precisely the same thing: we took a picture together and so that was the [last] picture before the war. It was a very strange thing. … It never occurred to us that we were before a war."

By most standards, the Jewish community of Luhansk was small. Gopin has estimated that there were between 5,000 and 6,000 Jews living in the city and its surrounding environs. Out of those, between 1,300 and 1,400 were in touch with the community in one form or another at least once a year, while only 300 to 400 engaged in organized Jewish life on a regular basis. These people comprised Luhansk's core community.

After holding referendums in mid-May, the separatists in both Donetsk and Luhansk had declared independence from Ukraine, paving the way for the escalation of the conflict and sparking an ongoing refugee crisis. "The city began to shrink," Chana Gopin wrote. "Many residents, Jews among them, began to leave. We tried over and over to hold off the end, but it was like layering bright paint over a gloomy picture." As the likelihood of armed conflict grew, the Gopins decided to send their older children out of harm's way. "The only way out was a 22-hour train ride to Kiev … and from there, a flight to Israel. All those hours that they were traveling, we were in suspense. Would they get there safely? I stayed home with just the two little ones and prayed for them."

During the early hours of June 2, a group of separatist fighters made their way through the city streets and, acting with the element of surprise, attacked a government border control base. Their initial attack repelled, the militants then laid siege to the building for several days, firing automatic weapons and RPGs from a neighboring rooftop. Residents, including the Gopins, were terrified at the sound of the battle in the middle of their once peaceful city.

Several hours later, the rabbi was chairing a meeting in the synagogue when he heard a large explosion and felt the building shudder. Running outside, they discovered that there had been an aerial assault on the city. A Ukrainian military jet had strafed the separatists' headquarters and an adjacent park, killing a number of civilians. "The whole building shook. The phones did not work, you could not talk to anybody. … So I told my wife that … there is nothing to do, we need to leave already." At one o'clock the next morning he and his wife, two small children in hand, boarded a train to Kharkiv. The trip usually lasted six hours but on that day it took eleven.

In her account of their *hegira* (exodus), Chana Gopin described a scene reminiscent of the stories many contemporary Jews grew up hearing from grandparents who had survived the Holocaust. "I didn't know what to take and what to leave, or for how long the conflict would last. We left at midnight, a couple with two children. The darkness was thick; the city was a ghost town. We stood at the train station and didn't know whether to laugh or cry. We just hoped the train would come before another siren sounded." As she waited on the crowded station platform, she prayed and hoped that her family's service as emissaries of the Lubavitcher Rebbe had earned them enough of a heavenly merit to protect them.[108]

> "We heard the rattle of the train's wheels, and we got on—me carrying the stroller and my husband carrying the suitcases. My eyes closed immediately. If at any time in the last three months I'd felt like a war refugee, it was then. There were tens of bunk beds in the train's carriages, occupied by sleeping farmhands and their wives. Finally, I broke down. 'What am I doing here? Am I going to have to spend the next 12 hours in such crowded quarters?' But I'm not one for self-pity. I quickly decided that while I may have lost control of some things, I was going to remain in control of how I responded. It's said that everything starts in the head, and apparently, that's true."

Thankfully, the children were too small to fully understand the situation and the family arrived safely at their destination by noon the next day, only hours before the start of Shavuot, a two-day holiday during which orthodox Jews are religiously proscribed from engaging in actions as mundane as buying a soda or flipping a light switch. As such, there must have been an awful amount of pressure on the Gopins as they disembarked far from home on the eve of the festival.

New lodgings were quickly acquired, however, and the erstwhile leader of the Luhansk Jewish community found himself celebrating his first holiday as an internally displaced person (IDP). A week later, the Gopins were aboard a flight back to Israel and safety.

RIDING OUT THE STORM

"I can't leave because I have a responsibility to the people who remain here, and, no matter how hard or dangerous, I remain to discharge my obligation to these people and to heaven."

—Pinchas Vishedski

Somewhere in the Donbas
May 29, 2014

The train rattled over the tracks, the rhythmic percussion of its passage coming up through the soles of my feet. A Ukrainian man dozed fitfully in the seat opposite as episodes of "Kukhnya," a Russian sitcom, played on a television bolted overhead. Sitting awkwardly to accommodate the flak jacket and helmet wedged under our cabin's small table, I removed an iPad from my bag and began to read a novel by Terry Pratchett. It was an attempt to distract myself from thinking about my destination.

I had boarded the geriatric train, which looked to have been manufactured during the Soviet period, after two days in Kharkiv, where I had been conducting interviews with members of the Jewish community. Scrolling through Twitter in my hotel room the night before leaving for Donetsk, I had run across an image of a woman in a blue dress, limbs akimbo, lying in a puddle of her own blood. A middle-aged man, clad in white athletic gear and a pair of cheap plastic sandals, was covering her face with a piece of cardboard. The woman had been killed by a shell while walking outside the Donetsk Rail Center.[109] It was hard to relax on the train ride after that.

Kharkiv
May 27-28, 2014

Back in Kharkiv, life had seemed to be continuing normally. Stores in Ukraine's second city were open, with shoppers thronging the downtown streets. None of Kharkiv's imposing brick and stone buildings showed any sign of the violence that was convulsing the country. Everything appeared, on the surface, no different than any other major western city. However, such an outcome had been far from a forgone conclusion.

During the revolution, many local dignitaries, including the city's Jewish mayor Hennadiy Kernes, had come out strongly in favor of the Yanukovych government and it was to Kharkiv that the president initially fled at the end of the revolution. Unlike western Ukraine, which had been forcibly incorporated into the USSR after centuries of Austria-Hungarian (and later Polish) rule, Kharkiv had long been an integral part of Imperial Russia. The city had even served as the first capital of the Ukrainian Soviet Socialist Republic.

Culturally and linguistically, Kharkiv's residents were among the most Russophile in the country,[110] and it was therefore no surprise that in early April, when separatists took control of government buildings in Donetsk and Luhansk, they also rose up in Kharkiv. However, unlike in the Donbas, Ukrainian forces were able to quickly quash to revolt and retake the occupied structures.[111] By the time I arrived in Kharkiv in late May, the city seemed totally at peace, a fact that local Chabad rabbi Moshe Moskovitz, a Venezuelan who had relocated to Ukraine 24 years earlier, deemed nothing short of a miracle.

I met with the rabbi in Kharkiv's domed red-brick Choral Synagogue. Finished just over a century before the current crisis, the synagogue was a marvel, full of columns and arches. Painted in a rich cream, the interior was decorated with sky blue highlights and gorgeous red appointments. A blue and white star surmounted the interior of the window-filled cupola, allowing light to fall on the holy ark below. As is typical in the post-Soviet space, the organized Jewish community in Kharkiv is dominated by Chabad. This sectarian affiliation was on full display at the Choral Synagogue, whose exterior wall is graced by a large colored mosaic of 770 Eastern Parkway, Chabad's worldwide headquarters and the former residence of the late Lubavitcher Rebbe.[112]

"When everything started they mentioned Kharkiv, Donetsk and Luhansk. Kharkiv was [one] of the cities that people thought would be trouble," Moskovitz said,[113] adding that while that trouble was largely nipped in the bud, the ongoing conflict to the south was having an impact. Many of his congregants were beginning to consider emigration because they didn't see a future in a region rapidly tearing itself apart and dragging down the entire country's economy with it.

While most of the city's Jews were trying to get on with their day-to-day lives, some parents had expressed worries over sending their children to school, requiring the rabbi to sooth their fears. He found it ironic that people looked to him for answers when he was just as much in the dark as everyone else. What Moskovitz did know was that, like Kruskal in Odessa, he resented the Jewish world's lack of concern over his community's fate.

The following day I went to meet with Oleksandr Feldman, the minor Jewish oligarch who represented Kharkiv in the Rada. It immediately felt as if he were trying to impress me. Before being ushered into his office, I was given an extensive tour of the lawmaker's collection of indigenous African art, a preview of the strutting that was to follow.

Where once he was one of the Maidan's strongest critics, especially on the issue of antisemitism, he had now made a complete turnaround, praising the country's new revolutionary rulers. "There is strong domestic antisemitism, [but] the government is trying to fight it," he told me, leaning forward across a conference table of rich, burnished wood. He thanked God that there had not been any antisemitic incidents in Kharkiv (a development for which he was quick to take credit) and repeated his standing request that Israel send representatives to organize the Jewish community's security. Why that was necessary if he and the government were so effective in combating antisemitism was unclear.

The omnipresent luxury of Feldman's surroundings stood in stark contrast to the brutal realities of life 300 kilometers to the south. Two days earlier, rebel forces had launched an assault on Donetsk's Sergey Prokofiev International Airport and its imposing, ultra-modern glass-walled terminal. Still held by forces loyal to Kyiv, the airport was a critical foothold for Ukraine's overstretched armed forces. For the rebels, it was an essential strategic target whose capture would deprive the enemy of its ability to easily supply and reinforce its troops.

As control of the airport seesawed back and forth between the separatists and Ukrainian forces, I was in another, altogether surreal, world. Men were spilling their blood upon the earth while I was chatting with a short, pudgy-faced businessman who insisted on showing me pictures of his lavish lifestyle on his iPhone.

One image in particular stands out in my memory. Interrupting our discussion, he casually asked if I was interested in seeing a picture of his son. I agreed and he pulled out his phone, scrolling to a shot of a young child sitting in a plastic bathtub at the edge of a swimming pool. There was a shapely blond woman, presumably the boy's mother, lounging in the background. It was totally unremarkable save for the chimp scrubbing the boy's back.

"That's my monkey," Feldman beamed.

My unexpected animal adventures continued, with Feldman insisting that I go on a guided tour of the Feldman Ecopark, his eponymous zoo, before leaving for Donetsk. Knocked slightly off balance by the strange offer, I agreed and soon found myself being led from cage to cage by another one of the oligarch's employees. I didn't think anything could be more nerve-wracking than my pending journey, but I was shocked back into the moment when we reached the lion cage. "Would you like to hold him," my guide asked, gesturing toward a lion cub. The next thing I knew I was inside his cage and stroking his back. I smiled and posed for a photo. That evening I read in the news that the first battle of the Donetsk airport had left dozens dead.

Donetsk
May 29, 2014

I had finally arrived in Donetsk. Getting off the train in the occupied city, I was confronted with an unremarkable scene. There were no gunmen in sight, and the station appeared to be humming along, the crowds unhurried and relaxed. Almost immediately I was met by a driver in a beat-up old clunker. He was a member of the local community and spoke neither English nor Hebrew. I buckled on my vest, leaving my helmet aside, and we set off through the streets of what was then still a city of more than a million people.

While definitely a major metropolitan area, the city still had the slightly worn-down look common to Ukraine's industrial heartland. As we drove along, my guide pointed wordlessly to various roadblocks and checkpoints thrown up across strategic roads around the city center. These were manned by a heterogeneous group of randomly equipped separatists armed with everything from modern Kalashnikovs to grandpa's old shotgun. I snapped away with my DSLR. This wasn't necessarily the smartest move. People get suspicious when a man in body armor takes their picture from a moving car.

I aimed my camera at a young man in a blue poncho who was guarding a building. As we drove past he yelled something in Russian and began to raise his double-barreled shotgun. The driver accelerated and we quickly breezed past. I was breathing hard. While we continued to pass the occasional barricade blocking a side street, I was surprised to see that there were still a significant amount of pedestrian and vehicular traffic about. Life doesn't stop, even in wartime.

We soon turned onto Zhevtneva Ulitsa, a leafy side street filled with overgrown lawns and private homes in various states of disrepair. Across from a decrepit house with peeling paint stood the Bet Menachem Mendel Synagogue, the headquarters of the Donetsk Jewish community. Only 14 kilometers from the airport, the building was guarded by a burly Ukrainian with a shaved head and a black bulletproof vest over blue-tinted camouflage fatigues. He was unarmed.

I stopped briefly in the synagogue's restaurant, really a glorified cafeteria, for a filling, if uninspired, lunch, before walking upstairs to the office of Pinchas Vishedski. Like his colleagues across the former Soviet republic, Vishedski was a Chabad rabbi from Israel. He was similar in appearance to many of his compatriots, with a scraggly black beard going gray around the edges, spectacles, and the slight pudginess that seems to come with middle age. Sitting behind a pale wood veneer desk in a bare cell of an office, he appeared careworn and drained of the vitality and levity which always seem to be the hallmarks of Chabad rabbis. This, I thought, was a man who, if not yet defeated, had certainly been hammered hard on the anvil of life.

"Truthfully, the situation is very, very tense," he opened. "The situation is very bad, people are not in good spirits, people are tense. I myself am not longer in good spirits. I have no strength anymore. All the time we think this will end but it doesn't end. I don't know what will be … I don't know."

Anxiety over antisemitism had receded since the previous month's incident with the flyers, but the day before I arrived Vishedski found himself having to engage in frantic damage control after leaked Israeli documents again forced Ukrainian Jewry into the spotlight.

On May 28, Israel's Channel 2 reported that the Israeli foreign ministry was up in arms, accusing the Jewish Agency of "leaking" its plans to evacuate the Jews of eastern Ukraine, a "dangerous" move that created a situation conducive to allegations of dual loyalty.[114] The agency responded by denying that it was planning any sort of large scale exodus.[115]

"I really screamed yesterday … it went out in all of the press in Ukraine that the Jewish Agency is organizing a rescue operation—the evacuation of all Jews in Donetsk. This [caused] great damage," Vishedski told me. "Yesterday I received phone calls from all of the newspapers in Ukraine … I told everyone that it is nonsense and nothing like that exists."[116]

According to Vishedski, the Jewish community was still functioning, but many were facing economic hardship. Five hundred families had signed up to receive regular food packages, a number that the rabbi thought likely to grow. Daily prayer services continued to be well attended despite the violence, and Torah classes were still taking place in the evenings. Attendance at the synagogue and nearby Jewish community center was down, but Jewish life had not stopped.

At the community center, the director of cultural programs, Olga Pypenko, said that hundreds of people were still coming to take part in classes and activities, and between 25 and 30 families with small children were expected to take part in a communal Shabbat that week, "no fewer [than] since the violence started."

The Jews' anxiety was manifesting itself in other ways. Vishedski had been forced to temporarily close the local day school because parents were keeping their children home. When classes resumed after a short hiatus, only 30 out of 150 pupils returned to their studies. He sent his own children, but would have kept them home if he hadn't needed to set an example for his congregants. Some, like Yaakov Virin, a bearded Hasid who was the editor of Donetsk's Jewish newspaper, were wary, fearing that patriotism and nationalism might eventually turn into anti-Jewish incitement. "It's a tradition that the Jews are always guilty for all of our problems," he told me dolorously.[117]

***

While Virin was worrying about antisemitism, many other Ukrainian Jews were celebrating what appeared to be a major setback for the Ukrainian nationalist camp. On May 25, the day before the separatists launched their offensive against the Donetsk airport, citizens across the country headed to the ballot boxes to select their first post-Euromaidan president. Chocolate king Petro Poroshenko won handily with more than 54 percent of the vote, a sign that moderate forces could still mobilize a broad swath of the electorate.

Even more reassuring was the showing for dark horse candidate and Jewish oligarch Vadim Rabinovich. Coming in at a little more than two percent, he still received more votes than both Oleh Tiahnybok and Dmytro Yarosh, who were unable to capitalize on their role in the revolution. Rabinovich had run in order to "destroy the myth of antisemitic Ukraine,"[118] and his "victory" over the right was fêted as a sign that Ukrainians had repudiated hate.[119] This election presaged major political changes, and within two months the coalition would crack up, leading to parliamentary elections and the downfall of Svoboda.

✳✳✳

This new era did not immediately bring relief, and antisemitic incidents (mostly vandalism) actually increased over the course of 2014.[120] Within days of the election, a group of armed men attacked a guard outside Rabbi Bleich's home in Kyiv, pushing him to the ground and threatening to kill him before setting the building alight. Bleich, who was abroad at the time, denied that there was any antisemitic component to the incident.[121] Later that month, a yeshiva student was beaten during an attempted robbery in a *mikva* (ritual bath) near the grave of Rebbe Nachman in Uman. The *mikva*'s restroom was also vandalized by the assailants.[122]

✳✳✳

Regardless of developments in the west, in the east things were going from bad to worse. With the Ukrainian army tightening the noose around the capital of the self-declared People's Republic of Donetsk, retaking suburbs surrounding the city of one million inhabitants, and rebel leader Alexander Borodai promising Kyiv "another Stalingrad," many residents with the wherewithal to leave had sought refuge elsewhere. By late June, 54,000 Ukrainians had been displaced internally, and more than double that number had fled to Russia, Poland, and other countries.[123] By the beginning of July, Donetsk had been dubbed a ghost town by the *Guardian*, which reported that 30,000 residents had fled the city.[124] The situation had grown serious enough that Germany announced that it would begin to ease limits on immigration specifically for Ukrainian Jews.[125]

Despite escalating violence and the concomitant mass exodus of refugees, the Jewish communities of the Donbas were doing their best to hold together. In the western city of Zhytomyr, Chabad, with the backing of the IFCJ, had established a transit camp for IDPs, likely the first camp for Jewish war refugees in Europe since the displaced persons (DP) camps of the post-war period.[126] Built on the grounds of a summer camp, the new refugee center primarily serviced those displaced from Luhansk. By the end of July, Shalom Gopin had returned from Israel and was there, ministering to his flock.

By that time, everyone with the means to do so had left, but those too sick or old to move had been left behind, Gopin told me. Only "a few hundred out of several thousand still remain[ed]" in the city, he said.[127]

The exodus from Luhansk also split up families. Sixteen-year-old Daniel Sklyarov said that both of his parents, who held dual Ukrainian-Israeli citizenship, had opted to remain behind. He was very worried. "How can I not feel badly when my family is in Luhansk?" Moshe, aged 23, was one of the few remaining young people in Donetsk. He said that most of his contemporaries had already fled and that he was looking for an exit as well. In the meantime, he was helping Vishedski provide aid for other Jews stuck in the city. "Most [of my friends] are currently not here, some of them left with their families and some stayed with their families, but for the most part they are not here," he said. "There are almost no people on the streets."

Back in Donetsk, Vishedski, who was "attempting in this impossible situation to maintain communal life," had called on families with small children to leave the city and offered financial aid to help cover the costs of a move. But while the organized community had facilitated the flight of hundreds of its members, many remained. For those left behind, the rabbi set up an emergency hotline that operated even on Shabbat, when orthodox Jews traditionally do not use electronics. "We bring them help, food or medicine, or anything else. We are here for them," he told me.

Earlier that summer, the rabbi had sent his own family to the United States. His children were enrolled in a Chabad-run summer camp in Detroit, while his wife stayed with their married daughter in New York. He refused to leave the city. "It's dangerous here but there is no situation where one hundred percent of the people can leave," he explained. "And so we are here to help people. I can't leave because I have a responsibility to the people who remain here and no matter how hard or dangerous, I [must] remain to discharge my obligation to these people and to heaven."

A CRIMEAN SHOW

"Once Crimea became a part of Russia, the Jewish community turned to us to try to help them … we tried to stay out of politics."

—Berel Lazar

Sevastopol, Crimea
July 10, 2014

Every year since 1992, the Jews of Sevastopol have held a sparsely attended Holocaust memorial ceremony. Never a large event, it invariably failed to garner the kind of attention lavished on similar gatherings in more prominent cities. Following Russia's annexation of the Crimean peninsula, however, the event ballooned from a few dozen participants to several hundred.

Large delegations of rabbis and journalists, flown into Crimea from Moscow in a chartered plane and whisked through the streets by a police escort, mingled with locals at a "spruced-up monument" guarded by Russian troops.[128] This was a logical next move for Russia. Vladimir Putin had previously made himself out to be the savior of the Jews, first during his March 3 press conference, when he used the issue of antisemitism as a justification for military intervention, and later at a meeting of rabbis shortly before the commemoration.

Addressing Israeli and European rabbis in Moscow on July 9, Putin had made a statement widely interpreted as intimating that his western neighbor had slipped into fascism. Praising his own country's efforts to preserve the memory of pre-war Jewry, the Russian president stated that he wanted "to assure you that in Russia, we will not only always remember these tragedies, but also forever carefully maintain the memory of those who perished."

> "And we will do everything to ensure that such tragedies do not reoccur in the future. Of course, the revival of Nazi ideas here and there is particularly alarming. I want to thank the Jewish community and public organizations that are actively and bravely ... continuing to uncompromisingly fight against any displays and any attempts to revive Nazi ideology. I want to say that in this regard, we consider you to be our closest allies and I am asking you to view us in the same light."[129]

The next day in Sevastopol, there was little illusion about the fact that the entire spectacle had been arranged in order to make Moscow look good. Rabbi Boruch Gorin, a spokesman for Berel Lazar, was incredibly blunt about what was happening. "You can't hide the fact that it is very important for Putin and the Kremlin that everything takes place in an orderly fashion in Crimea," he told the JTA. "There's much more media interest in this ceremony this year. And, of course, this is also in the interest of propaganda, to show that everything is going all right there and that there's no anti-Semitism but [rather] peace and quiet."

It was obvious from the beginning that the main purpose of the event was to give a gloss of legitimacy to the occupation by presenting it as beneficial to local minorities,[130] and media outreach during the run-up to the commemoration demonstrated clearly that Russia was also interested in promoting a narrative of international acceptance of its conquest. In invitations to the event sent to reporters by the Russian public relations firm Mikhailov and Partners, Chief Rabbis David Lau and Yitzhak Yosef were listed among a number of influential Israeli rabbis expected to attend.[131] Bringing senior Israeli officials would have indicated an Israeli acquiescence to Russian revanchism. Unfortunately for the Russians, both rabbis' offices denied any knowledge of the event, with Lau's assistant calling it a "scam."

"No one invited him," he told me. "He would never go there. It's crazy."[132]

The questionable claims kept piling up. Despite assertions by both the Federation of Jewish Communities of Russia and Mikhailov and Partners that the Crimean Jewish community was involved in organizing the event, local Chabad rabbi Benjamin Wolf was clear that he was not and had received minimal advance information. By the time of the event itself, however, Wolf and other locals interviewed were effusive in their praise for their new masters. Speaking with the JTA, Wolf asserted that "the situation has changed for the better" and that the government was giving the Jews everything they needed. "Jews feel at ease here," he told the news agency. "They are not ashamed to identify themselves as Jews, and it's partly because of instructions that come from the top, from high-level bureaucrats to junior ones, that Jews are to be respected and assisted."[133]

Predictably, several prominent Ukrainian Jewish leaders condemned the visit, with one calling it a "cynical use of the Holocaust for political ends" and alleging that the event's organizers were "jeopardizing the Jews of Ukraine" for "personal interests." The Dnipropetrovsk Jewish community issued a scathing statement, essentially calling the European rabbis who participated in the event, at best, useful idiots.[134]

✳✳✳

Not everyone connected to the Kremlin acted in as friendly a manner as Wolf claimed. In late May, only weeks before the Sevastopol commemoration, the Kremlin's philo-Semitism offensive was marred by the appearance of a more traditional strain of antisemitic sentiment. In an interview with the pro-Russian *Crimean Pravda* newspaper, Aleksandr Dugin, a far-right political philosopher close to Putin, accused the Jews of running Ukraine, a theme that would later be picked up on by the Donbas separatists.

> "The nationalists who set the tone for the 'Maidan' spoke of the need to choose an ethnic Ukrainian. As a result, *they chose a Jewish president*, not a Slav, whatever he was. They talked about the nation, but it disappeared after the separation of the Crimea and the uprising in Novorossia. ... This is the result of Euromaidan ... Ukraine without Ukraine. *It is in the hands of homosexuals and Jewish oligarchs.* It's just a freak state, it would be ridiculous, if it was not bloody."[135]

On the day of the commemoration itself, Putin's imperialist tendencies were emulated by representatives of the Russian Jewish community, exposing internecine Jewish enmities at odds with the image of fraternal comity that Lazar and Putin were trying to create. That afternoon, a group of Russian Jews led by Lazar—accompanied by men wearing camouflage fatigues—entered Simferopol's Ner Tamid Synagogue. It was, in the words of Anatoly Gendin, an unwarranted "occupation." Gendin, who was not present at the time, posted a lengthy (and colorful) description of the incident on Facebook, accompanied by grainy footage from the synagogue's security camera.

> "In the synagogue there remained the community worker Kira and the youth activist Katya. ... The doorbell rang at the door of the synagogue. Katya opened the door [and] two men in camouflage pushed [it open] and went to examine the corridors and open the premises of the synagogue[136] (as it turned out, it was the guard of Rabbi Berel Lazar, who was looking for terrorists in the ancient synagogue building). They were lucky that I did not open it, otherwise this 'guard' would have to spend the night in our policeman's [lockup] for unauthorized intrusion into the synagogue. ... And the whole delegation, [feeling] at home, went to inspect the premises of the synagogue. When Kira

asked, 'did you call Anatoly Isakovich about his arrival' [she was told] 'we are such that we do not need an invitation—we are all happy!' I do not know what the rules of etiquette are for Chabad in Moscow, but I would not have entered into a foreign synagogue without the permission of the host."[137]

According to Gendin's account, the Russians then proceeded to inspect the synagogue, including the offices, which were closed to the public. The Crimean Jewish leader described the the visit as part of a larger conflict between orthodox and non-orthodox Jews. "You need to respect not only yourself, but also the people you go to visit," he said. "And I do not understand … why only the representatives of Chabad [are part of] the power structures of the Russian Federation. Why did the representatives of Chabad take upon themselves the responsibility to represent all [Jews]?"[138]

The Russians had a different interpretation. Gorin vigorously denied Gendin's accusations, describing a pleasant afternoon devoid of tension or confrontation,[139] while Lazar stated that he had come to the occupied peninsula for only the most altruistic of reasons. "Once Crimea became a part of Russia, the Jewish community turned to us to try to help them," he said. "We tried to stay out of politics."

Lazar and company may have been bullish on the potential for a Jewish renaissance in Crimea, but as the Ner Tamid episode proved things were much less idyllic than Russia would have us believe. No matter what problems roiled the Jewish community of Crimea, however, things were nowhere near as bad as they were about to get for the Jews of the Donbas.

ESCAPE FROM DONETSK

"On Shavuot [June 3-4], there was shooting right under the window of our home. The next day, nobody came to the synagogue; they were afraid. That Monday after the holiday, we left."

—Ania, an IDP from Luhansk[140]

Zhytomyr
August 6, 2014

As the exodus from the Donbas swelled to a flood, local Jewish communities began to wither away. While exact figures are hard to come by, we do know that by mid-September Lyudmila Saprikina, the head of the Donetsk branch of Hesed, estimated that somewhere around 70 percent of the city's Jews had fled.[141] By the end of November, over 1,300 Jews from the territories of the newly formed People's Republics had immigrated to Israel.[142] Most of the rest would resettle around Ukraine, waiting for a chance to return.

It was early on the morning of August 6 when Yechiel Eckstein and I landed at Boryspil International Airport and set off on the highway for Zarychany, a town just outside Zhytomyr. There, Eckstein, the gregarious and voluble founder of the IFCJ, had funded the establishment of a refugee center housing some 150 of the displaced. Run by Shlomo Wilhelm, the local Chabad emissary, the camp was now home to a wide range of Ukrainian Jews: from young orthodox families to elderly pensioners.

We pulled up to the entrance of the impromptu camp's dining hall, a red-roofed building with yellow walls, where dozens of refugees waited for Eckstein's arrival. Some were carrying balloons and most wore tee shirts with the logos of the IFCJ and the Federation of Jewish Communities. A sign on a nearby fence proclaimed the "safe summer fellowship program for families from the war-stricken areas of eastern Ukraine." The Federation and Fellowship logos were prominently displayed.[143]

As the refugees recalled their travails, the sounds of music and laughter echoed from outside, where the children were taking part in a carnival that appeared to have been specially arranged to coincide with Eckstein's arrival. The youths ran about, yelling through mouths jammed with cotton candy, making their way from one attraction to another.[144]

"This is a 21st century refugee camp, even if it does not look like it," Eckstein told me.

The temporary festive atmosphere seemed at odds with the reality of the situation in Ukraine. After they first arrived in the city, many of the children would cringe and run to their parents whenever an airplane passed overhead. Traumatized by the war, they thought that they were under air attack.

One of those children was four-year-old Vadim Sytnikova. A towheaded youth with sad brown eyes, he had escaped Luhansk with his grandfather Vladimir the previous month. He was lucky to be alive. In mid-July, Vadim's mother Anna and grandmother Svetlana decided to take him out to buy shoes. At the last moment Vladimir intervened, saying that he would like to spend some time with his grandson. Minutes later, Anna and Svetlana were dead, killed by an artillery strike.[145] More than twenty civilians were said to have died in the shelling that day as Ukrainian forces attempted to retake Luhansk. After receiving word of the loss of his family, Vladimir took the child and fled, leaving everything behind. As he and his grandson sat and spooned up soup in the camp's dining hall, Vladimir—a thin man with a lined face, receding hairline, and close-cropped salt-and-pepper goatee—strove for positivity. "We want to return to Luhansk when the war is over," he told me. "God willing, it will be okay."

Lurking just behind the celebratory facade of the camp was a deep and abiding sadness. One small child, a girl who couldn't have been more than five or six years old, cradled a broken arm and stared at me wearily. Trudging behind a building to catch my breath, I found an elderly woman wearing an old housedress. Her lined face was set in a look of utter dejection. I had heard the phrase "thousand-yard stare" in movies but now I was witnessing it in real life. She turned and looked at me apathetically as I snapped a series of pictures.

One woman recalled huddling on the floor of her bathroom with her daughter and granddaughter for a week, three generations doing their best to avoid the deadly artillery fire that raked their neighborhood. Isaac Mohelievsk, another of the displaced, described not only hearing the shelling but "feel[ing] the explosions" through his feet. Recounting her own exodus, Chana Gopin expressed nothing but contempt for both sides, accusing the rebels and Ukrainian army alike of indiscriminately firing into civilian areas. Both were just "like Hamas." Michael, an elderly escapee, said that the rebels in Luhansk had confiscated his company, leaving him without a means of support. Once a prosperous businessman, he was reduced to spending his days learning Hebrew and pondering an uncertain future.

When reporting from Donetsk I had met Yaakov David, a young Hasidic father of three. He had insisted on taking a picture while wearing my body armor. Now, running into him in Zhytomyr, he told me that he had been in the camp for two weeks. Pushing a stroller, he described how he planned on moving his family to Dnipropetrovsk, where the local Jewish community was doing its best to resettle the displaced. Although he was anxious about the possibility of the war spreading, he still held onto the hope of returning home.

As the day progressed, I found myself sitting on a boat in the middle of the campground's lake as Eckstein, surrounded by newly homeless children, shot a fundraising video. Gopin, sitting next to me, repeatedly—and obsessively—checked his smartphone. He had been cut off from his community in Luhansk for three days. While in Zhytomyr, he had hired drivers to go door-to-door, begging residents to abandon their homes.[146] It wasn't going quite as well as he had hoped. The situation there, he told me as Eckstein droned on in the background, was "a catastrophe."

Not long after, a number of IDPs gathered in the camp's synagogue where Eckstein tried to sell them on *aliya* (immigration to Israel), a prospect that one attendee said was becoming more attractive the longer they were displaced. Despite the horrors they had just escaped, however, many IDPs initially showed little appetite for leaving Ukraine. According to Jewish Agency chairman Natan Sharansky, most Jews around the world have shown themselves to be less concerned about moving to Israel than with continuing their day-to-day lives, even during times of conflict. This was especially true in the case of Ukraine, where the local Jews constituted the "hard core" of those who had declined to leave during the great migration following the collapse of the Soviet Union.[147]

Many were "still trying to gain some time and postpone the decision," Sharansky said, describing the economic worries of those who fled the Donbas.[148] "Whether [they want] to sell this property to survive here or to have some money to start their new lives in Israel … their main fear is that the moment that the authorities or the locals know that they have made *aliya*, their property will be confiscated. Many people will try to postpone their choice another month [after] month."

Addressing a meeting of the Jewish Agency's board of governors in late 2015, Roman Polonsky, director of the agency's unit for Russian-speaking Jews, discussed the situation in striking terms. Describing the wildly oscillating figures on a chart marking immigration from Ukraine as reminiscent of the "temperature of a very sick man," he pointed out that the numbers spiked and sagged according to the state of the conflict. "It drops when there is hope for a cease-fire and there are sharp increases when this collapses," he said.[149]

Alena, the aid worker who had braved the Maidan to bring food to elderly Jews, also described the extreme reluctance of some aging Ukrainians to abandon their homes. One Jewish pensioner, a resident of a frontline village, told her point blank that he was "getting used" to the clamor of war. Alena believed that his views were shared by many of his contemporaries. They just could not conceive of making their lives elsewhere. "There are many people who are thinking the same way because for them it's better to die in their own apartments with their cats, with their carpets on the wall, with their pickles in the jars," she laughed. "This is what they said, some of them, yes. Like 'I made pickles for next year and now you want me to leave?' It's a metaphor … but this is true."

✳✳✳

Certainly, the Jews who fled Donetsk did so with only the greatest reluctance, and none more so than Pinchas Vishedski. He had been living alone ever since sending his wife and children to Detroit at the end of June, a move designed to ease the psychological burden on the entire family. It backfired. Shorn of his emotional support system and struggling under the double load of managing an evacuation and providing aid for those left behind, the rabbi slowly broke down. A flood of refugees was fleeing the city, and Vishedski had encouraging as many of his followers as possible to join them. He never expected that the conflict would last and was operating under the assumption that after a matter of weeks or months most of those he had sent away would be able to return. Those with Israeli citizenship he pressed to fly home, while others were sent to Zhytomyr, Mariupol, Dnipropetrovsk, and other cities in government-controlled territory. For those without the means to leave, Vishedski provided financial assistance out of funds he had received from the IFCJ and the Russian Jewish community. Anyone who turned to the rabbi would have his or her travel and rent covered for free. At the same time, Vishedski strove to maintain some semblance of normalcy. Services were held in the synagogue, and all of the community's institutions continued to operate despite the ongoing exodus.

Between June and September, around forty families affiliated with Vishedski had made their way to Mariupol, an industrial city located two hours south of Donetsk on the Sea of Azov. Vishedski and his representatives worked with Mendel Cohen, the local Chabad emissary, to rent dozens of apartments, an effort somewhat complicated by surging prices driven by increased demand.

Most of those Vishedski had sent to Mariupol were young Orthodox families with children who would have found the longer trip to Zhytomyr excessively onerous. They were also among the most active in the community and had resisted going too far from their homes. They hoped to soon return and rebuild their shattered communal life. Rosh Hashanah was coming up at the end of September, and many expected that the conflict would calm down enough for them to return home for the holidays. While Mariupol's Jews welcomed their coreligionists, their arrival did pose a logistical problem that had to be solved. Prior to the war, only a small number of Mariupol's Jews were actively affiliated with the synagogue, and Rabbi Cohen's resources were stretched to the limit by the influx of IDPs requiring kosher food.[150] "In our community today, there is almost nobody who is Shabbat and mitzvah observant," Cohen explained. "Therefore when the Jewish community arrived from Donetsk it was very special, it was very interesting. Suddenly we saw religious Jews in the streets, suddenly the synagogue was full of ultra-orthodox people. Too bad it happened in such circumstances and too bad that it was for such a short period of time."

Back in Donetsk, Vishedski was struggling to maintain his equanimity. "I couldn't take it anymore, you couldn't sleep at night from the sound of the bombardment," he recalled. "You can't think, your head ceases to operate. And think about this as well, that I sat there for months alone, without my family. And when you're alone, it's much more difficult for you to deal with all these things, you know?"

✳✳✳

One of those who left during this period was Yaakov Virin. Short and slight with thinning hair, glasses, and a prominent nose above the obligatory unkempt Chabad beard, Yasha, as he was known to his friends, was a pillar of the Donetsk community who had edited its Jewish newspaper for two decades.

On July 10 he was in Kyiv, inspecting a company for Vishedski's kosher certification agency, when he received a call from his wife Rachel. The situation was dire, she said, announcing that she was taking their thirteen-year-old daughter Miriam to Dnipropetrovsk. Yasha, who had unfinished business in Donetsk, came home to an empty flat but was sure that he could cope with the loneliness. For nearly two weeks, he lived a solitary life under fire. By day, he would frequent the synagogue, and at night he would lay awake, thinking frenzied and panicked thoughts as he listening to the crump of incoming artillery. Mostly he prayed and hoped that the conflict would pass so that he and his family would be able to resume their lives. During this period, Yasha kept himself busy producing one last issue of the community newspaper. He didn't think it would be the final edition, but he never returned to publish another.

By July 22, he had finally had enough. Pushed by Vishedski to leave, Yasha packed a small suitcase and hopped on a trolleybus headed to the central railway station. As he approached the station, the sound of an explosion rent the air. A separatist stepped out into the road, halting traffic. Snatching up his belongings, Yasha descended from the trolley and began to make his way down the street on foot until he encountered a rebel checkpoint and could go no further. He had chosen to escape in the middle of a battle. The day before, government forces had retaken the airport and were currently in the process of tightening a noose around the rebel city. Fighting in Donetsk had already led to several civilian deaths,[151] and the municipal government was warning residents living near the train station to stay inside their homes.[152] "The sounds of shooting and explosions were quite loud," Yasha would later recall, describing the sight of tanks and buses full of armed men making their way past him to the central station. The fighting went on for hours, with civilians scrambling for shelter in basements to avoid the apparently random rain of heavy ordinance.[153]

As the sounds of battle drifted across the city, Yasha, unable to escape, returned to his office at the JCC. He booted up his computer and went online to look for an alternate escape route. As luck would have it, trains were still running through a small station just outside the city limits. He had his way out.

Hours later, after a long and grueling overnight journey, Yasha finally found himself alighting on a dim platform in Dnipropetrovsk. It was two o'clock in the morning and he was beyond exhaustion. But he wasn't yet in the clear. An unidentified man, presumably linked to local law enforcement or one of the newly raised volunteer battalions, approached him, demanding to know who he was and why he had come from Donetsk. Yasha identified himself as a Jewish refugee. The man was unimpressed and demanded proof. He opened his bag and produced his *tallit* (prayer shawl) and *tefillin* (phylacteries), which appeared to satisfy his interlocutor. Tired and stressed, Yasha cast about, spying Rachel standing on the platform. Overjoyed to see his wife, he hurried over to her, and together they left the station. Within a day, the Virins were on their way to Zhytomyr.

In the camp, he was finally able to decompress, taking long, meditative walks in the forest and day trips with his family to museums in Vinnytsia. In the evenings, Yasha and the other displaced would sit together, laughing, reminiscing, and talking about what the future would hold "but nobody had any answer to that question."

Donetsk
August 13, 2014

It was a warm August afternoon when Pinchas Vishedski finally left Donetsk. Several factors conspired to push the rabbi out of his adopted hometown. Above all, Vishedski was worn out by the constant shelling. He realized that, if he wanted to "stay a sane person" who could help those looking to him for assistance, he would have to leave and find a "quiet and calm place" to continue his work. Staying in Donetsk was becoming counter-productive. "I understood that, if I remained there, I wouldn't do any good for the Jews of Donetsk but the opposite. I couldn't help them anymore," he recalled.

At the same time, many of those closest to Vishedski had already fled and were begging him to follow. One member of the community, whose wife had given birth to a boy after they left Donetsk, went so far as to threaten not to circumcise his son unless the rabbi was present. Vishedski's family was due to arrive back in Ukraine around this time anyway, and, buffeted by rocket-fire and the pleas of his congregants, he decided that a war-zone was no place to bring his wife and children. It was decided that he would evacuate for two weeks and then reassess the situation.

"We thought we were in a bad dream and we didn't believe what was happening in front of our eyes," he later recalled. "Our city was a booming city, and suddenly everything falls apart before our eyes. We assumed that we needed to find a city of refuge, a temporary city of refuge, and then return and every-thing would continue as it was. It was very, very traumatic. I was certain that I would return within two weeks and my family, at maximum, in another month. I already started to think about what we would do for the holidays. I would send my family to Israel and be alone there for the holidays."

Acting on that assumption, Vishedski barely packed anything for the trip to Mariupol. He only brought with him a bag with his personal papers, his *tefillin* and letters and dollars from the Rebbe,[154] as well as a few changes of clothes. Despite his faith that he would soon return, the decision to leave was wrenching for Vishedski. As the hour of his exit approached, the rabbi attempted to distract himself from his troubles by engaging in busy work. He didn't want to think about everything he had built and was leaving behind.

As in much of eastern Europe, the Jewish community of Donetsk (then known as Stalino) was virtually destroyed during the Holocaust, and while Jews managed to reestablish an active community following the war, the renaissance wasn't to last. By the late 1950s, the Soviet authorities shuttered the synagogue and banned the practice of ritual slaughter.[155] Decades of enforced atheism, followed by mass emigration after the fall of communism, had left the Jewish community of Donetsk all but defunct when Vishedski arrived to revive it in the mid-1990s.[156] Now it was dying again and there was nothing he could do.

Fully aware of that history and what he had done to revive a dormant community, Vishedski couldn't bring himself to leave and continually procrastinated, pushing off his inevitable departure. His phone rang. It was his driver calling to ask when he wanted to go. Give me "a little bit, a little bit," he replied, playing for time. "It's already four in the afternoon, we have to leave," the driver insisted. He reminded Vishedski that in several hours it would be dark, increasing the risk of an already dangerous trip through the lines. With a heavy heart the rabbi assented.

"This is the synagogue to which I gave 21 years of my life," he later recalled. "This is the synagogue I built. When I arrived it was a ruin, and I built it with my strength and my blood. I arrived 21 years ago in a community that was nothing and built it and reconstructed it and it became a strong and vibrant community. [Now] everything is destroyed. You can't live with this."

Heaving himself up from his chair, the rabbi made his way downstairs for one last look at the synagogue. He entered the sanctuary—a long room with wooden floors, green and pink walls, and an arched, coffered ceiling—and made his way past row after row of pews to the *aron kodesh*. Standing before the ornate red-brown ark, light streaming in from the stained glass windows on either side, Vishedski drew back the curtain to face the Torah scrolls and began to sob.

"I cried as I stood near the ark across from the Torah scrolls, and I requested mercy from God. 'Have mercy upon us, we don't know what we are doing.' And I requested a blessing, that he would watch over all of us, that he would watch over all of the members of the community, that he would watch over the synagogue. That he would watch over everything."

Vishedski then closed the curtain, turned away from the ark, and was driven into exile.

Kyiv
September 4, 2014

The vestibule of the Brodsky Choral Synagogue was packed with refugees as members of the Donetsk Jewish community-in-exile gathered to pay tribute to one of their own. In the middle of the marble floor, surrounded by sobbing mourners, stood a coffin bearing the mortal remains of Georgiy "Garik" Zilberbord, a senior member of the community's board and a generous contributor to its coffers. The middle-aged developer had been extremely close to Vishedski ever since the rabbi's arrival decades earlier and was, at the time of his death, preparing to join him in the capital.[157]

The previous Friday, only hours after the start of Shabbat, Zilberbord was informed that a unit of separatist fighters had been spotted breaking into houses in a development he had built on the outskirts of the city. He rushed over to save his property but was less than successful. The 47-year-old husband and father was shot to death along with a security guard.[158]

Recovering Zilberbord's remains was a complicated affair that entailed working with people on both sides of the conflict. No doubt the difficulty of the task served to strengthen his friends' and family's grief. For Vishedski, it was a shattering experience. "It was one of the most tragic events of my 21-year career as a rabbi," he told me. Despite his grief, however, at least the rabbi had finally been reunited with his family, who had returned to Ukraine in late August. For many others, especially those who had fled to Mariupol at Vishedski's urging, this period held little, if any, consolation. Within days of Zilberbord's funeral, many of them would be forced to flee once more.

✳✳✳

Despite the relative calm that greeted the Jews of Donetsk upon their arrival in Mariupol, the city had only just emerged from several months of chaos as it seesawed between separatist and government control. Following fierce fighting, Ukrainian forces had withdrawn from the city in early May, only to launch an offensive that wrested back control the following month. By late August the situation was once again growing tense, although so far few members of the city's small organized Jewish community had actually picked up and relocated.[159] That was about to change.

On August 28, separatist forces, backed by Russian troops and armor, launched an offensive aimed at retaking Mariupol, a key port whose capture would be crucial in establishing territorial contiguity between separatist Donetsk and Russian-occupied Crimea. Over the course of late August and early September, separatist and Russian forces continued to advance on the city, taking several outlying towns and, on September 4, attacking Ukrainian troops guarding the city itself.[160]

"It seemed for a while that all was lost, and the pro-Russian separatists were poised to break through the Ukrainian lines and overrun the city," wrote journalist Nolan Peterson. "People were packing as much as they could into their cars and fleeing. Restaurants were shut down. The streets grew empty."[161]

As Ukrainian troops dug in around the city in preparation for battle and artillery thundered in the distance, many residents, including those who had recently escaped Donetsk, were busy preparing for the possibility of flight. Under Rabbi Cohen's direction, the Jewish community began preparations to evacuate its members, especially families with small children. Within days, the community had moved hundreds of Jews to temporary accommodations in Dnipropetrovsk, Odessa, Kyiv, and Zhytomyr. Out of the forty families that had recently arrived from Donetsk, only about ten or so people elected to remain behind in Mariupol.[162]

The Jews of Donetsk "left their homes and came here to find a safe place, and they got it for a month, but now the situation is very hot," Aaron Kagnovski, a 29-year-old community activist and father of two, explained at the time.[163] While he helped others evacuate, Kagnovski was initially unsure of whether he could bring himself to follow. "I can't leave the synagogue, I can't leave the community, I can't leave the people," he said at the time. "Maybe I'll send my family and live here. ... It's a very difficult decision, because my wife is getting more and more nervous. My head is almost exploding, but I know one thing for sure: I feel that I can't leave the people here." Within days, he too was on the way to Dnipropetrovsk, wife and children in tow.

REFUGEE RESETTLEMENT

"A lot of times we would have people calling from the road that they were coming. There was no discussion. It was just taking care of people. ... It was successful but it was a spontaneous and chaotic operation."

—Zelig Brez

Outside Mariupol
September 16, 2014

Our car decelerated and pulled over to the side of the highway after passing the final checkpoint on the road leaving Mariupol. Walking over the cracked asphalt, the driver, my translator Alexandra and I approached the uniformed soldiers manning the concrete barricade to ask for permission to take their photograph. As we stood under the vivid blue sky of eastern Ukraine, I noticed that the verdant fields and leafy trees lining the way provided the scene with a pastoral feel that contrasted sharply with the harsh lines and drab colors of the Ukrainian military position bisecting the decrepit road.[164]

I ambled behind my Ukrainian companions and walked up to one of the infantrymen. After an exchange in rapid-fire Russian, my translator turned and answered in the negative. "He says you can't photograph the checkpoint, but you can ask his commander for permission. He's just up that way," Alexandra said, gesturing to a small temporary fortification comprised of sandbags and concrete blocks 30 meters down the road. As we reached the command post, an officer came out. He was a burly man in full battle kit and sunglasses, a Kalashnikov assault rifle slung barrel-down across his back and a Ukrainian flag sewn to his camouflaged combat harness. "No, you can't take photographs of my soldiers," he said. "But you can take a picture with me."

Hoping that such a shot might include the checkpoint itself in the background, I handed my camera to the driver and walked over to the commander. A sudden smile distorting his broad face, he grabbed me across the shoulders and hugged me in tight, just as another soldier ran up and thrust a loaded rifle into my arms. Standing there in shock—I was a noncombatant after all—I reverted to training, looping the gun-strap over my neck as I had been taught in the Israeli army, just before the driver snapped a picture.

Moving on, with the sun setting over the highway, I reviewed that day's notes, reflecting on the signs of the Ukrainian civil war evident in a city only a few kilometers from the front. Having left prior to the imposition of that night's military curfew, we had a long drive ahead of us. I knew that in the hours to come I would have to work out the best way to tell the stories I had collected.

Dnipropetrovsk
September 14, 2014

Several days earlier, I had stepped off a Ukraine Airlines flight to Dnipropetrovsk, eager to come to grips with the refugee situation in the east. After landing in Dnipropetrovsk, I immediately made my way to a holiday resort comprised of small green dachas—Russian-style bungalows—where the Jewish Agency maintained a small way station for Jewish refugees awaiting transport to Israel. Since January, nearly 4,000 Jews had immigrated or were in the process of immigrating and I wanted to meet some of them.

Birds sang among the trees as teenagers rushed past, teasing each other in Russian. A woman in her twenties sauntered past in a bikini, an indication of the continued use of this facility by vacationers even in wartime. Life, even in eastern Ukraine, went on.

As my car pulled up, Maxim Luria and his wife, Nataly Nabitovsky, the Jewish Agency's representatives in Kharkiv, came out to greet me. We ambled over to the campground's communal dining hall, and the pair began to sketch out a picture of what it meant to emigrate from Ukraine.

The vacation village setting was necessary because not all of those seeking to move to Israel felt safe in an urban environment after their war experiences, Luria said, explaining that he had settled on this specific location because it was one of the only campgrounds to keep the heat on over the winter. Given the time necessary to work out the bureaucratic issues involved in *aliya*,[165] the Jewish Agency had to provide temporary shelter for its clients, many of whom did not have Ukrainian passports. Obtaining a passport, dealing with the Israeli consulate, and providing all of the paperwork required to prove one's Jewish identity all conspired to make the process far less smooth than it could otherwise be, especially given the dearth of documentation among those who fled the conflict zone.

"You [have to] understand that now there are many people who suddenly decided that they want to either immigrate or undergo a consular check, just in case. This is something that can take a week or two, [or] even more, and [then] there is also the whole matter of how long it takes a person to prepare and to be ready to leave." In the meantime, many of the soon-to-be-emigrants spent their days filling out forms, learning Hebrew from Jewish Agency employees, and speculating on what their new lives in the Jewish state would hold.[166]

Like Roman Polonsky, Nabitovsky noted how there seemed to be a correlation between flare-ups in the war and the demand for *aliya* services. The Jewish Agency's office in Dnipropetrovsk would "fill up every time that there [were] new incidents," and dealing with those who had just escaped the war-zone could be immensely difficult, especially when the Israelis had to request documents that the displaced had left back in the Donbas.

On the afternoon I visited the camp, there were 28 refugees present, down from 42 only a few days before. The camp's population fluctuated as people arrived, were processed, and then placed on flights to Tel Aviv. Despite the rise in *aliya* figures, many of those who had escaped the war still harbored hopes of returning and "rejected" the reality of the situation, Luria asserted.

"There are volunteers whose services we are using who are going to, more or less, every Jew who remains in Luhansk," he said, explaining that, like Rabbi Gopin, the Jewish Agency was also attempting evacuate people from the separatist enclave. "In a city where there is no electricity and no water and sometimes gunfire, [many of the elderly] simply don't want to leave. ... When we start to discuss *aliya*, they say, 'No, no, no, it's okay, it'll all work out.'"

Olga, an evacuee from Donetsk in her mid-fifties, confirmed Luria and Nabitovsky's account. She and her geriatric mother had been rescued from Donetsk by Christian volunteers in August and were waiting on the final paperwork needed for their move to Israel, where Olga hoped to stay temporarily with her daughter in Ramat Gan. Most people wanted to leave, but many had no place to go, she explained. Non-Jews with the financial resources to do so were able to escape, but many of them began to return once their money started running out. The Jews, however, "don't have to return" if they choose to go to Israel.

There was a pervasive gloom in the camp, indicative of the reduced circumstances that had pushed its inhabitants to choose what amounted to exile.

Igor and Larisa, a couple in their forties, together with their twenty-year-old son, Alexander, had also recently escaped the Donetsk region. Sitting on a bench among the trees, Igor slumped over, a frown above his short gray beard. His eyes were only half open behind his glasses as he clasped his hands between his knees. The picture of misery, he listened as his wife recalled how they closed their cell phone repair shop in the town of Makiivka during the turbulent days of the Euromaidan and lived on savings until the separatist uprising forced them to flee.

As soon as the separatists took over, they began looting, stealing cars right out of local dealerships' showrooms. While engaging in lawless behavior, the separatists also placed draconian restrictions on the local civilian populace, imposing martial law and a curfew.[167] "Pharmacies, bakeries, cafes—all the small businesses were closed as well, because people had no money," recalled Larissa, looking visibly distressed. Even if there had been money to spend, however, the curfew and the evening's "regular explosions" made any sort of nightlife impossible.

Angry at what was happening to their city, she and her husband refused to vote in the DNR's May independence referendum, and three months later their anger and fear became a catalyst for action. One evening in late August, unable to go outside, Larissa walked out onto her third story balcony. Looking down, she was confronted with a column of tanks moving down her once quiet street. Above the armored vehicles fluttered Russian and Soviet flags alongside the banners of South Ossetia and Abkhazia, two breakaway regions of Georgia backed by Moscow. At that moment she made a decision. "I realized that we all needed to leave. There was no reason to tarry, nothing good was happening here."

Alex Evshinko, another resident of the camp, also got the feeling that nothing good would happen when his friends began to disappear. During the early stages of the crisis, Evshinko, a 44-year-old Hebrew teacher, had attended several pro-Ukrainian demonstrations in Donetsk, and when the separatists seized power he says he was warned that he had to "shut up or die." "It simply became more and more dangerous, very much like the Soviet period and the Stalinist period when people simply shut up and people disappeared [at the hands of the] the [secret] police," he said.

One Friday in particular was seared into his memory. He was going about his business, anticipating Shabbat dinner, when he received a call informing him that a young man who was supposed to join his family that evening had been taken. As he worked to process what had happened, he received another blow. One of his friends, a priest, had also been kidnapped. That evening, at the end of a horrible day, his wife decided to blow off some steam and take a stroll in their building's courtyard. Within minutes Evshinko, who was sitting inside, heard the pop, pop, pop of bullets and his wife burst into the apartment, her face drained of blood. Panicked, she blurted out that a car had driven into the courtyard and disgorged four men armed with automatic weapons. "She was certain that they had come to arrest me. ... They broke down [the door] right next to our [ours] and began firing," he recalled. Utterly terrified, his wife turned to him and issued an ultimatum. "I don't know where, but we're leaving now."

★★★

Evshinko's worry was not without basis. As the Donetsk People's Republic consolidated its control over its newly captured territory, it clamped down on dissent, declaring the Orthodox Church the new state religion and detaining anyone questioning its right to govern. This included local priests, journalists, and outspoken Ukrainian patriots.[168] Hundreds of Ukrainians disappeared into the night[169] during the course of the conflict, and human rights organizations have accused both sides of kidnapping and torturing civilians.[170] According to Human Rights Watch, the DNR also began impressing civilians into "punishment brigades" which provided the separatists with "unpaid labor."[171]

Wishing the soon-to-be-Israelis good luck, I left the camp and made my way to Dnipropetrovsk, where I was met by the community director general, Zelig Brez, who had agreed to brief me on the local Jews' efforts to accommodate their coreligionists fleeing the war-zone. I first saw Brez—an open and friendly looking Chabad Hasid with a bald pate covered by a black velvet kippa and a full, bushy beard tipped in gray—standing inside the Menorah Center, a seven-building complex billed as the world's largest Jewish community center. Built with funding from oligarchs Gennadiy Bogolyubov and Ihor Kolomoisky, it had opened just over a year before the outbreak of the Euromaidan protests and was widely seen as a symbol of Jewish revival in Ukraine.

Known as Yekaterinoslav during the Czarist period, this eastern Ukrainian city had historically been a major Jewish center, with Jews comprising a third of its population by the 1890s. Battered by waves of pogroms over the course of the first decades of the twentieth century, organized Jewish life came to a virtual standstill after the Russian revolution, when "most of the synagogues in the city were either closed or turned into clubs or kindergartens."[172] The Second World War further ravaged the city's battered Jewish population. Most but not all of Dnipropetrovsk's Jews managed to evacuate to the east before the Nazis took the city, and some 20,000 were murdered. And while the Jewish population rose to more than 50,000 by the end of the 1950s, Jewish life did not recover. By 1970 only one synagogue was left operating in a city that had once boasted nearly forty.[173]

The Menorah Center stands adjacent to the resurrected Golden Rose Synagogue, an austere nineteenth century structure, built in the classical style and fronted by four white stone pillars and a pediment bare of all decoration save a lone star of David. The center itself comprises seven marble and glass fronted towers which were erected in a staggered formation, with the tallest in the center and two sets of three buildings, each slightly shorter than the last, radiating out from the center, forming a "v." Viewed from the right angle, it has (no surprise) the appearance of a Hanukkah menorah.

The timing of my arrival, Brez told me over lunch, was serendipitous. Within an hour the complex—which housed a Holocaust museum, several restaurants, a luxury hotel, the city synagogue, a hairdresser, a Jewish Agency office, and the Israeli consulate—would be the site of a fascinating event. The Jewish community had arranged for a mass wedding ceremony for nineteen couples, several of them refugees from the war, who had never married according to Jewish law.[174] It was a chance for a celebration in the midst of horror. All of the brides had been provided with hairdos, makeup, and clothing courtesy of the center's stylist. Such pampering must have been an incredibly surreal experience for those who had fled the war only a short time before.

After checking into the hotel I made my way onto the roof, where ten wedding canopies had been set up (the pending nuptials would have to take place in shifts). Hebrew music played softly in the background as refugees and locals mingled. Standing on the side, one enterprising Hasid had set up shop and was offering guests the opportunity to lay *tefillin*. I wandered around, chatting with guests and snapping copious photos until the wedding parties began making their way onto the roof in a festive procession. Spotting Yaakov Virin, I made my way over and was introduced to his in-laws, Shimon Leib and Esther Zuckerman. Octogenarian refugees from Luhansk, the pair were not new to displacement, having fled to save their lives during the Holocaust. Living in the Soviet Union they had been unable to marry according to the laws of their fathers, and now, displaced once again, they were determined to rectify that oversight. Flanked by younger couples under their own canopies on either side, Shimon stamped down, shattering a linen-wrapped glass in the culmination of the traditional ceremony, and his family burst into applause. To both sides of the Zuckermans, other families were also celebrating.

The Zuckermans had lived in Luhansk since graduating from university, and Shimon had spent more than half a century there as a university instructor. He bemoaned being forced, once again, to bear the title of refugee, telling me that he regarded it as a badge of shame. "First we [fled] to Donetsk [where] we stayed with our children ... but we realized that Donetsk was already under such bombing and military activities that we had to abandon it and come to Dnipropetrovsk," Shimon told me, recalling that even after his father had died and he was forced into an orphanage during the Second World War "it wasn't as scary as it is now." Despite the situation, the reception that he received in Dnipropetrovsk—where he and his wife were put up with other refugees at the Bet Baruch assisted-living facility— went a long way to ameliorating his misery. "I have no words to express the feeling of the revival of our souls since we always see how we are being cared and loved ... I feel like I went from hell to paradise."

Others displaced by the fighting, including son-in-law Yaakov Virin, while happy to have escaped, were markedly less content with their current situation. "It's very good for us here, and we would like Donetsk to be at least 50 percent as good as it is in Dnipropetrovsk," the former journalist told me. "We are hoping that negotiations will lead to something. We are hoping that the fighting sides will reconcile and negotiate and find compromise and there will be peace and people from Donetsk will come back."

By this time Virin, a man who until recently had both an apartment and a job, was underemployed, doing what was essentially make-work for the local Jewish community and sharing a small room with his wife at Bet Baruch. It was a jarring dislocation. Only that morning, hours before the wedding, he had been travelling on a bus through downtown Dnipropetrovsk with his daughter Miriam when a young man whose clothing bore several Ukrainian nationalist symbols began ranting about "building [a] Ukraine without Jews."

Asked by the driver why he cared about the Jews, the churlish nationalist replied with a diatribe about "Rothschild and Rockefeller's" alleged control over Ukraine by way of the country's central bank. A number of passengers irately respond, telling the young man either to get off willingly or to be ejected by force. As he stormed off, the nationalist turned and pointed at Virin, his hand twisted into the shape of a gun. "Are you scared of this?" he asked, and with one final shout of "glory to Ukraine, death to the Jews!" he was gone.

✷✷✷

Unlike many other orthodox communities across Ukraine, the one in Dnipropetrovsk was not shy about expressing nationalist or patriotic sentiments or publicly aiding the war effort, Brez told me. While communal leaders in Donetsk, Luhansk, and other cities had professed neutrality, wishing to remain separate from a conflict in which their communities had become little more than propaganda tools, "our community took a strong position for supporting the independence of Ukraine and territorial integrity," he said. The local Jewish school helped raise funds for the war effort and one Hasid living in the city even voluntarily enlisted, taking part in the fight on the front lines near Donetsk.

Josef Zissels has posited that a new Ukrainian political identity that transcended ethnicity had been born as a result of the conflict and that a new national Jewish identity was being forged in the process.[175] This idea tracked closely with Brez's thinking. He believed that the war had served to unify many of the disparate ethnic groups of Ukraine and create a sense of patriotism among its Jews, many of whom were "very rooted ... culturally, mentally, linguistically, and socially, to this place."

This new affinity for the Ukrainian nation, despite opening up possibilities for new forms of personal identity, did nothing to sunder the ethno-religious bonds between the country's various Jewish communities. As such, when refugees began arriving in Dnipropetrovsk, Brez and Kaminezki worked hard to accommodate them. As Orthodox Jews, both would have been well aware of the Talmudic dictum that "all of Israel are responsible for one another."[176]

While feeding and housing the refugees had strained the exchequer, "the ideology of the Jewish community of Dnipropetrovsk and the city rabbi is that we don't refuse help to anyone," Brez told me. "Even if we don't have a place, we find one." It was a struggle. As the trickle of refugees turned into a flood, the local community began responding on an ad hoc basis, sticking refugees in any available space.

"[We put people] in the boarding home for boys, the boarding home for girls, the assisted living [center] for the elderly, the teaching college, many apartments and also the hotel of the Menorah Center," he said.

Many of the newcomers had to be provided with everything from food and lodging to medical care and education, all on the community's dime. However, as its expenses mounted, the community's cash flow was decreasing precipitously. Ukraine, already one of Europe's poorest countries, had slid into recession, causing a contraction in the middle class, a major source of domestic financial support.[177] During 2014 alone, donations to the Dnipropetrovsk Jewish community declined by up to 35 percent,[178] and rampant inflation devalued whatever contributions did come in.[179] Supplemental funding from Jewish organizations abroad helped,[180] but the local community definitely felt the squeeze. Still, Brez told me, nobody was turned away.

"We did not have any discussion. We had absolutely no time for any discussion. It was every single person's separate project. There were times where we were panicked and had no idea where to put people. So we were adding institutions and thinking 'we can use this place and that place.' A lot of times we would have people calling from the road that they were coming. [There] was no discussion. It was just taking care of people. … It was successful but it was a spontaneous and chaotic operation."

Ohr Avner Day School, Dnipropetrovsk
September 15, 2014

The Ohr Avner Levi Yitzchak Schneerson Day School was a multi-story, gray stone and brick building, imposing in its size and very solidly built. Outside it exuded a sense of faded grandeur, but its drab and dismal facade belied the bustle of the young life within. A staircase just inside the main entrance was filled with children, ascending and descending next to art projects painted in the blue and white of the Israeli flag.

At the time of my visit, around 450 children, including a number of refugees, were enrolled in the community's three schools, Yehudit Bar'am, an Ohr Avner administrator, told me as we strolled in the schoolyard. We entered the building and made our way past the art exhibits up to the second floor, where several displaced children had been taken out of class to speak with me. Most of them provided almost identical reports of their ordeals, describing fleeing the city as the conflict began to heat up and, after escaping, being forced to adjust to a new life away from home. Daniel, a fourteen-year-old from Luhansk, summed up the prevailing mood when he told me that "Dnipropetrovsk is a beautiful city and the school is okay but I still miss my city and my school." Not everybody wanted to return home, however. Nine-year-old Miriam, an IDP from Donetsk, who had spent the beginning of the war hiding in her house as explosions reverberated through her neighborhood. told me that she was embarrassed to admit it but she liked Dnipropetrovsk and didn't want to return home. "It's good for me here," she said.

All of the teachers I met expressed real warmth toward the refugees, but at the same time expressed concerns regarding the cost of their upkeep, especially in light of the community's principled refusal to turn anyone away. Interrupting his Bible class to speak with me, Moshe Neuman, an Israeli Judaic studies teacher, described the services the youngsters received. "We admit them into our institutions. They don't pay. The community takes care of everything: their food, their transport, their living solutions. They eat and drink and study for free, and [we all] hope they will return home in peace." Lomi Segal, another Israeli expatriate instructor, echoed this sentiment, telling me that "we'll have to tighten our belts and save," although she held out hope that Rabbi Kaminezki would somehow pull a "miracle" out of his hat and obtain additional funds.

✶✶✶

While the school provided education, it couldn't provide accommodation. That was the job of the Bet Baruch assisted living facility, a low-slung concrete and glass building on General

Zakharchenko Street. Peach colored, with a red tile roof and a large glass skylight above the entrance, it was a cheery looking building originally constructed to house the community's elderly, many of whom had difficulty scraping by on their meager pensions. Since the beginning of the conflict, it had opened its doors to the displaced and, at the time of my visit, had found room to accommodate 41 of the more than 200 Donbas Jews currently receiving housing assistance from the Dnipropetrovsk community. Ten of the new residents, Bet Baruch director Malvina Ruvinskaya told me, were children.

When I entered, several of them were seated with their parents, eating lunch in the communal dining hall just off the lobby. As an older woman with a cart circulated from table to table ladling out bowls of soup, a bearded Hasid strode purposefully out into the center of room brandishing a *shofar*, the ritual ram's horn whose ethereal wail is used to urge the faithful to repentance on Rosh Hashanah. The residents stood and the Hasid let out an extended blast on the *shofar*, his cheeks puffing with the effort. Religious duty done (orthodox Jews blow the *shofar* every day in the month leading up to Rosh Hashanah) the man turned around and left the refugees to their lunches.

Among those dutifully eating the retirement home's kosher fare were Sofia and Gregoriy Minyuck. A retired couple in their early seventies, the Minyucks had been forced to go their separate ways by the war, each making the treacherous journey to Dnipropetrovsk on their own. A small woman whose gay and vibrantly dyed red bowl cut only served to highlight the deep frown lines etched into her downcast visage, Sofia cried several times when she recounted her last days in Donetsk. When the conflict began, she had been anxious to flee but her husband's health issues precluded an immediate exit.

Gregoriy had been suffering from an adenoma, a kind of benign tumor requiring surgical removal, and had already undergone a procedure in early May, when he spent the day of his city's independence referendum in the hospital. By June, the tension was too much for Sofia, who could no longer tolerate the sound of falling shells. "I began to cry every day, I could not hear the roar," she described. By June the last of their children had left Donetsk, and Sofia decided that, as little as she wished to do so, she would have to leave Gregoriy to finish his treatments alone. They made their way to the train station where Gregoriy bought his wife a ticket to Dnipropetrovsk and then returned to an empty house. The nights were filled with the sounds of high explosives as rockets rained down on the embattled People's Republic and Gregoriy, like many other Donetskers, moved into his basement in an effort to shelter himself from the carnage.

Looking down at the floor of Bet Baruch from behind his thick glasses, his wrinkle lines converging in a pair of pursed lips, Gregoriy was a picture of misery as he recounted his lonesome subterranean existence. For more than two months he hid inside at night, emerging during the day to stroll in his yard and trade for food with his neighbors. Nobody from the Jewish community brought him any supplies. "Maybe someone from Hesed or the Jewish community called me, but I had no opportunity to answer because I just tried to hide," he said, adding that the only contact he could remember was a telephone call from the local Hesed, asking "Why are you here? Why didn't you leave?" The basement quickly became intolerable. There was no light, no gas, no water. Toward the end he subsisted for several days on potatoes that he baked over an open fire. Finally, he decided that his precarious existence was unsustainable and that he would also have to flee.

Now, reunited at Bet Baruch, the couple were lavish in their praise of the Dnipropetrovsk Jewish community's aid efforts but, like many of the displaced, expressed a fervent desire to return home.

✶✶✶

Many others had depressingly similar experiences. At the Dnipropetrovsk Hesed later that week, I listened to IDP Andrei Frumkin describe how he hired an ambulance to evacuate his mother, an infirm septuagenarian, from Donetsk. Sitting around a table at the Jewish social service organization, Andrei and other escapees described harrowing circumstances reminiscent of refugee testimonies from the Second World War.

As the war intensified, Andrei and his sister began seriously considering *aliya* but decided to remain in Ukraine out of concern for their mother, who was all but immobile due to illness and age. Like Gregoriy Minyuck, it was Andrei's experience with the shelling that convinced him that flight was the only answer.

Andrei was walking down the street one day when shells began raining down on the city. He threw himself on the sidewalk. As he hugged the ground, the rough pavement pressed against his body, he saw a woman, who had exited a nearby building only moments before, struck down by flying shrapnel. He was scuttling over to offer assistance when she suddenly stood up, one of her arms severed completely, and walked off, evidently in shock. After that, he told me, "it became impossible to be in the city anymore."

Arrangements for housing were made through the Donetsk Hesed and travel plans were set. Dipping into his small savings, Andrei hired an ambulance to transport his mother through the lines into government-controlled territory, but when they came to a checkpoint the separatist militants on guard initially refused to let them pass. After an invasive search for valuables they finally relented. But this was not to be the end of their adventures and shortly after passing the checkpoint someone began firing on the Frumkins. When they arrived in Dnipropetrovsk, with almost nothing but the clothes on their backs, Andrei descended and looked at the ambulance. There were six bullet holes in the side.

Gregoriy Bitman also witnessed terrible suffering as a result of the shelling. A solitary pensioner, the 69-year-old Donetsk resident recalled separatists firing Katyushas from atop a vehicle just outside his apartment bloc. As the shelling grew worse Bitman, like Gregoriy Minyuck, largely hid inside. "The water and electricity supply were cut off because of the destruction. It was summer and it was quite hot … so all the products in the fridge went bad," he recalled. Things soon got much worse. "My building was hit on the third floor. It was just above my head and the family above me died," he told me. "My first thought was that I needed to run away from here." Not long after, he received a call from the Dnipropetrovsk Hesed asking him if he wanted to leave. He didn't require any urging. Packing a small bag, Bitman fled.

Unlike Bitman or the Minyucks, however, many elderly Jews remained behind in Donetsk, said Lyudmila Saprikina, the head of Hesed in Donetsk, who was in Dnipropetrovsk to meet with the heads of the other Donbas branches of the social services network.

While she estimated that approximately 70 percent of the city's Jews had already fled, her team on the ground was still caring for 1,650 elderly residents who either could not or would not relocate.[181] Estimates of how many Jews remained behind in Donetsk varied wildly, with Vishedski putting the figure at anywhere from several hundred to a thousand while a source within the Kyiv Jewish community familiar with resettlement efforts asserted that the real number was somewhere between 2,000 and 3,000. In addition to those in the Donetsk region, an additional 1,300 Hesed clients remained behind in Luhansk and its environs, according to Yoni Leifer, the Joint Distribution Committee's representative in Dnipropetrovsk. This statistic, of course, revealed nothing about how many younger people remained behind.

Back in Donetsk, the Hesed's operations continued as its employees brought supplies into the city and spirited elderly clients out. Around fifty of these evacuees were being temporarily housed in an IDP center in Prymorsk, just over 100 kilometers down the coast from Mariupol on the Sea of Azov. A local driver contracted by Hesed made the dangerous runs out of the city on back roads that were less heavily patrolled by the separatist militias than the main highways, dodging bullet and rocket fire to bring Jews out.

"[Our] psychologist left the city around three weeks ago … and even now she is trying to make phone calls to clients … to help them remotely," Saprikina told me. "The main question which we ask the clients is 'do you agree to [leave] the city?' Maybe not all of them wanted to leave the city, but it was important for them to feel that they can come to Hesed or make a phone call to Hesed and say 'I want to leave the city' and to know that Hesed will help."

Mariupol
September 16, 2014

Early on the morning of September 16, I came downstairs and met with Alexandra Budilova, a local translator, in the lobby of my hotel. It had been difficult to secure the services of a driver willing to make the trip into Mariupol, which, despite being once again in government hands, was uncomfortably close to the front line. I had been lucky that Alexandra was willing to make the trip and had managed to arrange transportation.

Our driver Andrei ushered us into his black Chevrolet sedan, and we set off. It was a more than five-hour drive on crumbling highways, and I barely looked up at the scenery flashing by as we bounced up and down over the cracked blacktop. Instead, I pulled out my laptop and focused on finishing an overdue feature story that I had promised would be filed several days earlier. I may have been slightly nervous about the trip to Mariupol, but I was terrified of incurring my editor's wrath.

As I finished my story, we arrived on the outskirts of the city, which was protected on the Ukrainian side by multiple checkpoints, each manned by armed fighters and flanked, on both sides of the road, by anti-tank barriers made of rusty I-beams welded together to form giant caltrops. At each checkpoint, our trunk and my passport were inspected. Finding no weapons or evidence that we were Russian provocateurs, the militiamen allowed us to pass.

A rundown city known for its heavy industry, Mariupol presented an unexpectedly jaunty appearance as we travelled its roads, looking out at the crowds of pedestrians thronging beneath flag-draped streetlights. The positive vibes didn't last long though, as Andrei soon pulled up alongside the burnt-out husk of the city's police station, which had gone up in flames during clashes between separatists and government forces several months earlier. The station, once a cheery-looking three-story yellow and white building a full city block long, was a charred ruin. The roof and interior floors had collapsed, and it was possible, looking up through empty windows, to see the sky. Bullet holes pocked its exterior walls.

While Mariupol appeared largely undamaged at that point, there were still a number of ravaged structures spread out across the city to remind its residents that the violence which had upended their lives could return without warning. One of these buildings was a local branch of Ihor Kolomoisky's PrivatBank. It had been torched several days before the police station, and when I arrived all that remained were the building's exterior walls and roof. The front facade was completely gone, exposing the bank's interior to the elements, and the green letters of its rooftop sign had melted, endowing the scene with a sort of post-apocalyptic quality. Someone had already cleaned out most of the debris, and there was almost nothing left except for a badly charred safe in a graffiti-filled back room. City Hall, which we passed on the way to the Hesed, was similarly decimated, a boarded-up wreck.

Hesed Mikol Anashama is located in nondescript, slightly tatty brick building with a small lawn on a green, tree-lined street. For the displaced, it is an island of sanity and kindness in an unforgiving sea of conflict.[182] Director Liudmilla Khaikin, a diminutive woman with short black hair and thick glasses, was waiting for us when we arrived.

The 63-year-old grandmother had been born in Mariupol and had no intention of leaving. Sitting in her red and cream-colored office, a large bas-relief of the Jerusalem skyline opposite her particleboard desk, she explained that one of her biggest priorities was convincing her clients not to panic.

Hoping to avoid becoming a target, the Hesed initially removing all Jewish symbols from its facade during the initial rounds of fighting. Khaikin worked hard to calm tensions, comparing the local clashes to the latest round of fighting between Israel and Hamas. "Often we used Israel as an example, and although some said that the war in Israel was different from here … I personally believe that war is similar everywhere so [we told people] that [they] are not supposed to leave, make a mess out of their lives or panic." It was a hard sell.

"The war has definitely not affected the Jewish life of the city in a positive way, but our Jewish life still goes on," she said. "People really started to panic when they saw tanks on the streets and heard gun shots. People were fighting in the streets."

Aid worker Yana Burmistrov, a thin blond woman in her early thirties, recalled one battle, describing how she "heard people screaming and saw military planes flying above [her] house" near the Hesed. She hid in the bathroom as gunfire split the air. From the screams she "could tell someone was badly wounded." She later learned from neighbors that people had been shot just outside her apartment building.

During the worst of the fighting in the city, "no one went out on the street; everyone tried to stay at home and hide," Khaikin added, noting that despite the violence very few Jews had fled the city. Four local families left for Zhytomyr, three for Crimea, and a couple packed up and took their children over the border to Russia, she said. And despite the flight of Vishedski's congregants out of the city, nearly sixty Donetsk Jews remained in Mariupol.[183] Some of them were gathered at the Hesed in order to share their stories.

They sat waiting, nine of them, at a gray folding table in a small room filled with cardboard boxes of supplies. Twinned Israeli and Ukrainian flags, a large menorah, and pictures of Hesed activities lined the walls, lending the space a festive look totally at odds with its inhabitants' miserable expressions. All were elderly except for two children: Misha Ginzburg, a tall, lanky sixteen-year-old wearing a black tee shirt adorned with a British flag, and his sister Sofia, a soft-faced ten-year-old with black bangs and an incipient double chin.

At the start of the conflict, the Ginzburg children lived with their mother in an apartment near Donetsk's hospital. After two weeks of shelling ("it was very close and we could hear them very well," Misha said) their grandmother, Natalia Lazakova, took them, along with an eight-year-old cousin, and escaped, leaving their mother behind to take care of their other grandmother. Lazakova, a bespectacled woman with gold teeth and a white mass of Ben Gurion-style hair atop her head, began crying as she described their flight. There was no room on the bus out of town, she said, but "because I had three grandchildren with me the driver allowed us stand in the bus." Despite their escape, a feeling of security was still elusive. "We were terribly worried about having to leave and if the Russians start bombing [Mariupol] we really don't know where to go," she continued, as Khaikin placed a hand on her shoulder. "Everybody desperately wants to go home."

Asked how it felt to escape Donetsk only to remain in the Russian line of advance, Misha and his grandmother replied that they tried not to think about it. "When we came here, Liudmilla convinced us nothing [bad] will happen [here], [that] we have shelters and places to hide," Lazakova said to the accompaniment of sobs from around the table. "When we came here Liudmilla hugged everyone with kindness … she is the right person to be in Hesed." Sonia, staring at her grandmother's beet-red, tear-soaked face, said that all she wanted was to return home and go to school. In the meantime, Misha added, all they did was read and try to pass the time.

Not everybody around the table had as easy an escape as Lazakova and her grandchildren. Emma Borodina, a portly 76-year-old pensioner with flaming red hair and bright pink lipstick, recalled her own journey to safety, which almost ended before it began. On the evening of July 24, Borodina was sitting at home when she heard a plane flying overheard. Within seconds the sounds of the bombing started. At six o'clock the next morning, she called her son Oleg and said "we're leaving." Pausing only long enough to pack their "documents and some essential things," they fled.

"We were at the bus station and we were waiting for the bus [when] the bombing began," Borodina recalled. "It hit the houses near the station where we were waiting … a crowd of people boarded the bus and we quickly left. I was basically only praying and asking God to keep me and my family safe and our apartment safe because the rest you can buy and this is the most important thing to have."

Most of those whom I had interviewed up until this point had told me remarkably similar stories, and I had no reason to think that this would change. However, Vyacheslav Aksentsev's story was anything but commonplace.

His narrative started conventionally enough, at least in terms of refugee stories from the Donbas. On July 21, only days after

Malaysia Airlines Flight 17 was downed by a Russian-made Buk-M1 missile system while overflying the conflict zone,[184] heavy fighting broke out in Donetsk. Both sides engaged in shelling targets within the city limits. It was, the 67-year-old pensioner, and trained philologist, would later recall, "like hail falling from the sky." He and his wife Natalia ran to a bomb shelter in a nearby school. Hunkered down, the pair were less than eager to go back into the deserted streets. However, as they say in Yiddish, man plans and God laughs. Soon, two men in uniform ran up and informed him that "the bombs will be falling on the bomb shelter and we had better run somewhere else." The scene they encountered upon emerging from their subterranean sanctuary was grim. "We went out just to see what was going on and saw a car burning because of an explosion. If we had been there we would have died." When their daughter-in-law returned home from work at the end of the day, they told her that they had had enough. Taking their divorced daughter, their son, and his family, they fled.

Asked if he had any grandchildren who had also made the journey, Aksentsev offhandedly replied that he had two grandsons, one in Russia and one in Syria, as if it was an entirely unremarkable for an elderly Jewish man from eastern Europe to have progeny living in the charnel house of Assad's Arab republic.

Perhaps sensing my confusion, Aksentsev elaborated, explaining that in 1995 his daughter, then at university, had fallen for a Kurdish man. They married and soon had a son who they named Jameel. Shortly after Jameel's birth, Aksentsev's daughter and her new family moved to the Middle East. The marriage, however, didn't last and the pair divorced. His daughter returned to Ukraine, but her husband and Jameel remained.

At that point, the Syrian civil war had been raging for three years. More than 200,000 people had been killed and another 10.8 million displaced.[185] Jameel was stuck in the middle of a conflict many times worse than the Russo-Ukrainian war, although he remained in touch with his worried Ukrainian relatives via Skype. The nineteen-year-old Jewish Kurd had wanted to emulate his father and come to Ukraine to study, but his plans had been stymied by the outbreak of war. His brother Daniel, meanwhile, was safe in Russia, where he was studying medicine. If he had made it to Ukraine, Aksentsev noted, Jameel would have been like his mother, "who tried to escape from one war and found herself in the other." It would probably have been an improvement.

Later that day I went to visit the synagogue. Hidden behind a low-key set of green gates on a quiet side street, the Chabad-affiliated house of worship served as the headquarters for Mariupol's organized orthodox community.

I sat down with Ludmilla Beyter, assistant to local rabbi Mendel Cohen, and Alisa Rostovtseva, the community's press secretary, in the synagogue's small dining hall. Decorating the walls were educational art exhibits and an oversized logo of Tzivos Hashem, the Chabad youth movement. According to Beyter, approximately 500 families attended the synagogue at least once a year, and most of those affiliated with the synagogue had opted to remain in the city.

Few had followed the example of their coreligionists from Donetsk, and those who wished to leave (mostly families with small children) received "door-to-door" transport courtesy of the community. Out of the ten families who had fled, Beyter told me, several had already returned, while others were "still afraid of coming back" and had moved on to Dnipropetrovsk and Zaporizhia where they received ongoing financial support from the Mariupol Jewish community. The problem was the media, which had "spread very scary information," Beyter asserted. "The people from Donetsk who managed to escape from the bombing in their own city got very afraid of what [might] happen and left for different cities and towns."

Fewer people had been leaving Mariupol since the signing of a ceasefire in Minsk, Belarus, earlier that month. However, the separatists continued to sporadically shell the city, and local media was reporting the possibility of a separatist attack. As a result, "many people [were] in a panic" and were "afraid of staying here," Beyter continued. "It has been quiet for the last few days, but I live close to the airport and the other day I heard some gunshots and similar sounds and it makes everyone kind of nervous."

Asked about the widespread Israeli belief that Ukrainian Jews should abandon their homes and move to the Jewish state, Beyter replied that such a solution wasn't very realistic. Many people had jobs and families and homes and cannot just move on, she said, The Israelis should understand that "Israel is home for them as much as Ukraine is home for us."[186] Interjecting, Rostovtseva told me that, while she had her bags packed and had topped off her car's gas tank, "we are not going to leave this city and I am going to be here until the last moment."

Russian aggression aside, were the local Jews nervous about being defended by members of the Azov Battalion, I asked. A Ukrainian volunteer militia with neo-Nazi ties, Azov was at that time a critical component of Mariupol's defense. Commanded by Andrei Biletsky, the leader of the neo-Nazi Social-National Assembly and its affiliate Patriot of Ukraine,[187] Azov proudly flew the Wolfsangel as its symbol. In interviews, its members expressed sympathy for Adolf Hitler, questioned the Holocaust, and identified as Nazis. Biletsky himself had previously called for "a crusade against the Semite-led *Untermenschen* [subhumans]."[188]

Rostovtseva looked at me and replied in a casual manner, indicating a surprising indifference to the heavily armed anti-semites only kilometers away. However, she added, while she was unconcerned, the city's elderly were "very afraid and scared when seeing Nazi symbols."

One of these elderly Jews was Chaim Shubarev, whom I visited in his well-furnished fourth floor walk-up in a Soviet-era apartment bloc. He pugnaciously asserted that, even should artillery begin to fall, he would not move from his house. "I am a Jew," the 97-year-old retired Red Army colonel declaimed in fiery Yiddish. "Whenever I go to bed, I always pray to God to save and support those who are close to me."

Shubarev may have been resigned to whatever fate awaited him, but my driver and translator were somewhat skittish. We had to leave, Alexandra insisted, pointing out that it would soon be dark. Aside from the dangers of driving through an area that close to the front after nightfall, we also had to contend with the curfew that had been imposed on Mariupol several days earlier.[189] After passing through three checkpoints, we were on the cracked and broken highway. Stopping off at a gas station, I picked up a small bottle of vodka and began putting my notes in order.

The day after my return from Mariupol, I was sitting in a hotel room at the Menorah Center sorting through my notes, when I realized that I had significantly more material than I could possibly fit into a news dispatch. I had a great deal of sympathy for my interview subjects, stemming from my own family history. Both of my grandparents had fled to the Soviet Union following the German invasion of Poland. There my grandfather survived on the margins as an economic "criminal," dealing in boots and other small items on the black market. My grandmother wasn't as lucky. She was pressed into hard labor by the communists, forced to work long hours in an asbestos mine. After the war, they both ended up in a displaced persons camp in Ulm, Germany, where they met, married, and had my mother. She was born a refugee.

I also knew, from personal experience, how terrifying huddling in a shelter with one's family during a bombardment could be. Several months earlier, Hamas had kidnapped and brutally murdered three yeshiva students in the Etzion settlement bloc. In response, the Israeli military had initiated a wide-ranging crackdown on the US-designated terrorist organization. Refusing to sit still while its operations in the West Bank were dismantled, Hamas forces in the Gaza Strip began firing rocket barrages into Israel, forcing hundreds of thousands of Israelis, including my family, to take refuge in shelters. It became a familiar, if always terrifying, ritual. Whenever the siren went off, we would grab the children and huddle in our *mamad,* the concrete and steel-reinforced safe room built into every Israeli apartment since the Gulf War.

Given my affinity for the topic and the large amount of material I was collecting, I thought it might be a good idea to write a book chronicling the travails of Ukraine's Jews. From now on, I would collect as many testimonies as possible when reporting, and in the course of time maybe something would come of it. My decision made, I realized that it was getting late and that I ought to turn in. That night I dreamt that I was on the sidewalk with Andrei Frumkin watching people get blown to bits. I woke up screaming, my body drenched with sweat.

Arriving at the Dnipropetrovsk International Airport for my flight home, I was greeted by the sight of dozens of new immigrants to Israel being shepherded by a Jewish Agency emissary. Wandering about the duty free shop, aimlessly taking in the alcohol, cigars, and knickknacks, I noticed Igor and Larissa, their long thin faces drawn down into expressions of misery. Their paperwork had finally gone through, and they too were on the way to Israel. For me, it would be a quick and unremarkable flight home to my wife and children, but for Igor and Larissa it was a journey into the unknown, to a country with a strange language and culture, thousands of miles away. It must have been excruciating.

UMAN AND DONETSK

"On Wednesday evening when we started the Rosh Hashanah prayers, at that precise moment, the shelling started."

—Yehoshua Vishedski

Ben Gurion International Airport, Israel
September 22, 2014

Despite the war, everyone was coming to Uman. Since the fall of the Soviet Union, increasing numbers of Jews from Israel, Europe, and the United States had come on a pilgrimage to this small central Ukrainian city to spend Rosh Hashanah at the grave of the eighteenth-century Jewish Hasidic rabbi and mystic Nachman of Breslov. For several days every year, it was like a *shtetl* revival, with tens of thousands of worshippers, many of them dressed in the black suits, hats, and side curls of Hasidim, thronging the streets and filling the air with the sounds of Yiddish and Hebrew.

It was a warm, clear morning in Tel Aviv when I arrived at Ben Gurion International Airport's old Terminal One building. Long since supplanted by the ultra-modern Terminal Three, it was still in use by budget airlines and, that morning, a flight of incoming immigrants. Inside, within a special hall reserved for the Ministry of Immigrant Absorption, 140 Ukrainian Jews sat in rows of orange chairs under strings of small plastic flags listening to welcome speeches by Jewish Agency Chairman Natan Sharansky and Immigrant Absorption Minister Sofa Landver.[190]

Small children wearing Jewish Agency tee shirts milled about, eating chocolates wrapped in foil embossed with the Israeli flag, as their parents sat filling out forms in a row of small offices to the side of the hall, putting the finishing touches on the paperwork necessary to receive their official identification cards and become Israelis. It was a touching scene and one totally at odds with what was happening only a few hundred meters away at the other end of the terminal. As the newcomers, fleeing war and recession, breathed a sigh of relief at finally reaching Israel, only meters away, hundreds, if not thousands, were excitedly preparing to make the same journey in reverse.

The main entrance to the terminal was packed with excited Hasidim pulling suitcases. Many of them had saved the entire year in order to afford the airfare, leaving their wives and children behind to celebrate the Jewish new year alone. Rebbe Nachman, a charismatic spiritualist and the founder of the Breslov Hasidic movement, had requested to be buried in Uman so that he could be close to the Jewish martyrs of the 1768 massacre of the town's Jews. He had promised his followers that whoever visited his grave, donated to charity, and read a selection of psalms would be saved from the torments of hell.[191]

By the beginning of the second decade of the 21st century, around 25,000 Jews were showing up in Uman every year.[192] Previously a custom restricted to members of the Breslov Hasidic sect, such visits had exploded in popularity alongside growing interest among non-Hasidim in Rebbe Nachman's ecstatic philosophy, which focused on attaining joy through worship. The pilgrimage has also created friction with local residents, which has spilled over into violence on several occasions.[193] In 2010, a group of Hasidim were deported and banned from Ukraine for half a decade for fighting with an evangelist, and a Jewish man was murdered, possibly in response to the stabbing of a Ukrainian man by a pilgrim two weeks earlier.[194]

During the run-up to Rosh Hashanah, organizers of the pilgrimage expressed confidence that, despite the war, attendance would not be much lower than in previous years. Several weeks before the holiday, Rabbi Chaim Kramer, a Breslover involved in arranging accommodation for the pilgrims, told me that he did not believe that the conflict would deter Israelis, who had just gone through their own war with Hamas. Israelis, after all, are "used to it," but "there are people that I know from North America and England staying away this year because they are afraid of what's going on. I assume that it will be noticeable, the drop in tour groups that come, but I think we'll have a pretty well-attended Rosh Hashanah anyway."[195]

"A lot of people were not going to go because of the war, but as soon as they heard about the ceasefire a lot of people started buying tickets," Yoni, an American living in Israel and a frequent visitor to Uman, told me. The fighting "wasn't in that area anyway but people are still afraid fighting could break out anywhere. Apparently now it's a ceasefire so I'm planning on going." Among his friends, interest in Uman was actually on the rise, he added, explaining that "Israelis had their summer of rockets and threats and war and all that and a lot of people feel like they need to let loose a little bit. That's what you do in Uman, you let loose." In fact, as the pilgrimage grew in popularity, Uman had indeed become known as a destination for those looking to relax on the holiday, with reports of drug use, prostitution, and other problematic recreations filtering back to the orthodox community in Israel.[196]

On that sunny September morning at Terminal One, as I watched the Hasidim celebrate their upcoming flights to Ukraine I suddenly got the feeling that I was watching people stream through a revolving door. At one end of the massive building Jews were thanking God for their escape and at the other end their coreligionists were excitedly embarking on a journey to the same place, oblivious to their brothers' sorrows. It was a surreal scene.

✶✶✶

This sense of dissonance would carry over to the different ways in which the pilgrims and those affected by the war marked the incoming new year. Back in Kyiv, the exiled leaders of the Donetsk Jewish Community worked hard to create a comforting atmosphere for their constituents. In a hall provided by the capital's Jewish community, 150 Donetsk Jews assembled for the holiday. Gathered by Rabbi Pinchas Vishedski, the exiles prayed, ate, and discussed their futures.

"It was very emotional and very painful," Vishedski recalled, explaining that Rosh Hashanah was supposed to be a holiday spent at home with family and not on the run from a war. "We wanted to be in our synagogue and not in another location. On the one hand it was very hard, but on the other hand we rejoiced to be together, to pray together, to eat together and lend each other strength."[197]

According to Chief Rabbi Yaakov Dov Bleich, Jewish refugees from Kharkiv to Dnipropetrovsk took part in the services held by local communities, but he believed that Vishedski's efforts to gather at least some of his congregants in the capital for the holiday put "a bit of light in their lives." "I think it meant a lot to them that they were able to get together again," he said. "They are able to see that their community still exists even though they are in exile."

The war and the Jewish community's imperative to care for refugees also dominated Bleich's holiday sermon, in which he cast Ukraine's war against the separatists as a battle of "good against evil." It must have seemed grimly appropriate to his listeners. Earlier that day, an unknown assailant had thrown a firebomb into the Podil synagogue compound. And while the fire was quickly extinguished, the hate behind the attack must have made the rabbi's congregants particularly receptive to such a Manichaean message.[198] Only three days before, a swastika had been daubed on a Holocaust memorial at Babi Yar.[199] It would not be the last time.[200]

At the same time as the exiles in Kyiv celebrated Rosh Hasha-nah, the remnants of the Jewish community in occupied Donetsk were also holding their own services, led by two Hasidim whom Vishedski had sent back into the war zone for the holiday. One of these Hasidim was Vishedski's cousin Yehoshua, a hirsute rabbi with a bushy black beard and close-cropped, graying hair, who wanted to create the same kind of comforting atmosphere of continuity in Donetsk that his cousin was endeavoring to promote in Kyiv. Upon his arrival in Donetsk, Vishedski imme-diately threw himself into the distribution of aid and the organi-zation of the synagogue's communal meals. He also put the word out that the rabbinic leadership had not abandoned the city's Jews. Anybody who wanted to leave would receive assistance.

In the end, around 100 people participated in the synagogue program, which got off to something of an inauspicious start when the prayers were interrupted by the thunder of explosions reverberating across the city. "On Wednesday evening when we started the Rosh Hashanah prayers, at that precise moment, the shelling started," Vishedski recalled. "And it was very serious the whole first evening and the first day, all of the time it was shelling [but despite everything] we continued everything like normal." From nearby the sounds of separatist counter-fire could be heard, with the violence lending a poignancy and sense of urgency to the prayers for a peaceful and prosperous year. "[We] just had a very special prayer," he said. It was "very special and moving."

In Uman, meanwhile, the festivities went on as usual, with little to no apparent awareness of the plight of the Jews praying under fire less than a day's drive to the east. "No one seemed to know about it," one pilgrim succinctly put it. Some participants, however, showed a hyperawareness and concern for others affected by the conflict. Specifically, the soldiers themselves.

The Hasidim set up collection boxes at several locations, solic-iting donations "for the soldiers wounded in the hard war in eastern Ukraine." In a news report about the campaign broadcast on local network ICTV, a number of Hasidim were filmed putting money in one of the boxes and declaring "Slava Ukrainy" ("Glory to Ukraine"), a greeting closely associated with the OUN which had become popular following the Euromaidan.[201] It is unlikely that they were aware of the phrase's connotations.

Responding to the report, Bleich praised the initiative of the Hasidim, emphasizing the tensions between locals and pilgrims and asserting that "the act of raising money to assist the injured soldiers may very well turn the tide and give them the opening of positive PR." Back in his internal exile in Kyiv, however, Vishedski had a different take, lamenting that it was "very unfortunate that people are not aware of, and may not seek to know, the difficult situation of so many Jews in eastern Ukraine."[202]

Ironically, despite the Kremlin's rhetoric regarding the dangers facing Jews in Ukraine, Russia itself was far from immune to antisemitic violence. On the second night of Rosh Hashanah, a group of men disrupted a holiday concert in Moscow, screaming abuse at musician Andrey Makarevich and lobbing pepper spray canisters throughout the hall. In covering the incident, Russian television ignored the Jewish nature of the concert, describing "the attack as a legitimate expression of outrage at Makarevich 'for his friendship and support of the fascist junta in Ukraine.'"[203]

The state media's response to the Rosh Hashanah attack was reminiscent of a recently aired "propaganda film" which had slammed an opposition activist as a "disgrace to the Jewish people," noted historian David Fishman. The message, he averred, was clearly "a not-so-veiled warning by the state-controlled propaganda machine: Jews should be quiet and not join the protests, or they will face an anti-Semitic backlash."[204]

CHAPTER FOUR

DISINFORMATION

"Putin's politics of memory has created a lens through which the only analog to the contemporary Ukrainian movement for national liberation is the Banderivsky (Ukrainian nationalists, followers of Stepan Bandera) of World War II, who were traditionally depicted in Russia as Nazi collaborators. … The politics of memory that was based on the cult of the war had managed to produce a worldview within which new acts of war could be justified.… It has also created a language of political mobilization against the external enemy, which the regime needed in order to marginalize the in-country opposition."

—Nikolay Koposov[1]

Odessa
October 1, 2014

In the autumn of 1905, after nearly a year of swelling unrest across his empire, Czar Nicholas II promulgated a series of reforms known as the October Manifesto. Celebrations broke out across Russia, even as many monarchists blamed their country's shifting political landscape on the perennial scapegoat of the Jews. The predictable result was that "in many Ukrainian cities jubilation ended in pogrom."[2] In the Black Sea port city of Odessa, the center of Russia's Jewish cultural renaissance, 400 Jews were murdered and thousands injured in an orgy of violence that lasted three days.[3]

In 2014, revolution was again in the air, and Putin's Russia was working overtime to disseminate propaganda that was, in journalist David Patrikarakos's words, "designed to make the Ukrainian government look ridiculous and the threat of Ukraine's supposed 'fascists' look grave."[4] A significant part of this effort was focused on pushing the narrative that the country had been overrun by violent antisemites whose aggression had caused a mass exodus of Ukrainian Jews. Three weeks before the 109th anniversary of the 1905 Odessa pogrom, Russian newspapers *Pravda*[5] and *Izvestia*[6] reported that members of Pravy Sektor were terrorizing the Jewish community of Odessa and had beaten more than twenty people. Local leaders were reported to be in the process of preparing an appeal to the World Jewish Congress, asking the international Jewish organization to intercede on their behalf. "Pravy Sektor is just destroying us, it is pure militant Nazism," Mikhail Maiman, described by *Izvestia* as the leader of Odessa's Jewish community, was quoted as saying. "We will not allow our people to be beaten, to be robbed of our future. … We must disarm and disperse the 'right wingers!'"

This story, however, was a complete fabrication. Its veracity was vociferously denied by local Jewish leaders, all of whom denied any knowledge of the fictional Maiman. To a man, they stated that there had not been one incident of violence directed against their community.[7]

"People are worried [about us]," Chabad emissary Rabbi Avraham Wolf told me. "We received hundreds of emails and calls. We clarified what happened, and there were no antisemitic incidents. [There] has been no rise in antisemitism."[8] Rafael Kruskal of the city's Tikvah organization agreed, stating that there was no climate of fear in Odessa.

One communal representative, speaking on condition of anonymity, said he believed that both sides in the Russo-Ukrainian conflict were making use of antisemitism in their propaganda as a way of disparaging their enemies. "There is no question that from the beginning we became a tool. Both sides are trying to say [they] are the protectors" of the Jews, he told me, adding that the authorities had expressed a commitment to combat antisemitism not only because it was right but also because "they realize that any antisemitic attack could reflect badly on them." It was possible, he continued, speculating, that the low-key response among Jewish groups to the attempted firebombing of the Podil synagogue the previous month was because the security services had asked the Jewish community not to make a fuss, as this would "play into the hands of the other side."[9]

The Ukrainian response to the firebombing incident had been instructive. Alongside the pro-forma condemnations of the event and reassurances that the authorities in Kyiv would not tolerate prejudice, another, less anodyne narrative about antisemitism in Ukraine was also taking shape. Asked about the firebombing, the Second Secretary of the Ukrainian Embassy in Tel Aviv responded by describing it as the action of "stupid people or provocateurs."[10] The idea that antisemitic incidents could and should be attributed to outside agitators became increasingly widespread as vandalism against Jewish sites surged in the period following the Euromaidan.

According to the Vaad of Ukraine, occurrences of graffiti and attempted arson more than doubled over the course of 2014, with the most popular targets being Holocaust memorials such as Kyiv's Babi Yar. Synagogues in Zaporizhia, Simferopol, Mykolayiv, Kyiv, and Hust were also targeted. In a contemporaneous report, Vyacheslav Likhachev contended that the increase in the desecration of Jewish sites could be explained by the fact that "symbolic violence has now been legitimized in Ukrainian society."

"The psychological barrier between theoretical intolerance and symbolic violence has become quite transparent for persons leaning towards radicalism," he wrote. "One needs to take into account that thousands of young people in Ukraine have gained experience making and using incendiary mixtures in the winter struggle, as well as undergoing even more extreme and traumatic experiences that have seriously shifted the boundaries of what is acceptable."[11]

It was after one of these repeated attacks against Babi Yar that one of the most high profile instances of blame-shifting occurred. On the first night of Rosh Hashanah 2015, unknown assailants piled tires around the menorah-shaped monument at Babi Yar and lit them on fire. Photographs of the monument showed it blackened and covered with soot. It was the sixth attack on the site that year and the ninth since 2014.[12]

The Jewish community was indignant, accusing the government and civil society of ignoring the incidents and doing little, if anything, to prevent them. At a memorial ceremony at Babi Yar several days later, the leaders of seven Ukrainian Jewish organizations issued a statement demanding that Kyiv move to protect Holocaust sites across the country.

"The last act of brutal vandalism at Babi Yar—the site of the massacre of tens of thousands of Jews—is not just a public insult of honor and dignity of the Jewish people, but also a humiliation for the country and its government, whose inaction made possible this crime as well as other similar acts of abuse in Kyiv and other Ukrainian settlements," the leaders of the Jewish groups wrote in a joint letter. "We demand immediate and effective steps to prevent vandalism in the future, along with the strengthening of criminal responsibility for vandalism and punishment of the organizers and executors of this crime. [The fact that there was] almost no reaction of civil society and mass media, no feedback from authorities and law enforcement agencies in respect to the events in Babi Yar clearly indicates the ignorance of society in respect of the large-scale tragedy that happened to the Jews of Ukraine during the Holocaust."[13]

Prime Minister Arseniy Yatsenyuk's response to the vandalism took a somewhat different tone. Rather than directly addressing the Jewish community's concerns regarding the fact that no concrete steps had been taken to secure the site, he claimed that the vandalism at Babi Yar was, in reality, a direct attack on his government. In a letter to World Jewish Congress CEO Robert Singer, Yatsenyuk wrote to stress "the firmness of me personally and of the government of Ukraine regarding the fight against anti-Semitism and all kinds of xenophobia [sic] manifestations."

> "The government of Ukraine deeply concerns [sic] regarding the acts of vandalism in Babyn Yar site. There are convincing evidences [sic] that enables us to assert we are facing well planned and thoroughly prepared provocations. The purpose of these provocations is twofold—to throw discredit upon Ukrainian authorities and to destabilize the internal political situation in Ukraine. Respectively, I have given full instructions in order to provide extremely comprehensive and impartial investigation of these shameful incidents."[14]

With one letter, Yatsenyuk had artfully shifted the focus from Ukraine's inability to prevent antisemitic violence, instead placing all of the blame on outside, presumably Russian, actors. This approach of blame-shifting and ignoring antisemitism would eventually become so blatant that even Boreslav Bereza, the Jewish ultra-nationalist, would call out what he described as the "shameful silence of the Ukrainian leadership."[15]

That being said, it seems quite likely that Russia was behind at least some of the incidents that occurred during the course of the Ukraine crisis.[16] There have been credible reports of agents of Russian influence "fomenting ethnic tensions within Ukraine" by way of attacks on local Polish and Hungarian targets.[17] In one high profile case in late 2017, Ukrainian police arrested three men who had been caught smuggling explosives over the border. The Ukrainians blamed the trio for a long list of crimes, including a number of previous antisemitic incidents.[18]

However, not all—or even most—of Ukraine's racial problems could credibly be laid at Russia's door, and just as Kyiv sought to shift the blame for its domestic antisemitism onto

Moscow, the Kremlin was likewise working to exaggerate its neighbor's Judeophobia. Asked about the widespread reports regarding anti-Jewish violence in Odessa, Evgeny Piskunov, Second Secretary of the Russian Embassy in Tel Aviv, stated unequivocally that he believed that violence against minorities was frequently concealed by the Ukrainian authorities. Following the revolution, the new government had done its "utmost to cover up extremists' attacks on ethnic and religious minorities, including Russians and Jews, and prevent their coverage in the media." Despite its best efforts, however, Kyiv still "failed to hide some crimes against representatives of the Jewish community of Ukraine," he told me.[19]

Like Patrikarakos, historiographer Nikolay Koposov has argued that the utility of this kind of rhetoric lay in its ability to strengthen support for Russia among certain sectors of Ukrainian society.

> "The politics of memory is the main instrument that Putin's government has used to divide Ukraine and render it politically dependent on Moscow. That politics, and in particular the cult of the Great Patriotic War, has become central to the ideology of Putin's regime. ... With regard to Ukraine, though, the cult was used to demonize all 'anti-Russian' forces in that country, from liberal nationalists to far-right groups, by presenting them as 'Nazi allies.' Putin's 'Battle for Ukraine' could thus be viewed as a continuation of Russia's struggle against Nazi Germany, in which all 'good [meaning pro-Russian] Ukrainians' should support Moscow against the 'neo-fascist' West and its Ukrainian 'accomplices.'"[20]

These tactics were feasible because Ukraine had been "one of the most Russified Soviet Republics," Koposov wrote, explaining that "most Ukrainians were therefore personally attached to the symbols of [the] Soviet community, and the cult of World War II was deeply rooted in Ukrainian culture of the Soviet period."

Such a conceptual approach provides much needed context for understanding Putin's claim that Ukrainian forces in the Donbas were conducting themselves like Nazis.[21] Spread through Russian-language media, these talking points became articles of faith for many of Yanukovych's Russophone supporters who felt disenfranchised by the revolution. And while Russian propaganda outfits like Russia Today vehemently opposed any efforts to tar them with the brush of fake news, they also saw their promotion of the Kremlin's narrative as a critical component of their country's war effort.[22]

Faux antisemitism became a regular leitmotif in Russia's propaganda over the course of the first two years of the conflict. One of the vectors for such disinformation was the Kremlin's network of trolls. Much has been made of the role of troll farms in disrupting the 2016 US election, but before the Kremlin used its online warriors to advocate for Donald Trump they had their eyes on different targets, including the "secret Jewish roots" of Ukraine's leaders.

In mid-2015, internet researchers Lawrence Alexander and Aric Toler (of Bellingcat fame) discovered a "sprawling network of pro-Kremlin websites," one of which was the aptly named "Who is Who," an ersatz Ukrainian outlet purporting to provide critical background information on members of the new government. "A strong theme of antisemitism runs through the site, with a large number of articles accusing Ukrainian leaders [such as Poroshenko and Yatsenyuk] of being part of a Jewish conspiracy," Alexander and Toler wrote.[23] This message would also be taken up by the DNR's propagandists, who, in conjunction with the Internet Research Agency, a notorious Russian troll farm, produced a plethora of online videos attacking Ukraine. In one, the separatists ridiculed their Ukrainian adversaries for "living under a 'Jewish occupation.'"[24]

It is not unreasonable to speculate regarding the negative ramifications of this kind of vilification. The Kremlin's propaganda offensive may have been responsible for the gas attack in Moscow described in the previous chapter, and it is possible that the intentional linking of Jews and Ukrainians may have had something to do with the Russian Communist Party's November 2014 demand that Russian Jews "distance themselves from Kolomoisky and make him understand that his crimes are denounced by his own people."[25]

This demand, which was panned as "vulgar and primitive anti-Semitism" by a spokesman for Chief Rabbi Lazar,[26] was reminiscent of a similar statement made by Turkish President Recep Tayyip Erdoğan several months earlier, when he insisted that his country's Jewish community "adopt a firm stance and release a statement against the Israeli government."[27]

However, there are those who argue that belief in Jewish control may not be as indicative of antisemitic sentiment as one would think. According to Matthew Kupfer, a reporter at the *Kyiv Post*, it is "very common in Ukraine to believe that many of the leaders are Jewish," and, although "these rumors' origins are almost certainly antisemitic, there are also a lot of Ukrainians who believe it but say there's nothing wrong with that."

"So, there certainly are antisemitic rumors that exist and are widely believed, but many of the people who believe them don't personally hold antisemitic beliefs," Kupfer told me. "That's one thing I've often found surprising about Ukraine. The former USSR has a high tolerance for stereotyping. I suspect this has a lot to do with the Soviet approach to nationalities, which reified (and occasionally invented) different 'national groups.' The Soviet Union essentially posited that each nationality had a distinct territory, language, culture and, therefore, 'national character.' And this was part of official policy. So Caucasians are 'hot blooded,' Ukrainians are rustic salo-eaters, and Jews are cunning."[28]

Kyiv
October 26, 2014

If anything could have put the lie to Russia's claim that the levers of Ukrainian power had been seized by antisemites, it would have been the results of the 2014 parliamentary elections. On a freezing late October day, citizens across the country (excluding Crimea and the occupied Donbas) went to the polls to vote for their country's first post-Maidan Rada. It was a singular test for the new Ukraine. Would the nationalists, who had made huge strides only two years earlier, continue to increase their representation, or would the electorate reject them, even after their decisive role in ending Yanukovych's kleptocracy?

The results were a thorough repudiation of the far right. Svoboda, which had 37 MPs going into the elections, failed to pass the five percent threshold for entry into the legislature. (However, because parliamentary mandates in Ukraine are apportioned through an odd mix of proportional representation and direct election by district, Svoboda managed to hang on to six of its seats.) Right Sector also failed to pass the electoral threshold. This collective failure buoyed the spirits of the country's Jews.

Svoboda was "back where it should have been" now that Yanukovych was gone, Bleich told me, conjecturing that the ousted leader had "boosted their popularity" to make the opposition "look bad." Reuven Stamov, the leader of Kyiv's Conservative Jewish community, agreed, asserting that "they didn't have as much support as they say in Russia. It's simply not like that." Josef Zissels prognosticated that Ukraine's diminished ultranationalists would henceforth direct their attention "exclusively against Russian aggression ... and in this regard will not be distracted by the migrants ... and—even more so—the Jews."[29]

Among the new deputies was Jewish oligarch and failed presidential candidate Vadim Rabinovich, who had been elected as a member of the Opposition Bloc, a newly-formed party consisting of Yanukovych loyalists and others disinclined to support the new government. Rabinovich's decision to join the opposition was a shock to Ukrainian Jews and led to a split with his long-time collaborator Ihor Kolomoisky. This caused some Jews to fret that this would "make the Jewish community look like we are in opposition."[30] Such worries were mitigated, however, by the choice of Poroshenko loyalist Volodymyr Groysman as speaker of the Rada a month later.[31] Even more heartening for the Jewish community was the fact that, within weeks, Svoboda's representatives in the cabinet had announced their resignations, clearing the board for the emergence of a more moderate government.[32]

Why had Svoboda's fortunes declined so dramatically? One possible explanation is that the cooption of the party's anti-Russian agenda by more mainstream political actors sapped it of its attraction. While Svoboda's prominent role in the revolution could reasonably be expected to have led to further electoral gains, Anton Shekhovtsov has posited that the party's support was already drying up prior to the Euromaidan. The developments of the revolutionary period merely accelerated this trend, providing the final nail in the party's coffin.

> "Svoboda's relative failure to mobilize its former electorate can be attributed to the demise of former president Viktor Yanukovych's regime: Svoboda was successful in 2012 because it was considered an anti-Yanukovych party, so with Yanukovych ousted, almost half of Svoboda's electorate was gone too. Furthermore, in 2012, Svoboda was also considered almost the only 'patriotic' party, but now all democratic parties are patriotic, so Svoboda has lost its 'monopoly' on patriotism."[33]

Moreover, while a portion of Svoboda's voters fled for more moderate factions, the formation of additional right-wing parties also served to split its base. "Where did Svoboda's former electorate go," Shekhovtsov asked. "I presume that more moderate voters went back to the national-democratic forces, such as the

People's Front or Samopomich ['Self-help']. Part of Svoboda's former electorate apparently went to the Right Sector and Oleh Lyashko's Radical Party."

It would be misleading to assert that no antisemites or extremists entered the Rada in 2014. Among those elected were Azov commander Andrei Biletsky,[34] Artyom Vitko, who would later be filmed singing a song in praise of Adolf Hitler,[35] and Yuri Shukhevych, whose father Roman headed the UPA during the Second World War.[36] However, it would be even more misleading to assert that fascists or antisemites had won any sort of victory in Ukraine (although any such statement must be qualified by the caveat that the exigencies of the emerging war in the Donbas led the Ukrainians to ignore the antisemitic and ultra-nationalist leanings of many of those fighting on their behalf).

Vadym Troyan, Biletsky's deputy at Azov, is a perfect example of this phenomenon. After an unsuccessful bid for the Rada as a member of Arseniy Yatsenyuk's People's Front party, Troyan was chosen to head the Kyiv Oblast regional police by Interior Minister Arsen Avakov, who feted him on Facebook as a respected commander who could form "the basis of a new national police force." Despite Avakov's fulsome praise, others were less enthusiastic, with Efraim Zuroff stating that Troyan's appointment sent "the worst possible message about the intentions of the new Ukrainian government."[37]

Overall, however, the events of late 2014 sent a message of Ukrainian moderation that was totally disregarded in Moscow. Addressing the Duma not long after the election, Russian Foreign Minister Sergei Lavrov asserted that a lack of Russian involvement in post-Soviet Ukraine was actually responsible for the putative rise in extremism.

"I believe that Ukraine did not get enough attention after the breakup of the Soviet Union," he declared. "We could have done more to defend the rights of Russians there. Frankly speaking, it could never occur to anybody that radicals and neo-Nazis could come to dominate Ukrainian politics and that responsible politicians would be forced to make statements—maybe, even against their will—that are influenced by radicals and neo-Nazis."[38]

Russian claims aside, it was actually quite difficult to gauge the real level of antisemitic sentiment that existed in Ukraine at the time, given the lack of accurate data on the subject. In mid-2014, the Anti-Defamation League released a global survey which found that 38 percent of Ukrainians—some 14,000,000 people—harbored Judeophobic views. (Russia came in at 30 percent and Poland at 45.[39]) However, some experts questioned the results of the survey, which labeled respondents as anti-semites if they agreed with six or more stereotypes out of a set of eleven presented by pollsters, on methodological grounds.[40]

Researcher Ivan Katchanovski, writing in the journal *Communist and Post-Communist Studies*, has cited studies "indicat[ing] that, since the 'Euromaidan,' public attitudes in Ukraine have become relatively more supportive toward the OUN, the UPA, and Bandera." His report contrasted a 2013 Kyiv International Institute of Sociology (KIIS) survey showing a 19 percent approval rating for Bandera with an April 2014 poll which found that 31 percent of Ukrainians viewed the nationalist leader in a positive light.[41]

However, despite Bandera's checkered legacy, these numbers cannot necessarily be used as a substitute for polling on racial prejudice. While many Ukrainian antisemites lionize Bandera, not all of his admirers are necessarily antisemites, especially given the tendency in Ukraine to focus on his legacy of anti-Soviet activity while denying his racially charged ideology. Citing a 2009 KIIS survey, Katchanovski noted that some 35 percent of Ukrainians believed the UPA and Bandera's OUN(b) faction had been been complicit in war crimes but this number dropped precipitously precisely in the western parts of the country in which support for Bandera was highest.[42]

One 2015 survey by Ukrainian firm RatingPro indicated that 26 percent of Ukrainians would react negatively to one of their children becoming romantically involved with a Jew although it did not explore the issue further.[43] Another survey released in 2010 found that, while 63 percent of Ukrainians manifested tolerant attitudes toward Jews, such sentiments had been trending downward since the early 1990s.[44] Overall, there has been little in-depth research on antisemitic attitudes in Ukraine and, as we have just seen, those polls that did address the issue did so in passing and provided little context.[45]

The research that is available, however, paints a picture of a country that is in many ways unremarkable and strikingly similar to its neighbors. The post-Soviet region, the Kantor Center's Irena Cantorovich explained, "continues to be characterized by 'classic' anti-Semitism: anti-Semitic propaganda together with desecration of Jewish facilities and a relatively small amount of physical violence against Jews."

The taboo against public antisemitic expression, so strong in the west, is much weaker in Ukraine, just as it is in the rest of the former Soviet Union. Examples of public figures engaging in public antisemitism include Artyom Vitko's videotaped ode to Adolf Hitler ("Adolf Hitler, together with us, Adolf Hitler, in each of us, and an eagle with iron wings will help us at the right time"), reserve general Vasily Vovk's Facebook post threatening to "destroy" the Jews,[46] and Ukrainian war-hero-turned-lawmaker Nadiya Savchenko's claim, made during a televised interview, that Jews hold disproportionate control over the levers of power in Ukraine.[47]

Former Prime Minister Yulia Tymoshenko, one of Ukraine's most prominent opposition leaders, was forced to apologize after she was filmed laughing at an antisemitic comedy act at a gathering of her Fatherland party.[48] Former Georgian President Mikheil Saakashvili, who was brought to Ukraine to serve as the governor of Odessa Oblast, fired his press secretary for indulging in the conspiracy theory that President Poroshenko was a hidden Jew.[49] Even Poroshenko himself would be tarred with the brush of antisemitism after his office announced that he would award Vasyl Kvasnovsky, an author who had falsely accused Jews of perpetrating the worst crimes of the Soviet state, with the prestigious Order of Freedom. (A spokeswoman later stated that his inclusion in the list of award winners was the "result of a technical mistake.")[50]

In the immediate post-Euromaidan period, however, most of these incidents were yet to occur. And after the 2014 election and the appointment of Groysman as speaker of the Rada, one might have expected the Russians to develop another line of attack that didn't involve accusations of antisemitism and fascism. But the Kremlin wasn't willing to allow reality to get in the way of a good story. In 2015, keenly aware of the growing number of Ukrainian Jews leaving for Israel, Russia's Vesti news program ran a segment blaming the exodus on the new government.[51]

As proof of its assertions, the program cited a letter purportedly written by Rabbi Menachem Margolin of the European Jewish Association (EJA), a Brussels-based advocacy group, which claimed that an EJA investigatory commission had uncovered "cases of compulsory closures of Jewish organizations and schools" and the "revocation of licenses from newspapers published in Hebrew and Yiddish." (Needless to say, Margolin vehemently denied drafting the letter.[52])

> "There have also been registered multiple cases when uniformed people with the insignia of voluntary nationalistic battalions, participating in combat actions in eastern Ukraine, destroyed Jewish historical and cultural monuments. Unlawful calls for forced banishing of Jews are often made during mass demonstrations in big cities across the country. *This outrageous revival of Nazi Germany traditions* [sic] *in a modern state threatens Europe and European ideals* and it is of utmost importance for top European Union officials to immediately respond to the threat!"[53]

For expert commentary, Vesti brought on Yevgeny Satanovsky, former president of the Russian Jewish Congress, and Avigdor Eskin, once an aide to aide to Israeli far-right politician Rabbi Meir Kahane (and latterly a close collaborator of Russian hyper-militarist philosopher Aleksandr Dugin).[54] Satanovsky, it should be noted, had recently come under fire, both in Russia and Ukraine, for publicly calling for the deaths of Ihor Kolomoisky and Josef Zissels.[55]

Reinforcing the segment's questionable thesis, Eskin told Russian television viewers that "we see hints of antisemitism in all levels of Ukrainian society," adding that the *Jerusalem Post* had reported "that Putin is telling us that neo-Nazis are governing in Ukraine and it looks like Putin is right."

Eskin, whose credibility with Russian audiences likely came from his overtly Jewish appearance (he wore a beard and skull-cap), was more than just a useful tool, he was the perfect cover for Putin's campaign against Ukraine's "fascists." Addressing a television audience less than a month after his Vesti appearance, Eskin again claimed that Kyiv was at the forefront of a Nazi resurgence and, somewhat shockingly, "equated Russian speakers in Ukraine's east to Jews murdered by Nazi Germany in the Holocaust."[56]

Despite Eskin's heated vitriol, however, not all—or even most—of Ukraine's fighters were neo-Nazis. Some were even Jews.

JEWS AT WAR

"It's not right for people to make statements that Jews will run if there will be a war. The Jews didn't run during the Maidan and were represented on both sides of the barricades. They are a part of this society."

—Yaakov Dov Bleich[57]

Kyiv
February 20, 2015

Yossi Azman chanted the *kaddish*, the mourner's prayer, as the rain-drenched coffin was lowered into the cold, damp earth, accompanied by the sharp crack of rifle fire. The young rabbi and a team of volunteers had worked for days to make this moment possible, searching among the dead for the body of Evgeny Yatzina, a 25-year-old infantryman who had died during the fierce combat of the Second Battle of Donetsk Airport.

Holding out against heavy odds, fighting for every meter of ground against the separatists in frigid winter conditions, the defenders of the airport had come to be known as the "Cyborgs," symbols of Ukrainian resistance. Sent in with the 90th Battalion as reinforcements in mid-January at the height of the battle, Benya, as he was known to his friends, was wounded almost immediately, his cheek ripped open by a piece of shrapnel. Despite his injury he fought on for two days until the separatists detonated part of the terminal building he was tasked with defending, bringing down the ceiling and crushing his legs. He succumbed to his injuries the next day, a fact his mother Svetlana only discovered when she came across a video of her son's body laying among the dead.

"Neither the Ministry of Defense, nor the military, nor any other state structures have made any effort to find guys," she told Ukrainian media. "I turned to all the volunteers who could at least somehow search for soldiers. Everyone answered me that they could not get there."[58]

With no help forthcoming, Benya's uncle in Israel called Rabbi Moshe Azman, describing the video and asking for the Jewish community's help in locating his nephew. The rabbi in turn spoke with his son Yossi, tasking him with bringing Benya home.

"The same day that they called my father from Israel I contacted the soldier's mother and I was constantly updating her, because we have friends that are still located [in Donetsk and] we got in touch with them," the younger Azman recalled. "They drove over to the airport and looked for the body while [dodging] bullets since [according to] Jewish law we had to bury him properly. It was a very difficult operation and it probably took about two to three days before they were able to get his body out of there."

As the two sides battled over the airport, the volunteers searched, checking each body they came across. It was a difficult task as "these bodies were in terrible condition [and] some were unidentifiable," Azman said. Finally, however, the volunteers identified Benya through a birthmark and, with help from members of the volunteer battalions, brought his body by armored car to Dnipropetrovsk. From there, Svetlana accompanied her son back to Kyiv, where he was given a Jewish burial with full military honors. As Benya's comrades, some on crutches and others in wheelchairs, looked on, soldiers fired volleys into the air and Azman recited psalms for the soul of the young infantryman.

"We buried him on a Friday. They say that anyone who's buried on a Friday goes to heaven," Azman said. "Later after the funeral I spoke to his mother. This was the first time I met her in person … she was crying and saying 'thank you so much that you did this work, this deed, because many of his friends weren't found and we don't know where they are.'" Benya "was a very proud Jew," Azman continued. "His mother told me that after the army he really wanted to move to Israel. [She] showed me pictures and he was often holding the flag of Israel, he was a Zionist. He was a calm guy, wise, and everyone loved him."

✶✶✶

Nearly a year earlier, following the appearance of Russian troops in Crimea, Chief Rabbi Bleich had responded angrily to reports that yeshiva students were looking for ways to dodge the draft, stating that "Jews didn't run during the Maidan" and wouldn't shirk their responsibilities in time of war. However, given that the Jewish community represents only a small fraction of Ukraine's population and skews toward the elderly, not many Jews, relatively speaking, ended up serving. And despite Bleich's belligerent words, no full-time yeshiva students ended up in uniform. However, one aging Hasid did end up enlisting and, like Benya, took part in combat operations near Donetsk.

With his long, salt-and-pepper beard, lined face, velvet kippa, and side-curls, Asher Joseph Cherkassky was the very picture of a middle-aged husband and father. A veteran of the Red Army, the 43-year-old had picked up his wife and children and left Crimea for Dnipropetrovsk soon after the occupation.[59] As the separatist insurgency grew in the east, he joined the Dnipro Battalion, organized and funded by Ihor Kolomoisky, out of a sense of "civic obligation."[60]

"I felt obligated to serve in the army to defend the country and the citizens of Ukraine," he would later explain. "If you live in this country, you must serve this country."

After being wounded by a grenade in a village several kilometers from Donetsk,[61] Cherkassky was removed from frontline service and put on tour, making the rounds with Dnipropetrovsk Deputy Governor Borys Filatov, who promoted him as "a hero and a symbol of the resistance."[62] Selfies taken with the Hasidic soldier proliferated across social media, images of a man whose very existence seemed to disprove Russian claims of rampant antisemitism. Media outlets vied for interviews with the battle hardened Hasid who suddenly found himself a minor celebrity due to his role as public defender of Ukraine's image. In interviews, he fulfilled that role with vigor, telling reporters that "Muslims, Jews and Ukrainians [had] fought together" and claiming that Pravy Sektor leader Dmytro Yarosh (whom he considered a friend) had even floated the idea of forming a special

Jewish unit.[63] As he explained it, Cherkassky saw it as his duty to combat what he saw as Russian efforts to use his "image in the informational war against Ukraine." There were "many other Jews" fighting in the Ukrainian army, and by participating in media interviews the "Russian information war was defeated," he explained.[64]

✶✶✶

Cherkassky wasn't the only Jew from Dnipropetrovsk to contribute to the war effort. From Kolomoisky and Kaminezki on down, the local community was one of the most engaged in Ukraine. Among the city's most fervent Jewish patriots was Pavel Khazan. An ecologist and environmentalist who had emerged as a prominent anti-Yanukovych activist during the revolution, Khazan soon became one of the more important players in the so-called Anti-Terrorist Operation Zone (ATO Zone or ATO for short.)

Unlike Cherkassky, Khazan, a thin and balding 40-year-old, didn't pick up a rifle and go to the front. As his associate Kolomoisky struggled to raise troops to stabilize the east, Khazan engaged in a parallel effort to provide the poorly equipped Ukrainian army with supplies and technical assistance. In a war in which the civilian sector was highly involved in the provision of logistics, organizations like Khazan's newly established NGO, the National Defense Foundation (NDF), were incredibly important.[65] One of Khazan's primary goals was the establishment of a secure military radio network. The Ukrainian military's aging analog communications infrastructure was especially vulnerable to Russian surveillance and desperately required an upgrade.

Despite also bearing the status of a reserve officer, Khazan regularly went out into the field on behalf of the NDF as a civilian volunteer, donning fatigues and combat kit to set up encrypted radios for frontline units, including those belonging to the Dnipro Battalion.[66] While not strictly observant, Khazan was very proud of his Jewish identity,[67] and during one trip to the front at Kodema, just outside DNR territory, he decided to use it to troll the separatists.

He had arrived in the village, where the 43rd Infantry Battalion was holding the line, and set up shop upgrading the unit's communications equipment. Along with his gear, he also brought along a personal present for his old friend Yuriy Formenko, the 43rd's commander. Trudging up a hill overlooking the separatist positions, Khazan and his comrades planted the present, a large Israeli flag, right where their foes could see it. "We put it on the hill and after that [we intercepted communications] from the other side [claiming] that the Israeli army came to Ukraine," he recalled, laughing. "But for us it was very funny. Yuriy Formenko is very Ukrainian … everybody was Ukrainian there and [I was the only Jew] but … the Russians and separatists said 'oh it's the Israeli army.' But after that we decided to destroy their minds and [later] we came with an American flag. And it was serious, not just humor. It was trolling of Russians and separatists … the next time we came with a Canadian flag."

✳✳✳

Like any modern military conflict, the Russo-Ukrainian War attracted foreign fighters. While the total number of volunteers on both sides was low by the standard of struggles such as the Syrian civil war, it wasn't insignificant. Hundreds of fighters were estimated by the Atlantic Council to have picked up arms for both the Ukrainian and separatist causes, including far-right extremists who volunteered to serve with the Azov Battalion and units linked to Right Sector.[68] There were also, according to DNR Foreign Minister Alexander Kofman, a significant number of Israelis involved in combat operations.

In an interview with a Jewish news website linked to Lazar, Kofman—an agnostic Jew and self-described former Jewish Agency youth program counselor—railed against the Ukrainian Jewish community, deeming it "offensive that Jews take the most active part in this Nazism." He never could have imagined, he said, that he would have cause to be "ashamed of my fellow tribesmen." He also took time to brag about what he described as "representatives of Israel who are fighting here because of their nationality."

"Basically, it's reconnaissance and sabotage units, snipers," he said. "Among them are the guys who served in the IDF, and those who came to Israel, already experienced fighters. We have dozens of such guys."[69] However, while there are multiple documented cases of Israelis training or fighting with Ukrainian troops, we only know of two cases of citizens of the Jewish state taking up arms on behalf of the separatist cause.

One of those was Ina Levitan. Born in Baku, Azerbaijan during the communist period, Levitan grew up in Israel and never expected to return to the territory of the former Soviet Union. However, when a friend disappeared in eastern Ukraine in late 2014, she began investigating. She was able to track him down within a few days but continued following the conflict from Israel and within a month and a half had "decided to go to Novorossiya."[70] In an open letter published on the website of Maki, the Israeli Communist Party, Levitan described how she decided to "fight against fascists, pro-Nazis, and oligarchs." The Ukrainian people, she claimed, were in danger from "pro-Nazi activists" who "torture and murder civilians and soldiers of the Ukrainian army who do not share their grievances."

"I met a mother who told me about her 14-year-old daughter, who was raped by a group of neo-Nazis and then abused to death," she explained. "Her body was sent to her parents in a wooden box. I myself saw a man who returned from neo-Nazi captivity. They cut off limbs from his body and tattooed swastikas on his body. We are fighting against these horrors, which occur repeatedly and harm civilians. ... As an Israeli, I personally feel a deep hatred for the fascists. I hope there will be time when everyone will understand what is really happening in Ukraine. I hope and believe that we will succeed and win, we are building a new land—for the people."[71]

Like Kofman, Levitan said that there were a number of Israelis fighting for the separatists, although she provided no proof of her assertions. According to Lazar confidant Boruch Gorin, for the most part Israeli citizens fighting in Ukraine were adventure seekers of Russian and Ukrainian origin relegated to support roles.

"For both sides, the Jewish factor was very important in the beginning of the war," he explained. "It's less important now but then it was very important to show to both sides that they have the Jews fighting for them [and] the Israelis, and that the Jewish community abroad are their supporters. … I think that this is … PR as usual and there's nothing to talk about."[72]

Levitan, however, disagreed, retorting that "it is precisely here that it is now possible to do something for the principles which I have always believed in—helping others, building, defending, [pursuing] justice. In addition, didn't Israel teach me who is a Nazi? Doesn't Israel honor Holocaust Remembrance Day every year? … I grew up on these principles. We all did—it is only that we are not all aware that in the land of Ukraine all the pro-fascist horror has come back to life."

✶✶✶

Around the same time that Levitan was thinking about volunteering for the LNR, another Israeli, named in local media reports as Alex "Pavel" Vetko from Rehovot, was released during a prisoner swap along with 37 other separatists. However, unlike Levitan, it was unclear just who Vetko really was. A spokesman for the Israeli foreign ministry declared that the separatist prisoner had "nothing to do with Israel" and that, while he may or may not have been Israeli, "his action's are his, not Israel's."[73]

Alex Kogan, editor of the Israeli-Russian language news site Izrus, cast suspicion on the Ukrainian reports, echoing Gorin's concern that both sides were "trying to show that they are not antisemitic because they have Jews fighting with them" and adding that it was hard to vet much of the information coming out of the war zone. "You can't rule out that there is somebody who has Jewish blood [fighting], but the only thing that troubles me with all these stories is that we don't see them. We have no physical proof of their existence."

Whatever the truth regarding Israelis in the people's republics, the situation was much clearer when it came to the government. In mid-2014, Natan Chazin, who had previously exaggerated both his Israeli military record and his role in the Euromaidan, had finally found an important niche.[74] Noticing that the Ukrainian military lacked any sort of drone reconnaissance program, Chazin and several others established the Aerorozvidka, a crowd-funded volunteer unit using off-the-shelf consumer technology to produce weaponized UAVs for use in intelligence gathering and combat operations.

By early 2015, the unit—which would later be integrated into the army—comprised twenty men operating sixteen drones, some of which were retrofitted to allow them to carry ordinance.[75] Chazin, instantly recognizable by his custom insignia combining a Star of David with the red and black nationalist flag, was made an advisor to the Chief of the General Staff. Defense Minister Stepan Poltorak was certainly impressed with Chazin, writing on Facebook that he was "pleasantly staggered by those results that they have already succeeded in attaining."[76] (Ironically, while Ukraine's drone program was getting off the ground with the help of an Israeli, Jerusalem was reportedly selling its own advanced UAVs to Russia, two of which were downed by Ukrainian forces in the ATO.[77])

Back in Israel, supporters of both sides were busy gearing up to provide support from abroad. While hundreds of thousands of Russian-speaking Jews had immigrated to the Jewish state since the end of the Cold War, most were not particularly involved in the conflict, but those who were went the whole hog. On one side there were activists like Ravid Gur, an Odessa native who held a series of small demonstrations attempting to rally Israeli support for the separatist cause, while on the other there was Victor Vertsner, a graying professional photographer with a triangular face and jutting jaw from Tel Aviv.

A Ukrainian Jew raised in Israel, Vertsner ran Israel Supports Ukraine, an activist group he established in the aftermath of the Maidan massacre. By November 2014, the group had over 5,000 Facebook followers, and its more active supporters took part in their own demonstrations against what they saw as Russian aggression against their homeland. Protesting, however, was not the group's raison d'être, which was crowdfunding the purchase of relief supplies. Through Vertsner's efforts, multiple shipments of clothing weighing hundreds of kilos each were shipped from Tel Aviv to Kyiv and from there to the Donbas, where they were used by both frontline Ukrainian troops and displaced civilians.

In an interview in late 2014, Vertsner described his frustrations with Russian-speaking Israelis, most of whom he believed to be "on the Russian side." The reason? They were watching same Russian propaganda that had helped set off the Donbas conflict in the first place, he said. "The broadcasting of Russian TV channels [in Israel] is disproportionate. Open your TV set and you will see ten Russian channels against one or two Ukrainian. Propaganda is much more aggressive on the Russian channels."[78] While his countrymen may not have been doing enough to satisfy him, Vertsner himself would soon go on to contribute a lot more than just clothing to the Ukrainian cause. This was largely thanks to another Israeli expat who heard the call.

During the immediate aftermath of the Maidan, Tzvi Arieli had established a small self-defense force to protect the Kyiv Jewish community. It was a short-lived project, and by the end of the year the Latvian IDF veteran had moved on to the east, determined to create a similar force in Mariupol. In a fundraising video posted online, he pled for funds, asserting that his proposed group was "of [the] utmost importance as the situation is volatile and can erupt at any moment. Some Jews have already fled the city, but most remain and need protection."[79]

Arieli never did manage to establish a Jewish self-defense force in Mariupol. Instead, he ended up training local National Guard units stationed nearby.[80] Around that time Vertsner, a commissioned officer in the IDF reserves, offered the newly-minted instructor his assistance, leading to an invitation to deliver a lecture at a military academy in Kyiv.

"In the academy I was supposed to lecture for a week [but] instead [gave] a [single] lecture for seven hours," Vertsner recalled, describing how he was asked to continue teaching but declined in order to help several officers who were in the process of establishing a new, rapid reaction unit. Over the next two years, Vertsner travelled to Ukraine some 25 times, training soldiers and adapting the tactics he learned in Israel to Eastern European realities. He was, he claimed, one of at least ten such Israelis volunteering for the Ukrainian cause.

Why would an Israeli, albeit one who was born in Ukraine, choose to leave his home to take part in a war thousands of kilometers away, especially if his efforts were not always rewarded? For Victor, part of the answer lay in his connection to the Russian Federation. While born in Ukraine and largely raised in Israel, Vertsner also spent five years in Russia as a child. As an adult he travelled there often and "had many friends" in the country. "Basically I was a witness to this brainwash[ing] that they [were] doing in Russia. People I spoke to, [who] I thought were friends of mine—very educated people, journalists, profes-sors—they were just brainwashed. They lived in an atmosphere of hatred and fear. When I expressed at first my support for Ukraine on Facebook during Maidan, the day after I had maybe 80 percent less friends from Russia. Approximately 200 people unfriended me. I got inspired by all this Maidan spirit."

While Vertsner, for the most part, found the patriotic post-Euromaidan spirit incredibly uplifting, he did have one "really bad experience" with a neo-Nazi that left him especially angry. Apart from his work as an instructor, he had also been donating his time to a initiative that provided wounded servicemen with prosthetics. He was sitting with the program's doctor when one of his clients, who was aligned with Pravy Sektor, walked in for his final fitting wearing the tee shirt "of an SS brigade." "[We] gave him his prosthesis and kicked him out," Vertsner told me, recalling with anger how he later saw the same man presented as a hero at a photographic exhibition about the war.

Vertsner's antagonism toward the far right was not shared by all of the Israeli volunteers on the Ukrainian side. Grigory Pivovarov embraced it. Like most of the Israeli volunteers, Grisha, as he was known, had been born in the Soviet Union. However, unlike many of his comrades, he was originally from Russia. He got involved in the conflict almost by accident while passing through Ukraine during a hitchhiking trip across Europe.[81] A veteran of Israel's storied Golani infantry brigade, Pivovarov ended up in the Aidar Battalion, a controversial volunteer unit whose soldiers have been accused of committing war crimes.[82]

In an interview with Israeli journalist Edward Doks, Pivova-rov was rather blasé about the allegations against the battalion, stating that he could "not say we are so kosher, that's how it is in war, everything happens." He also admitted that Aidar contained Nazi elements but insisted that this was not a source of conflict and that they were his "brothers in arms."[83]

Despite it's initial reliance on Aidar, Azov, and other units, the Poroshenko administration was decidedly uncomfortable with this state of affairs and strove to exert its control over all of the armed groups operating on Ukrainian territory, which were seen as a destabilizing influence. (Some would go on to turn their guns against the government, which would take various measures to reassert control and integrate most of these units into its official forces.[84]) However, even as the Poroshenko administration endeavored to tame Aidar, Azov, and others, it was also working on a parallel effort to rehabilitate their spiritual forebears, the terrorists of the OUN and UPA.[85]

THE STRUGGLE FOR HISTORY

"War is a myth-creating experience in the life of every society. But in Eastern, Central and Southern Europe it is continuously a source of vivid, only too often lethal, legitimization narratives."

—Jan Gross[86]

"I'm absolutely sure that history at the moment is one of the platforms where the struggle and the war with Russia is being held."

—Volodymyr Viatrovych[87]

Verkhovna Rada, Kyiv
January 16, 2014

One of the turning points of the Euromaidan revolution was the passage of the "Dictatorship Laws," a set of bills which severely curtailed Ukrainians' freedom of speech and assembly. Aimed at crushing the revolution and saving the Yanukovych government, these "draconian" statutes were also a weapon on another battlefield, that of history. As the world focused on the more repressive aspects, including one provision allowing the trial of suspects in absentia,[88] Yanukovych loyalists in the Rada also pushed through two measures intended to reshape local perceptions of Ukraine's wartime legacy. The first[89] increased the legal penalties for the desecration of the graves of "Soviet soldier-liberators," while the second, apparently aimed directly against the Ukrainian nationalist right, banned the glorification of Nazi collaborators and the rationalization of their crimes.

These two bills, passed as President Yanukovych was fighting for his political life, highlighted the centrality of memory issues to the political discourse of the former Soviet Union. Their language, which specifically called out the "Waffen-SS [and] its subordinate structures … and [those who] collaborated with fascist occupiers,"[90] referred to the Waffen-SS Galizien, Schutzmannschaft Battalion 201, and Nachtigall Battalion, three formations organized by the Germans and staffed in large part by Ukrainian nationalists affiliated with the OUN. And while the government behind these bills fell just over a month after their passage, the political transition did not mark the end of Ukraine's history wars. In fact, the battle for the past was only heating up.

Kyiv Hilton
November 18, 2014

By November, Yanukovych had long since fled to Russia, Crimea was occupied, and the war in the Donbas was raging, but none of that was apparent inside the luxurious Kyiv Hilton. Members of the Ukrainian elite mingled, clutching drinks and chatting in the hotel's wood-paneled ballroom. Classical music played a soft accompaniment to the low-voiced conversation as uniformed waiters circulated, handing out hors d'oeuvres and making sure that the capital's rich and powerful were well taken care of. Everyone were there to pay homage to Victor Pinchuk, an influential Jewish oligarch and son-in-law of former president Leonid Kuchma, who was receiving the Metropolitan Andrei Sheptytsky Medal of Honor Award.[91]

The prize was the brainchild of Yaakov Dov Bleich. Now in its second year, it had become a joint venture between the Jewish

Confederation of Ukraine and the Ukrainian Jewish Encounter, a group dedicated to, among other things, helping Jews and Ukrainians "understand each other's historical experience and narratives." Ukrainian Jews appeared to believe that Sheptytsky, the controversial wartime leader of the Ukrainian Greek Catholic Church, could serve as a role model for reconciliation. Speaking at a press conference prior to the award ceremony, Bleich explicitly stated that the idea came from "trying to find a way of bringing together the Jewish community and Ukrainian community." Given Russia's increasingly strident propaganda campaign against Ukraine's purported "fascist junta," it is likely that efforts to promote the Metropolitan as a national hero were also aimed at reframing the debate around the country's past as much as they were intended to create common ground between Jew and Gentile. "Look at Sheptytsky," one could imagine the organizers thinking. "He represents us better than Bandera."

However, while Sheptytsky was certainly a better role model than Bandera from the Jewish perspective, he was still a deeply flawed hero. On the positive side of the ledger, the senior clergyman had been relatively well disposed toward the Jews for a man of his time and place. It was this sympathetic attitude that eventually led him to risk his own life by hiding some 150 Jews from the Nazis. His 1942 pastoral letter "Thou Shalt Not Kill" was a rare contemporaneous public condemnation of the destruction of European Jewry. Written in response to the increasingly brutal treatment of civilians by both the Germans and their local allies,[92] the letter, which never explicitly named the Jews, called for social ostracism of those who, by engaging in political murder, have "chosen execration" and "separate[d themselves] from human society."

> "Those who delude themselves and others that political killing is not a sin do so in a strange manner, as if politics releases a man from obedience to God's law and justifies a crime that is abhorrent to human nature. This is not so. A Christian is required to

observe God's law both in private and in political and social life. A person who sheds the innocent blood of an enemy, a political opponent, is as much a murderer as a person who does this in the course of a robbery and deserves the same punishment from God and excommunication from the church."[93]

Sheptytsky had previously made a similar plea in his pastoral letter "On Mercy," in which he wrote of his "profound pain" at seeing "how in many communities there live people whose souls and hands are stained with the unnecessarily spilled blood of their neighbors." He was also said to have written to SS leader Heinrich Himmler, protesting the treatment of the Jews and requesting "that the Ukrainian police, which is composed exclusively of his faithful, not be used in action[s]" against them.[94] The Metropolitan was especially pained by the role played by Ukrainians in the killings, writing in one pastoral letter that "the most terrible of all these plagues [brought about by the war] is the plague of crimes voluntarily committed by our people."[95]

Extolling Sheptytsky 72 years later, Bleich (addressing a crowd that included Prime Minister Arseniy Yatsenyuk, former presidents Leonid Kravchuk and Leonid Kuchma, and Ukrainian Greek Catholic Archbishop Sviatoslav Shevchuk) quoted the Talmudic dictum that one who saves an individual life has saved an entire world. The senior cleric, he declared, had "saved many worlds" through his actions, in the process providing an invaluable lesson. Continuing in that vein, former Polish president Aleksander Kwaśniewski called on Israel's Yad Vashem Holocaust remembrance center to recognize Sheptytsky as one of the Righteous Among the Nations.

This title is bestowed upon those who risked their lives to save Jews during the Holocaust. Despite lobbying from various quarters over the years, Yad Vashem has consistently declined to recognize Sheptytsky, due to what a museum spokeswoman described as the "great deal of ambiguity regarding his active support for the Nazis."

This support, which must be distinguished from support for violence against Jews, can be traced to the very beginning of Nazi rule in Ukraine, when the Metropolitan declared "the victorious German army as the liberator from the enemy." As Himka has noted, although he would grow increasingly disaffected with the occupiers as the full extent of their murderous plans and their opposition to Ukrainian independence became clear, Sheptytsky initially lobbied them to form a "Ukrainian unit to fight the Soviets" that he hoped would "form the nucleus of a national army."[96] This unit, the 14th Waffen SS Grenadier Division, would go on to commit exactly the kinds of war crimes that so disturbed Sheptytsky.[97]

United Nations, New York
November 21, 2014

Only days after Bleich and the Ukrainian elite gathered in Kyiv to honor a man whose legacy was inextricably tied to the SS, the Russians, who were pushing their own wartime narrative in order to legitimize a vastly different set of foreign policy aims, proposed a resolution in the United Nations condemning the "glorification" of Nazism, neo-Nazism and "other practices that contribute to fueling contemporary forms of racism, racial discrimination, xenophobia, and related intolerance."

Russia portrayed Ukraine's opposition to the resolution, whose passage had become something of an annual ritual, as alarming, prompting the Ukrainians to counter that Moscow was actively supporting extremism at home and engaging in "nationalistic, xenophobic, and chauvinistic policies" in occupied Crimea. Excoriating Russia for its own dismal human rights record, the Ukrainian delegation evoked the memory of the Holodomor, the massive famine caused by forced collectivization that devastated Soviet agricultural regions in the early 1930s, killing millions. The Holodomor is viewed by many Ukrainians as an intentional genocide planned by Soviet dictator Joseph Stalin. In a statement, the Ukrainians asserted that while Kyiv was committed to fighting the glorification of Nazism, they also "equally condemn[ed] Hitler and Stalin as international criminals for what they have done to us."

> "We have always demanded that Russia should stop glorifying Stalinism and neo-Stalinism, because of their misanthropic and xenophobic nature. Until and unless the notions of Stalinism and neo-Stalinism are equally condemned along with Nazism and neo-Nazism and other forms of intolerance, Ukraine will not be able to support the draft presented by Russia."[98] ·

Ukraine's response to the Russians was noteworthy in that it represented both a general effort to use history as a weapon against the Kremlin and a specific use of Double Genocide theory. Promoted by a number of former communist states, especially in the Baltics, this theory is premised on the idea that the crimes of Nazi Germany and Soviet Russia were morally equivalent. Enshrined in the 2008 Prague Declaration on European Conscience and Communism, which called for, among other things, the "adjustment and overhaul of European history textbooks so that children could learn and be warned about Communism and its crimes in the same way as they have been taught to assess the Nazi crimes,"[99] Double Genocide theory has become especially popular in countries where local collaborators were complicit in the Holocaust.

The theory, argues Professor Dovid Katz of Vilnius Gediminas Technical University, has a number of implications, the first of which is that "some 'Double Genociders' see a need to mitigate the history [of their countrymen's involvement in the Holocaust] by discrediting the victims." Such tactics, he explains, "often have their roots in Eastern European anti-Semitism, where the phrase, 'many of the Jews were Communists, and they got what they deserve,' is still widely heard."[100]

In other words, Double Genocide theory puts those who lived under communism on an equal footing with the victims of the

Holocaust and allows them and their descendants to cleanse themselves of any guilt regarding wartime collaboration or contemporary antisemitism. Moreover, Katz argues, Double Genocide theory is frequently linked to the idea that "Holocaust collaborators, and even perpetrators, are often redeemable as contemporary national heroes."

> "The common denominator has been that 'national heroes' who were anti-Soviet are thought to deserve national hero status, regardless of their affiliation to Nazi Germany or their status of being Holocaust collaborators or perpetrators. In Latvia and Estonia, this usually takes the form of adulation for those nations' Waffen SS groups, which came into existence after most of the Jewish population had been annihilated. These were battle units that were mobilized against the Soviets and swore oaths of loyalty to Hitler; they were racist, pro-Nazi, often comprised of Holocaust perpetrators who were retrained for battle. In Hungary, there has been adulation for political leaders who carried out the Nazis' bidding regarding deportation of the Jews. In Lithuania, there are streets, public plaques and sculptures, and a state university lecture hall that have been named for Holocaust collaborators and perpetrators."[101]

Katz's explanation is especially relevant when examining Kyiv's treatment of the Holodomor. Local legislation in countries promoting this doctrine frequently goes beyond merely equating communism and Nazism as enshrined in the Prague Declaration, instead legislating a narrative in which the "Soviet genocide was much greater or, in fact, 'the real one.'"[102] This approach complements the glorification of Nazi collaborators, because, if Soviet crimes were equal or worse than Nazi crimes, those fighting the communists would perforce have been on the right side of history. Like the glorification of Bandera, efforts to create a new Holodomor narrative began in the North American Ukrainian diaspora in the latter part of the 1970s and 1980s. This effort came about partly as a result of increasing Holocaust awareness in the west, which highlighted the role of local collaborators. This, Rudling explained, "infuriated Ukrainian diaspora nationalists," who "feared that … Holocaust collaboration would be perceived as a defining feature of these nationalities." In fact, prior to the coining of the term Holodomor, Ukrainian émigré scholars intentionally referred to the famine as a Ukrainian Holocaust.[103]

This new historiography eventually made its way to Ukraine under Yushchenko, who characterized the Soviet Union as a "a genocidal occupation regime bent on exterminating the Ukrainians" and the Holodomor as a genocide that had wiped out more than ten million victims.[104] Like Yushchenko's Banderist agenda, efforts at Holodomor commemoration flagged under Yanukovych, only to be revived in the post-Maidan era. Over the course of the next several years, President Poroshenko would go on to breathe new life into the exaggerated casualty counts of the diaspora nationalists, claiming that "7 to 10 million Ukrainians" had died during the course of the famine.[105] This is significantly higher than most scholarly estimates. (According to Himka, the total number of victims in Soviet Ukraine was somewhere around four million. In his book *Bloodlands*, scholar Timothy Snyder put the figure at closer to 3.3 million.[106])

Critics of this approach contend that such inflated numbers have traditionally been intended to create a moral and conceptual equivalence between the Holocaust and the Holodomor as part of a "competition for victimhood."[107] This is a view reinforced by Poroshenko's juxtaposition of the two tragedies in a way which gives them co-equal status. Speaking at a state Holodomor commemoration in 2017, Poroshenko made this comparison explicit. Stating that "not recognizing the Holodomor is as immoral as denying the Holocaust," the president called for the passage of a law "on the responsibility for not recognizing these two unprecedentedly horrible tragedies."[108]

To many western historians, efforts to conflate the Holocaust with communist crimes (as horrendous as they were) is problematic, because it obscures the Holocaust's status as a unique event in human history. The Holodomor and other crimes against humanity carried out by the Soviet Union deserve to be marked, both as a tribute to the victims and as a warning to future generations, but they ought to be allowed to stand on their own without needless comparisons to the Holocaust or ahistorical embellishments. As Israeli Holocaust historian Yehuda Bauer wrote after the adoption of the Prague Declaration: "One certainly should remember the victims of the Soviet regime, and there is every justification for designating special memorials and events to do so. But to put the two regimes on the same level and commemorating the different crimes on the same occasion is totally unacceptable."[109]

Oświęcim (Auschwitz), Poland
January 27, 2015

As I crunched through the snow outside of Auschwitz, the path trodden into mud by hundreds of pairs of feet, I reflected that it was ironic that I had come all this way and was not allowed inside the death camp. I and the other assembled journalists grumbled and complained as we were relegated to a massive heated tent in the parking lot, about 100 meters away from the main tent covering the Auschwitz-Birkenau gatehouse and guard tower. In the heated press tent, Jews, Poles, and Germans were united in their frustration that they had come so close but were denied entrance to the main event.[110]

Many of the journalists present had been given the opportunity to explore Auschwitz, but those from the Israeli press delegation to which I belonged had arrived too late to tour the camp. In the hour prior to the ceremony—which marked 70 years since the camp's liberation by the Red Army—journalists were herded into the main tent in groups of 100 to stand at the back and stare at the brick tower under which the inmates of Auschwitz had all traveled on their final journey. The tracks under our feet, which once vibrated with the rush of passing death trains, were covered by flooring installed as part of the massive structure protecting the now fragile survivors from the harsh winter elements.

The enormous tent dwarfed the camp gate, while inside it the survivors—many of them wearing kerchiefs with the colors of their camp uniforms—sat alongside world leaders on row upon row of plastic chairs. Standing in the back, I noted that the contrast between the tent, its sides luminescent from the floodlights, and the gate to the concentration camp, which seemed somehow reduced. Its presence in the tent somehow changed it from an intimidating structure into something of a parody of itself. It was hard to connect the gate to the crimes that had been committed just beyond the borders it delineated. Wanting to speak with some of the survivors, I ducked under the rope separating them from the members of the fourth estate, but I was quickly caught and expelled by a Polish official. It appeared that they did not want their guests inundated with a barrage of questions from the large press contingent. Fuming, I headed to a side door of the press tent, where one of my compatriots was slowly smoking a cigarette, the tobacco smoke gently mingling with the fog of his breath in the frigid Polish winter. Looking out over the snow covered landscape, I began muttering darkly, venting my anger over the limits imposed on me by my Polish hosts. In a way, my situation was similar to the larger drama playing out in Auschwitz, not between journalists and ushers, but between nations.

For months leading up to International Holocaust Remembrance Day, Russia critics in Poland had lobbied hard to prevent Putin from attending the ceremony. Representatives of the populist Law and Justice opposition party condemned the Russian leader for following a "foreign policy modeled on Stalin and Hitler" and asserted that, as long as his government continued to "raid neighbouring countries," he should be "persona non grata."[111]

Around the same time, members of the Czech Jewish community launched their own protest following the European Jewish Congress's decision to invite Putin to its own commemoration ceremony in Prague. The Federation of Jewish Communities in the Czech Republic was harsh in its condemnation of Russia, accusing the Putin "regime" of disrespecting international treaties, acting aggressively, and using "its power to occupy the territory of a neighboring state." Surprisingly, given his record of strong criticism of Russia, Bleich disagreed with the protest, saying that he understood why his coreligionists were upset but that he "would imagine that an event marking the end of the Holocaust should be above all forms of politics."[112]

In the end, the internal political pressure must have been overwhelming. In practice, while Poland did call for Russia to take part in the Auschwitz ceremony, it did so in an unusual manner which seemed calculated to appease voters opposed to any effort to solicit Putin's presence. Rather than send out conventional diplomatic notes to the various heads of state who would be participating, the Poles used what is known as a *note verbale*, a kind of semi-formal communiqué that fell short of a full invitation. This political maneuvering was interpreted as an intentional slight by the Kremlin, which announced that Putin would not attend.[113] Predictably, Jewish leaders in Russia voiced strong objections to what they saw as the politicization of their history.

Putin's absence from Auschwitz was a "very big and shameful scandal, and to commemorate the events of 70 years ago without the head of the country that was at the center of this event is … questionable," protested Rabbi Boruch Gorin, a senior official of the Federation of Jewish Communities of Russia and an adviser to Chief Rabbi Berel Lazar. When the Red Army arrived in Auschwitz in 1945, he said, it "also wasn't sent by the democratic angels, but was sent by Stalin, so nobody invited them when they came."[114] Others, especially in the Polish government, disagreed.

In a radio interview not long after the Kremlin announced Putin's non-attendance, Polish Foreign Minister Grzegorza Schetyna attempted to obscure Russia's role in the liberation of Auschwitz, telling Radio Poland that "the First Ukrainian Front and Ukrainians liberated" the camp.[115] Soon after, a senior member of the Ukrainian presidential administration also took up this theme, telling reporters in Kyiv that "Ukrainians made up the majority of those who freed Auschwitz."[116]

Despite Jewish entreaties to keep the commemoration free of politics, neither Poroshenko nor Putin found themselves able to separate their conflict from the legacy of the Holocaust. Addressing the assembled world leaders and Holocaust survivors at the gate of the former death camp, Poroshenko subsumed the Jews under the overall count of Ukrainian casualties, stating that "Jews were a quarter of [the] six million Ukrainian civilians who became victims of the [sic] World War II."[117] He also attempted to link the Holocaust with the Russian occupation.

> "Having gathered here today, we remind Europe and the world of the greatest tragedy, the apocalypse of the XX century— the Holocaust and all its victims. Similarly, we remind of the tens of millions of victims of the World War II caused by imperial madness, aggressive nationalism and xenophobia. ... And today, grandchildren and great-grandchildren of those who defended Ukraine more than seven decades ago left their homes to protect the loved ones and their Homeland from the aggressor. ... *I will not mention clear and obvious parallels between the events in Europe in the 1930s and present developments.* The threat of continental war is now great as never before. ... Thus, I call on the entire world to prevent the recurrence of tragic events. *We must not only remember the innocent victims of the past, but also think about how to prevent the recurrence of the tragedies similar to Holocaust and the World War II.* We must jointly oppose the new imperial madness, new claims for supremacy in Europe."[118]

As Poroshenko was linking the Holocaust to the Kremlin's aggression, Putin was also giving a speech which was in some ways the mirror image of his Ukrainian counterpart's. Standing in Moscow's Jewish Museum and Tolerance Center in the presence of senior Russian rabbis, Putin alluded to his government's frequent claim that Ukraine had been taken over by a fascist junta. He warned that the failure to learn the lessons of Nazism had led to new war crimes in the Donbas.

> "We continue coming across attempts at dividing humankind on ethnic, racial or religious grounds and demonstrations of anti-Semitism, Russophobia and aggressive intolerance of other ethnic groups, cultures and traditions. Nazis made use of these primitive instincts back in their times, while now they are used by neonationalists [sic], extremists and terrorists in a number of countries and regions. ... We all know how dangerous and destructive double standards and indifference to others may be. Take, for instance, the current tragedy in the southeast of Ukraine, where the peaceful population of Donetsk, Luhansk and other towns and cities have been shot for months in cold blood."[119]

And while Poroshenko had focused on presenting Russia as the Germany of the twenty-first century, Putin chose to use the occasion to highlight Ukrainian involvement in the Holocaust, stating that "Banderites and other collaborationists and Hitler's henchmen were themselves involved in the destruction of the Jewish people."

Any attempt to rewrite history was "unacceptable and immoral," the Russian strongman said, contending that "frequently such attempts cover up the desire to conceal one's shameful behavior—cowardice, hypocrisy and treason, and to justify one's direct or indirect, silent collusion with the Nazis in implementing their criminal policy." While used in the service of propaganda intended to delegitimize Ukraine, Putin's rhetoric contained a grain of truth, one that would soon become apparent as Ukraine's new rulers pushed through a legislative agenda aimed precisely at obfuscating their country's wartime record.

Kyiv
April 9, 2015

Less than half a year after the first post-Maidan parliamentary elections, Ukrainian nationalist historiography was back with a vengeance as the Rada passed a package of four bills known collectively as the Decommunization Laws. Intended both to make a clean break with the country's Soviet past and to enshrine the OUN/UPA in Ukraine's national pantheon of heroes, the legislation was a deliberate repudiation of Russia and its own national conception of history. The bills—which banned the denigration of groups which had fought for Ukrainian independence,[120] opened the old Soviet secret police archives,[121] memorialized the victory over Nazism,[122] and (ostensibly) banned the use of communist and Nazi symbols[123]—were the result of a compromise between two sets of proposals, one promoted by the government and prepared by Volodymyr Viatrovych of the state-funded Ukrainian Institute of National Memory (UINM) and the other put forward by Oleh Lyashko's Radical Party.[124]

Listing the OUN and UPA among the groups it was "granting legal status," Bill #2538-1 (On the Legal Status and Honoring the Memory of Fighters for Ukraine's Independence in the Twentieth Century) mandated the enactment of "measures aimed at increasing awareness and drawing public attention to the history of struggle and fighters for Ukraine's independence in the twentieth century." These measures were to include the development of new school "curricula, textbooks, programs, and activities" as well as the "creation of memorial complexes" and other monuments. Beyond merely glorifying Ukrainian nationalists, however, the law went further, prohibiting "denial of the legitimacy of the struggle for independence of Ukraine in the twentieth century," said denial being both an "insult to the memory of fighters for independence" and a "disparagement of the Ukrainian people." Showing "contempt" for such groups and their members was now legally prohibited.

While Bill #2538 was prescriptive, Bill #2558 (On the condemnation of the Communist and National Socialist (Nazi) regimes, and prohibition of propaganda of their symbols) was prohibitive, enshrining the Holodomor as "a genocide of the Ukrainian people" and banning the display and distribution of Communist and National Socialist symbols and propaganda. It also required local authorities "to rename districts, streets and landmarks whose names contained "symbols of [the] communist totalitarian regime."

Ironically, decommunization, despite enacting sweeping changes, did not actually ban Nazism. Numerous events have been held in memory of the Waffen-SS Galizien (with Nazi symbols prominently displayed) since the passage of the laws,[125] and Viatrovych, who has since become the public face and main proponent of decommunization, has explicitly stated that that he does not believe that the unit's symbols are legally problematic.[126] A close reading indicates that Viatrovych's interpretation is indeed correct as the Waffen-SS Galizien's name does not appear on the list of organizations whose symbols are prohibited.[127] As the authorities have not cracked down on such events, it appears that glorifying the SS is legally acceptable in contemporary Ukraine. This, at least, is the view of scholar Tarik Amar, who has asserted that "the otherwise misleading term 'decommunization' reflects well that the laws are not—as pretended—targeting Nazism and Communism equally, in a spirit of 'anti-totalitarian' and 'double-genocide' evenhandedness." Rather, he contends, "Communism is the main target [and] the purpose of condemning Nazism is clearly rhetorical—to reinforce the attack on Communism."[128]

The new official narrative drew immediate fire. Outside of Ukrainian émigré circles, the scholarly consensus is that the

OUN, UPA, and Waffen-SS Galizien did indeed engage in war crimes. As Rudling explained, following the German invasion of the Soviet Union in 1941, the OUN(b) declared statehood in L'viv, and "Yaroslav Stets'ko, its self-proclaimed 29-year-old prime minister, enthusiastically declared his dedication to the new Europe and endorsed 'German methods of exterminating Jewry.'"[129]

> "Organized by the OUN(b) militia, pogroms broke out in at least 58 localities across Western Ukraine. The number of pogroms differ significantly, from 35 to over 140, as does the estimates of number of victims, which ranges between 13,000 and 35,000. The Germans from 1940 trained OUN men for military service, and OUN-organized formations in German service took part in the mass murder of Jews. When Hitler refused to recognize the OUN as allies, much of the OUN leadership, including Bandera and Stets'ko, was arrested and incarcerated, whereas many of the local rank-and-file members continued as collaborators.
>
> The battles of Stalingrad and Kursk were major turning points in the war, and foreshadowed the demise of the Third Reich. Many nationalists who had collaborated until 1943 now felt emboldened to break with the Germans. In the spring of 1943 the OUN(b) violently took over the control of the Ukrainian Insurgent Army, UPA. About 50% of its leadership had been in German service before joining the ranks of the OUN-UPA in 1943. This year saw some battles between OUN-UPA and the German forces, but the collaboration was again resumed in the fall of 1944, when Bandera, Stets'ko, and some other OUN leaders were released from prison. Whereas nationalist history writing has greatly exaggerated the OUN-UPA fighting with German forces, its fighting with the Germans was a secondary priority to its campaign of ethnic cleansing of Galicia and Volhynia, in which up to 100,000 Poles were killed in 1943 and 1944."

It was this history that was cited by seventy Ukraine specialists who co-signed an open letter calling on President Poroshenko to refrain from signing the bills into law, calling them a direct threat to Ukrainians' freedom of speech.[130] They were far from alone. The United States Holocaust Memorial Museum (USHMM) condemned the legislation and urged the Ukrainian government to "refrain from any measure that preempts or censors discussion and politicizes the study of history,"[131] while a representative of the Organization for Security and Cooperation in Europe (OSCE) opined that the new rules "could easily lead to suppression of political, provocative, and critical speech, especially in the media."[132] The Simon Wiesenthal Center asserted that the laws proved that the Ukrainians "clearly lack the Western values which they claim to have embraced upon their transition to democracy."[133]

However, countered former Prime Minister Arseniy Yatsenyuk—one of the leading proponents of the laws—the impetus for decommunization was inherently democratic. In an interview for this book, Yatsenyuk dismissed the idea that the laws may have been intended as a sop to the nationalist right after the revolution, instead putting them in the context of shedding a tortured historical legacy.

"When the Bolsheviks invaded Ukraine, Ukrainian people suffered from the Holodomor, from political repressions, from [the] killing [of] Ukrainian priests, from [the] killing [of the] Ukrainian (I would say) nation and from antisemitism that was brought by Bolsheviks to my country. Both Bolsheviks and Communists. So the idea was very clear, to get rid of this dire and dark part of Ukrainian history where Ukrainian people had been humiliated by Bolsheviks and Communists and Jewish people were humiliated too."

Asked about the nationalists' problematic legacy, he seemed to imply that there was nothing particularly unique about the OUN or the UPA, stating that "you have your own heroes, we have our own heroes. We do respect your history. I strongly believe that you do respect our history. I am not a historian. I am a politician, so I strongly believe that this is a perfect spot for historians to dig into details, to elaborate on the different stories and narratives and to eliminate all Soviet-style propaganda that was imposed in Ukrainian history."

Remarkably, the state of Israel refrained from issuing a statement in response to the new laws or the sustained campaign of state-sponsored historical revisionism that followed, despite Jerusalem's policy of not "relinquish[ing] historical memory in favor of other interests." This restraint becomes less surprising, however, when put in the context of Israeli history policy in the post-Soviet period, in which efforts at diplomatic outreach in the former Warsaw Pact frequently override the demands of Jewish memory.[134]

Ukrainian revisionism did not emerge *ex nihilo* after the Maidan revolution. During his presidency (2005-2010), Viktor Yushchenko put the full weight of government backing behind efforts to promote the creation of a Ukrainian narrative which "juxtaposed the genocidal Soviet rule with the self-sacrificial heroism of the OUN-UPA, producing a teleological narrative of suffering (the famine) and resistance (the OUN-UPA) leading to redemption (independence, 1991)."[135] This program, which Rudling has dubbed Yushchenkoism, was pursued through a number of official and semi-official channels, notably the Ukrainian Institute of National Memory and the OUN(b)-linked Center for the Study of the Liberation Movement (TsDVR) in L'viv.[136]

Yushchenko articulated the reasoning behind his memory policy quite clearly during a November 2007 speech to the Israel Council on Foreign Relations in Jerusalem. Stating that issues related to the conduct of Ukrainian nationalists during the war should be "relegate[d] ... to the institutions entrusted with national memory," the president asserted that the Ukrainian nationalist organizations were innocent of any wrongdoing:

"I think that it is high time for us to live with open minds. Therefore, I would like to draw your attention to the fact that there was not one Ukrainian freedom organization (including that of General Roman Shukhevych) involved in persecuting Jews. During the Nuremberg trials, no freedom organization of Ukraine was recognized or exposed as one that fought against society. In the proceedings of that trial, there were no Ukrainian organizations mentioned on the list of those committing atrocities."[137]

Having worked as both the head of the TsDVR and the director of the SBU archives, Volodymyr Viatrovych, a young historian from L'viv, quickly became one of the most prominent drivers of the new history policy. During this period, Viatrovych "made the promotion of OUN-UPA mythology a fundamental part of his legacy, rewriting school textbooks, renaming streets," and publicly glorifying the OUN and the UPA.[138] It was during this period that Yushchenko famously named Stepan Bandera a "Hero of Ukraine," a move later reversed by Yanukovych.[139]

Viatrovych worked hard to promote a view of the UPA as an egalitarian and democratic movement, arguing that it could not conceivably have been antisemitic. His 2006 book *OUN Attitudes Towards the Jews*, in which he makes this case, has been harshly criticized by historians such as John-Paul Himka, who have said it demonstrates a deliberately shoddy approach to scholarship:

"[Viatrovych's book] attempts to exonerate the OUN of charges of antisemitism and complicity in the Holocaust by employing a series of dubious procedures: rejecting sources that compromise the OUN, accepting uncritically censored sources emanating from émigré OUN circles, failing to recognize antisemitism in OUN texts, limiting the source base to official OUN proclamations and decisions, excluding Jewish memoirs, refusing to consider contextual and comparative factors, failing to consult German document collections, and ignoring the mass of historical literature on the subject written in the English and German languages."[140]

Among Viatrovych's proofs that the UPA was not antisemitic was the highly misleading claim that it had included Jews in its ranks. Aside from referencing historical fabrications such as the fictitious autobiography of Jewish UPA member Stella Krentsbakh, he also allegedly warped the facts about Jews like Leiba Dobrovskii who actually did join the nationalist militia, painting them as willing participants in the struggle.[141] However, as UCLA historian Jared McBride has noted, Dobrovskii's KGB file paints a reality sharply at odds with Viatrovych's elysian vision, showing that he "actually concealed his Jewishness [from] his nationalist 'compatriots' and was no enthusiastic supporter of Ukrainian nationalism."[142] Most of the small number of Jews who served in the UPA likely had similar experiences. Himka paints a vivid and frightening picture of what it must have been like to be a Jew among the nationalists.

> "What about the Jews in UPA? They definitely served as doctors. It was a way of staying alive, at least for a time. As a result of the Holocaust and because of the increased demands of war, there was a shortage of medical personnel throughout Eastern Europe, and UPA felt that shortage as well. There was a marriage of convenience between a partisan unit desperately in need of doctors and nurses and Jews desperately in need of a place that would keep them out of the hands of the Germans. It is not a good sign, however, that we have few indications that Jewish physicians and medics survived their service with UPA, that the fullest accounts we have are by persons who escaped UPA, and that the picture they paint of the nationalist partisans is so negative."[143]

In 2007, Viatrovych took his show on the road, flying to Israel and challenging Yad Vashem over the legacy of Roman Shukhevych. Responding to Yad Vashem Council Chairman Joseph (Tommy) Lapid's claim that the Holocaust remembrance center had "an entire file that certifies that Shukhevych participated in mass murder," Viatrovych headed to Jerusalem and demanded a copy.[144] In response, Yad Vashem chief archivist Haim Gertner stated that no such collection existed, but rather that the relevant testimonies remained dispersed throughout Yad Vashem's copious collection of documents.[145] Returning to Ukraine, Viatrovych held a press conference in which he said Yad Vashem had effectively exonerated the Ukrainian nationalist leader because its "archive does not contain any dossier concerning Roman Shukhevych, which would prove his participation in anti-Jewish actions in Lviv."[146]

The Israelis were not amused. In a scathing response published on its website, Yad Vashem protested the "glaring and offensive inaccuracies regarding our institution" presented by Viatrovych. "Academic research, conducted and published around the world," the memorial asserted, "points to the support of, and intensive and widespread collaboration with, the German Nazi occupation of Poland and Ukraine, by Nachtigall and its commander at the time, Roman Shukhevych."[147] Regardless of the historic truth, Viatrovych had skillfully outplayed Yad Vashem, demonstrating his high value to the revisionist enterprise.

Ukrainian Institute of National Memory, Kyiv
February 3, 2016

Located in a run-down, two-story, pink stone building at 16 Lipskaya, only a ten-minute walk away from the Presidential Administration on Bankova Street, the headquarters of the Ukrainian Institute of National Memory (UINM) is decidedly low key given the wide-ranging impact its inhabitants have had on the historiography and toponymy of Ukraine.

I met with Viatrovych in his office, a massive, high-ceilinged room dominated by a large map of Ukraine hanging over a polished wood conference table. Ensconced at the table, his translator seated across from him, the 39-year-old historian appeared much too young to be at the center of such controversy. Even though his hair was receding, his thin Slavic face and neat little beard, reminiscent of Russel Crowe's in *Gladiator*, provided him with something of a boyish appearance. Leaning back in a richly upholstered leather chair with his hands clasped over crossed legs, Viatrovych appeared relaxed, although subtle cracks would appear in his bonhomie over the course of our interview.

Appointed to head the Institute shortly after the revolution, Viatrovych had been very busy and seemed eager to explain the motivations underlying his controversial activities. He argued that, from the beginning of his presidency, Yanukovych had sought to rehabilitate the country's Soviet past, with the Great Patriotic War as its central defining feature. This policy, which was "closely connected with other methods used by Mr. Yanukovych," such as the "restriction of freedom of speech [and] restrictions of freedoms of conscience [and] censorship in media," led to the Euromaidan. As such, Viatrovych contended, the revolution was as much a "struggle against Soviet values" as an effort to promote a more European Ukraine.[148]

Explaining that he saw his role as part of a larger ideological battle for the national narrative, Viatrovych asserted that "history at the moment is one of the platforms where the struggle and the war with Russia is being held." The Russians, he said, were attempting to impose their own view of history on their neighbors. In turn, the UINM was pushing back and "trying to get rid of that Soviet point of view of the Ukrainian past and show real, true Ukrainian history." He dismissed any concerns about the potential politicization of history—even during a period of war, when truth is often the first casualty—by explaining that while Russia was attempting to peddle "myths," all the Ukrainians were doing was "trying … to tell the truth."

"I don't like to talk about Ukrainian propaganda because the term propaganda is something that is one of the methods of the totalitarian regimes … because propaganda is the way the state or the country is trying to have the only one correct version of what was going on and we are not trying to do that," he said.

Viatrovych also applied this thinking in explaining the rehabilitation of the OUN and UPA, stating that aside from a desire to show gratitude to those who fought for Ukrainian independence, the new law was also passed because "it was very important to ruin Soviet myths calling members of those organizations criminals," especially as such narratives were still being actively promoted by the Russian Federation.

He also asserted that the passage of the law honoring Ukrainian nationalist fighters had been partly motivated by a desire to raise up a pantheon of national heroes to inspire the country during a time of crisis. The militants of the OUN and the UPA had been seen as exemplars of heroism by the Maidanistas, and decommunization was a response to that, "a kind of answer to the mood that was spreading through society." Moreover, he added, "for our soldiers that are struggling now in the eastern part of Ukraine … those people are heroes" and an example of "the struggle with totalitarian methods."

"We tried with the law to [create] some kind of legal [framework] for [the] moods and atmospheres that [Ukrainian] society was already engaged in," he said.

Viatrovych believed that critics of this policy were ignorant and that there was a "huge gap … in the knowledge possessed by Ukrainian historians and foreign historians." Moreover, critics' denunciations were off-base, as the new laws said "nothing about glorification [or] about people being heroes or not."

While those "struggling for Ukraine" and Soviet troops had both violated the laws of war and while nationalists had committed "some crimes," it was illegitimate to label their organizations as being guilty of war crimes. To claim the contrary was to endorse the "totalitarian method of so-called common responsibility." What Viatrovych was in effect saying was that any crimes against humanity which had occurred had been carried out by scattered individuals and were unconnected to the OUN or UPA leadership. Nowhere was this approach clearer than when Viatrovych addressed the Volhynian massacres, establishing a moral equivalence that obscured the deliberate nature of the UPA's ethnic cleansing campaign.

"I am absolutely sure and I can state that there exists no one army [the] soldiers of which committed no crimes at all," he told me. "That's true of each army that participated in the Second World War. So definitely [if we are] talking about the Polish-Ukrainian conflict we should talk about mass killing of [the Polish] civil population committed by the Ukrainian Insurgent Army as well [as talking] about the mass killing of the Ukrainian civil population committed by the Polish underground. Definitely we should talk about this and that."[149]

This obfuscation also extended to his approach to the Holocaust. Asked about the role of the UPA in the ethnic cleansing of Ukraine's Jewish population, he replied that, while some Ukrainians assisted the Germans in killing Jews, others, including nationalists, tried to save Jews and that it was "wrong to pay attention only to one part of the people and ... say either that all Ukrainians were killing Jews or visa versa that all Ukrainians were trying to save Jews." This approach is highly misleading, as it presents a false dichotomy that ignores the very real role of organized Ukrainian formations in the killing.

While his public activities and explanations may have given the impression that Viatrovych was only intent on rehabilitating Ukraine's national image (even at the expense of minority groups' feelings), on more than one occasion his rhetoric has deviated from what might be termed "standard" historical obfuscation into the promotion of antisemitic stereotypes. During his tenure at the SBU, for example, the security agency published a document identifying the Soviet officials said to be responsible for the Holodomor. Many of those listed were Jewish.[150]

The myth of Jewish communism was central to Ukrainian ultra-nationalism, and the identification of the Jews with the Soviets played a significant role in mobilizing Ukrainian participation in anti-Jewish actions such as the 1941 L'viv pogrom.[151] This phenomenon had deep roots in Polish nationalism as well, dating back to the late nineteenth century.[152] Needless to say, there is little truth to the claim that the NKVD was inherently Jewish, despite the fact that in its early days Jews were overrepresented in the Soviet Union's security organs. Its Jewish members were overwhelmingly against organized religion, especially their own, and did not pursue of any sort of Jewish ethnic or religious goals.[153]

Later on, as decommunization gathered steam, Viatrovych again veered into apparently antisemitic territory when he responded to a critical *New York Times* op-ed by Eduard Dolinsky. In his article, Dolinsky, a vocal critic of Ukrainian memory policy, condemned both the Poroshenko administration and the UINM for "whitewashing" history. Dolinsky also linked Viatrovych's revisionism to what he asserted was a growing "climate of anti-Semitism."[154] In response, Viatrovych took to Facebook to accuse his Jewish bête noire of fabricating Ukrainian antisemitism and selling it "in the country and abroad to everyone who will pay for it." He also claimed that Dolinsky was "tearing open old wounds in order to generate new fear" in order to turn a profit. The activist, he alleged, was even worse than those who "made money by hiding Jews from Nazi persecution."[155] For his part, the voluble Dolinsky did not remain silent, countering on his own Facebook wall that such statements constituted "an old and well-known antisemitic lie [that] the Jews themselves invent and disseminate antisemitism ... [and that] of course, they make money on it." It was Viatrovych himself, Dolinsky continued, who was spreading false information by claiming that members of the OUN and the UPA had engaged in the rescue, rather than the destruction, of Ukrainian Jewry.[156]

★★★

One of the primary ways in which decommunization was implemented was through the renaming of locales throughout the country. By the end of 2016, nearly 1,000 cities and towns and over 50,000 streets had been renamed.[157] Many places were given new designations connected to Ukrainian nationalists and collaborators. In the western city of Kalush, a street was renamed after SS Hauptsturmführer Dmitro Paliyiv, while in the capital the names of two main boulevards were changed to honor Stepan Bandera and Roman Shukhevych.[158] In what may have been an effort to appease the local Jewish community, the city of Dnipropetrovsk, which had decided to rename a street after Shukhevych, also named one local road after Rabbi Menachem-Mendel Shneerson, the Lubavitcher Rebbe.[159] While the gesture was welcomed by the local community, Kyiv's toponymic policy was not particularly well received by many Ukrainian Jews.

By July 2016, with decommunization in full swing, a number of the country's Jewish organizations (including the Dnipropetrovsk community but not the Vaad) issued a joint statement denouncing the new policy and the "irresponsible" UINM.

> "The antisemitism of OUN and UPA led to the murder of many thousands of Ukrainian Jews and is a proven historical fact supported by a great deal of eye-witness accounts, documents and other research materials. That we, as Ukrainian Jews, suffered from, among others, OUN and UPA is a well-known fact. *We believe that attempts to rewrite the history, to suppress and deny the antisemitic ideology and practice of these organizations is none other than an abuse of the memory of more than one million Ukrainian Jews murdered by Nazis and their local collaborators. More than that, it is a denial of the Holocaust.* Our other concern is with renaming of streets after persons whose names cause not only the Jews but also other peoples to shudder. We consider inappropriate the decision of the Kiev City Council to rename one of the city's boulevards after Stepan Bandera (leader of OUN), as well as the existing plan to rename another street after Roman Shukhevych (leader of UPA). *We are also concerned by the fact that, despite numerous invitations*

by member governments and appeals from civil society, Ukraine continues to refuse membership in the International Holocaust Remembrance Alliance. We are patriots of our country, wholeheartedly supporting Ukraine's sovereignty and territorial integrity. We call on the Ukrainian Parliament, the Cabinet of Ministers, the Kiev City Council, national and international institutions to support interethnic peace in Ukraine. We call on all Ukrainians to listen to our voice. There are many challenges before us all on the road to building a European democracy. Realization of these plans will require concerted efforts from all citizens of Ukraine, whichever ethnicity they may be."[160]

In a separate letter a year later, prominent Kyiv rabbi Moshe Azman also protested official efforts to honor antisemites, stating that while he fully supported decommunization as part of a "purification" process necessary to jettison the country's communist past, "the Kyiv City Council's decision to name a street after Shukhevych had "caused outrage in our Jewish community." He contended that Ukrainians needed "names that unite people" rather than "sow[ing] discord and intolerance." He was sure that the Ukrainian people had "many other figures" worthy of honor.[161]

Regardless of Jewish opposition, the rehabilitation of Ukrainian nationalists continued unabated, and in February 2017 the UINM announced a new public information campaign intended, in Viatrovych's words, to "refute one of the key myths of Soviet propaganda about the UPA's collaboration."[162] Timed to coincide with the 75th anniversary of the group's founding, *UPA: The Answer to the Unbroken People* focused on publicizing the group's "anti-Nazi and anti-communist" struggle through traveling exhibitions, a film festival, and various other initiatives.[163] A website was set up to "give history back to [the] people."[164] Members of the UPA were held up as members of the anti-fascist coalition, equal to the Russians, French, and Americans, and photos of UPA and Ukrainian Red Army veterans shaking hands were plastered on glossy posters to "remind contemporary Ukrainians that the victory over Nazism is common to all parts of Ukraine."[165]

Efforts were also made to dispel "myths" of Ukrainian nationalist participation in the Holocaust, with the UINM and the Ukraine Crisis Media Center sharing information purporting to exonerate the country's new national heroes. The language used is instructive:

> "Unfortunately, the local population was taking part in the pogroms and other anti-Jewish actions in Ukraine guided by personal motives. However, these were not only Ukrainians, but also Russians, Poles, and people of other nationalities. Among them, there could have been some members of the Ukrainian nationalist organizations or persons of nationalist views. However, even German war-time documents mention that the Jewish pogroms and anti-Jewish actions did not have wide support among the population."[166]

Decommunization in all of its forms was supported at the highest levels of government. President Poroshenko publicly celebrated the legacy of the UPA on a number of occasions, describing its members as "heroes" who "contributed to the independence of our state with iron, blood, and sweat." This legacy, he asserted, was an inspiration to Ukrainian servicemen fighting in the Donbas.[167] Poroshenko actively promoted this viewpoint and issued instructions to government representatives as to how they could do so as well. In a letter sent to officials across Ukraine, Poroshenko described how they could "provide citizens with objective information."[168] An appendix to the letter prepared by the UINM reiterated the myth of enthusiastic Jewish participation.

> "There is evidence that Jews fought in the UPA. They considered their stay in this army as real salvation from physical extermination by the Nazis. That's why so many Jews moved there after

escaping from the ghetto, others were released from there by Ukrainian insurgents. They positively proved themselves not only as ordinary soldiers, but also as qualified doctors. The volumes 'Chronicles of the UPA' contain information about the heroics of Jews who fought in the ranks of the UPA both against Nazism and against communism, and many of them died in the fight for the will of Ukraine and the honor of the Jewish people."[169]

The Ukrainian authorities also reached back to the early twentieth century for heroes, honoring the legacy of General Symon Petliura, leader of the Ukrainian National Republic (UNR). One of several competing governments that formed in Ukraine following the Russian revolution, the UNR initially appeared as a positive force for Ukrainian-Jewish relations, enfranchising the Jews and establishing a Ministry of Jewish Affairs.[170] However, as the civil war between the UNR, the Reds (communists), and the Whites (Russian nationalists) progressed, reasons for optimism disappeared. Estimates vary, but somewhere between 50,000 and 200,000 Jews were killed in the ensuing pogroms, up to 40 percent of which were perpetrated by Petliura's troops.[171] In 1926, Petliura was assassinated in Paris—where he lived in exile—by Sholom Schwartzbard, a Jewish man seeking revenge for the murder of his family.

The question of Petliura's responsibility for the pogroms is one that is still hotly debated. According to historian Serhii Plokhy, while Petliura believed that "attacking Jews was equivalent to betraying Ukraine," he did not take serious steps to rein in his troops. On the one hand, he saw the Jews as "natural allies of the Ukrainians in the struggle against national and social oppression," but on the other "he only rarely or belatedly punished perpetrators." Petliura, Plokhy explained, "was reluctant to enforce his orders, as he had limited control over his army."[172] In short, while Petliura may not have approved of pogroms, he did almost nothing to stop them.

However, this controversial legacy did not prevent the Poroshenko administration from honoring Petliura, and on May 25,

2016, the entire country observed an official minute of silence to commemorate the anniversary of his assassination. The following year a statue of Petliura was unveiled not far from a synagogue in Prime Minister Volodymyr Groysman's hometown of Vinnytsia.[173] While some local activists and Israeli lawmakers complained, others, such as Josef Zissels, defended the monument. The head of the Vaad, who had previously implied a moral equivalence between Ukrainian and Jewish actions, seemed to think that the furor was counterproductive and said that merely moving the statue would be sufficient to end the controversy.[174] Not content with breaking with other Jewish leaders to defend Ukrainian memory policy, Zissels went further, intimating that it was the assassination of Petliura that precipitated the Holocaust. "When we say that 'all Jews are responsible for one another,' do we also mean [in] this case?" he asked in a post on Facebook. "And if we do, do we realize that, for many other reasons, this murder paved the historical path to the Shoah?"[175]

Petliura wasn't the only pogromist honored in Ukraine following the revolution. In late 2015, residents of Uman unveiled a statue commemorating Ivan Gonta and Maxim Zheleznyakov, who led a 1768 uprising against Poland and carried out a pogrom in which, according to some estimates, between 20,000 and 30,000 Jews were murdered.

According to Russian-language media reports, the five-ton granite monument was built with funds donated by local businesses, a fact that enraged Russian Jewish Congress president Yuri Kanner. A large part of Uman's economy rests upon the annual high-holiday pilgrimage to the grave of the Hasidic master Rebbe Nachman, who requested to be buried there to be close to the victims of Gonta and Zheleznyakov. Calling it "a monument to thugs built by Jewish money," Kanner asserted that building such a memorial near the mass grave of the victims was "not just blasphemy [but] savagery" and the "glorification of those whose hands are stained with blood." Taking the opposite tack, as usual, was Zissels ally Vyacheslav Likhachev, who said that most Ukrainians "don't know that there were Jewish victims of Gonta and Zheleznyakov" and that the pair had been placed in "a pantheon, a long historical list of persons from Bohdan Khmelnytsky to Stepan Bandera who struggled for Ukrainian independence."[176] Like Gonta and Zheleznyakov, Khmelnytsky led a peasant revolt against Polish rule in the seventeenth century in which tens of thousands of Jews were killed, making him simultaneously one of Ukraine's greatest national heroes and perhaps the greatest villain in pre-Holocaust Eastern European Jewish historiography.[177]

✷✷✷

The veneration of figures such as Gonta, Zheleznyakov, and Bandera did not go unnoticed in Warsaw. Despite their contentious shared history, Poland and Ukraine had cultivated strong bilateral ties following the dissolution of the Soviet Union. While certain issues, such as the Volhynian massacres, had always been a sore spot, the conflict over history only really began to prove a sticking point in the two countries' relationship in 2015. Two factors contributed to the growing tension. The first, as we have already discussed, was the passage of the Decommunization Laws, and the second was the ascension to power of Poland's populist-nationalist Law and Justice Party (PiS) several months later.[178]

Like the Poroshenko administration, the new Polish government was set on enacting a exculpatory historical agenda focused on the events of the Holocaust. Unlike Ukraine, however, Poland had made great strides in coming to terms with the seamier aspects of its legacy prior to 2015, angering many on the right. As a result, when PiS took over in 2015, one of its primary policy goals was to push back against the emerging scholarly consensus regarding the war years and "forcibly introduce a sanitized, feel-good narrative that has nothing to do with our knowledge of the past, but everything to do with national myths."[179]

In a campaign of state-sponsored historical reinterpretation paralleling that of Ukraine, Poland attempted to deny the extent of Polish antisemitism and collaboration during the war. Those who saved Jews were highlighted, while unpleasant episodes, such as the destruction of the Jewish community of Jedwabne at the hands of the town's Polish residents, were downplayed.[180] Historians complained of pressure to conform to ideological restrictions on their scholarship, while activists protested what they described as government efforts to delegitimize their work.[181]

While there were significant similarities in how Poland and Ukraine attempted to revise their respective histories, the contradictory nature of the neighbors' preferred narratives, especially when it came to divisive issues such as the Volhynian massacres, all but ensured conflict. Early efforts at reconciliation were unsuccessful, and in July 2016, shortly after the passage of the Decommunization Laws, the Polish parliament passed its own bill declaring the killings a "genocide."[182] (It should be noted that the Decommunization Laws were passed during an official visit to Kyiv by the Polish president.) For years, Poland was Ukraine's strongest advocate within the European Union, but ties between the two countries began to fray as decommunization accelerated. Ukraine, PiS leader Jaroslaw Kaczynski threatened, would never "enter Europe with Bandera."[183] President Andrzej Duda went even further, calling on Poroshenko to purge his government of officials holding anti-Polish views that "destroy" Polish-Ukrainian relations.[184]

Things really came to a head in 2018 with the passage of Poland's own history bill, which prohibited falsely accusing the Polish state and Polish people of "crimes against peace, crimes against humanity or war crimes."[185] While most of the criticism worldwide focused on what was widely seen as an effort to ban criticism of Poland's wartime record, in Ukraine the law was controversial for an entirely different reason. In addition to its other provisions, the new bill also criminalized the denial of "crimes committed by Ukrainian nationalists and members of Ukrainian units collaborating with the Third Reich." To the Ukrainian right, this was tantamount to a ban on "Bandera ideology."

✶✶✶

While the Volhynian killings were a major source of friction, it was another massacre, carried out by the Germans just outside of Kyiv, that I believe best exemplified the conflict over memory in contemporary Ukraine.[186] Over a period of two days in September 1941, the Nazis shot 33,000 Jews in the secluded Babi Yar ravine. The massacre would go on to become one of the most infamous incidents of mass murder in the so-called "Holocaust of bullets."[187] According to Yad Vashem, "local collaborationists played an important role in the extermination." The Ukrainians "knew the local population, could easily tell the Jews from the rest, and it was therefore local councils and local police that were entrusted with registering the Jews, escorting them to the murder site, and cordoning off the site itself."[188] All told, up to a 100,000 people, including but not limited to Jews, captured Soviet troops, and Roma, were murdered at Babi Yar during the course of the German occupation.

Prior to Ukrainian independence, it was the stated policy of the Soviet state to eschew and even eradicate any separate mention of the Jewish victims of this atrocity, a policy carried on by the nation's post-Soviet leadership, which has put into effect a policy of "minimization."[189] Speaking in Kyiv in September 2016 at an event marking the 75th anniversary of Babi Yar, Jewish Agency chairman and former Soviet dissident Natan Sharansky described how, as a young man in communist times, he would be briefly detained every year along with other active Jews in order to prevent them from marking the date of the massacre. Soviet efforts along these lines prevented any reference to Jews, as such, on the Soviet memorial statue erected at the site in the 1970s.[190]

For a long time, even the utterance of the name "Babi Yar" was suppressed, although the picture became somewhat more complicated in the 1960s, and even more so during the late Soviet period.[191]

Soon after Ukrainian independence in 1991, a wooden cross was erected on the site in memory of the OUN/UPA members killed there, and while a menorah was also erected, it was only one of many small memorials to different groups placed across the site. That menorah, as we have seen, was vandalized repeatedly over the course of 2015-2016, prompting then-Prime Minister Arseniy Yatsenyuk to claim that the incidents were "well planned and thoroughly prepared provocations," intended to "throw discredit upon Ukrainian authorities and to destabilize the internal political situation in Ukraine." While we have previously explained this statement in the context of the Russo-Ukrainian conflict, it can also been seen as indicative of a preexisting appropriation of the Babi Yar killings as a general Ukrainian, rather than narrowly Jewish ethnic, experience.

However, this narrative is complicated by the fact that the Ukrainian authorities have also made efforts, parallel to their attempts at historical revisionism, to reach out to the Jewish community and acknowledge local Ukrainian complicity in the destruction of their country's Jewish population. Speaking in the Knesset during a state visit in late 2015, Poroshenko invited Israeli and Jewish leaders to attend the upcoming 75th anniversary commemoration of Babi Yar and raised the issue of collaboration. Evoking the memory of Babi Yar, Poroshenko stressed the "need to remember the negative episodes of our history, when collaborators, who could be found, unfortunately, in almost all European countries that had been occupied by the Nazis, were helping those monsters in bringing about the so-called 'Final Solution of the Jewish Question.'"[192]

Preparations for the anniversary of the massacre were not without controversy, however. Several months after Poroshenko's

Knesset speech, it emerged that Ukraine was again attempting to revamp the site in preparation for September's commemorations and transform it into a generic symbol of human suffering. An architectural competition was organized in which contestants were invited to focus on overcoming the "problem" of the "discrepancy between the world's view and Jewry's exclusive view of Babi Yar as a symbol of the Holocaust." The original language used in describing the competition's purpose is instructive: "The chief challenge that the organizers (and thus also the future entrants of the competition) are facing is the need to achieve an organic unity of all the aspects of history, *whereby the Holocaust would be transformed from a unique occurrence into a symbol of all tragedies of the previous century*, while the mass shooting of Kyiv's Jews would become a core event of the entire history of Babyn Yar." The text also referenced members of the OUN killed at the site following their public break with their former German allies and called for their memorialization.[193]

The Ukrainians quickly backtracked and amended the text following a outpouring of anger by Jewish groups around the world incensed over what they perceived as an attempt to diminish the site's Jewish significance. Yad Vashem denounced the initial language as "very problematic," while World Jewish Congress CEO Robert Singer, a Ukrainian Jew, stated that "given the sanctity of the grounds at Babi Yar, the final resting place of tens of thousands of Jews who suffered an unimaginably horrifying end, any attempt to 'universalize' or 'contextualize' their suffering and death would constitute an unacceptable distortion of the truth."[194]

Babi Yar
September 29, 2016

Crowds of Ukrainians and foreign diplomats made their way along the road leading to Babi Yar, past displays highlighting the faces and stories of the victims. They had converged on Kyiv from around the world to commemorate the 75th anniversary of the massacre in a way that would have been unimaginable only a few short years before. President Poroshenko, addressing the gathered dignitaries, commented on the significance of the evening's events while also managing to politicize them to a remarkable degree.

Opening with a boast about the more than 2,500 Ukrainians who had been declared "Righteous Among the Nations," Poroshenko again apologized for collaboration by his countrymen (adding the caveat that collaborators did "not represent their people.") He then went on to link the culture of silence that had previously prevailed in Ukraine to Stalinist bigotry, which he asserted was still extant in today's Russian Federation.

> "I thought a lot why the Soviet regime first stonewalled the Babyn Yar tragedy for decades, and then tried to dilute its Jewish component in the general martyrology of World War II. Might it be because Stalin, in the depth of his black soul supported the so-called 'final solution of the Jewish issue?' After the victory over the Nazi, the repressive national razor mechanism was launched again and the first, who the razor cut, were the Jewish Antifascist Committee members, the so-called 'rootless cosmopolites' and 'doctors-saboteurs.' It was Stalin's death that saved the USSR's Jews from a deportation similar to [those that] the Crimean Tatars and other ethnic groups had suffered. By the way, today the Supreme Court of Russia issued a xenophobic judgment banning the Mejlis—so Stalin's cause is still alive!"[195]

Poroshenko's comments came off as somewhat insincere given both his government's prior effort to turn Babi Yar into a generic symbol of human suffering and the efforts to memorialize members of the OUN alongside the Jews. While members of the OUN were undoubtedly killed at Babi Yar, many Jews took umbrage at what appeared to be an effort to assert a moral equivalence between Jews and nationalists. Among the informational signs placed along the promenade leading to the ravine was a display memorializing members of the underground movement, including several members of the Melnykite faction of the OUN.[196] The juxtaposition of virulently antisemitic Ukrainian nationalists with the Jewish victims of the site was jarring in the extreme. One of those mentioned by name on the sign was Ivan Rohach, the editor of *Ukrainske Slovo*, an OUN(m) mouthpiece. Ukrainian revisionist panegyrics to the contrary, the newspaper was virulently antisemitic. Only days after the slaughter began in Babi Yar, it ran an article decrying the fact that there were still Jews hidden in Kyiv—disguised as members of other ethnic and religious groups—and called on ethnic Ukrainians to turn them over to the Gestapo:

> "The Yids who still remain in Kiev pretend to be people of other ethnic backgrounds—Greeks, Armenians, Ukrainians, Russians; they pay hundreds of thousands of rubles for the appropriate documents. But Ukraine has many true patriots, who are dreaming to cleanse their life, their villages, thick forests and beautiful cities as soon as possible from partisans, inciting Yids, and red Commissars. These patriots come every day to the little house on the Shevchenko Boulevard (Gestapo) and give information about the enemies."[197]

While waiting for the ceremony to commence, Eduard Dolinsky was extremely angry, complaining that having to sit together with those who would honor the OUN was "awkward and terrible" and asserting that Kyiv's new and improved approach to Babi Yar was merely "the continuation of the Soviet tradition" of minimizing the unique Jewish character of the site.[198]

Poroshenko's apology also rang hollow when put in the context of the responses of government figures, such as Viatrovych, to an oration by Israeli President Reuven Rivlin two days prior. Addressing the Rada, Rivlin delivered a fiery speech denouncing the OUN's collaboration with the Nazis and the "sin of concealment and destruction of the [victims'] memory." In a stark rebuke of Ukrainian policy, Rivlin forcefully asserted that "we must not be partners in a second crime. We must not play a part in the sin of forgetting or denial." It was true, he said, that "there were more than 2,500 Righteous Among the Nations, lone candles who shone in the darkness of humanity. Yet the majority remained silent."[199]

While applauded in parliament, the speech was greeted with opprobrium by Ukrainian nationalists, both in and out of government. In a series of posts on Facebook, Viatrovych excoriated Rivlin, accusing him of repeating "the Soviet myth of OUN participation in the Holocaust."[200] (Zissels agreed, telling me that he believed that Rivlin had been taken in by old Soviet propaganda.) Paul Podobyed, a fellow at the UINM, stated that Rivlin's speech was comparable to the hypothetical situation of Poroshenko telling the Knesset that Jews were responsible for the Holodomor. Bohdan Chervak, head of the current incarnation of the OUN and a senior official at Ukraine's state-run broadcast regulator, went even further, accusing Rivlin of "spit[ting] in the soul of Ukrainians" and "disrespect[ing] the Ukrainian nation."[201]

Another development that generated controversy (though primarily among nationalists) was the announcement of the establishment of the Babi Yar Holocaust Memorial Charity Fund, a private-public partnership dedicated to building a Holocaust museum at Babi Yar in time for the 80th anniversary of the massacre in 2021. Unveiled at a press conference featuring the president, the prime minister, the chief rabbi, the mayor of Kyiv, and the head of the Jewish Agency, the new initiative appeared to have a chance of finally creating a memorial complex at the site. This was especially significant, given the many difficulties in getting such a project off the ground in the years since Ukrainian independence.

Efforts had been made on a number of occasions but had always ended in failure due to a number of ideological and practical issues. During one such attempt in 2002, which pitted Bleich against Zissels, "the controversy had expanded to include the Ukrainian intellectual and cultural elite [and] shifted to whether there should be any memorial at all, or whether it should be a Holocaust memorial or one that commemorated all victims." Efforts at memorialization were further stymied by Yushchenko's 2007 decision to place Babi Yar under the administration of the UINM.[202]

As in 2002, the new project saw Bleich and Zissels come into conflict, with the head of the Vaad siding with Chervak, who complained that the new initiative was headed by foreigners who ignored members of the OUN killed at the site.[203] A number of Ukrainian historians, including Jewish scholars Anatoliy Podolskyi and Vitaliy Nachmanovych, also objected to the project, condemning "the erroneous attempt to combine Babyn Yar with the Holocaust only, ignoring other victims and other dramatic moments in its history." The museum, they claimed, was not only removing Babi Yar from the larger context of the Holocaust but also ignoring the plight of the rest of the victims buried there, including but not limited to the Roma, Soviet prisoners, nationalists, and the mentally ill.[204]

Echoing Chervak and Nachmanovych's concerns, Zissels panned the project as "paternalistic," pointing out the foreign origins of its backers and stating that Babi Yar was "only partially" about the Holocaust. "The Holocaust," he wrote, "is limited to considering only the Jewish and Roma murders of that time. The rest [of the victims] are not included in it."[205] Instead of throwing his support behind the memorial, Zissels lobbied hard for the creation of a competing initiative, which was established by presidential proclamation in October 2017.[206] The new committee, which aimed to "approve a plan of measures for the long-term development of the National Historical and Memorial Reserve 'Babi Yar,'" proved somewhat controversial, primarily because both Chervak and Viatrovych were given roles alongside prominent Jewish leaders such as Bleich, Singer, and Dukhovny.[207]

While Dolinsky asserted that the two far-right members' inclusion had created "a very awkward situation where Jewish leaders have to sit together in the Babi Yar committee with those who praise and glorify antisemites and murderers of Jews," the Jewish members of the committee seemed rather unperturbed.[208] Several indicated that they had been unaware of Chervak's appointment to the commission when they agreed to participate. One local rabbi, speaking on background, stated that he felt it was more important to "create light than to fight the darkness." For his part, Zissels stated that he had absolutely no issue with such hardened nationalists providing input.

Despite its shortcomings, the Ukrainian emphasis on reintegrating Jewish narratives into the story of Babi Yar was a positive development, especially in light of previous failures. However, despite all the progress that had been made, Ukrainian efforts still seemed infused with a moral equivalence at best, a leitmotif of displacement at worst. In a letter to this author, Himka stated that "the Holocaust has developed some moral universality, but especially outside the places where the murders were committed." He also noted that:

> "In Ukraine, the Holocaust is looked at more as the tragedy of the Jews rather than a universal lesson. The attitude to the Holodomor in Ukraine is also not universalistic: it is a specifically Ukrainian tragedy. The world, [former President] Yushchenko had campaigned, should recognize the Ukrainian genocide. [He had] no desire to look at the famine in the wider context of the entire Soviet Union. Given these prevailing attitudes, and in the context of Ukraine's execrable failure to admit the crimes against Jews and Poles of people it wants to honor as heroes, I think any 'universalizing' on the part of official Ukraine is just an attempt at dilution."

There has always been a struggle between the particular and the universal when it comes to memorializing the Holocaust. On the one hand, depicting the event as an exclusively Jewish one makes it hard to foster sympathy among those who cannot see themselves in the victims' place. On the other hand, failing to honor the uniquely Jewish nature of these events can be tantamount to killing the victims again by erasing their unique identities. It is in the conceptual space between these two poles that all memorials operate, but in Ukraine it sometimes seems as if, rather than merely attempting to drift toward the universal, a sort of replacement theology is at work, with Ukrainians seeking to compete with the Jews in a game of victimhood.

In late 2013, hundreds of thousands of Ukrainians took over Kyiv's central Maidan square during protests against pro-Russian President Viktor Yanukovych. (Sam Sokol)

Svoboda supporters march in memory of Ukrainian nationalist leader Stepan Bandera, the wartime leader of the Organization of Ukrainian Nationalists. (Oleh Tiahnybok on Twitter)

Josef Zissels, a former Soviet dissident and the head of the Vaad of Ukraine, addresses protesters during the Euromaidan. Zissels has been criticized by a number of prominent Jewish organizations who have claimed that his spirited defense of Kyiv's historical memory policy does "not represent the Jews of Ukraine." (Vaad of Ukraine)

Eduard Dolinsky, the pugnacious director of the Ukrainian Jewish Committee, is one of the most outspoken critics of Kyiv's historical memory policy. (Courtesy)

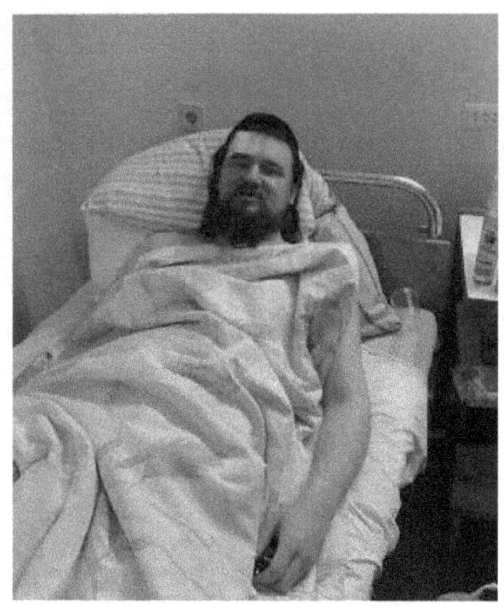

Dov Ber Glickman was stabbed in an apparent antisemitic attack in Kyiv during the Euromaidan. (Hatzalah Ukraine)

The Great Choral Synagogue in Podil. The community went into lockdown after two community members were physically attacked nearby during the Euromaidan. (Sam Sokol)

American born Chief Rabbi Yaakov Dov Bleich. He is pictured here with former Jewish Agency chairman Natan Sharansky. (Sam Sokol)

Oligarch and former Foreign Minister Petro Poroshenko, who was elected following the revolution, was responsible for bringing back the revisionist historical memory policies of the Yushchenko period. (Sam Sokol)

Russian Chief Rabbi Berel Lazar with President Vladimir Putin. Following the Euromaidan, Lazar pressed the Simon Wiesenthal Center "to declare that any attempt to install pro-fessed antisemites in the political establishment will cause irreparable damage not only to the prestige of the new Ukrainian authorities but to the Ukrainian state as a whole." (Kremlin)

Rabbi Pinchas Vishedski fled Donetsk after enduring months of occupation and shelling, moving to Kyiv in order to try and rebuild his community in internal exile. Here he can be seen standing next to the Holy Ark in his synagogue in Donetsk. (Sam Sokol)

Jewish IDPs from Donetsk grieve at the funeral of Georgiy "Garik" Zilberbord, a prominent member of their community who was shot by separatist militants. (Courtesy)

The Menorah Center in Dnipropetrovsk, with its seven towers reminiscent of a Hanukkah menorah, claims to be the world's largest Jewish community center. It quickly became one of the nerve centers for the effort to resettle displaced Jews during the Russo-Ukrainian conflict. (Sam Sokol)

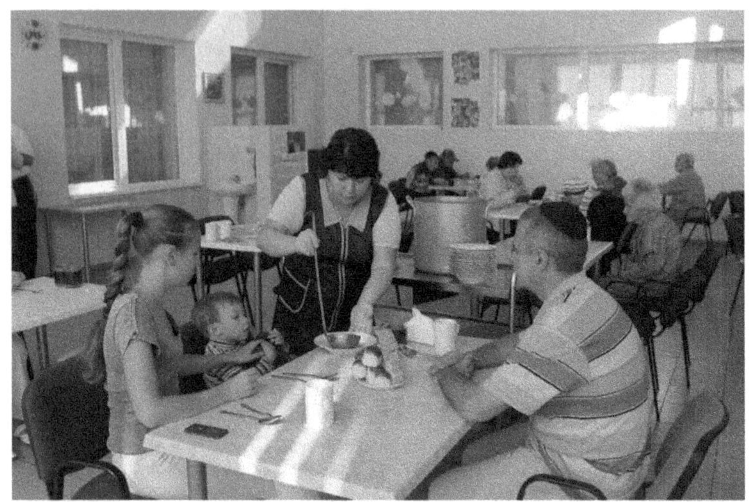

Young IDPs from the Donbas eat at the Beit Baruch assisted-living facility in Dnipro-petrovsk. (Sam Sokol) 2

Rabbi Shalom and Chana Gopin, along with many of their congregants, left Luhansk as part of a massive wave of Ukrainians fleeing the war. They ended up in Zhytomyr at a refugee camp run jointly by Chabad and the IFCJ. (Sam Sokol)

Shimon Leib and Esther Zuckerman, octogenarians from Luhansk, get married at a Chabad-organized mass wedding for IDPs from the Donbas at the Menorah Center in Dnipropetrovsk. (Sam Sokol)

Yaakov "Yasha" Virin, the erstwhile editor-in-chief of the Donetsk Jewish newspaper, fled the separatist stronghold, reuniting with his wife and daughter in Dnipropetrovsk. (Sam Sokol)

Between 2014 and 2018, some 30,000 Ukrainians immigrated to Israel, including those pictured here standing in line to check in at the Dnipropetrovsk International Airport. (Sam Sokol)

Young refugees in Zhytomyr. At first, many of the children in the camp, traumatized by the fighting, would cringe and run to their parents whenever an airplane would pass overhead. (Sam Sokol)

Rabbi Moshe Azman (third from right) supervises the laying of the foundation of a building in Anatevka, a gated compound he established just outside Kyiv to serve as a home for displaced Jews. (Sam Sokol)

Volodymyr Viatrovych, the head of the Institute of National Memory, is a controversial figure who has drawn scorn from many mainstream historians for his rehabilitation and glorification of Ukraine's wartime fighters. (Institute of National Memory)

Asher Joseph Cherkassky, a Hasidic Jew and Red Army veteran, enlisted to fight when war broke out with Russia. He said he "felt obligated to ... defend the country and the citizens of Ukraine." (Courtesy)

Volodymyr Groysman, Ukraine's Jewish Prime Minister, was the speaker of the Verkhovna Rada during the passage of the Decommunization Laws in 2015. (Sam Sokol)

CHAPTER FIVE

ANTISEMITISM AND COUNTER-PROPAGANDA

"How can I react to Russian propaganda? It's simple. Nobody in the world believes the Russians during this war—this is just another form of war, not only on the battlefield but using propaganda spanning hundreds of millions of dollars to create a negative image of Ukraine."

—Petro Poroshenko[1]

Kyiv
April 26, 2016

While the Russians initially had a head start when it came to propaganda, the Ukrainians were quick to catch up. By mid-2016, the Ukrainian foreign ministry announced the appointment of Borys Zakharchuk, a career diplomat, as the first Special Representative for preventing and combating antisemitism, racism, and xenophobia.[2] His installation came a little over a year after the initial announcement of the post's creation, during a period when the Poroshenko administration was struggling to counter a concerted Russian propaganda campaign labeling it as antisemitic.[3] From the beginning, it appeared that Zakharchuk's appointment was merely window dressing designed to protect the government's image.

In an extended interview with this author published in the *Jewish Chronicle*, Zakharchuk stated that his job was to coordinate Ukraine's fight against antisemitism at home and abroad, a claim contested by several prominent figures in the field.[4] Ira Forman, who had served as the US State Department's Special Envoy to Monitor and Combat Antisemitism under President Barak Obama, said he had never spoken to his Ukrainian counterpart. This message was echoed by European Commission Coordinator on Combating Antisemitism Katharina von Schnurbein and OSCE antisemitism point-man Rabbi Andrew Baker. Akiva Tor, who worked on antisemitism issues for the Israeli foreign ministry, stated that he had "never heard of this guy," and while Israeli ambassador to Kyiv Eli Belotserkovsky admitted to meeting Zakharchuk on several occasions, he could not recall anything substantive coming out of their interactions.[5] Zakharchuk also claimed that, despite declining to join the International Holocaust Remembrance Alliance, Ukraine was cooperating "very closely" with the organization. However, sources close to the IHRA indicated otherwise, stating that there had been "no official attempts by the Ukrainian government to work more closely."

It seemed that the Ukrainians had no intention of becoming active in international efforts to combat antisemitism and that Zakharchuk's appointment was largely a propaganda ploy.[6] In fact, it was a sign of the Ukrainians' willingness, like their Russian antagonists, to instrumentalize the struggle against antisemitism in the interests of propaganda.

Donetsk
January 21, 2015

One of the first apparent examples of elements within Ukrainian society picking up on Russian methods came in early 2015, when several Ukrainian media outlets reported that Yehuda Kellerman, a senior Jewish communal leader, had been murdered. According to the reports, which cited European Jewish Congress president Moshe Kantor as a source, Kellerman had been beaten to death by separatists in Donetsk. This claim was immediately branded a fabrication by community representatives.[7]

"Thank God he's all right and God bless him with health and long life, up to 120 [years]," the community wrote in a Facebook post in which it demanded apologies from both the media and Kantor, who had also been quoted as saying that terrorists and antisemites had taken over Donetsk. As with Menachem Margolin of the European Jewish Association, to whom false quotes had been attributed by the Russians, Kantor was livid at the appropriation of his name for propaganda purposes. "He most certainly did not give such an interview," EJC spokeswoman Orly Joseph protested. "At a time when there are all too real attacks on Jews across Europe, the EJC certainly has no intention or need to pay any attention to false ones."

In the end, Kellerman turned up alive in Dnipropetrovsk, where he was living as an IDP. Speaking through a senior leader of the local Jewish community, he said that many of his fellow Donetskers believed that the articles constituted an "effort to pull [the Jewish community] into the political game."[8]

A similar incident occurred less than three months later when Ukrainian newspapers reported that separatist fighters had entered Luhansk's Jewish school, killing two people and seizing the building. As with Kellerman's "murder," community leaders immediately denied the reports.[9]

Donetsk
February 2, 2015

Despite Ukrainian allegations to the contrary, antisemitic harassment was not a pressing concern for the Jews living in the Donbas. However, the reality on the ground did not stop Ukrainian leaders from making such claims, nor did it mean that separatists leaders did not occasionally traffic in antisemitic sentiments, giving Kyiv fodder for its propaganda.

Speaking at a joint press conference with LNR chief Igor Plotnitsky in Donetsk in February 2015, DNR President Alexander Zakharchenko declared that the Jews had taken control of Ukraine and that the government was comprised of "miserable representatives of the great Jewish people."[10] Several months later, Plotnitsky made similar comments, intimating that there was a connection between Jews and the revolution, because the Russian word for Jew, "Evrei," sounded somewhat, to his mind, like "Euro."

> "I'd like to ask the historians … or maybe the philologists … why was it called the 'Euromaidan'? Where did the name come from? From the area? Or perhaps from the people? Those same people who now make up the majority of leaders of what was once our Ukraine? I have nothing against … Valtzman, Groysman, and many others … I have nothing against the Jews as a people, as the 'Chosen People' … but the crux of the matter is that when we call what has happened a 'Euromaidan,' we infer that the leaders now are representatives of the people who have been harmed the most by Nazism."

Such statements were not surprising given that the rebel leaders had "allowed themselves to employ fully antisemitic rhetoric on previous occasions," Lazar associate Boruch Gorin commented at the time. "It is also no secret that, on the side of the separatists, war is also being waged by real Russian Nazis. The trouble, though, is that they are often confronted by those with the same ideology but with a trident [the Ukrainian national symbol]."[11]

Expressions of separatist antisemitism were not limited to Zakharchenko and Plotnitsky. One article, posted on the official page of the Donetsk municipal TV station, claimed that Israel deliberately provided Ukrainians with poisoned medications containing barbed wire.[12] In another incident, a separatist-linked media outlet announced that it would strike "a powerful blow to the biblical matrix" by combating "zombie Zionists."[13] Asked about Zakharchenko, DNR Foreign Minister Alexander Kofman denied that he was a racist, adding that he considered him "personal friend."[14] Rather than admitting that its leaders had indulged in antisemitic conspiracy theories, the DNR announced in November 2015 that it would hold a roundtable to discuss the "importance of fighting against occurrence[s] of national, ethnic and race hatred."[15] In a press release, the DNR stated that the participants had "exchanged views on [the] anti-fascist struggle of the Donetsk and Luhansk People's Republics as a continuation of the struggle of the Soviet people in the Great Patriotic War" and expressed opposition to "the rise of Nazism, xenophobia and antisemitism in modern Ukraine."[16] Of course, the Ukrainians had a different take on the matter, and Zakharchenko and Plotnitsky had just made their job immeasurably easier.

Jerusalem
December 22, 2015

Petro Poroshenko, sitting at a small table in a conference room at the David's Citadel hotel in downtown Jerusalem, gave me a strange look as he compulsively fingered a set of rosary beads in one hand. I had just queried him about Russia's claim that his government was antisemitic. "How can I react to Russian propaganda," he asked, offended. "It's simple. Nobody in the world believes the Russians during this war—this is just another form of war, not only on the battlefield but using propaganda spanning hundreds of millions of dollars to create a negative image of Ukraine." Look at how the far right did in the 2014 elections, he continued, asserting that its failure provided the "best evidence" that Ukraine did not provide fertile ground for hate. As for Jewish concerns regarding the rehabilitation of the UPA, Poroshenko was sanguine, stating that his government was merely paying tribute to those who fought for national independence. "Let's not try to find the black cat in the black room, especially if there is nothing there," he commented dismissively.[17]

Poroshenko did not only downplay Ukrainian antisemitism; he also made a concerted effort to portray his enemies as dangerous xenophobes. Addressing the Knesset, the Ukrainian president stated that he was worried for the Jews of Crimea because the Russians had "started to cultivate the anti-Semitism issue."[18] He expanded on this theme during a conversation with Russian-born Knesset member Ksenia Svetlova, claiming that Crimean Jews were being "oppressed" and had been banned from attending synagogue.[19] These comments did not go unnoticed by the Crimean Jewish community. As we saw earlier, while Jewish leaders in mainland Ukraine had pledged allegiance to Kyiv, the Jews of Crimea mostly sided with Russia. This loyalty was reflected in their response to the president's speech, which was extremely harsh. "The Jewish organizations of Crimea firmly state that these allegations are false and are a clumsy and hopeless attempt to distort the true picture of the existing inter-ethnic peace and harmony in the Russian Crimea," community leaders from cities including Simferopol, Yalta, and Sevastopol countered in a joint statement. "Today, we are under the protection of the Russian state. However, we love and remember the real Ukraine, with its national colors, rich culture, hospitable people, where it was before the rampant nationalism and Bandera."

Elena Raigorodskaya, a spokeswoman for the All-Crimean Jewish Congress, put her constituents' outrage in even starker terms, saying that Poroshenko had "no moral right to speak about the Jews of the Crimea."[20]

✳✳✳

If Poroshenko didn't have a moral right to speak about the Jews, then Josef Zissels certainly thought that he himself, as a prominent Jewish personality, did, and he exercised this right as much as he could, weighing in on a variety of issues as the Ukrainian media's go-to-Jew. An older figure whose star had been in decline prior to the revolution, he suddenly found himself held up every-where as the quintessential patriotic minority. He certainly acted the part, defending the government's revisionist agenda against all critics, including prominent Jewish ones such as Eduard Dolin-sky.[21] As a former dissident and one of the builders of the first Jewish institutions in the post-communist period, Zissels had credibility that the Ukrainians could use.

In off-the-record comments and whispered asides over the years, a number of prominent Ukrainian Jews had complained about the press's focus on antisemitism and Holocaust distor-tion. One prominent figure described the issue of Ukrainian complicity in the Holocaust as inconvenient, while others took refuge in silence, refusing to speak out one way or the other. Zissels was different. He repeatedly waded into the political fray, issuing statements and granting interviews in which he defended Ukrainian narratives and harshly denounced critics.

A prime example of the Vaad leader's tendency to bend histo-ry can be seen in an interview he gave to Britain's *Daily Mail* tabloid, in which he asserted that most Ukrainian collaborators were, in reality, ethnic Russians. "There are certain stereotypes about participation of Ukrainian nationalists in pogroms in the early war years which were planted by Soviet history," he was quoted as saying. "It is true that the local population did cooper-ate with German Nazis in the occupied territories but the majority of them were Russian. Russia makes a point about Ukrainian nationalists because it is keen to divert suspicion from itself."[22] While Zissels would go on to dispute the accuracy of the quotation, it fit in well with both his prior rhetoric and subse-quent statements, which were duly reported by the Ukrainian press.[23]

Zissels was eagerly sought for interviews so that he could speak, ostensibly, on behalf of the country's Jewish community. One local outlet stated this explicitly, writing that Zissels, "as a member of the European and World Jewish Congress, assumed the functions of a public lobbyist for the interests of the state of Ukraine."[24] This approach proved to be a source of tension almost immediately. Within months of the revolution, the Moscow-based home office of the Euro-Asian Jewish Congress suspended funding of its Ukrainian branch due to Zissels's outspoken condemnations of Vladimir Putin.[25] However, instead of pulling back, Zissels doubled down, spending the next several years waving away problems and discouraging his coreligionists from criticizing Ukraine. In statements to the English media he disavowed any sympathy for Bandera, Shukhevych, and other nationalist figures, but insisted that "the Jewish minority, or any other ethnic minority, should not interfere with the choice of the Ukrainian people as they name their national heroes."[26] Protests against decommunization could only lead to "unnecessary assignment of blame that serves only retrospection but fails to offer a vision for the future."[27]

Speaking with local media, Zissels's rhetoric took on a different tone. He denied the UPA's crimes and insisted that Ukrainian police units organized by the Nazis be re-designated as Soviet formations.[28] In one Facebook post criticizing the Simon Wiesenthal Center's Efraim Zuroff and his Lithuanian writing partner Ruta Vanagaite, Zissels mused that "if Soviet propaganda did not insist on the ethnic origin of collaborators with the Nazis, perhaps the Lithuanians would not insist on the ethnic origin of the NKVDists." Since "most of the collaborators with the Nazi regime were Soviet citizens before the war," he wrote, it would be appropriate to label them "Soviet policemen under the Nazi administration" or "Soviet collaborators with the Nazis."[29] It appeared that in order to defend Ukraine against allegations of Holocaust distortion and the glorification of collaborators, Zissels had determined that he had to prove that nationalist collaborators did not exist as such and that these war criminals belonged only to the all-encompassing category of Soviet collaborators. Any argument to the contrary was false and stemmed from Soviet or Russian propaganda. After all, if Zuroff and Vanagaite's claims regarding the Lithuanians were historically accurate, logic dictated that the same might hold true for Ukraine. But if it became impossible to categorize collaborators according to nationality, then the Ukrainians could continue decommunization without having to face up to the moral implications of their policy.

Zissels and his colleague Likhachev also appear to have had little compunction about fabricating information that would create the impression of a harmonious relationship between Jews and contemporary ultra-nationalists. Within weeks of the end of the revolution, the pair had cooked up a narrative in which three of the protesters who had died on the Maidan had been Jews killed while fighting alongside their nationalist Ukrainian brothers.[30]

According to Likhachev, the deaths of Josef Shiling, Alexander Scherbanyuk, and Evgeniy Kotlyar disproved allegations that the revolutionaries had been antisemites.[31] The lie had its intended effect. The story of Jews fighting and dying alongside Ukrainian nationalists was too good for many Jewish and Israeli reporters (including this author) to resist, especially as masked members of Right Sector showed up at Scherbanyuk's funeral in Chernivtsi to fire off a salute with handguns. Citing Likhachev's post, the Jewish *Daily Forward* reported that this incident showed "how Jews and right-wing nationalists get along in today's Ukraine."[32] However, when I later followed up on Likhachev's claims, his story quickly fell apart.

While it is true that Scherbanyuk's son Dan attended a Jewish school and that the family was affiliated with the local (Messianic) Beit Simcha synagogue, the Afghan war veteran wasn't actually a Jew. Leonid Milman, the leader of the Chernivtsi Jewish community described him as a gentile member of a Jews for Jesus group who was "very close to us, but not Jewish."[33] It was the same story when I looked into the background of Josef Shiling, who Likhachev had claimed was "well-known in the Drogobych

Jewish community of L'viv Oblast." Adel Dianova—the director of the L'viv Hesed told me that she had offered Shiling's family support after his death, only to be rebuffed. "Josef Shiling has never considered himself a Jew," she said. "His family denies their Jewish roots and they refused Hesed's help."[34] Asked about Evgeniy Kotlyar, Rabbi Moshe Moskovitz of Kharkiv likewise disavowed any knowledge of the putative Jew, asserting that "no one here knows who he was."[35]

✱✱✱

While accusations and counter-accusations of antisemitism proliferated, actual manifestations of the "oldest hatred" remained stable over the course of 2015 and actually dipped in 2016.[36] However, as Kantor Center researcher Irena Cantorovich noted, not only was distinguishing between real incidents and provocations difficult, but the published numbers likely did not accurately reflect reality because many incident just weren't being reported.[37] Also contributing to the confusion was the sometimes blurry line between antisemitism and run-of-the-mill crime. An example of this is the fatal beating of Rabbi Mendel Deitsch in Zhytomyr in 2016, which appeared to have been a robbery rather than a racially or religiously motivated attack.[38] Such incidents could be safely put aside by those eager to minimize antisemitism. Higher profile incidents with obviously racist motivations were harder to ignore and provoked predictable reactions from the Ukrainian authorities.

Uman
December 20, 2016

The attack occurred suddenly, stoking fears of violence. Shmuel Cohen was standing in the synagogue built atop Rebbe Nachman of Breslov's grave when the vandals appeared, hurling a severed pig's head and blood-red paint into the holy structure before running back into the night. "I thought there was going to be a pogrom," Cohen later recalled. Two men "entered and within three seconds threw the head and red paint, and left. I didn't see their faces, it was fast. One of the goyim [gentiles] filmed it when he was doing it. They had a jeep [waiting outside] and they fled."[39]

The Ukrainians wasted little time in condemning the incident, characterizing it as an unacceptable attack on a cherished minority and placing the blame squarely on supposed outside agitators. Volodymyr Groysman, the Jewish politician who had succeeded Yatsenyuk as prime minister earlier that year, theorized that the vandals had sought to harm bilateral relations between Ukraine and Israel while Deputy Prime Minister Vyacheslav Kyrylenko attributed the attack to "third countries [that] are trying to scold Poles and Ukrainians."[40] Prosecutor General Yuriy Lutsenko categorized the vandalism as a "very rough anti-Ukrainian provocation" with which "true Ukrainians" were not involved, while the Jewish nationalist MP Boreslav Bereza blamed it on "useful idiots" in the pay of the Russians.[41] The attack, he wrote, had been intentionally carried out in a demonstrative and clumsy manner in order to create "the 'correct picture' for the media," which would then "be disseminated by Russian technologists on Israeli and Western TV channels in order to influence the attitude of Jews all over the world towards Ukraine and spoil the image of our state."[42]

As we saw earlier, the Ukrainian authorities eventually announced the apprehension of three suspects, linked to Russia, whom investigators accused of carrying out a series of attacks targeting Jewish sites. While it is true that the Russians had indeed engaged in precisely this kind of provocation, there are several reasons to be wary of Ukrainian attributions of blame. The most obvious cause for skepticism was, of course, the cozy relationship between senior Ukrainian law enforcement officials and the far right. Interior Minister Arsen Avakov, who oversaw the national police, maintained close ties with members of extremist groups, such as Patriot of Ukraine and the Azov Battalion, promoting their members to high positions within his ministry and turning a blind eye to vigilante activity.[43] One extremist brought into government service by Avakov was former Azov Battalion deputy commander Vadym Troyan. Initially appointed as head of the Kyiv Oblast regional police, Troyan had advanced quickly, becoming acting head of the national force a little over a month before Rebbe Nachman's grave was targeted.[44] A former member of Patriot of Ukraine, a group which has "espoused xenophobic and neo-Nazi ideas [and] engaged in violent attacks against migrants," Troyan was a less than ideal choice to head a department whose officers were tasked with investigating antisemitism.[45] Aside from problems of bias, the credibility of the Ukrainian police was also undercut by the corruption plaguing the force, a problem which persisted despite post-Maidan efforts at reform.[46] Reports that the SBU misused terrorism laws to crack down on independent media and tortured detainees captured in the east further undercut the security services' credibility.[47]

The Ukrainians' policy of burnishing their national reputation by distorting reality was pursued through the use of two distinct but related strategies. The first, as we have seen, was Kyiv's effort to co-opt Russian propaganda methods, minimizing domestic antisemitism and attributing racially motivated crimes to the Kremlin. The second was the government-sanctioned effort to prohibit any foreign media it considered propaganda. Russian television networks and websites were proscribed,[48] while a number of foreign correspondents, including several from Israel, were blacklisted. The Jerusalem Journalists Association, a branch of the National Federation of Israeli Journalists, harshly denounced the decision, calling it "another example of a state moving away from freedom and freedom of the press."[49]

As part of this censorship campaign, the State Committee for Television and Radio Broadcasting—in an effort managed by OUN leader Bohdan Chervak—banned nearly 40 foreign books containing "anti-Ukrainian content."[50] One of the proscribed works was the Russian translation of respected British historian Antony Beevor's history of the battle of Stalingrad, which earned Kyiv's ire for its description of Ukrainians murdering children.[51]

To the civilians trapped between government troops and separatists in the Donbas, however, these history battles paled in comparison to to the day-to-day struggle for survival.

CHAPTER SIX

WINTER IS COMING

"The Kyiv authorities didn't help us with work or with anything else. When you look for work here they call you a terrorist and if you should be paid 4,000 [hryvnia] they will only pay you half."

—Ilya Tokachov[1]

Kyiv
November 17, 2014

Walking up the steps of Kyiv's Great Choral Synagogue, I ran into Yaakov Virin, the erstwhile editor of Donetsk's Jewish newspaper. It seemed like we kept running into each other during each stage of the war. I had met Virin in Donetsk during the initial occupation, in Dnipropetrovsk after he fled into exile, and now in Kyiv where he was attempting to reassemble the shattered remnants of his previous life. His exodus was emblematic of that of the Jews of Donetsk, Luhansk, and other cities engulfed in the Ukrainian crisis. As I caught up with my fellow newspaperman, he related that he was happy to have arrived in the capital, where Rabbi Pinchas Vishedski had set up shop.[2]

Vishedski and I had remained in touch ever since our first meeting in Donetsk that April, and I had come to Kyiv to follow up on his story for the *Jerusalem Post*. Shortly after my fortuitous meeting with Virin, I made my way to Vishedski's new office in the Gulliver Center, an upscale shopping and office complex a short walk from the Maidan. It was from a glass enclosed office high up in the 35-story tower that he was attempting both to coordinate aid efforts for his former congregants scattered across the country and to refashion a demoralized group of IDPs in Kyiv into a coherent community.

Greeting me warmly in the building's spacious polished wood, tile, and glass lobby, Vishedski took me up to his twelfth-floor office. It was a large and imposing space with floor to ceiling windows and a commanding view of Kyiv's bustling downtown. Ignoring the beautiful panorama just outside, several community members sat engrossed at their work, typing on their computers and making phone calls in a coordinated effort to feed, house, and support their coreligionists spread across the country.

At the time, Vishedski believed that as many as 3,000 out of Donetsk's pre-war population of 10,000-11,000 Jews, many of them elderly, remained trapped in Donetsk. He said that since arriving in Kyiv his days were mostly spent caring for those left behind and those who had fled. He and his staff of ten were consumed with the challenge of sending supplies through the lines and coordinating the provisioning of community members scattered throughout the country.

One of the rabbi's most important assistants was community director Nadiya Goncharuk. A blond 29-year-old with wide, prominent cheeks that dimpled when she was happy, Goncharuk had been put in charge of coordinating the organized community's aid efforts. Her work didn't give her much to smile about. When I met her, she had just returned from a long road trip checking in on Donetsk Jews scattered across the country.

"I visited ten cities all over Ukraine [including] Novgorod, Kremenchuk, Poltava, Cherkassy, Dnipropetrovsk, Zaporizhia, Kirovohrad, and Zhytomyr," she said sadly. "Jews from Donetsk now live all over, and it's hard even to tell you what we are seeing. People who had everything—their homes, their stuff—who had a good life in Donetsk now live in bad conditions."

Many Jews who fled Donetsk have no income with which to pay rent or fill their refrigerators, she continued, describing how many of those living in government-controlled territory exploited and discriminated against refugees from the east. Smaller cities were cheaper than the big urban centers like Kyiv and Dnipropetrovsk, but even in such places rents were extortionate. Staying in Mariupol prior to her arrival in Kyiv, she had to pay $1,000 a month for a two-bedroom apartment in a region where the average monthly salary is only several hundred euros. "They're broke. They have no food, no money to pay for rent," she said of the refugees. "They don't know what to do next. Nobody cares. Not the Ukrainian government, nobody. They moved from Donetsk and our government didn't [provide] them [with housing], money or jobs. Nothing." Many refugees with families felt unable to provide for their children and consequently "are depressed [and] don't know what to do next."

She recalled one family whose husband had not been paid in months, one in which the children play on top of bags packed for continued flight at a moment's notice, and one whose fridge was starkly empty. The children of another family she met with, the Kaiminovichs, were playing in their garden when the bombing started. The parents grabbed their children, stopping only to take one bag and a menorah, and got on the first available bus to Poltava, where the entire family ended up crowded into a small one-room apartment.

"When I see these people, I want to give everything that I have," she said.

✳✳✳

Back in rebel territory, the humanitarian situation was growing increasingly grim as fall shaded into winter. By December, the United Nations was reporting that more than one million people had fled the conflict zone and that many of those left behind were "on the brink of survival, facing continued hardship due to the conflict, and their condition may deteriorate with the onset of winter."[3] The International Crisis Group issued a similar warning:

> "The first sign of winter weather brought fragmentary but disturbing reports of a decline in living conditions for many residents of Donetsk and Luhansk. … Around the same time one of the separatists' main websites, Rusvesna, claimed that eighteen people in one village had died of starvation. A recent visitor to the Luhansk towns of Pervomaysk and Stakhanovsk reported lines of pensioners and disabled, who had not received pensions for the last six months, waiting to receive a quarter of a loaf of bread each. … People who have cash must decide between food, medicine or fuel. Health care is under severe strain."[4]

Among those fleeing the horrific situation in the Donbas were some 1,310 Jews from Donetsk and Luhansk who made their way to Israel over the course of 2014. More that 5,800 Ukrainian immigrants in total had arrived in Israel since the beginning of the conflict, an increase of 190 percent over the previous year. Immigration from Ukraine had become second only to that of France.[5]

Despite everything happening, however, Jewish life still continued, even if at a greatly reduced level. Donetsk's Jewish kindergarten and grade school remained open for their 28 remaining students, and the synagogue still held regular services, even in the absence of Vishedski and many of the community's more religious members. According to Aryeh Shvartz, whom Vishedski had appointed to replace him as interim rabbi for the duration of the crisis, by November 2014 some 250 people were being fed hot meals at the city's synagogue every day. By February 2015, this number would rise to nearly 300.[6]

Life was also difficult in Luhansk, where more than 500 people were still receiving aid from the local Hesed branch. While the majority of the city's Jews had fled, the elderly, who were "low mobility, bed ridden, homebound, [and] lonely" were left behind, recalled Hesed director Valeria Studenikina.

"When the situation was on the most hardest level these clients didn't have the opportunity to receive any services," she said during an interview in Dnipropetrovsk in September 2014. "Now they are trying to renew the process of receiving services: food, medicines. So now clients are receiving food packages and medicines. For two months the city was under constant fire and moving around the city was quite dangerous and it was better to stay at home, not to leave the house. So people stayed at home and hid in the basements of buildings." Supplies were brought in by hired drivers who took back roads to ferry in their life-saving cargos.

Studenikina described how, during the worst of the fighting, the Hesed's four remaining staffers "were afraid to go to work due to the proximity of separatist positions." She would not remain there with them for long. Even though hundreds of her clients remained in the city, Studenikina eventually fled. She was terrified by the shelling, which, she recalled, sounded like something out of a World War Two movie. The city's utilities, knocked out during the previous months of harsh fighting, had been restored but only worked fitfully, and many residents worried about how they would heat their homes. In an interview with eJewishPhilanthropy, Igor Leonidovich, the sexton of the local synagogue, described how people would heat up bricks on their stoves to attenuate the bone-chilling cold of the long winter nights. "It works better in smaller apartments," he said. "It's not ideal, but it helps a little. It's more complicated for people with electric stoves when there's no electricity, however."[7]

The remaining members of the synagogue, mostly elderly pensioners, continued to get together for prayer services on the three days a week when Orthodox Jews read from the Torah. After services in the unheated synagogue, the men would gather around a fire and drink tea to keep warm. "We survived the shelling and life without water and without light, so we can say that now it's a bit better, although far from perfect, of course," Leonidovich said. "Still, we can gather, read from the Torah—we even have our own Cohen [member of the hereditary priestly class]—and now we see people coming to the synagogue who haven't been here in a long time. People come because at the synagogue, the soul is warmed."

Those who left Luhansk suffered terribly both from the traditional privations which accompany displacement and from the hostility of their countrymen, who tended to blame the conflict on the residents of the Donbas. This was the experience of Eira Karzvina, a Jewish resident of the city who fled with her husband and mother-in-law in August, after shells began landing near their home.

The Karzvinas stayed for a time with friends who owned a cottage in the suburbs just outside Kharkiv, sleeping together on the cold floor of a spare room while waiting for an opportunity to return home. The government provided no help and Karzvina eventually turned to the local Hesed, which gave them "money and the cards for the supermarkets where they could buy food and other stuff." The local Jewish community went out of its way to make her feel welcome but others were less understanding.

Driving into Kharkiv to go grocery shopping, Eira was stopped at a checkpoint by a traffic policeman who demanded to see her identification. Seeing that she was from Luhansk, he began yelling that she and her companions were "separatists and rebels."

"The traffic policeman started to threaten our driver," she recalled. "The policeman claimed that the driver was drunk but he wasn't. He asked him to take a [breathalyzer] test but hid the results. The policeman began to threaten the driver and demanded that he take off his shorts. He wanted us to pay because he thought were supporting the rebels. I was very afraid and began taking public transportation."

Following the signing of the Minsk ceasefire agreement in early September, the Karzvinas decided to return home. The war was winding down, they thought, and in any case they "had no other place to live." Stocking up on supplies, the IDPs once again took to the road, retracing their steps back into separatist territory. On the way they arrived at a Ukrainian checkpoint. As they pulled up to the barrier, a militiaman in a balaclava approached them and began yelling. Raising his gun, he let off a burst of fire into the air and ordered the terrified Eira out of the car. "He just wanted to show us his power because we were from Luhansk," she said.

When they finally arrived at the outskirts of their shattered hometown, it was like stepping into an alternate reality. "There was a feeling that the city was dead because [it] was empty," she described. "We went through the city and saw a lot of broken windows and smashed roofs. Our flat ... also had broken windows. There was no such area in the city where everything was okay. There was no place that wasn't shelled. The stadium, the circus, the nursing home, they were shelled as well. We thought that there would be more destruction as shown in the cinema in the films about the Second World War, but fortunately there was no firing from aircraft. We lived in the south of the city but drove in from the northwest so we got to drive through all of Luhansk and on the way saw [maybe] ten cars. The city was completely empty. We saw several supermarkets that were completely burned out, but the firefighters were working and the garbage was being taken out [and] the streets were swept so the services were working. In our house we saw the gas pipe was broken and that our roof was damaged. We repaired it, but there were a lot of houses near us that were completely burned out."

✳✳✳

Hunger and cold weren't the only issues brought about by the war. For those who were religiously observant, the war brought additional hardships. While the Jews of Donetsk were now growing increasingly reliant on outside food aid, prior to the war their city had been the primary certifier and producer of kosher comestibles in Ukraine. Vishedski's agency, the Kashrut Committee of Ukraine, had certified products across the country, including the prepackaged kosher meals served on Ukraine International Airlines flights. Since fleeing the Donbas in August, the rabbi had been struggling to reestablish the committee, forging ties with new producers to replace its old partners in Donetsk. As the war intensified, the *kashrut* inspectors began fleeing the city until only those supervising the production of dairy products remained. By January 2015, they had left as well, throwing the kosher food industry into turmoil. It took two months to establish new partnerships, during which time kosher milk was largely unavailable.

"Whenever it was up to us, we did everything we could to advise to keep prices down," he recalled during an interview in mid-2015. While many non-Jews—including vegetarians, Muslims, and people who perceive such fare as generally more healthy than the alternatives—have created a large market for kosher food in the United States, making certification a big business, in Ukraine it's "far from being a business [but] more of an ideological matter." After all, "Jews need kosher food." Ramping up production to prewar levels "wasn't simple," he added, noting that as of June there was still no locally produced kosher cheese.[8]

While the bulk of the suffering was on the Ukrainian side, the conflict created religious challenges for Russian Jews as well. In late 2014, a group of rabbis affiliated with Russia's Congress of Jewish Religious Organizations (KEROOR) gathered in a Moscow yeshiva to discuss how to handle the influx of sabbatical produce coming into the country from Israel as a result of Kremlin counter-sanctions against European food producers. As the Europeans found their exports blocked, the Israelis stepped in to fill the void. However, while this was certainly a boon for Israeli farmers, the massive increase in their produce on Russian super-market shelves added an unsought complication to the lives of kosher consumers there. *Shmitta*—the sabbatical year in which farming in the land of Israel is Biblically prohibited—had begun in September, and the rabbis were worried about how to prevent their congregants from violating the law by consuming forbidden produce.[9] "This is the first time we are really confronted with this on such a major scale," said Rabbi Pinchas Goldschmidt, a rabbinical court judge from Moscow and president of the Conference of European Rabbis.

Various legal justifications are utilized to prevent the land from remaining fallow, a number of which are not universally accepted among the ultra-orthodox. More moderate rabbis rely on a legal mechanism known as the *heter mechira,* in which the titles of fields are transferred to non-Jews, freeing up the Jewish farmer to engage in normal agriculture. Others rely on Arab produce or on a system called *otzar beit din,* in which rabbinic courts supervise the harvesting and distribution of crops, the price of which is supposed to only cover costs and does not constitute a proper sale of the produce in question. Many of the ultra-orthodox are careful not to buy *heter mechira,* which they consider of questionable validity. Those looking to abide by the strictest interpretations of Jewish law, however, were stymied by the lack of branding on produce that would have allowed them to differentiate between the various standards employed by the farmers back in Israel. As one rabbi put it, the situation was a complete *balagan,* a Hebrew word of Russian origin used to signify a mess or confusion.

Jerusalem
October 30, 2014

For much of the first year of the conflict, there were a number of Ukrainian Jewish leaders who were extremely frustrated. They felt that the Israelis and much of the wider Jewish Diaspora had abandoned them. Pinchas Vishedski described how, after the outbreak of hostilities in the Donbas, he had received calls from both the American and Japanese embassies, inquiring after his community's welfare. He claimed that he had never heard from the Israelis.

However, by the fall of 2014, Jerusalem had stepped in. The Ministry of Diaspora Affairs, a little known and relatively small government department, earmarked two million shekels (more than half a million dollars) to provide "members of the Jewish community who have been affected by the fighting" with food, clothing, and shelter. Initially, the ministry did not publicly acknowledge the program. A source with knowledge of the matter told me that, given the sensitivities of the situation, "much of the aid need[ed] to be delivered through non-conventional channels," a veiled reference to the American Jewish Joint Distribution Committee (JDC).[10]

While Ukrainian Jewish leaders praised the Israeli move, calling it a "a big shift," there were also complaints that it had taken Jerusalem too long to get involved. "Who could wait so long," one communal official asked. "They have to clean up their bureaucracy. Some things just can't take so long." There were those in the ministry itself who seemed to agree with their critics, with one official baldly stating that the funding was "not enough" and that as "another wave of refugees" fled the Donbas even more money would be required. The ministry, a spokesman said, was "looking into the resources needed to continue the project."[11] By March 2015, the government money, which the JDC was using to support some 2,500 people, had run out. Luckily for the Jews of the Donbas, the ministry had managed to obtain a budget to continue the aid project and was able to provide a fresh tranche of funds.[12]

At the same time that the Ministry of Diaspora Affairs was trying to help the Jews of Ukraine survive in place, the Israeli Interior Ministry's Population, Immigration and Borders Authority also began to reach out, easing bureaucratic requirements in order to facilitate the flow of refugees to Israel. In a decision it touted as a much needed humanitarian gesture, the authority announced in late 2014 that it was relaxing guidelines concerning the paperwork required for *aliya*. The refugees were freed from the necessity of pre-translating certain documents, including those attesting to their lack of criminal records.[13] "If he [the immigrant] is missing paperwork, the directive says he won't be turned down," a spokeswoman for the Immigration Authority explained at the time. "It's not that we don't request the documents. We request the documents, but if someone comes and doesn't have a certain document it doesn't disqualify him." Jewish Agency officials had previously noted that the issue of paperwork had been a vexing one for Ukrainian Jews, many of whom did not have passports and had left documents attesting to their Jewish identity at home.[14] One immigrant to Israel even recalled how her parents had been required to return home to the conflict zone, even after fleeing at the behest of Israeli officials, in order to collect the documents necessary to obtain their citizenship.

The newcomers were also asked to provide papers establishing their religious heritage in order to satisfy the requirements of the Law of Return, the Israeli legislation governing immigration.[15] For many, this was easier said than done. Due to generations of assimilation, it is sometimes difficult to ascertain the Jewish identity of those coming from the former Soviet Union. A lack of paperwork only compounded the problem. "Many Jews have issues and problems in proving that they are Jewish," explained Dnipropetrovsk rabbi Shmuel Kaminezki. Proving one's status often involves traveling to far-flung former Soviet republics and digging through dusty archives, and many prospective immigrants "don't have the finances or organizational ability to do it. I know many people who have been denied the possibility of making *aliya* because they just didn't have enough documents.

Many people say 'I'm really Jewish but won't be able to prove it so forget about it.' It's a pity."[16] The problem was sufficiently pressing that by mid-2015 Israel's Tzohar rabbinical organization had opened an office in Dnipropetrovsk in a bid to prove the status of Ukrainians according to Jewish law before they arrived in Israel. According to Tzohar executive vice president Yakov Gaon, up to a quarter of a million Israelis from the former Soviet Union are Jewish according to *halacha* (Jewish law) but lack the documentation to prove it. As such, they are unable to marry in Israel and exist in a limbo in which they are considered Jewish by secular state institutions but not by the Chief Rabbinate. "To preserve a Jewish Israel we try to get them all relevant documentation when they are in Ukraine or Russia, so the process [of absorption in Israel] is more user friendly and [so it is] easier to be part of the Jewish people in the Land of Israel," he explained.

Just as the Israeli government was changing its policies to deal with the issues raised by the war, the Jewish Agency was likewise adapting in order to operate more efficiently in a conflict zone. In an interview with the *Jerusalem Post* in mid-2015, Roman Polonsky and Bilana Shakhar, respectively the head of the agency's unit for Russian-speaking Jews and the official responsible for *aliya* and Israel experiences in the FSU, stated that the war had forced several changes in how they prepared prospective immigrants, due to the limited amount of time available when dealing with escapees from the Donbas.[17] "We are doing all needed internal adjustments [so that] no one who wants to come to Israel will be abandoned [and so they can] receive all needed help," Polonsky said, explaining that the agency was serving "vulnerable and shaken communities" through summer camps, Sunday schools, and other programs.

According to Shakhar, the agency was "dealing with a new phenomenon of Jewish internally displaced persons. It means people are escaping from conflict areas. They don't have a lot of time and in a very short period we have to provide them with as much as we can [in terms of] information about the opportunities in Israel." She recalled one woman from Donetsk, whom she met in the agency's refugee transit center in Dnipropetrovsk, whose four-year-old daughter died due to the shortage of medicine in the occupied territories. She "died in front of her mother," and the entire family—including her 10-year-old brother—would require psychological help once in Israel, which would complicate their integration. According to Shakhar, such stories were common enough that they required the agency to adopt a new approach to integrating refugees into Israeli society, including boosting the amount of time that some immigrants would spend in agency-run absorption centers.[18] Such extended stays would be necessary to deal with their traumas as well as to make up for the time lost due to their accelerated immigration process. "We are adjusting specially to these kinds of problems," she said. "We will try to find them programs that can give them the opportunity for a more gradual process."

Kramatorsk
February 10, 2015

Back in the east, the war continued and civilians on both sides of the line were suffering. In Kramatorsk, Hesed director Galina Gabinskaya was eating lunch when she heard a rocket strike in the courtyard of the nine-story building housing the social services center. Looking out her first-floor window, she saw its tail sticking up out of the ground. It was a dud. As she stared out and contemplated how close she had come to death, there was a sickening crash. A second rocket had hit the building's roof. It also failed to explode. Shaking themselves out of their shock, Gabinskaya and her employees called emergency services and bundled the dozen elderly clients in the building at the time into cabs.[19] At first "we were in shock and didn't understand what was going on and that we were under shelling. The fear came later," she recalled.

"I can't say we are nervous or scared, but we all have our bags packed," said Tanya Shapkovsky, a member of the local Jewish community. "If there will be any hot situation or more conflict, probably we will all have to leave the city."

In total, separatists fired twenty rockets at Kramatorsk that day, and not all of them were faulty. Although Gabinskaya and her clients survived, others weren't as lucky. Across the city, twelve civilians were killed and dozens wounded.[20] That day in Donetsk, a member of the Jewish community was killed by a rocket that struck her apartment. The victim, Shelkaeva Irina Grigorievna, had worked for the local Jewish community for the better part of a decade, both as a guard and at the local kindergarten, and her death hit those who knew her hard.[21] I have "no words. I can't cry anymore," Nadiya Goncharuk told me only hours after Grigorievna's death. "She was funny, intelligent and very talented. She created pictures and information for kids and parents on the walls of the kindergarten. Her family is very poor. They have no money because of the war. Our community paid all the expenses for her funeral. People are afraid, they are crying. Imagine … every hour I am getting horrifying news from our home city."

Only hours later, a rocket hit a bus full of passengers several hundred meters from the synagogue. "In the middle of the morning prayers, the walls shook with noise," described Pinchas Vishedski, who was in touch with the community after the incident. "There was … a commotion and hysteria [but] later, when the place calmed down after the evacuation of casualties, [life] returned to normal."

Dnipropetrovsk
February 11, 2015

The incessant shelling had already driven out many of the city's residents, and the exodus was far from over. Only a day after Grigorievna's death, three buses pulled up to the curb outside of the Dnipropetrovsk Regional State Administration building and dislodged their passengers. Bearing signs declaring "Don't shoot! Children," the buses were the result of long and intense three-way negotiations between regional governor Ihor Kolomoisky's staff, the JDC, and the Donetsk People's Republic over the extrication of members of the Jewish community trapped behind the lines in the occupied territories. All told, 130 Jews were removed from the war zone, including 22 children and many geriatrics.[22]

Some time earlier, the JDC's Yoni Leifer had contacted Boris Traigerman, a Jewish senior advisor to Kolomoisky, and asked for assistance. "He said that he had some trouble in Donetsk and the surrounding areas as these elderly Jews couldn't leave the area," Traigerman later recalled. "Most of them couldn't move. It was basically their lives [on the line] because they were incapable of moving cities, of moving anywhere. The Joint has tried contacting, you know, the separatists to get the problem solved but they weren't getting anywhere with it. So they simply came and asked for help." Together with Deputy Governor Hennadiy Korban, another Jew, Traigerman began planning a rescue operation. "The first point was to get all of those people who wanted to get out of there to one place at one time in Donetsk with everything they wanted to take out" and then bring them to the no man's land between the lines. "We had to agree with both the Ukrainian army and the separatists to stop fire, for a ceasefire for that period of time."

According to Traigerman, the operation was initially complicated by the need to arrange a second set of decoy buses, because he had received intelligence "that the separatists ... [had] planned [a] terrorist attack to ... show the Ukrainian army was shooting at the buses with Jewish people." (He did not provide any corroborating evidence to back up this claim.) "So at first we had planned for an empty bus to go with windows closed with a different track, a different journey track, to distract attention but when we agreed completely with everybody—including the separatists, the Ukrainian army and special forces—and we were sure there would be no terrorist attacks, no shooting, we changed the plan and basically just went together in one group. The separatists gave them the green light. They guaranteed that there wouldn't be any searches on any checkpoints and there would be a cease-fire during this time. They completely realized they were carrying responsibility for the lives of these people."

Kyiv
March 22, 2015

For many, escaping Donetsk only led to a set of new and difficult problems. According to Lena Tarasova, the head of family services at Kyiv's JDC-run Beytenu youth center, by March 2015, her organization had provided assistance to around 280 families—more than 640 people. IDPs, she said, were eligible for rent subsidies for up to three months after their arrival (up to six months for families with children or the elderly). In total, the displaced received between 5,000-6,000 hryvnia a month, equivalent to about $250. The problem, she told me, echoing Nadiya Goncharuk, was that many in the capital would still not rent apartments to their countrymen from the east.[23]

"The Kyiv authorities didn't help us with work or with anything else," Ilya Tokachov told me, sitting in a cramped one-room apartment he was sharing with his wife, one-year-old son, and mother-in-law. A 26-year-old white-collar professional from Luhansk, Tokachov was Jewish on his father's side and said he was planning on moving to Israel shortly after our interview, joining more than ten of his friends who had already left. Meanwhile, things were tough. According to Tokachov, many local businesses only paid refugee hires half of what they would pay those hailing from government-controlled territory. "When you look for work here they call you a terrorist and if you should be paid 4,000 [hryvnia] they will only pay you half and say 'it's enough we will find someone else from Luhansk who is looking for work,'" he explained.

Even for those earning full salaries, life was difficult. The precipitous decline of the Ukrainian economy since the outbreak of hostilities meant that it was growing increasingly challenging to make ends meet. Vadim Dorofeev, another IDP, said that he had found work in Kyiv paying roughly what he had made before the war but that inflation had made it nearly impossible to survive.

For people like Tokachov and Dorofeev life was hard enough, but for others things were even worse. In February, a local Jewish news website reported that a number of IDPs from Donetsk had lost their life savings to theft. The money, which was being held in a safety deposit box at a branch of Alliance Bank belonging to a fellow community member, had disappeared and, according to a letter obtained by Ukraine's *Jewish News*, Pinchas Vishedski believed that the SBU had stolen the funds.[24]

"In December of last year, the Jewish community of Donbas was shaken up by events that took place at one Kyiv bank. Under strange circumstances, large sums were stolen from safe boxes, including money belonging to Donetsk refugees," Vishedski wrote. "On December 22, law-enforcement officers entered a bank ... and broke into the depository, using force, destroying video cameras and entry detectors. The boxes were opened without an investigator, witnesses and bank employees. During the 'search' the entire contents of the boxes disappeared, including boxes in which Jewish refugees from Donetsk kept their savings."

"The depositors and owners of the stolen money are private individuals, Jews from Donetsk, who attended our synagogue and were part of the community," Vishedski told Jewish News. "They went to Kyiv, a city that was not familiar to them. They didn't go there because they wanted to but because they were forced to leave their native Donetsk, taking what they had with them."

Kyiv
March 23, 2015

"Welcome to Israel, even if we still are in Ukraine," Ofer Dahan told the crowd in rapid-fire Hebrew. As his words were translated, the largely somber crowd of refugees chuckled, their grim faces breaking into smiles. Addressing the gathering of soon to be Ukrainian émigrés, Dahan—at the time the head of the IFCJ's newly established *aliya* department—described how his organization had made arrangements with over 200 municipalities across Israel to ease the newcomers' transition. "Everyone who comes to a city, a representative of the local authority will be in touch with you personally," he assured them.

As their luggage was being loaded into large tractor trailers outside of the hotel in which they were meeting, IFCJ staffers began handing out tickets for the flight, the second such *aliya* charter plane organized by the group. The IFCJ had begun flights for Ukrainian Jews in late 2014, putting it into conflict with the Jewish Agency, which accused it of "attempting to go rogue, to the ultimate detriment of those they purport to serve." The IFCJ dismissed the agency's claims, and a spokesman for the Ministry of Immigrant Absorption said that those brought by the NGO would "receive exactly the same treatment from our ministry as all other immigrants."[25]

Later on, at half past one in the morning, I stood outside the hotel watching the just over 100 Jews climb onto the buses that would take them to Boryspil International Airport for their flight to Tel Aviv.[26] It was dark on the bus, with the streetlights outside casting a sinister pall over the refugees, but the mood, at odds with the lighting, was jubilant if somewhat restrained given the late hour. Leaning forward, his pitted and scarred face wreathed in shadow, one immigrant grinned widely, a fitting avatar for the contradictions inherent in that moment. Many of the immigrants expressed happiness at their escape to Israel. Alex, the scarred young man, said he "didn't know" why he hadn't made *aliya* before, but he was happy to go with his father now that his mother and younger brother had already left and were waiting for them in Israel. A second young man with a kippa proudly pulled out an Israeli passport and said that he had briefly lived in Israel years ago and that it was good to return.

There was none of the gloom I had witnessed among a similar group of immigrants almost a year earlier with whom I shared a nighttime flight to Israel out of Dnipropetrovsk, and, while their departure seemed bittersweet, those who spoke to me were all enthusiastic about the chance to start over in a nation without war. After seeing the refugees off I made my way to domestic departures, where I planned on sleeping on a bench for the rest of the night. In the morning I had a flight to the east.

Dnipropetrovsk
March 24, 2015

The next morning, after a restless night, I arrived in Dnipropetrovsk to meet up with Mendel Cohen, the rabbi of Mariupol, whose community was located just behind the front lines. Hopping in his car, we began the five-hour drive over Ukraine's decrepit highways. Even outside the combat zone, the roads were so neglected that one could be forgiven for thinking that the potholes were shell-holes from artillery fire. Eventually we reached a government checkpoint where an armed Ukrainian serviceman pulled us over and inquired as to our business. Cohen, knowing that he had been stopped because his license plates showed him to be a resident of the Donetsk Oblast, smiled and identified himself as a rabbi. Receiving a smile in return, we were allowed to proceed and continued on our way. As he drove, Cohen told me that he remained upbeat about the future, despite the war and the economic downturn, and described how hundreds of people received food, clothing, and other aid from the organized community. Despite all of these efforts, however, people had begun leaving, with at least 100 members of the "circle closest to the synagogue" having made *aliya,* and he believed that the following summer would see a "large wave" of emigration.

Mariupol and Chermalyk
March 25, 2015

The next morning, I met up with Elena Mozgina, my fixer, and Dima Shapovalov, a local Jew who had volunteered to act as my translator, and we set off to meet with representatives of the Dnipr Battalion, a privately funded pro-government militia affiliated with Kolomoisky.[27] We were planning on visiting Chermalyk, a dusty little farming village separated from separatist territory by the Kalmius River which had been heavily bombarded in recent weeks. After a short wait, a van retrofitted with armor plates pulled up and we were off. Making our way to Chermalyk, we passed several checkpoints with heavy weapons emplacements and concrete bunkers hidden behind mounds of dirt and sandbags. Antitank obstacles bracketed the road and checkpoints. As we rattled down the crumbling blacktop, slowly navigating around potholes and shell holes, I noticed a Kalashnikov and two shoulder-fired rockets on the floor between the two militiamen sitting up front. They slid around as we drove.

Once in the village, a spread-out collection of fields and farmhouses with a number of larger buildings interspersed for variety, we traded the armored van for a pickup truck and went on patrol, driving along the dirt roads between the farms lining the Kalmius. Sitting in the back of the truck among the militiamen, I struggled to keep my balance as we made our way down the uneven roads, occasionally stopping when flagged down by the locals. One woman reported that a rocket had landed in her field and asked them to take a look. Jumping out, we made our way across the bare dirt until we reached the hole. The troops looked inside, shrugged and went back to the truck.

Pulling up to a house with a shattered roof, one of the militiamen told me that the river had frozen during the winter, enabling the separatists to launch several raids. As we approached the house, a dog barked and pulled at its chain. Hearing the noise, an elderly woman peered outside, saw us, and slammed her door shut. She reemerged a minute later with a geriatric man in tow. They introduced themselves as Volodya and Olga and told me that they were living in an outbuilding next to their farmhouse while its roof was being repaired. It had been hit by a separatist rocket two weeks earlier. "If [the shelling] sounds too loud we go down to the basement," they said, adding that they lived in fear but couldn't afford to leave.

Later that day, after returning to Mariupol, Cohen told me that many of his congregants frequently left because separatist forces were so close to the city, but unlike in the people's republics they usually returned, creating something of a revolving door effect. "People are always coming and going. [It's an] absurd situation."

Among those who wanted to leave was Michael, an older man who had been shot in the foot during clashes between government troops and separatists earlier in the conflict. I met with him in the dim living room of his home as he convalesced on his sofa. He had already undergone two separate surgeries at the community's expense.

Julia Evashenko, another resident, had fled Mariupol twice, both times returning, and told me that she was planning to leave again. She had given birth while staying with relatives in Melitopol during one of her stays outside Mariupol. Her husband, Andrei, who had stayed behind in Mariupol to support their extended family, had come to visit her for the birth but had to return in order to work. "It's hard to make a living for all of us on my husband's salary," she told me. "My mother is on a pension and my brother has no work and there is no work to find. Andrei's parents have no work as well." Sitting on their cream-colored couch next to his wife, Andrei said it was lonely staying in Mariupol by himself but that he had no plans to leave. They would wait out the war in Ukraine.

Others, like 36-year-old Yulia Mashtanir, were less sanguine about their prospects in Ukraine. She said that her seven-year-old son Eitan had been traumatized by the shelling and would shake and cry whenever he heard the sound of rockets. Like the Evashenkos, the Mashtanir family had initially fled, heading to Crimea for a spell, but had elected to return and had since begun the process of applying to make *aliya*. She said that, while she did not know what would happen in Israel, in Ukraine her children were certain to face the prospect of even more horror and war. When I asked him if they were excited to go to the Jewish state, Eitan and his younger brother Yisrael shouted "yes." They were raring to go.

✶✶✶

At the same time that I was driving around Mariupol and Chermalyk, a political bomb had gone off in Kyiv and Dnipropetrovsk. President Poroshenko had sacked Kolomoisky. The previous week, Kolomoisky had sent armed men into the offices of the state oil company, UkrTransNafta, in response to the firing of its director, who was one of his associates. That led to a crackdown on Kolomoisky's inner circle. A number of months later, Deputy Governor Hennadiy Korban, who was also a member of the board of trustees of the Dnipropetrovsk Jewish community, was arrested during a massive raid conducted by the SBU. The authorities accused him of running an organized crime operation,[28] and prosecutors claimed that he was guilty of embezzlement and had masterminded several kidnappings. Shortly after the raid, which also targeted the Kolomoisky-linked National Defense Foundation, Kolomoisky advisor Pavel Khazan left Ukraine for Israel. While he maintained that he had gone to receive medical care for an eye ailment, it was hard to accept that his timing was unconnected with the political and legal maelstrom that had engulfed his circle.

"When [Korban] was arrested … the police came to my home during the night," Khazan later recalled during an interview in Jerusalem. "My wife called me and said to me that the police want to search, and when I came home they had already broken doors and tried to make this terrible search. Two guys with machine guns came to the room of my younger son when he was sleeping and I don't know why, maybe they wanted to find terrorists in the room of my son, but it was [a] really dangerous action and I think the aim of this action was to explain to us volunteers that the government has power and maybe this was to scare us to be silent. Actually, before this action I had given many interviews where I criticized our government very much. I said very critical [things] and I believe that it was an action to [force me to] be silent and not say very critical things about our government."

In a statement on its website, the Dnipropetrovsk Jewish community slammed the arrest. Calling Korban "a respected member of the Jewish community, philanthropist and benefactor" and a "political figure of great stature," they noted that he had recently undergone heart surgery. The statement accused the authorities of denying Korban adequate healthcare and of having "flouted the rule of law, human rights, and the principles of humanism and humanity."[29]

However, the community didn't go nearly as far as Korban, who compared himself to Mendel Beilis, a Kyiv factory worker who had been the defendant in the Russian empire's last blood libel trial just over a century earlier. Accused of murdering a Christian child in order to use his blood for Passover matzah, Beilis had eventually been exonerated, despite the Czarist government's concerted efforts to ensure a conviction. Korban invoked the Beilis affair, which had became synonymous with politicized justice and judicial antisemitism, telling reporters that "history repeats itself."

"One hundred years ago, here in Kiev in 1913, a trial of the Jew Beilis took place. This is the famous lawsuit that even then could show the absurdity of justice. Today, 100 years later, here in Kyiv, we can draw a full analogy between that kind of justice and [contemporary justice]. Then the 37-year-old father of five children was accused of all mortal sins—of eating babies, and God knows what else. Then it was a process related to antisemitism, and the Black Hundreds," he said, referring to a notorious Russian anti-Jewish organization. Shortly thereafter, Korban's UKROP party doubled down on his claims, issuing a press release which described "clear parallels between the cases of Beilis and Korban." Party advisor Nikita Poturayev claimed that it was clear from social media postings that there was "an organized antisemitic informational campaign against Korban. We are seeing lots of repeated hate comments about the Jews stealing from the state and not being welcome in Ukraine. This is very dangerous and feeds into social tensions in Ukraine."

Many Jewish leaders, already wary of previous attempts to politicize the issue of antisemitism, cast doubts on Korban's claims. Eduard Dolinsky stated baldly that there was "no connection between his arrest and the Jewish community." Vyacheslav Likhachev called "the comparison with the Beilis case … an impermissible speculation." Rabbi Boruch Gorin of the Federation of Jewish Communities of Russia was extremely caustic, calling on his coreligionist "not to make a joke of himself" and accusing him of "provoking" antisemitism.[30]

Kyiv
March 31, 2015

Pinchas Vishedski was relieved. He had been working for weeks to convince the army to allow him to send a shipment of Passover matzah through the lines to Donetsk in time for the holiday, and he had finally succeeded. "Thank God the matzot arrived in Donetsk and Luhansk and there will be a big Seder both on the first and second nights of the holiday," he enthused, referring to the traditional festive meal in which Jews recount the Exodus from Egypt and celebrate their freedom from bondage. In addition to the communal meals in Donetsk, Vishedski had also organized similar events for IDPs in Kyiv, where representatives of the JDC had been busy distributing matzah to needy Jews. In total, the JDC said that it had distributed 48,000 free boxes of matzah. Working with the JDC, the IFCJ claimed that it had donated 35,000 food boxes and 3,500 cards redeemable for children's clothing, as well as arranging Seders for some 15,000 people in 260 communities across the country, with a further 60 Seders organized through Chabad.[31]

Holidays can be among the most difficult times of the year for refugees, and Jewish organizations across the country were working hard to make sure that their displaced coreligionists had a place to celebrate. In Dnipropetrovsk, the Jewish Agency had organized a practice Seder in which children "learned about the holiday for the first time" ahead of their "imminent *aliya* and first Passover in Israel." Like the agency, the local Jewish community there had decided to engage in a widespread educational effort, which included creating a video showcasing how to run a Seder according to *halacha*. "Most of those who come to the public Seders aren't deeply observant, and it's important to have a connection to the emcee of the Seder," said community director Zelig Brez. "This Seder in [the Menorah Center] is one of the biggest, with 1,500 people who come and want to be part of it, but with such a large number one person without a microphone can't lead, so the community [has launched] a new project to teach every single father and person what the Seder is all about, how to do it and how to live it."

Luhansk
April 3, 2015

Despite all of the efforts to make it a pleasant holiday, Passover was still difficult in the occupied territories. In Luhansk, the community was "unable to arrange a public Seder … because the Seder starts in the evening, and people do not go out at night now," Rabbi Shalom Gopin told the news section of Chabad's website.[32] "Since people don't want to leave their homes at night, we arranged for fifteen Seders to be held in private apartments around the city. Everyone got traditional kosher-for-Passover food, matzah, and wine from our kitchen, and then people signed up to attend a Seder held in their neighborhood."

The rabbi denied reports in the Ukrainian media that the separatists—who had raided his synagogue in the initial months of the conflict—had begun nationalizing Jewish communal property outright. He asserted that, while in late March representatives of the Luhansk People's Republic had "entered our school building in Luhansk and told our guards that it appeared that the Jewish community was forfeiting the building, and they were taking it," the issue was soon cleared up. The separatists had given him assurances that the building was safe.

✶✶✶

As we have seen, the uncertainty engendered by living under such a capricious regime, coupled with the ever-present dangers of living in a conflict zone, drove people out of the Donbas en masse. According to Israel's Ministry of Immigrant Absorption, more than 30,000 people immigrated to Israel from Ukraine between 2014 and October 2018. Of those immigrants, 1,985 were from Donetsk, nearly 687 from Luhansk, and 280 from Mariupol. According to the Jewish Agency,[33] 3,170 Jews in total immigrated to Israel from the Donbas and Ukrainian-controlled cities in the vicinity during this period.[34]

Those who stayed in Ukraine had to be resettled and supported until they could reestablish themselves. Even many of those living outside the conflict zone required help due to the country's shrinking economy. By early 2016, the JDC was providing aid to some 2,800 IDPs.[35] At the time, the Jewish Agency estimated that there were around 2,500 Jews from Donetsk and Luhansk living in the Kyiv metropolitan area, with another 100-150 families in Odessa.[36] Resettling all of these people was a challenge that community leaders approached in radically different ways.

Anatevka
February 4, 2016

One of these approaches was that of Moshe Azman, who had purchased a tract of land outside of the capital in mid-2015 in order to construct a self-contained refugee compound named after the fictional village of Anatevka from *Fiddler on the Roof.* "Located only 30 minutes from the Kiev city center, the community will serve as a basis for refugees to find work, receive medical and psychological rehabilitation, and begin new lives," a website established by Azman boasted, adding that eventually the compound would include "housing in small apartment blocks, a school, an orphanage, an old age home, a synagogue, and a community center." A spokesman for the project predicted that Anatevka would eventually become the home of 300-500 people.[37] When I visited the site in early 2016, construction was in full swing.

The ankle-deep mud sucked at my boots as I slogged along, ducking under a cement mixer's chute just before it began disgorging its cargo into a ditch dug out of the frozen soil. A construction worker with a shovel began smoothing the concrete, Azman tossed a symbolic spadeful into the foundations of the newest building to be erected in Anatevka. As the foundations for what I was told would be a residential building were being filled, I turned and took in the temporary housing already erected in the months since the rabbi launched his resettlement program, a wooden structure rising together out of a sea of muck. At first glance it wasn't an especially impressive site, but inside the buildings were well put together, with a smell of freshly cut wood that brought back memories of summer camp in upstate New York. Workers swarmed over the building, hammering, sawing, and making a god-awful racket.[38]

At the time, around 100 IDPs were living in the camp, although when I visited, in the middle of the day, only a handful were present. After praying the afternoon service in Anatevka's small but well appointed synagogue, I chatted with the residents, most of whom were from Luhansk. Elena Yaremchenko, who had come to Anatevka by way of Zhytomyr, told me that she was satisfied with her accommodations and that her husband had been hired to complete its construction. Sitting on a stool in the hallway of the wooden barracks, alongside several other women and children, she looked at me and said that being resettled in Anatevka has given her a sense of "security and a feeling that there will be a tomorrow." "It's kind of like a kibbutz, a Ukrainian kibbutz," interjected Svetlana, another IDP whom Azman had hired to coordinate services for the displaced. "It was a different life in Luhansk. They had friends and a house and everything. Here it's different. They live as a group that does everything together, it's completely different," she explained, standing across from the entrance to the dormitory's communal kitchen, where two women were busy preparing a meal. With a full-time job helping other displaced people and a rental apartment in Kyiv that she shared with her six-year-old daughter, Svetlana said that she did not like to be called a refugee, recalling how she had helped Azman find and develop the plot of land on which Anatevka was being constructed.

Another approach to resettlement was that of Pinchas Vishedski, who fundamentally disagreed with Azman's establishment of a latter-day *shtetl*, calling it "part of the Jewish nation's past." To Vishedski, the compound represented "the wandering of the Jews." Instead, the rabbi and his team worked to resettle members of the Donetsk expatriate community in apartments across Kyiv. "I think it's more important to help people in places where they can have a future," the rabbi explained. "People need hope, the hope is to rebuild one's life." By the beginning of 2016, he had left his offices in the Gulliver tower, establishing a synagogue cum community center in a small, sky-blue stone building a short walk from the Great Choral Synagogue in Podil.

Sitting in his small office behind the small sanctuary/event hall, Vishedski opined on the differences between his and Azman's respective approaches, reiterating his skepticism regarding Anatevka's viability. His community was comprised of "normal people with cars and livelihoods who had lost everything and just wanted to raise their children in a normal place."

"You can't tell them to live in a refugee camp," he explained. "They want to be in the city where there is a good education for their kids. I don't judge and [I] honor anyone who acts for refugees," but as a displaced person himself, he said that he recognized that for most people like him, the resumption of a normal life was the highest priority. "If I don't want to live there no one wants to. I want a day to come when they don't need my help." In the meantime, however, he admitted that it was "very hard to find work. People turn to us and we worry for them. For the majority of families, it continues to be a struggle. The economy isn't good, businesses are closing and don't want to hire people. People don't know what they will do tomorrow."

While Chabad rabbis are usually not big promoters of *aliya*, Vishedski told me that he had been pushing the Israel option as a good solution for many in the Donetsk émigré community. "We, my family and I, are living without certainty. I can't say that we have found our place and will live in the future in Kyiv. I don't know what will be tomorrow [but] I don't have the privilege of giving up on the community," he said, expressing a sentiment widespread among those who had fled the war. Later that evening, the rabbi delivered a lecture on the Torah to a small group of IDPs in the back of the synagogue. Among those present was Alexander Gordon, a middle-aged businessman who was out of work. While he had been able to resettle his family somewhat comfortably, he said, "people who don't have money are having a very hard time living in Kyiv. It's very hard for many people. It's impossible to say how difficult, but we have no choice."

Interjecting, Pavel Zaranken, another IDP, seemed to speak for all of Ukraine's Jews, stating, to the murmured assent of those present, that "we have no plans for the future. We are finding a way to live without making plans."

CHAPTER SEVEN

REBIRTH

"We came to Kyiv with our luggage in our hands and all the time the community grew bigger and bigger and bigger. Our halls didn't have enough room for the whole community [but] God helped us and gave us His hand."

—Nadiya Goncharuk[1]

A NEW SYNAGOGUE

Kyiv
January 26, 2020

Four years later, things had changed dramatically.

Just past a dark and unobtrusive arch leading off Nyzhnii Val, a tree-lined street in the heart of the Ukrainian capital, stands the Kedem Synagogue, a modest three-story red and white building whose existence is seen as almost miraculous by its habitués, many of whom were convinced only a few short years ago that their community was on the verge of being erased from the face of the earth.

Its halls echoing with the sounds of Hebrew and Russian, the rented building served as the new home of the Donetsk Jewish community in Kyiv. In January 2020, in what was to be my last international reporting trip before the Covid-19 pandemic disrupted international travel, I visited Ukraine one last time to see how Vishedski, Goncharuk, and the other IDPs had acclimated.

Inside the synagogue hall, a group of men stood around an electric kettle, brewing cups of instant coffee and chatting after the end of morning services. Grinning as one of their number cracked a joke, they appeared no different from their counterparts in synagogues around the world. But looks can be deceiving, and their smiles belied the horrors that each had experienced.

One of the men was Yaakov Virin, whose extended journey, which found him moving from city to city across the country, had finally led him and his family to Kyiv. Now, over half a decade after the outbreak of the conflict, Virin said that he and his wife had found a measure of stability working for local community organizations. They were, after a long time, able to support themselves once again, although the high cost of living made things more difficult than they would have preferred.

His wartime experiences taught him "that a person shouldn't make plans and calculations," Virin told me as we sipped our coffee. "I just live. I moved here with my family and it goes the way it goes."

"When you live in a rented apartment and you need to pay each month and go from one place to another and each year the price is rising, you feel like you are in a temporary place. Generally it's okay. I've come back to the community and the rabbi and, thank God, a job. It's not the same, but things have returned to normal," he said.

"On the one hand, I'm happy that there is a community that I can call my community, but on the other hand I would substitute all of the life that I have here for my life in Donetsk before the war."

Just like Virin, the community's synagogue has had to make its way in Kyiv, starting off in a small house in the capital's Podil neighborhood and moving twice, eventually to Nyzhnii Val.

"I'm grateful that I'm here," Zushi Plietnov, a 30-year-old refugee from Luhansk who translated for Virin, told me. "This is the best community ever. Vishedski really made a place for everyone here."

Plietnov recalled living through the "bullets and shots" during the initial takeover of his city but insisted that despite what he had gone through he is "not struggling at all."

"Sometimes you need to force yourself tell yourself a new story about your life and what happened," he said. "I don't feel sorrow or bad. I feel like we moved on and we never discuss what there was or how we used to live."

For others who might not be doing as well, the community maintains a WhatsApp chat group and "if someone needs help they get so much support from the community," he told me.

After coffee with Virin and Plietnov, Grisha Sagirov, an administrator in Vishedski's UkrKosher kosher certification business, volunteered to show me around the building, noting, as we toured its classrooms, event hall, and playroom, that while many community members were "getting along normally, some people still need help."

"All of the people rent apartments, which is very expensive in Kyiv, and if they want to be in Podil and keep Shabbat they need to stay near the synagogue," he said. "Kyiv is a very expensive city and most of your salary goes to pay for an apartment. The rabbi is still helping some people."

Noting that on an average Shabbat the synagogue prepares meals for around 100 people, he said that people from all over the city come to pray there, not only former members of the Donetsk Jewish community, and that the synagogue's name, which means forward in Hebrew, reflected the fact that the community had a "new soul" and identity.

A ROUGH LANDING

"It wasn't easy; it was very difficult," community administrator Nadiya Goncharuk recalled with a wry smile.

Sitting behind a desk in the synagogue office, she described the first hectic days of the exodus from the east when she and the rabbi struggled to coordinate the distribution of aid from a makeshift office in a high-rise office building in downtown Kyiv.

"We came to Kyiv with our luggage in our hands and all the time the community [in exile] grew bigger and bigger and bigger. Our halls didn't have enough room for the whole community [but] God helped us and gave us His hand."

"It's a great miracle," Vishedski told me. "We found ourselves in a situation where we couldn't plan our lives and we set a goal to help people, and we succeeded in helping people to find work, to arrange their livelihood, and not to be dependent on charity."

However, even with all of the progress that has been made, Vishedski said that, while many in the community no longer needed help to pay their rent, some 30 percent were still dependent on aid from abroad.

"It didn't happen in a day," Vishedski said, adding that for the first ten or so months of the war people still held out hope of returning to Donetsk and that most of his efforts during that period focused on providing immediate aid to his coreligionists rather than developing a new community.

But "people loved each other and wanted to be together," and as the situation stabilized, he said, he found himself presiding over a new and growing community with a membership drawn from displaced Jews and those already living in the capital.

But not everybody had been as successful is recreating their communities. In Kyiv's Obolonskyi District, Rabbi Shalom Gopin of Luhansk also established a synagogue, but only a couple of Jews from his old community had joined.

Luhansk always had a much smaller community than Donetsk, and when the war broke out Gopin traveled with many of his congregants to a makeshift refugee camp set up in the city of Zhytomyr, some 140 kilometers (87 miles) west of Kyiv. Many of them, including the rabbi (who is a native Israeli), ended up moving to Israel, and it was only in late 2016 that Gopin returned to Kyiv, determined to begin anew.

"Almost all of the observant Jews in our [former] community are either in Germany or Israel," he said. "Some came to Kyiv and I wasn't here so they joined the Donetsk Jewish community."

But while Gopin worked to send money to several hundred elderly Jews still living in the east, he said that he saw his return to Ukraine as an opportunity to build a completely new community, explaining that there were more Jews living in his current neighborhood than in all of pre-war Luhansk.

THE UNRECOVERED

While younger members of Vishedski and Gopin's communities were able to restart their lives, many of the elderly displaced by the war would have been unable to support themselves without continuing charitable assistance.

By January 2020, the Joint Distribution Committee (JDC) had helped 5,200 internally displaced people in Ukraine, 185 of them in Kyiv, officials said at the time. And while the total number of those requiring aid had decreased significantly, those who were still on the Hesed's rolls needed more help than ever, according to Kyiv Hesed head Raisa Gritsenko.

Sitting down for a conversation in a brightly lit conference room filled with greenery at her organization's Kyiv center, Gritsenko told me that rising prices, along with "all of the stress" placed on her elderly clients over the past six years, had made integration into life in the capital "rather difficult."

"Prices are increasing more quickly than pensions," she said, adding that due to how funding to the JDC is earmarked by its largest donors, Holocaust survivors receive more money than their non-survivor counterparts, which means that funding for IDPs was only around 30 percent of the level she thought appropriate.

According to Vishedski, in 2020 most of the aid money distributed by his community went to feed those who remained on the separatist side of the line, where around 100 people still queued up daily for meals at Donetsk's Bet Menachem Mendel Synagogue.

A POTEMKIN SHTETL?

Anatevka
January 14, 2020

Back in Anatevka on the outskirts of Kyiv, things had taken a turn for the surreal.

While Azman had claimed that his refugee compound was home to some 150 people, few were in evidence when my *Times of Israel* colleague Simona Weinglass visited on January 14, 2020.[2]

While it was indisputable that Anatevka housed at least some refugees, the actual number was a matter of dispute. According to an exposé published in *Bloomberg* the previous November, "residents who asked not to be named for fear of retribution" had said that the compound only housed around 20 IDPs and that only around 65 people in total actually lived there, most of them from Kyiv.[3]

Members of the Donetsk Jewish community in Kyiv said that they did not know of any members of their community living in Anatevka, while Rabbi Gopin of Luhansk said that there were "maybe 15-20" people from his city there and that the rest came from Azman's community.

Questions about what was really going on in Anatevka had been swirling around for several months prior to the *Bloomberg* report, given Azman's links to several figures implicated in the 2019 Ukrainegate scandal, in which then-President Donald Trump pressed Ukraine to criminally probe the son of a political rival.[4]

In May 2019, Azman was photographed in Paris smoking cigars with former New York Mayor Rudy Giuliani, President Donald Trump's personal attorney, fueling speculation among some in Kyiv that the president's representative and his colleagues were using the rabbi to provide cover for illicit Ukrainian lobbying activities.[5]

The Giuliani-Azman meeting seemed to have been arranged by Lev Parnas and Igor Fruman, two Jewish Giuliani associates who have been linked to those lobbying efforts. Both sit on the board of the American Friends of Anatevka nonprofit organization.

Trump was impeached in December 2019 after it emerged that he had pressed his Ukrainian counterpart, President Volodymyr Zelensky, to investigate Biden and his son Hunter during a phone call five months earlier between the two leaders. During the call, Trump asked Zelensky to look into allegations that Hunter Biden had engaged in illegal behavior while serving on the board of a Ukrainian firm that was being probed for corruption. The Senate acquitted Trump in February 2020.

According to the Organized Crime and Corruption Reporting Project, an international journalism network that works to uncover political corruption, Giuliani was being paid to deliver a speech at a fundraiser in Anatevka, where he had expected to meet with Zelensky "on the sidelines."[6]

Instead, after canceling his trip to Ukraine, Giuliani flew to Paris, where he attended a number of meetings—brokered by Parnas and Fruman—with senior Ukrainian figures. He also sat with Azman for two hours. Azman presented Giuliani with a giant novelty key declaring him "honorary mayor of Anatevka."

While neither Azman nor Giuliani agreed to tell me what they discussed in Paris, the rabbi wrote in a series of Facebook posts following the meeting that the pair had spoken about "pressing issues" and that the president's attorney "was very interested in current events in Ukraine."[7]

COMING "HOME"

Jerusalem
May 9, 2019

While some of the displaced within Ukraine were still struggling to find their footing, others who had decided that a better life was to be found outside of Ukraine's borders were struggling to adjust to life in Israel.[8]

By and large, Israel was an attractive destination. It is the home of one of the largest Russian-speaking communities in the world—more than a million Israelis are émigrés from Ukraine, Russia, and other post-Soviet states—and offers automatic citizenship and resettlement to anyone with at least one Jewish grandparent.

It boasts a vibrant Russian-language press, and in some cities, like Haifa, Russian can be heard as often as Hebrew on the streets. All this seemingly makes it an appealing place to build a new life.

But new arrivals from Ukraine face challenges. A large proportion do not qualify as Jewish under Orthodox religious law, even though they are considered Jewish for the purposes of immigration.[9]

This means that many of the newcomers will eventually face significant barriers when they attempt to marry through the state-controlled rabbinate, which maintains a monopoly over marriage and divorce. Many locals get around such regulations by getting married abroad, often in Cyprus. Such marriages are subsequently recognized by the Interior Ministry, if not by the religious authorities.

There are already several hundred thousand Israeli citizens who fall into this legal grey zone, prompting calls from politicians like Soviet-born Israeli lawmaker Avigdor Liberman, who represents a primarily Russian-speaking constituency, for religious reforms.

But the biggest obstacles are economic and professional.

"Many newcomers are people with professions, and for them it is not an easy task to find their place in Israel," Roman Polonsky, the then-head of the Russian-speaking department at the Jewish Agency, a quasi-governmental organization tasked with promoting and facilitating Jewish immigration, told me in May 2019.

"You have to take into account that they could have emigrated to Israel any time over the past thirty years, but didn't. Instead, they built their personal and professional lives in Ukraine and then had to abandon them," he said. Those hardest hit are the immigrants in their forties who are "not old enough to get pensions" but too old to easily integrate into the local job market, especially given the difficulty of learning Hebrew at a later age.

"This is the most pressing challenge for immigrants from Ukraine: jobs," he said. "If you are talking about blue collar workers, they have more chances to find a job in Israel immediately."

The security situation in Israel can also be a concern. But for many recent immigrants from Ukraine—particularly those from the conflict zone—it is worse back home.

"They compare the situation in Israel to that in Ukraine, and for them Israel is an island of stability, of prosperity," Polonsky said.

"No doubt when they come, they have a lot of psychological difficulties, starting with language, but in general I can say they are very informed about the situation in Israel thanks to their relatives and friends here and the internet. They know about Iran and Hamas and it doesn't scare them."

COFFEE AND KVETCHING

Sitting at a table in a sidewalk cafe on Jerusalem's busy downtown Jaffa Road, Anastasia and Katrin sat sipping their drinks and chatting in a steady stream of Russian peppered with Hebrew. From Donetsk and Sevastopol, respectively, the pair met in Israel and became friends. Both asked that I not publish their surnames in order to protect family members living in Russian-controlled regions.

Anastasia, a member of the Donetsk Jewish community, came in 2014 and settled in Jerusalem. She said that her transition to Israeli life wasn't overly difficult because she had already been thinking of making the move before the war erupted. It was harder for her parents.

"They had to uproot and make large changes, and when you're later in life it's harder to give up possessions. They had to leave their apartment and start fresh without language and skills," she explained, sipping her coffee. "For me, [it's] not my first time living abroad, so the transition was smoother."

While her parents' move was jarring at first, she said that their decision to move to the city of Carmiel, which boasts a significant Russian-speaking community, meant that "they didn't really have to adjust to the surroundings."

For Anastasia's family, it was the Russian-speakers from previous waves of immigration who posed one of the hardest challenges. They made fun of her mother's dreams and told her that she would "never find a good job," Anastasia said.

While her mother soon found work as a quality assurance engineer in a factory producing jet turbines, lingering doubts about life in Israel remained. Her non-Jewish father, on the other hand, quickly acclimated to life in Israel.

"He's a happy camper," Anastasia said. "I never saw him happier than here. He's the biggest Zionist in the family and wears an Israeli flag pin on his jacket."

For her part, Anastasia told me that she wasn't particularly happy in Israel, citing cultural barriers. Israelis generally have less respect for personal space and privacy and tend to be more outspoken than their Ukrainian counterparts, something that has caused resentment among some immigrants.

It's a "less cultured country," she explained, adding that the intersection of religion and state here can cause problems for the overwhelmingly secular Russian-speaking community. "I'm very much opposed to the fact that all the shops are closed [on the Sabbath] and the government is telling me what to spend my money on on my hard-earned day off."

Katrin largely agreed with Anastasia, adding that she had similar issues, especially when it came to dealing with the strikingly different cultural norms in Israel. But, she added, she didn't believe there was any future for her in Ukraine.

Like Anastasia and Katrin, Chana Zlobin was ambivalent about life in the Middle East.

Only sixteen when the war started, Zlobin fled Luhansk with her mother, ending up in the refugee center in Zhytomyr. By 2015, she was studying at a religious seminary in Israel but subsequently moved back to Ukraine, where she met and married her husband, himself an internally displaced person from Donetsk.

However, after a year that she described as one of the best of her life, they decided to return to Israel so that she could finish her degree, and by the summer of 2019 she was living with her husband and three-month-old son in the port city of Ashdod on the Mediterranean coast.

Things were initially tough financially, although her father, who remained in Luhansk, helped out by sending money to Israel, she said. Eventually, her husband, who did not speak

Hebrew, found a job at a company run by Russian-speaking Israelis. While things were tight, she believed that coming to Israel was the smart choice.

"We chose to move here because it is the only state that pays and helps [Jews to] come," she explained. "We had no money because of the war and no possibility to sell an apartment or car for money to start here. I really want to go back to Ukraine, [but] I understand that here there are more opportunities to make a living and build a life."

Chana, who described herself as a Ukrainian patriot and a reluctant émigré, said that people from the Donbas took flak from other Russian-speakers no matter what they did.

"People don't understand what's happening and it hurts when they say 'you don't love Ukraine and so you left.' Sorry, but you don't get it," she said. "There was a war there and I could have been in the ground. I know a woman who always says 'you left so you love Russia and your father is still there and he also loves Russia.' I don't speak about politics and the situation there."

"The problem is that most people only know the news from Russian television."

NEO-NAZIS AND JEWISH COMEDIANS

During the course of the conflict, Russian propaganda consistently painted Ukraine as a hotbed of antisemitism and fascism, while Ukrainians countered that such claims lacked any validity.

But while the situation was never anywhere near as dire as claimed by Ukraine's critics, it was neither as rosy as its defenders asserted. And nothing illustrated this as well as the careers of three politicians: Volodymyr Groysman, Volodymyr Zelensky, and Arsen Avakov.

Appointed as Interior Minister in 2014, Avakov had close ties to various far-right groups, especially the Azov movement, hundreds of whose members began patrolling Kyiv's streets as part of the newly established National Corps, a vigilante group which promised that it would "not hesitate to use force to establish order ... when government organs can't or won't help Ukrainian society."[10]

And while Avakov repudiated the new militia, stating that "in Ukraine, there is only one monopoly on the use of force—the state," it was far from clear whether the government had indeed cut its ties with the political fringe.[11]

Rights groups blamed Kyiv for intentionally ignoring attacks against members of the country's LGBT[12] and Roma communities, including an attack on a Roma encampment that left one dead and four injured, including a young boy. This incident followed several other violent incidents, which could more appropriately be called pogroms, in which Roma were chased from their homes, which were then burned to the ground.[13] According to Ukrainian news outlet Hromadske Radio, the extremist C14 group, which was responsible for some of these anti-Roma incidents, received more than $16,000 from the Ukrainian Ministry of Youth and Sport to support its activities, as had other groups with far-right ties.[14]

But at the same time, despite scattered antisemitic violence,[15] most Jews did not feel threatened, and Ukrainians, despite not cracking down on the far-right, rejected their views at the ballot box. (The National Corps won less than two percent of the vote in the 2019 election.[16])

In fact, where the far-right was failing, Jews were succeeding.

In 2016, the Verkhovna Rada approved President Petro Poroshenko's choice of Volodymyr Groysman as successor to the increasingly unpopular prime minister, Arseniy Yatsenyuk. And, while Groysman's appointment was for the most part greeted with a collective shrug of indifference by the country's Jews, the fact that a Jewish politician's ascension to this level of power was uncontroversial, and even boring, was seen by some as significant in and of itself. In post-revolutionary Ukraine, "every person can get any position independent of his ethnic origin," declared Eduard Dolinsky. "I think that it is just another proof that Ukraine is a normal multi-cultural society."[17]

Three years later, in 2019, Poroshenko was himself ousted by Jewish comedian-turned-politician Volodymyr Zelensky, who was best known in Ukraine for playing a schoolteacher thrust into the presidency on the sitcom *Servant of the People*. After Zelensky, who never made a secret of his Jewish identity, was swept to victory with over 73 percent of the vote, Ukraine temporarily became the only country outside of Israel where both the president and prime minister were Jews.[18]

CLEANING HOUSE

Zelensky's tenure was certainly not free of controversy, with his first year in office marked by a public clash with Israel and Poland over Holocaust memory[19] and criticism over the attendance of two senior officials at a benefit concert headlined by a neo-Nazi band.[20]

However, he also fired Institute of National Memory chief Volodymyr Viatrovych, who greeted the comedian's election by tweeting a photo of Germans performing the Nazi salute,[21] only four months into his administration.[22]

In his place, Zelensky appointed Anton Drobovych, the 33-year-old director of educational programming at the Babi Yar Holocaust Memorial Center in Kyiv.

A self-described "liberal," Drobovych was not a historian, but rather an educator, by trade. The holder of a PhD in philosophy, he had previously worked, among other things, as an assistant professor at the National Pedagogical University in Kyiv, an adviser to the minister of education, and the head of strategic development at a local modern art museum.

Ahead of his appointment in December 2019, he described how his approach would differ from that of Viatrovych in an interview with the Ukrainian newspaper *Istorychna Pravda* (Historical Truth), stating that he wanted to "make the official memory policy in Ukraine more balanced and liberal."[23]

If chosen, Drobovych said, he intended to "prevent the institution from being perceived as a mouthpiece for agitation, ideological struggle, or propaganda, and make it a tool for citizens to foster public dialogue and promote a healthy identity."

"Historical honesty [and] critical thinking in memory policy matters," he explained, adding that he wanted "to preserve the memory of the common history of Ukrainians and Ukrainian Poles, Jews, Armenians, Tatars, Greeks, Bulgarians, and others."

The following summer, as anti-racism protesters across the United States and Europe vocally demanded their own societies reevaluate the legacies of many controversial historical figures, I interviewed Drobovych for the *Times of Israel* and asked him point-blank about Ukraine's problematic memory policy.[24]

He appeared to repudiate the national effort, led by Viatrovych, to revise history along far-right, nationalist lines.

"We have to say the historical truth about all persons from our past without heroization but also without demonization," he declared, reiterating that he preferred to encourage dialogue over imposing a monolithic national narrative and that the way forward lay in "encouraging critical thinking in education" regarding the relationship between "historical truth and myth."

But while the institute appeared to have stopped actively promoting the legacy of far-right leaders, that did not mean that Drobovych had fully repudiated them.

Asked for his views on the kind of far-right figures favored by Viatrovych, he told me that "Soviet propaganda tried to destroy the reputations of persons who tried to build an independent Ukrainian nation. We must separate lies and truth and find out the real picture of these persons. The Institute of the National Remembrance of Ukraine has no intention to heroize anyone."

And while he condemned individual members, Drobovych disputed the assertion leveled by many non-Ukrainian historians that the OUN and the UPA were inherently criminal organizations.

While admitting that members of the groups had committed crimes against humanity and that this should be freely acknowledged—a significant change from previous institute policy which attempted to portray them as having saved Jews—he was insistent that "responsibility is a personal thing."

Despite this, he had harsh words to say about the Halychyna Division, a Ukrainian SS unit in which many nationalists served and whose emblem, according to Viatrovych, did not constitute a Nazi symbol.

"SS guys are bad guys and our policy is to say that Waffen SS [members] are bad guys," he declared, a statement which presaged his (and Zelensky's) unprecedented condemnation of a march in honor of the division the following summer.[25]

Beyond replacing Viatrovych, Zelensky also ousted Avakov in the summer of 2021,[26] which Michael Colborne, author of *From the Fires of War: Ukraine's Azov Movement and the Global Far Right*, told me caused the movement to "lose a bit of its moxie."[27]

But while Ukraine under Zelensky, despite its problems, was far from being a fascist regime, that did not stop the Kremlin from using the specter of Nazism and genocide to justify an aggressive war in early 2022.

CHAPTER EIGHT

INVASION

"I already went through this seven years ago, I don't have the strength to flee again."

—Shalom Gopin[1]

Tel Aviv
February 24, 2022

I had been working the phones all day, frantically trying to make contact with friends, colleagues, and sources within Ukraine as the bad news continuously poured in via Twitter and the wires. Despite a military buildup of over 150,000 troops that had been going on for more than half a year, nobody had really expected Russia to actually launch a massive ground incursion.

Early that morning, I had woken up to the news that Putin had ordered what he called "a special military operation" in order to "protect people who, for eight years now, have been facing humiliation and genocide perpetrated by the Kiev regime."[2]

"To this end," he explained, "we will seek to demilitarize and denazify Ukraine, as well as bring to trial those who perpetrated numerous bloody crimes against civilians, including against citizens of the Russian Federation."

Kremlin officials and state media had been making increasingly hysterical claims of genocide for weeks, with the head of the state-run RT network going so far as to demand Russian intervention before the Ukrainians "build concentration camps" and "gas their population."[3]

Zelensky, for his part, was having none of it, asking the Ukrainian people in a televised address the evening prior to the invasion how a people "that gave more than eight million lives for the victory over Nazism could be considered Nazis themselves."[4]

"How can I be a Nazi?" he indignantly demanded. "Tell my grandpa, who went through the whole war in the infantry of the Soviet Army and died as a colonel in independent Ukraine."[5]

Several days later, the Russians, angered by criticism of their genocide claims by Israel's official Holocaust remembrance organization, declared that "after this is all over, they will gladly invite Yad Vashem officials and show them mass graves."[6]

During the course of the day, I managed to get through to a friend in Kyiv, a local businessman and activist, who told me that he had woken up to the sounds of rocket fire and was planning to hide out in a basement with his family until the fighting was over. He eventually made his way to Lviv to escape the Russian bombardment of the Ukrainian capital.

Putin was, he declared, "totally nuts."[7]

"The Jews of Ukraine are an integral part of Ukrainian society, and we never faced Nazism here, or fascism, and we feel safe in Ukraine. [But] we don't feel safe when Russia says there are Nazis here," he told me.

Similarly, local rabbi Yonatan Markovitch said that he didn't understand what Putin was talking about.

"I can only say that, in terms of antisemitism, we're very secure here. Incidents are very rare, and the government takes care of them. We're now in a war situation and hear sirens and see smoke from our house, [so] I don't want to get into the issue of antisemitism. It's not relevant. We're in a war and we're all coming together."[8]

As the Russian attack intensified, videos posted online showed Jewish communities from Kharkiv to Uman praying in their synagogues, while the sound of explosions and gunfire could be heard outside.[9]

By that afternoon, the Jewish community of neighboring Moldova announced that it had established a refugee center in Chişinău (Kishinev),[10] and hundreds of Jews had fled from the Ukrainian port city of Odessa.[11]

During the days leading up to the fighting, rabbis across the country, including those who had been displaced during earlier stages of the conflict, vowed to stay on to support their congregations and began distributing emergency supplies.[12] In Kyiv, Pinchas Vishedski passed out 500 radios, while Markovitch prepared thousands of food packages.[13]

Azman, who only weeks earlier had stood in the snow at Babi Yar and begged Putin not to invade, invited anybody who could make his or her way to Anatevka to take shelter there. By February 26, there were reportedly more than 250 people staying at the compound.[14]

And while Ukrainian Jews showed little interest in leaving the country prior to the invasion, after the fighting started the Jewish Agency told my *Haaretz* colleague Judy Maltz that it had been "flooded" with requests from prospective immigrants.[15]

In a statement on February 26, the agency said that was preparing to open six aliyah processing stations along the Ukrainian border in Poland, Moldova, Romania, and Hungary "to immediately assist the expected waves of immigration due to the war in Ukraine."

But even with the prospect of another massive wave of refugees seeming to turn into reality, some held out hope for their eventual return.

In a heartbreaking video, which was shared widely on social media, the sexton of an Odessa synagogue promised that the Jews of his city would one day come home.

"Hadran alach," he declared, using an Aramaic phrase meaning "we will return to you."[16]

ON THE ROAD AGAIN

Over the coming days, things went from bad to worse, with the Russians unleashing indiscriminate bombardments against both military and civilian targets.

In Kyiv, a missile strike targeted the city's iconic television transmitter tower, located adjacent to Babi Yar, prompting President Zelensky to condemn Russia for violating the sanctity of the massacre site.

"To the world: what is the point of saying 'never again' for 80 years, if the world stays silent when a bomb drops on the same site of Babyn Yar? At least 5 killed. History repeating…," the Ukrainian leader tweeted following the attack.[17]

In Kharkiv, Ukraine's second city, Russian missile strikes decimated the city center, destroying government buildings, blocks of flats, and local Jewish institutions, such as the local Hillel House and the Chabad-affiliated Or Avner day school.

"February 23, the day before the war started, was thirty years since our school was opened in 1992. We had 400 children with balloons and flowers celebrating the thousands of alumni who went through the doors of our school. The next morning at five the bombing started and at six the director announced 'no school today,' but we never would have dreamed the school would have been part of this whole enterprise," Miriam Moskovitz, the wife of the local rabbi, told me.[18]

"We're trying to get people out. We're getting phone calls from desperate people [screaming] 'get me out' and 'I'm stuck in my home bring me food.' People are hungry. They haven't eaten in days and they are under fire and we can't get to them. We have a whole crew in the shul feeding people and there are people sleeping in the shul. We are sending food and medicine to all corners of the city."

Hillel members in the city were enlisting to fight the Russians, Hillel director Yulia Pototskaya said after the attack, telling me that she was devastated by the loss of her life's work.[19] One of them was Serafim Sabaranski, a 29-year-old who had enlisted in Ukraine's Territorial Defense Forces at the beginning of the war and who, Pototskaya told me, died when "a bomb from a plane destroyed his post."[20]

Shortly thereafter, Sabaranski was joined by Boris Romanchenko, a 96-year-old (non-Jewish[21]) Holocaust survivor who was reportedly killed when Russian forces struck his apartment building, highlighting, in the words of the Buchenwald and Mittelbau-Dora Memorials Foundation, "how threatening the war in Ukraine is for concentration camp survivors."[22]

It was certainly threatening for Holocaust monuments. Less than a week after Romanchenko's death, Russian forces shelled the Drobitsky Yar Holocaust memorial site on the outskirts of Kharkiv, damaging a memorial menorah and eliciting cries of Nazism from Kyiv.[23]

In response to the carnage, Azman recorded a new video, condemning what he described as the indifference of Russian Jewry. "I bless everyone who is indifferent, and if God forbid I will have to die let the curse be on those who are silent and silently participate in this horrible crime," he declared.[24]

For the Jewish community to publicly oppose Putin was no simple thing, with sources later telling me that Russian officials had applied "pressure on community leaders, including threats to shut down Jewish institutions, if no statements are made in favor of the invasion."

It felt, in the words of one community leader, as if the Russian Federation had gone "back to Soviet times."[25]

Nevertheless, the day after Azman's hostile demand, Russian Chief Rabbi Berel Lazar issued a statement indirectly condemning the invasion, a remarkable move for a religious leader long considered close to the Kremlin.

"The continuation of the current situation cannot be allowed" and "any conflict can and should be resolved only by peaceful means," he asserted, adding that he was "ready for any mediation, ready to do everything in my power, and even more, just so that the guns fall silent, the bombs stop exploding!"

As the destruction mounted, so did the exodus. By March 7, over 1.7 million Ukrainians,[26] including large numbers of Jews, had fled the country for neighboring states such as Moldova, Poland, and Romania, and the Jewish Agency was predicting that tens of thousands of immigrants would soon be arriving on Israel's shores.[27] By March 25, "almost a quarter of Ukraine's population" was displaced, with around 3.7 million people "forced to flee the country."[28]

"Our initial estimate was that the first wave of aliyah would be approximately three thousand people, and now [I] think it could be much higher, maybe ten thousand olim," the Jewish Agency's Roman Polonsky told reporters on March 2, less than a week before Prime Minister Naftali Bennett and Immigrant Absorption Minister Pnina Tamano-Shata announced the establishment of a special national task force focusing on integrating new immigrants from Ukraine and Russia.[29]

Ben Gurion International Airport
March 3, 2022

Surrounding by a crowd of flag-waving Israeli teenagers, I stood outside the arrivals hall of Ben Gurion Airport, chatting with my photographer as I awaited the arrival of an aliyah flight from Ukraine, one of the first since Russian forces breached the border a week earlier.

Suddenly, Yonatan Markovitch walked out of the doors, gathering journalists around him as he walked out of the terminal.

"The situation in Kyiv is a catastrophe. Explosions near residential buildings, near the train station, which is maybe 100 meters from where our son lives. It is very dangerous," the rabbi declared to an impromptu press scrum as airport officials attempted to stop us from blocking the doors.[30]

As the teenagers burst into song all around us and his wife crying nearby, I sidled up to the rabbi and asked him why he had left when he had previously pledged to remain come what may.

"From here we can do a lot more—not from Europe, not from Hungary or Romania," he replied, promising to "go and speak with whoever is needed [so] that they will open the gates to bring more Jews to the land of Israel."

As the teenagers singing reached a crescendo, I had to hold back tears, and it took a significant effort to maintain the outward appearance of composure and distance required by my profession.

The following afternoon, I finally managed to get through to Pinchas Vishedski, whom I had been unable to reach since the crisis began. He informed me that despite his earlier confidence that the civilian toll of any potential conflict would be less than that of the previous Russian invasion, he had once again been forced to flee.

The long-suffering rabbi described leading hundreds of the members of his newly re-established community, packed into dozens of cars, from Kyiv to the Romanian border, in a more than day-long trip through his war-ravaged country.

Asked how he felt about becoming a refugee for the second time in less than a decade, Vishedsky replied with resignation.

"I don't even know how it feels. I don't have time now to think about how to feel. Now I am working like a machine, simply doing what is necessary to help other Jews. After all of this I will get into thinking how I feel."

APPENDIX

ISRAEL'S CONTENTIOUS RELATIONSHIP WITH UKRAINE

The Russo-Ukrainian War of 2022 was marked not only by a military conflict between Kyiv and Moscow but also by simmering diplomatic tensions between the governments of Volodymyr Zelensky and Naftali Bennett.

Over the course of the weeks leading up to the invasion, Israel and Ukraine found themselves caught up in an extended low-grade diplomatic spat caused by what Kyiv saw as a lack of Israeli support. This anger over Israel's unwillingness to take a firm stand continued after the invasion, with the Bennett government—worried about undermining its military coordination with Russia in Syria—showing itself unwilling to potentially alienate Moscow by condemning the violence.

Notably, the Israeli government refrained from speaking out against Russian claims that the Ukrainians were Nazis carrying out a genocide in eastern Ukraine, while harshly condemning Ukrainian claims that the Kremlin was emulating the Nazis in its attacks on Ukrainian civilians.

And, while Ukrainian officials praised Israeli aid and mediation efforts, the government's decision to restrict Ukrainian immigration and refrain from selling weapons and body armor to the Ukrainian armed forces, were not well received in Kyiv.

As this is not a diplomatic history, I have not dealt with these issues at length. However, for those interested in Jerusalem's role in the conflict, I suggest the following reading list as a starting point for further research:

- Sam Sokol, "Why Israel Almost Had to Shut Down Its Embassy in Kyiv," *Haaretz*, February 1, 2022, https://www.haaretz.com/israel-news/.premium-israel-wanted-to-cut-hazard-pay-for-diplomats-in-ukraine-during-russia-crisis-1.10582395.
- Sam Sokol, "Israel Rebukes Ukraine Ambassador over Criticizing Lapid's 'Propaganda' on Russia," *Haaretz*, February 7, 2022, https://www.haaretz.com/israel-news/israel-rebukes-ukrainian-ambassador-over-criticizing-lapid-s-propaganda-on-russia-1.10594477.
- Sam Sokol and Jonathan Lis, "Israel Must Prepare for 'Immediate' Immigration of Ukrainian Jews, Minister Says," *Haaretz*, February 13, 2022, https://www.haaretz.com/israel-news/.premium.HIGHLIGHT-israel-must-prepare-for-immediate-immigration-of-ukrainian-jews-minister-says-1.10608833.
- Sam Sokol, "Ukrainian Envoy Calls for Israeli Mediation in Russia Crisis after Lapid Meeting," *Haaretz*, February 13, 2022, https://www.haaretz.com/israel-news/.premium-ukrainian-envoy-calls-for-israeli-mediation-in-russia-crisis-after-lapid-meeting-1.10609266.
- Sam Sokol, "Ukraine 'Disappointed' by Lack of Support from Israel during Russia Crisis," *Haaretz*, February 16, 2022, https://www.haaretz.com/israel-news/.premium-ukraine-disappointed-by-lack-of-support-from-israel-during-russia-crisis-1.10615569.
- Sam Sokol, "Israel Urges Hasidim to Evacuate Ukrainian Pilgrimage Site Amid Fears of Invasion," *Haaretz*, February 17, 2022, https://www.haaretz.com/israel-news/.premium-israel-urges-hasidim-to-evacuate-ukrainian-pilgrimage-site-amid-fears-of-invasion-1.10618115.
- Sam Sokol, "'You're Treating Us Like Gaza': Furious Ukraine Summons Israeli Ambassador," *Haaretz*, February 17, 2022, https://www.haaretz.com/israel-news/you-re-treating-us-like-gaza-furious-ukraine-summons-israeli-ambassador-1.10618462.

◆ Sam Sokol, "Israeli Officials Change Tune on Ukraine Crisis, Say They'll Side with Biden," *Haaretz*, February 21, 2022, https://www.haaretz.com/israel-news/israeli-officials-change-tune-on-ukraine-crisis-say-they-ll-side-with-biden-1.10624902.

◆ Jonathan Lis and Sam Sokol, "In First Official Statement, Israel Says It Supports Ukraine's Territorial Integrity, Sovereignty," *Haaretz*, February 23, 2022, https://www.haaretz.com/israel-news/in-first-official-statement-israel-says-it-supports-ukraine-s-territorial-integrity-1.10629699.

◆ Jonathan Lis and Sam Sokol, "Bennett Offers Humanitarian Aid in Call with Zelenskyy, 'Stands by Ukrainian People,'" *Haaretz*, February 25, 2022, https://www.haaretz.com/israel-news/.premium-bennett-offers-humanitarian-aid-in-call-with-zelenskyy-stands-by-ukrainian-people-1.10635326.

◆ Sam Sokol, "As a Jew, Zelenskyy Expects More from Israel, Ukrainian Ambassador Says," *Haaretz*, February 28, 2022, https://www.haaretz.com/israel-news/.premium.HIGHLIGHT-as-a-jew-zelenskyy-expects-more-from-israel-ukrainian-ambassador-says-1.10641412.

◆ Sam Sokol and Ben Samuels, "Ukraine 'Still Hopeful' for Israeli Weapons Despite Lukewarm Support," *Haaretz*, March 1, 2022, https://www.haaretz.com/world-news/europe/.premium-ukraine-still-hopeful-for-israeli-weapons-despite-lukewarm-support-1.10644335.

◆ Bar Peleg, Sam Sokol, and Jonathan Lis, "Fifty Ukrainians Denied Entry to Israel Since Russian Invasion," *Haaretz*, March 1, 2022, https://www.haaretz.com/israel-news/.premium-fifty-ukrainians-denied-entry-to-israel-since-russian-invasion-1.10645437.

◆ Noa Shpigel, Bar Peleg, and Sam Sokol, "Israeli Minister: 90% of Ukrainian Refugees Arriving Are non-Jews, Situation 'Cannot Go On,'" *Haaretz*, March 6, 2022, https://www.haaretz.com/world-news/europe/.premium-israeli-minister-90-of-ukrainians-refugees-are-non-jews-situation-cannot-go-on-1.10655497.

◆ Sam Sokol, "Israeli Mediation More Important to Us Than Weapons, Ukraine Envoy Says," *Haaretz*, March 7, 2022, https://

www.haaretz.com/israel-news/.premium-israeli-mediation-more-important-to-us-than-weapons-ukraine-envoy-says-1.10 658054.

◆ Jonathan Lis and Sam Sokol, "Kyiv's Top Diplomat Apologizes for Accusing El Al of Making 'Money Soaked in Ukrainian Blood,'" *Haaretz*, March 8, 2022, https://www.haaretz.com/israel-news/business/.premium-kyiv-s-top-diplomat-apologizes-for-accusing-el-al-of-evading-sanctions-1.10660302.

◆ Sam Sokol, "Israel's Diaspora Minister Calls for Unrestricted Entry of non-Jewish Ukrainians," *Haaretz*, March 9, 2022, https://www.haaretz.com/israel-news/.premium-israel-s-diaspora-minister-calls-for-unrestricted-entry-of-non-jewish-ukrainians-1.10664332.

◆ Sam Sokol, "Ukrainian Official Slams Yad Vashem Over Zelenskyy's Speech Request," *Haaretz*, March 14, 2022, https://www.haaretz.com/israel-news/.premium-ukrainian-official-slams-yad-vashem-over-zelenskyy-s-speech-request-1.10673766.

◆ Sam Sokol, "From Commons to Congress: Zelenskyy's Knesset Address Part of Worldwide Speaking Blitz," *Haaretz*, March 15, 2022, https://www.haaretz.com/world-news/.premium-from-commons-to-congress-zelenskyy-s-knesset-speech-part-of-worldwide-speaking-tour-1.10676267.

◆ Sam Sokol, "Zelenskyy Tells Israeli Lawmakers: Russia Is Plotting 'Final Solution' Like the Nazis," *Haaretz*, March 20, 2022, https://www.haaretz.com/israel-news/zelenskyy-tells-israeli-lawmakers-russia-plotting-final-solution-like-the-nazis-1.10686787.

◆ Sam Sokol, "Bennett Slams Zelenskyy's Holocaust Comparison as 'Forbidden,'" *Haaretz*, March 21, 2022, https://www.haaretz.com/israel-news/bennett-slams-zelenskyy-s-holocaust-comparison-as-forbidden-1.10687905.

◆ Sam Sokol, "Explained: Why Israel's Iron Dome Won't Help Ukraine Against Russia," *Haaretz*, March 22, 2022, https://www.haaretz.com/israel-news/explained-why-israel-s-iron-dome-won-t-really-help-ukraine-against-russia-1.10690475.

- Sam Sokol and Omer Benjakob, "Forget Iron Dome: Ukraine Wants Israel's Pegasus to Fight Putin," *Haaretz*, March 23, 2022, https://www.haaretz.com/israel-news/tech-news/forget-iron-dome-ukraine-wants-israel-s-pegasus-to-fight-putin-1.10693 506.
- Sam Sokol, "Israeli Intelligence 'Cooperating Very Closely' With Ukraine, Top Zelenskyy Aide Says," *Haaretz*, March 24, 2022, https://www.haaretz.com/israel-news/top-zelenskyy-aide-israeli-intelligence-cooperating-very-closely-with-ukraine-1.10696343.

Notes

PREFACE

1. Anatoli Kuznetsov, *Babi Yar* (New York: Pocket Books, 1971), 328-329.

CHAPTER ONE

1. The size of Ukraine's Jewish population has long been a point of contention between leaders of the local Jewish community and demographers. Community leaders affiliated with the Chabad Hasidic movement have traditionally liked to quote a figure of 1.5 million. Around the time of the Euromaidan, the Jewish Agency estimated that there were 200,000 Jews in the country. However, Hebrew University Professor Sergio Della Pergola, a leading expert, advances a credible argument that the population on the eve of the conflict was much lower, coming in at 71,500. See Darina Privalko, *Jewish Life in Ukraine: Achievements, Challenges and Priorities from the Collapse of Communism to 2013* (London: Institute for Jewish Policy Research, September 2014), http://archive.jpr.org.uk/object-ukr2. Privalko noted that "calculating the number of Jews in the former Soviet Union and in the contemporary post-Soviet states is often a contentious exercise, with official state data frequently mistrusted and all research further complicated by differences over the definition of Jewish identity." In the FSU, high rates of intermarriage, reluctance to identify as Jewish, ignorance of Jewish heritage and contending definitions of Jewishness combine to create a situation in which estimates of Jewish population size are sometimes no more than educated guesses. I ran

across a good example of this confusion in Kyiv in 2013 when I met a young man who believed that he could not be Jewish because he was uncircumcised and his father was a gentile. He was unaware that according to the definition under both Israeli law and *halacha* (Jewish law) he was completely Jewish. For further information, see Sam Sokol, "How many European Jews are there? It depends on who you ask," *Jerusalem Post*, April 7, 2015, http://www.jpost.com/Diaspora/How-many-European-Jews-are-there-It-depends-on-who-you-ask-396301.

2. Per Anders Rudling, "The OUN, the UPA and the Holocaust: A Study in the Manufacturing of Historical Myths," Carl Beck Papers in Russian and East European Studies, no. 2107 (2011).

3. Daniel Lazare, "Who Was Stepan Bandera?," *Jacobin*, September 24, 2015, https://www.jacobinmag.com/2015/09/stepan-bandera-nationalist-euromaidan-right-sector/.

4. Sam Sokol, "WJC Calls For European Ban On 'Neo-Nazi' Parties," *Jerusalem Post*, May 7, 2013, http://www.jpost.com/Jewish-World/Jewish-News/World-Jewish-Congress-urges-ban-on-neo-Nazi-parties-312395.

5. Per Anders Rudling, "The Return of the Ukrainian Far Right: The Case of VO Svoboda," in *Analyzing Fascist Discourse: European Fascism in Talk and Text*, ed. Ruth Wodak and John E. Richardson (London: Routledge, 2013), 228-255.

6. While Shekhovtsov's work on this topic was initially rather good, his approach became problematic after the Euromaidan. In a 2014 post on Facebook, Shekhovtsov seemed to justify the OUN's rhetoric against Jews by citing the conspiracy theory of Jewish Communism (*zhydo komuna*), writing that "the first Central Committee of the Revolutionary Communist Party comprised of 40% of Jews." See https://www.facebook.com/groups/52910686741/permalink/10152298449196742/?comment_id=10152302573156742&offset=0&total_comments=54. He also smeared scholar Per Anders Rudling and the Simon Wiesenthal Center's Efraim Zuroff, branding them "a leftist academic and a self-proclaimed 'Nazi hunter'" guilty of "blatant racism aimed at degrading East Europeans." See https://www.facebook.com/anton.shekhovtsov/posts/10209111734286287.

7. Anton Shekhovtsov, "The Resurgence of the Ukrainian Radical Right," *Europe-Asia Studies* 63, no. 2 (2011): 203-228.

8. Irena Cantorovich, "'Defending the Interests of the Ukrainians': The Empowerment of the Svoboda Party," *Israel Journal of Foreign Affairs* X:1 (2013): 95-104.

9. "TV host Larry King, Svoboda named in alleged Party of Regions black cash ledger," *Kyiv Post*, August 19, 2016, https://www.kyiv post.com/article/content/ukraine-politics/tv-host-larry-king-svo boda-named-in-alleged-party-of-regions-black-cash-ledger-421 401.html.

10. "Svoboda: The rise of Ukraine's ultra-nationalists," BBC, December 26, 2012, http://www.bbc.com/news/magazine-20824693.

11. "'Post' Journalist attacked by mob in Greece," *Jerusalem Post*, June 7, 2012, http://www.jpost.com/International/Video-Post-journalist-attacked-by-mob-in-Greece.

12. There were no violent antisemitic assaults in Ukraine in 2013 prior to the Euromaidan protests. See Dina Porat, ed., *Antisemitism Worldwide 2013* (Tel Aviv: Tel Aviv University Kantor Center for the Study of Contemporary European Jewry, 2014), http://www.kantorcenter.tau.ac.il/sites/default/files/Doch_2013 .pdf.

13. The title of Chief Rabbi has been hotly contested between several ultra-orthodox clerics, an issue which I will touch on later.

14. Rabbi Yaakov D. Bleich, Chief Rabbi of Kiev and Ukraine, House Foreign Affairs Subcommittee on Human Rights, "Anti-Semitism: A Growing Threat to All Faiths," Wednesday, February 27, 2013, http://docs.house.gov/meetings/FA/FA16/20130227/100336/H HRG-113-FA16-Wstate-BleichR-20130227.pdf.

15. Among the signatories to the letter were Vadim Shulman, the president of the Euro-Asian Jewish Congress, Anatoly Podolsky, the director of the Ukrainian Center for Holocaust Studies, Igor Kuperberg, the chairman of the Zionist Federation of Ukraine, and Prof. Alexey Khamray, the leader of the Conservative Jewish community in Kyiv.

16. Sam Sokol, "Ukrainian Jewish Leaders Spar Over JAFI Meeting," *Jerusalem Post*, March 15, 2013, http://www.jpost.com/Jewish-World/Jewish-News/Ukrainian-Jewish-leaders-spar-over-JAFI-meeting.

17. For more background on Dolinsky, see Sam Sokol, "Meet the Lonely Ukrainian Jew Fighting His Country's New Fondness for Nazis," *Haaretz*, December 6, 2018, https://www.haaretz.com/

world-news/meet-the-lonely-ukranian-jew-fighting-his-country-s-new-fondness-for-nazis-1.6722836.

18.   Sam Sokol, "Diaspora Affairs: 'We are ready to fight,'" *Jerusalem Post*, April 25, 2013, http://www.jpost.com/printarticle.aspx?id=311151.

CHAPTER TWO

1.   Simon Geissbühler, "The Ukrainian Crisis and the Jews: A Time for Hope or Despair," *Israel Journal of Foreign Affairs* (2015): 77-85. According to the Kharkiv Human Rights Protection Group (KhPG), a local civil society organization, members of Patriot of Ukraine have "espoused xenophobic and neo-Nazi ideas" and "engaged in violent attacks against migrants, foreign students in Kharkiv and those opposing its views." See http://khpg.org/en/index.php?id=1415367345.

2.   Svoboda and Right Sector were not the only far-right groups present at the Maidan. See Michael Moynihan, "The Swedish Neo-Nazis 'Volunteers' of Kiev," *The Daily Beast*, February 28, 2014, http://www.thedailybeast.com/articles/2014/02/28/the-swedish-neo-nazis-of-kiev.

3.   At the time, Forum Daily, a Russian-language American news site reported that "the artist has depicted the oligarch devouring chunks of Ukraine. The artist could draw any of the two dozen most prominent billionaires of the country, but as the eater of Ukraine, he portrayed a Jewish oligarch—Ihor Kolomoisky, co-owner of the Privat Group and the President of the European Jewish Union. To leave no doubt as to the nature of the Jewish oligarch, the cartoonist depicted Kolomoisky with a kippa on his head." "The Jew on the Maidan: Jews and antisemites in the midst of Ukrainian protest," Forum Daily, January 1, 2014, http://www.forumdaily.com/zhid-na-majdane-evrei-i-antisemity-v-epicentre-ukrainskogo-protesta/ (in Russian).

4.   "The Chocolate King Rises," *Spiegel Online*, May 22, 2014, http://www.spiegel.de/international/europe/profile-of-petro-poroshenko-in-the-run-up-to-the-ukraine-elections-a-970325.html.

5.   "Racism and anti-Semitism on the Euromaidan," YouTube video, 0:29. Posted by Nikolai Ganzha-Tselitsky, December 6, 2013, https://www.youtube.com/watch?v=kf5mbBaNKmU.

6. I am focusing on the ultra-orthodox here not because they form any sort of majority (or even a large plurality) of Ukrainian Jewry (they do not) but because many of the largest of the communal organizations in the country are run by them. As in much of the post-Soviet space, members of the Chabad Hasidic group have, since the early nineties, been involved in efforts to rebuild a Jewish infrastructure decimated by the Holocaust and decades of communist rule, leading to a situation in which organized communities largely composed of secular or moderately observant Jews are led by members of the orthodox sect. As such, the orthodox leadership will, of necessity, receive what could otherwise be considered a disproportionate amount of attention. Attention will, of course, also be paid to Reform and Conservative congregations and secular communal organizations. A fuller treatment of this subject will be forthcoming later in this work.

7. Gil Ronen, "Kiev Rabbi: This is a Revolution," Arutz Sheva, December 2, 2013, http://www.israelnationalnews.com/News/News .aspx/174715.

8. In an interview with the Jewish News, the better part of a year after the revolution, he would expand on his concerns, this time downplaying the fear that seemed to have driven him at the time. "A year ago in the center of Kiev, we planned a major event: lighting the menorah for Hanukkah, where many Jews gathered on one of the squares in the capital. It was at that moment a year ago that Maidan was dispersed. That time force was used: not far from the synagogue there was carnage. When we heard that the peaceful Maidan was becoming dangerous, I cancelled the entire entertainment program, which we had prepared especially for Hanukkah. A year ago we only lit the candles, there was no celebrating. I explained to the community that we could not make merry in a sincere way when people were being beaten up a kilometer away from us, and peaceful citizens were suffering." Liba Libovner, "Rabbi Moshe Asman: 'You need to start improving the world by first improving yourself,'" Jewish News, December 18, 2014, http://jewishnews.com.ua/en/publication/rabbi_moshe_asman_ you_need_to_start_improving_the_world_by_first_improving_ yourself.

9. Sam Sokol, "Ukrainian Jews Split on Dangers of Protest Movement," *Jerusalem Post*, December 4, 2013, http://www.jpost.com/

Jewish-World/Jewish-Features/Ukrainian-Jews-split-on-dangers-of-protest-movement-333907.

10. During the 1970s, Zissels became involved in dissident activities, eventually joining the Ukrainian Helsinki Group, leading to his ejection from the Komsomol communist youth movement and eventual incarceration for his anti-state activities, including the possession of Hebrew instruction manuals and Zionist literature. While many other dissidents would eventually emigrate to the United States or Israel when the Iron Curtain fell, Zissels stayed behind. In 1989, during the waning days of the Soviet Union, he made the leap to community leadership status when he helped establish the Vaad of the Union of Soviet Socialist Republics. See http://www.worldjewishcongress.org/en/bio/josef-zissels.

11. See http://www.ukma.edu.ua/eng/index.php/news/482-speech-of-josef-zissels-at-euromaidan.

12. In subsequent interviews, the septuagenarian activist would expand on this theme, explaining that he believed that, while previously the Jews of the Warsaw Pact countries saw themselves as Soviet Jews, the Maidan experience was a milestone on the road to a uniquely Ukrainian Jewish identity. See https://Ukrainian jewishencounter.org/en/josef-zissels-Ukrainian-jewry-created/.

13. "Call for Peace of Rabbi Hillel Cohen on Maidan," YouTube video, 3:52. Posted by Roman Vilenskiy, December 29, 2013, https://www.youtube.com/watch?v=JDNmhy7dPR0.

14. Amanda Borschel-Dan, "Ukraine Reform Shul Defaced by anti-Semitic Graffiti," *Times of Israel*, February 28, 2014, http://www.timesofisrael.com/ukraine-reform-shul-defaced-by-anti-semitic-graffiti/.

15. Several months later, Benyuk took part in the beating of the head of the National Ukrainian Television Company. Together with several Svoboda lawmakers, he led a mob into the office of Aleksandr Panteleymonov, assaulting the official and coercing him into signing a letter of resignation. See "Ukrainian TV boss assaulted and forced to resign by far-right Svoboda MPs," EuroNews, March 19, 2014, http://www.euronews.com/2014/03/19/ukranian-tv-boss-assaulted-and-forced-to-resign-by-far-right-svoboda-mps.

16. "Zhid on Maidan," YouTube video, 3:02. Posted by Shimon Briman, January 1, 2014, https://www.youtube.com/watch?v=Lnekp 54NMBw.

17. Oleksandr Feldman, "The Sad Progression of the Ukrainian Protest Movement from Democracy and the Rule of Law to Ultranationalism and Anti-semitism," *Huffington Post*, http://www.huffingtonpost.com/oleksandr-feldman/ukraine-protests-nationalism-anti-semitism_b_4588507.html.

18. For more on Ukrainians' views on Bandera during the period of the Maidan, see Ivan Katchanovski, "Terrorists or national heroes? Politics and perceptions of the OUN and the UPA in Ukraine," *Communist and Post-Communist Studies* XLVIII, Nos. 2-3 (2015), http://dx.doi.org/10.1016/j.postcomstud.2015.06.006; Sam Sokol, "Babi Yar as a Symbol of Holocaust Distortion in Post-Maidan Ukraine," *Israel Journal of Foreign Affairs* (2017), doi:10.1080/23739770.2017.1315694.

19. See "15,000 Ukraine nationalists march for divisive Bandera," Associated Press, January 1, 2014, https://www.usatoday.com/story/news/world/2014/01/01/ukraine-bandera/4279897/; Hanna Kozlowska, "Torches Lit, Ukrainian Nationalists Celebrate An Inconvenient Hero," *Foreign Policy*, January 3, 2014, http://foreignpolicy.com/2014/01/03/torches-lit-Ukrainian-nationalists-celebrate-an-inconvenient-hero/.

20. Marco Carynnyk, "Foes of Our Rebirth: Ukrainian Nationalist Discussions about Jews, 1929-1947," *Nationalities Papers* 39, no. 3 (2011): 315-352, doi:10.1080/00905992.2011.570327. Carynnyk provides extensive documentation of other instances of anti-semitism and incitement to violence by the OUN leadership. In 1940, the OUN split into two factions, the OUN(b) led by Stepan Bandera and the OUN(m) led by Andriy Melnyk, who represented the group's older, more conservative wing.

21. Sam Sokol, "Despite calls for neutrality in Ukraine protests, young Jews are on the front lines," *Jerusalem Post*, December 13, 2013, http://www.jpost.com/Jewish-World/Jewish-News/Despite-calls-for-neutrality-in-Ukraine-protests-young-Jews-are-on-the-front-lines-334907.

22. Yevgeniy Klig, "On the Ground in Kiev," eJewishPhilanthropy, March 10, 2014, http://ejewishphilanthropy.com/on-the-ground-in-kiev/.

23. This account is based on Vyacheslav Likhachev, "Anti-Semitism in FSU-2014," Euro-Asian Jewish Congress, Kyiv, 2014, as well as on a personal interview with Binyamin Gutfarb.

24. See Vladimir Matveyev, "Election of Third Chief Rabbi in Ukraine Splits Jewish Community," *Jerusalem Post*, October 27, 2005, http://www.jpost.com/Jewish-World/Jewish-News/Election-of-third-chief-rabbi-in-Ukraine-splits-Jewish-community.

25. Around the time Bleich left Ukraine, the Podil community was in turmoil. According to Bleich, he "left the Communal Rabbinate to try and concentrate on developing the Chief Rabbinate. Unfortunately, the Community split after I left. Basically between the Karlin-Stolin faction and the General Community." In a report written a year before the revolution, Jewish Agency Board of Governors member Betsy Gidwitz wrote that "the Chief Rabbi of Kyiv, Rabbi Yaakov Dov Bleich, appears to spend more time outside the country than within its boundaries, and no other individual has emerged as a leader of Kyiv Jewry." Bleich, she explained, was "increasingly an outsider, noted more for his absence from the country while attending to family matters, fundraising, and appearances at international conferences than for his local presence. Further, he is a Karlin-Stolin Hasid in a country in which Jewish religious life is dominated by Chabad. His outsider status, compounded by ongoing economic developments, is felt within his own institutions in Kyiv. Several of his umbrella organizations have shriveled, his publications have ceased, his day school is withering, and his own synagogue no longer is open on a daily basis." See Betsy Gidwitz, "Observations on Jewish Community Life in Ukraine (Dnipropetrovsk, Kharkiv, and Kyiv): Report of a Visit in May 2012," May 2012, http://www.betsygidwitzreports.com/pdfs/report33.pdf. Several sources claimed that Bleich had been pushed out due to "financial mismanagement," but I have been unable to verify these claims, which Bleich vehemently denied. "The bottom line is that my family moved back to the US ten years ago when my daughter got older and couldn't get the right schooling. I was commuting but still spending most of my time in Kyiv. It was taking a toll on the kids and my marriage and it was hard to stay separated." After several years of trying to make it work, Bleich "made the decision to retire from the communal rabbinate only and retain the position of Chief Rabbi which requires less of a presence in Kyiv."

26. Yaki Admakar, "They shouted 'Yid' and 'kicked with nails,'" Walla, January 19, 2014, https://news.walla.co.il/item/2713241.

27. Ibid.
28. Vyacheslav Likhachev, "Anti-Semitism in FSU-2014," Euro-Asian Jewish Congress, Kyiv, 2014.
29. Tali Farkash, "Kiev Jews alarmed at rising anti-Semitism," Ynet, January 19, 2014, http://www.ynetnews.com/articles/0,7340,L-447 8340,00.html.
30. Sam Sokol, "Jew stabbed in Kiev on way home from synagogue," *Jerusalem Post*, January 18, 2014, http://www.jpost.com/Jewish-World/Jewish-News/Jew-stabbed-in-Kiev-on-way-home-from-synagogue-338594.
31. "Zakharchenko promises to react tightly to anyone who does not want 'peace and quiet,'" Ukrainske Pravda, February 18, 2014, http://www.pravda.com.ua/news/2014/01/18/7009878/ (in Ukrainian).
32. David Herszehnhorn, "Unrest Deepens in Ukraine as Protests Turn Deadly," *New York Times*, January 22, 2014, https://www.nytimes.com/2014/01/23/world/europe/ukraine-protests.html?_r=0.
33. Andrei Kurkov, *Ukraine Diaries: Dispatches from Kiev* (London: Random House, 2014).
34. "Kiev clashes spur cancellation of annual Holocaust memorial," Jewish Telegraphic Agency, January 23, 2014, http://www.jta.org/2014/01/23/news-opinion/world/kiev-holocaust-memorial-event-cancelled-due-to-protests.
35. Alina Sharon, "Anti-Semitic violence frightens Ukrainian Jews amid Maidan protests," Jewish News Service, January 21, 2014, http://www.jns.org/latest-articles/2014/1/21/anti-semitic-violence-frightens-ukranian-jews-amid-maidan-protests#.Vf2vQyCqqkp=. The opposition was not alone in facing allegations of antisemitism during the revolution. See "Appeal to the President of Ukraine and the Head of the Ministry of Internal Affairs in connection with the anti-Semitic propaganda of the 'Golden Eagle' in the FB," Evreiskiy Kiev, December 22, 2014, http://evreiskiy.kiev.ua/obrashhenie-k-prezidentu-ukrainy-i-12689.html (in Russian); "Jews in Ukraine Outraged at "Berkut" Anti-Semitic Propaganda," Euro-Asian Jewish Congress, January 25, 2014, http://eajc.org/page32/news43180.html.
36. Vyacheslav Likhachev, "Attacks on Jews in Kyiv: Facts and Interpretations," Euro-Asian Jewish Congress, January 19, 2014, http://eajc.org/page34/news42755.html.

37. See Vyacheslav Likhachev, "Anti-Semitism in FSU-2014," Euro-Asian Jewish Congress, Kyiv, 2014.

38. See http://www.npu.gov.ua/ru/publish/article/989615; "The February revolution," *Economist*, February 27, 2014, http://www.economist.com/news/briefing/21597974-can-ukraine-find-any-leaders-who-will-live-up-aspirations-its-battered-victorious.

39. Katya Gorchinskaya, "He killed for the Maidan," *Foreign Policy*, February 26, 2016, http://foreignpolicy.com/2016/02/26/he-killed-for-the-maidan/.

40. "Opposition leaders call for people to join self-defense teams to protect EuroMaidan," *Kyiv Post*, February 9, 2014, https://www.kyivpost.com/article/content/ukraine-politics/kyivs-weekly-sunday-rally-under-way-as-several-thousand-euromaidan-demonstrators-gather-336551.html.

41. "Riots in Downtown Kyiv (Feb.18)—24 Hour Update," Maidan Translations, February 19, 2014, https://maidantranslations.com/2014/02/19/riots-in-downtown-kyiv-feb-18-24-hour-update/.

42. Andrei Kurkov, *Ukraine Diaries: Dispatches from Kiev* (London: Random House, 2014).

43. "At least four reported dead, more than 100 injured as violent clashes break out near Ukraine's parliament," *Kyiv Post*, February 18, 2014, https://web.archive.org/web/20140218165210/http://www.kyivpost.com/content/kyiv/renewed-violence-breaks-out-today-near-ukraines-parliament-at-least-one-injured-336993.html.

44. Ibid.

45. "Ukraine crisis: Police storm main Kiev 'Maidan' protest camp," BBC, February 19, 2014, http://www.bbc.com/news/world-europe-26249330.

46. Sam Sokol, "Jewish Groups 'deeply concerned' over Ukraine," *Jerusalem Post*, February 19, 2014, http://www.jpost.com/Jewish-World/Jewish-News/Jewish-groups-deeply-concerned-over-Ukraine-341928.

47. "Ukrainian Rabbi Tells Kiev's Jews to Flee City," *Haaretz*, February 22, 2014; Alex Nirenburg, "Opposition Leader: 'The dictatorship fell thanks to the demonstrators,'" NRG, February 22, 2014, http://www.nrg.co.il/online/1/ART2/556/432.html.

48. Interview with Hillel Cohen.

49. Alena thought they were Molotov cocktails, but they were more likely fireworks. See https://twitter.com/ChristopherJM/status/436843916051365888.

50. The full text of the agreement is available in English at http://www.auswaertiges-amt.de/cae/servlet/contentblob/671350/publicationFile/190051/140221-UKR_Erklaerung.pdf.

51. See http://euromaidanpress.com/2016/02/19/a-timeline-of-the-euromaidan-revolution/.

52. Alexander Dukhovny, "Ukraine's Reform Rabbi Cheers Protest's Victory," *Jewish Daily Forward*, February 24, 2014, http://forward.com/opinion/world/193313/ukraines-reform-rabbi-cheers-protests-victory/.

53. Zvika Klein, "Rabbi of Ukraine: We were saved by a miracle," NRG, February 23, 2014, http://www.nrg.co.il/online/11/ART2/556/788.html?hp=11&cat=1102&loc=9 (in Hebrew).

54. Menachem Posner, "Chabad Center in Ukraine Firebombed Amid Ongoing Violence," Chabad.org, February 24, 2014, http://www.chabad.org/news/article_cdo/aid/2502442/jewish/Chabad-Center-in-Ukraine-Firebombed-Amid-Ongoing-Violence.htm.

CHAPTER THREE

1. Anshel Pfeffer, "Apprehension Grips the Crimean Jewish Community," *Haaretz*, March 10, 2014, http://www.haaretz.com/jewish/features/.premium-1.578829.

2. David McHugh and Vladimir Isachenkov, "Lawmakers allow Putin to use military in Ukraine," Associated Press, March 1, 2014, https://www.yahoo.com/news/lawmakers-allow-putin-military-ukraine-152934357.html. Citing Ukrainian instability, Putin had explained that he was "submitting a request for using the armed forces of the Russian Federation on the territory of Ukraine pending the normalization of the socio-political situation in that country."

3. Anshel Pfeffer and Marcus Dysch, "Danger looms in Crimea for Ukrainian Jews," *Jewish Chronicle*, March 6, 2014, https://www.thejc.com/news/world/danger-looms-in-crimea-for-Ukrainian-jews-1.52820.

4. For more information about how local Jews responded to the takeover, see Cnaan Liphshiz, "In Crimea, some Jews feel safer after Russian intervention," Jewish Telegraphic Agency, March 4, 2014; Michal Margalit, "Israelis in Crimea: 'Putin's might is welcomed,'" Ynet, March 4, 2014, http://www.ynetnews.com/articles/0,7340,L-4494935,00.html. See also Talia Lavin, "In Crimea, a

Karaite community carries on, and welcomes Russia," Jewish Telegraphic Agency, March 26, 2014, http://www.jta.org/2014/03/26/news-opinion/world/in-crimea-a-karaite-carries-on-and-welcomes-russia.

5. "Putin reveals secrets of Russia's Crimea takeover plot," BBC, March 9, 2015, http://www.bbc.com/news/world-europe-31796226.

6. The other Svoboda members included in the cabinet were Minister of Agrarian Policy and Food Ihor Shvaika and Minister of Ecology and Natural Resources Andriy Mokhnyk. In early March, shortly after the formation of the cabinet, Right Sector leader Dmytro Yarosh would be appointed as National Security and Defense Council Secretary Andriy Parubiy's deputy, giving the far right another spot in the government. See http://www.kmu.gov.ua/control/ru/publish/article;jsessionid=7976FDB1704F14175FE9612E4BBA4B38?art_id=247059223&cat_id=244843950.

7. Lahav Harkov and Greer Fay Cashman, "Duma Chairman: Russia Concerned About Ukrainian Anti-Semitism," *Jerusalem Post*, February 26, 2014, http://www.jpost.com/Diplomacy-and-Politics/Duma-chairman-Russia-concerned-about-Ukranian-anti-Semitism-343609.

8. "Israeli Embassy urges Ukrainian authorities to find those guilty of beating Jews in Kyiv," Evreiskiy Kiev, January 21, 2014, http://evreiskiy.kiev.ua/posolstvo-izrailja-prizvalo-ukrainskuju-12764.html (in Russian).

9. In a resolution, Congress urged "all political parties to refrain from hate speech or actions of an anti-Semitic or other character which further divide the Ukrainian people when they need to be united." See https://www.congress.gov/bill/113th-congress/senate-resolution/319/text.

10. "Ukraine rabbi: New leader assured me he'll protect Jewish community," Ynet, February 26, 2014, http://www.ynetnews.com/articles/0,7340,L-4492704,00.html.

11. See James Kirchick, "Exclusive: RT Anchor Liz Wahl Explains Why She Quit," *The Daily Beast*, March 5, 2014, http://www.thedailybeast.com/exclusive-rt-anchor-liz-wahl-explains-why-she-quit; "Ukraine conflict: Turning up the TV heat," BBC, August 11, 2014, http://www.bbc.com/news/world-europe-28706461.

12. See https://twitter.com/KevinRothrock/status/442723062971383808/photo/1.

13. "Ukraine chief rabbi accuses Russians of staging anti-Semitic 'provocations,'" Jewish Telegraphic Agency, March 3, 2014, http://www.jta.org/2014/03/03/news-opinion/world/ukraine-chief-rabbi-accuses-russians-of-staging-anti-semitic-provocations.

14. See Guy Chazan, "In Russia, a Top Rabbi Uses Kremlin Ties to Gain Power," *Wall Street Journal*, May 8, 2007, https://www.wsj.com/articles/SB117858672536595256.

15. See Paul Berger, "Russian Chief Rabbi Tells Jews To Back Off On Criticizing Vladimir Putin," *Jewish Daily Forward*, September 9, 2013, http://forward.com/news/183459/russian-chief-rabbi-tells-jews-to-back-off-on-crit/. It must be said, however, that an ultra-orthodox rabbi taking a pro-LGBT stand is not something that one could reasonably expect, Lazar's relationship with Putin notwithstanding.

16. Yossi Melman, "No Love Lost," *Haaretz*, December 8, 2005, http://www.haaretz.com/news/no-love-lost-1.176188.

17. "Russia 'demands surrender' of Ukraine's Crimea forces," BBC, March 3, 2014, http://www.bbc.com/news/world-europe-26424738.

18. Sam Sokol, "Russian Jewish Leader Urges Silence Over Crimea," *Jerusalem Post*, March 4, 2014, http://www.jpost.com/International/Russian-Jewish-leader-urges-silence-over-Crimea-344188. See also Sam Sokol, "Chief Rabbi asserts Ukrainian Jews will not run away if war breaks out with Russia," *Jerusalem Post*, March 5, 2014, http://www.jpost.com/Jewish-World/Jewish-News/Chief-rabbi-asserts-Ukrainian-Jews-will-not-run-away-if-war-breaks-out-with-Russia-344434.

19. "Transcript: Putin defends Russian intervention in Ukraine," *Washington Post*, March 4, 2014, https://www.washingtonpost.com/world/transcript-putin-defends-russian-intervention-in-ukraine/2014/03/04/9cadcd1a-a3a9-11e3-a5fa-55f0c77bf39c_story.html?utm_term=.1028c860d59b.

20. Later on, when I asked Lazar about Putin's comments and both sides' weaponization of antisemitism, he replied by hinting at how Jews were traditionally made into scapegoats during times of conflict in the region and how recent trends seemed to mark an improvement in attitudes. "Anyone who wants to explain their actions says that they're trying to help the Jews, and I think that this is a very good sign," Lazar said. "This is happening on either side, whether it's condemning antisemitism or coming out against it,

making sure that any minorities, especially Jews, will be able to feel safe and comfortable. So I don't see anything wrong with anyone bringing out or showing [i.e. highlighting] antisemitism anywhere."

21. See https://maidantranslations.com/2014/03/05/open-letter-of-Ukrainian-jews-to-russian-federation-president-vladimir-putin/.

22. Sam Sokol, "Ukrainian official: Jews 'among the best protectors of our country,'" *Jerusalem Post*, October 2, 2014, http://www.jpost.com/Diaspora/Jews-among-the-best-protectors-of-our-country-377940. See also David Filipov, "Clashes and Crimea tension worry community that struggled to rebuild," *Boston Globe*, March 16, 2014, http://www.bostonglobe.com/news/world/2014/03/15/crisis-stirs-old-fears-among-ukraine-jews/JaWPzxrt68IjW872E55fiM/story.html.

23. Olga Rudenko, "Billionaire Kolomoisky takes over in Dnipropetrovsk Oblast, blasting Putin and Yanukovych," *Kyiv Post*, March 3, 2014, https://www.kyivpost.com/article/content/ukraine-politics/billionaire-kolomoisky-takes-over-in-dnipropetrovsk-oblast-criticizing-putin-and-yanukovych-338261.html.

24. "Rabbi Shmuel Kaminezki: A New Haman Came to Ukraine Today," Evreiskiy Kyiv, March 16, 2014, http://evreiskiy.kiev.ua/ravvin-shmujel-kamineckijj-segodnja-v-12915.html (in Russian).

25. See Batya Ungar-Sargon, "Russia's Chief Rabbi Cheers Crimea Annexation," *Tablet*, March 19, 2014, http://www.tabletmag.com/scroll/166779/russias-chief-rabbi-cheers-crimea-annexation.

26. See http://en.kremlin.ru/events/president/news/20603.

27. See https://www.facebook.com/permalink.php?story_fbid=646464742055475&id=450435081658443.

28. Asked about his presence at the speech, Lazar later told me that he had been invited by the president and that "the moment that I clapped was when he said that we should support all minorities, that they should have the rights, and I do believe that this is something that should be commended. I do feel that every minority should have the right to exist and live comfortably in their country. There was actually a lot of things about me being there that didn't even happen but I'm not going to try to disprove what newspapers write or I will be doing only that. But yes, I went, I was invited by the president, I think that it was a positive message for the Jewish community in Ukraine. At that point, I think I clapped once during the speech, so I don't think there's anything

wrong with that … [such large gatherings have] been going on for the last fifteen years at least. Every year all of the religious leaders are invited and I was one of them. The same way that the [Russian Orthodox] Patriarch was invited and the Mufti was invited, all of the different denominations. I was one of them. I don't think there was anything political."

29.   Kiril Feferman, "The Crisis in Ukraine: Attitudes of the Russian and Ukrainian Jewish Communities," *Israel Journal of Foreign Affairs* (2015), doi:10.1080/23739770.2015.1061259.

30.   In an email to this author, Feferman elaborated on his explanation. "I also posit that in those turbulent days (March 2014) no one could bet Putin would not advance further into Ukraine. This, alongside traditional rabbinical self-restraint in taking sides in local gentile politics, could explain why a significant number of Ukrainian rabbis co-signed Lazar's letter. After all, it is precisely by this pattern that the developments in Ukraine had been unfolding during the Civil War in 1918-20. It was extremely dangerous for the Jews to put all their balls in one basket and this seems to have been a lesson well learnt by Ukrainian rabbis. Even though a number of them were fresh newcomers, their centuries-old Jewish experience taught them to do precisely this, not to take sides."

Speaking with this author, one Chabad Hasid who is familiar with his movement's operations in the former Soviet Union expressed a similar view. Rather than being political, Lazar's letter was "a very mild, genial letter underlining that we as Jews are one, and that it's not the job of rabbis in Ukraine or Russia to get swept up by the politics of the day," he said, adding that it reflected a "general Chabad-Lubavitch outlook."

"What is the job of a shaliach [emissary] in his city? Is it to fight for democracy? Is it to lead or attend protests at the risk of alienating members of his community? Or is it to directly serve the needs of the local Jewish community, reaching out to each and every Jew to make sure they have what they need, to help them grow in their Jewish life, etc.[?] For Chabad emissaries as a whole, the latter is undoubtedly the goal, no matter what their personal feelings or opinions are. … As much as each individual rabbi may have their own thoughts and opinions on the politics of the day—and I assure you that Ukraine's Chabad rabbis all had their own personal takes—Chabad rabbis leave democracy activism to democracy activists. They chose a different calling in life, to serve their local Jewish communities, who were there when the flags on the government buildings were Ukrainian and who are still there now that they are Russian."

That also seemed to be the view of Donetsk's rabbi Pinchas Vishedski, whose community would later be overrun by the Russians. "Our intention was that there should not be found a 'Jewish point' to the conflict, God forbid, and that nobody from either side would come and, as usual, blame the Jews, so it was important for us to get the Jews out of the game," he said. "It was not a subject that had direct implications for Jews because they were Jews, but only because they were citizens of their countries, and it was important for us to keep it like that. By the way, I think we succeeded in that because, in general, neither in Russia nor Ukraine did they succeed to tie the Jewish issue to this conflict except for marginal actors."

Chabad is known for its tendency to maintain close relations with those in power in whatever country it operates in, including authoritarian regimes. This closeness to power frequently manifests itself in a tendency to minimize antisemitic trends and the use of antisemitic or historical revisionist tropes by governments. Good examples would be Chabad breaking ranks with the vast majority of Hungarian Jewish organizations during a period of tension between the community and the Orban administration in 2014, and the allegations by various Polish Jewish organizations that the Hasidic group had provided cover for Warsaw's toleration of antisemitism. See Lili Bayer and Larry Cohler-Esses, "Chabad Feuds With Jewish Leaders Over Cozy Ties To Eastern European Autocrats," *Jewish Daily Forward*, October 8, 2017, http://forward.com/news/world/384236/chabad-feuds-with-jewish-leaders-over-cozy-ties-to-eastern-european-autocra/; Sam Sokol, "Budapest Conference Highlights Jewish Battle over Communal Authority in Europe," *Jerusalem Post*, March 31, 2014, http://www.jpost.com/Jewish-World/Jewish-News/Budapest-conference-highlights-Jewish-battle-over-communal-authority-in-Europe-347048.

31. Sam Sokol, "Ukraine's Chief Rabbi to Post: 'We've Lost Most Local Donors," *Jerusalem Post*, March 14, 2014, http://www.jpost.com/

Jewish-World/Jewish-News/Ukraines-chief-rabbi-to-Post-Weve-lost-most-local-donors-345354.

32. Sam Sokol, "Ukrainian Jews adjusting to life in uncertain times," *Jerusalem Post*, February 27, 2014, http://www.jpost.com/Jewish-World/Jewish-News/Ukrainian-Jews-adjusting-to-life-in-uncertain-times-343680.

33. Talia Lavin and Cnaan Liphshiz, "Ukraine Jews hunkering down amid turmoil," Jewish Telegraphic Agency, February 25, 2014, http://www.jta.org/2014/02/25/news-opinion/world/ukraine-jews-hunkering-down-amid-turmoil.

34. Refael Kruskal, "Are you there? The Jews of Ukraine can't hear you," *Times of Israel*, March 21, 2014, http://blogs.timesofisrael.com/are-you-there-the-jews-of-ukraine-cant-hear-you/.

35. Judy Maltz, "Israeli Security Experts Head Out to Kiev to Train Local Jews in Self-defense," *Haaretz*, March 3, 2014, http://www.haaretz.com/israel-news/.premium-1.577683.

36. Anshel Pfeffer and Marcus Dysch, "Danger looms in Crimea for Ukrainian Jews," *Jewish Chronicle*, March 6, 2014, https://www.thejc.com/news/world/danger-looms-in-crimea-for-Ukrainian-jews-1.52820.

37. Sam Sokol, "Chief Rabbi asserts Ukrainian Jews will not run away if war breaks out with Russia," *Jerusalem Post*, March 5, 2014, http://www.jpost.com/Jewish-World/Jewish-News/Chief-rabbi-asserts-Ukrainian-Jews-will-not-run-away-if-war-breaks-out-with-Russia-344434.

38. "Israel Envoy Meets With Ukraine 'Anti-Semite' Dmitry Yarosh," Jewish Telegraphic Agency, March 7, 2014, http://forward.com/news/breaking-news/194014/israel-envoy-meets-with-ukraine-anti-semite-dmitry/. Yarosh stated that, while he collaborated and shared a common ideology with Svoboda, he rejected its "racist elements."

39. Oleg Sukhov, "Ukrainian nationalist Bereza looks to Israel as a source of inspiration," *Kyiv Post*, February 26, 2015, https://www.kyivpost.com/article/content/kyiv-post-plus/Ukrainian-nationalist-bereza-looks-to-israel-as-a-source-of-inspiration-381970.html.

40. Vladislav Davidzon, "Right-wing Ukrainian leader is (surprise) Jewish, and (real surprise) proud of it," *Tablet*, December 1, 2014, http://www.tabletmag.com/jewish-news-and-politics/187217/borislav-bereza.

41. Ibid.

42. Marco Carynnyk, "Foes of Our Rebirth: Ukrainian Nationalist Discussions about Jews, 1929-1947," *Nationalities Papers* 39, no. 3 (2011): 315-352, doi:10.1080/00905992.2011.570327. Carynnyk cited the following OUN nationality policy: "The national minorities are divided into … those that are friendly to us, that is, members of previously subjugated peoples [and] those that are hostile to us, Russians, Poles, Jews. [Members of the first group] have equal rights with Ukrainians; we help them return to their homelands. … Jews to be isolated, eliminated from official positions in order to avoid sabotage, Russians and Poles all the more so. If there should be an insurmountable need to leave a Jew in the economic administration, place one of our militiamen over him and liquidate him for the slightest offense. Administrators of various branches can only be Ukrainians, never hostile aliens. Assimilation of Jews is excluded."

43. See http://uacrisis.org/379-dmitrijj-yarosh.

44. Yarosh's about-face was especially suspicious in light of his prior statements and the timing of his purported change in idealogical orientation. According to *Der Spiegel*, in the pre-Maidan period Yarosh had written a book in which he mused about "how it came to pass that most of the billionaires in Ukraine are Jews." Jews hoarding a country's wealth is a classic anti-Semitic trope. See Benjamin Bidder and Uwe Klußmann, "Ukrainian civilians take up arms," *Spiegel Online*, April 16, 2014, http://www.spiegel.de/international/europe/Ukrainian-militias-prepare-for-possibility-of-russian-invasion-a-964628.html.

    Antisemitism was also obvious in the ideological program of Yarosh's Tryzub organization, which was one of the founding members of the Right Sector. In its declaration of principles, Tryzub stated that it existed in opposition to the following groups and ideologies: "Imperialism and chauvinism, communism and fascism, cosmopolitanism and pseudo-nationalism, totalitarianism and anarchism, every kind of evil that seeks to parasitize on the blood and sweat of Ukrainians." See http://banderivets.org/.ua/deklaratsiya-nashyh-pryntsypiv.html. Several of these terms have been used in the past to refer to Jews. During the Soviet period, the phrase "rootless cosmopolitans" was frequently used as a dog-whistle to stir up antisemitic sentiments. The phrase "every kind of evil that seeks to parasitize on the blood and sweat of Ukrainians" does not need further explication, especially in light of Yarosh's statement on the overrepresentation of Jews among Ukraine's hated oligarchic class.

45. See "'Death to the Jews': Anti-Semitic provocation in Odessa," Forum Daily, April 8, 2014, http://www.forumdaily.com/smert-zhidam-antisemitskaya-provokaciya-v-odesse/ (in Russian); "Right Sector came to the synagogue and will paint the Jewish cemetery," Forum Daily, April 9, 2014, http://www.forumdaily.com/pravyj-sektor-prishel-v-sinagogu-i-budet-krasit-evrejskoe-kladbishhe/ (in Russian).

46. Speaking with the Jewish Telegraphic Agency, Cohen described the Maidan period as follows: "Things began getting really uncomfortable when the rioters started setting up spontaneous roadblocks to keep police and army troops from reaching the action zone. It was very uneasy, being pulled over in a car full of orthodox Jews by club-wielding Cossacks." See "Kiev Rabbi Assaulted in Suspected anti-Semitic Attack," Jewish Telegraphic Agency, March 14, 2014, http://www.haaretz.com/beta/1.579873.

47. The Fast of Esther commemorates how how the Jews of ancient Persia fasted for three days in hope of divine salvation from the vizier Haman's plan to annihilate their community.

48. Ironically, that same day Ira Forman, US Special Envoy to Monitor and Combat Antisemitism, was quoted by the *Jewish Daily Forward* as saying that there was "no indication that what President Putin has been saying about anti-Semitism has been a true reflection of what's happening on the ground." See Nathan Guttman and Paul Berger, "Anti-Semitism Envoy Blasts Russian Effort To Play Ukraine 'Jewish Card,'" *Jewish Daily Forward*, March 13, 2014, http://forward.com/news/world/194458/anti-semitism-envoy-blasts-russian-effort-to-play/.

    Forman's statement came in response to the demonstrably false assertion by Vladimir Putin that there had "been mass attacks on churches and synagogues in southern and eastern Ukraine." See "President Putin's Fiction: 10 False Claims About Ukraine," https://web.archive.org/web/20170101013834/https://www.state.gov/r/pa/prs/ps/2014/03/222988.htm.

    Forman's *Forward* interview also clarified just how hard it was for outside observers to get a handle on the state of antisemitism in Ukraine. The Jewish state department official recalled how, in November 2013, Jewish leaders across Ukraine had told him that there was no antisemitism in the country, causing him to grow suspicious. He finally got an explanation when one rabbi broke ranks and told him that he had "been getting calls from local government officials to make sure I tell you there is no anti-Semitism."

49. Sam Sokol, "Ukrainian Jewish leaders blame Russia for anti-Semitic provocations," *Jerusalem Post*, March 16, 2014, http://www.jpost .com/Jewish-World/Jewish-News/Ukrainian-Jewish-leaders-blame-Russia-for-antisemitic-provocations-345516.

50. Ben Sales, Talia Lavin and Cnaan Liphshiz, "Wounded Ukrainian protesters airlifted to Israel for medical treatment," Jewish Telegraphic Agency, March 7, 2014, http://www.jta.org/2014/03/07/news-opinion/israel-middle-east/wounded-Ukrainian-protesters-airlifted-to-israel-for-medical-treatment.

51. The circle included nationalists such as Right Sector's Yarosh and revisionist historian Volodymyr Viatrovych, as well as figures such as the AutoMaidan's Sergei Poyarkova and singer Ruslana, among others.

Pekar described its formation as follows: "We saw that there was no specific leader that people believed or can trust, [so] we decided that a kind of collective leadership is necessary to be installed and we invented a specific body which we called the Circle of People's Trust and we invited a dozen of very different people who are representatives of different social groups and movements to be members of that and since we thought that if there are no leaders who can address to the whole community of Maidan maybe it would be possible to have some twelve leaders who will address different sub-communities or different small communities and then this way cover all of the community."

Or, as one of the group's members put it, the Circle was "an intermediary between Maidan and the managers who will be hired by the people." "Maidan representatives outline their demands for the new government of Ukraine," EuroMaidan Press, February 25, 2014, http://euromaidanpress.com/2014/02/25/maidan-representatives-outline-their-demands-for-the-new-government-of-ukraine/#arvlbdata.

52. See http://www.eajc.org/page6/news43744.html.

53. "Ukraine PM Joins President in Vow to Protect the Jews," *Haaretz*, March 17, 2014, http://www.haaretz.com/jewish/news/1.580332.

54. Kapustin wasn't the only rabbi to leave Crimea because of the crisis. Chabad rabbi Yitzchok Meyer Lipszyc and his wife Leah had already hurriedly fled in late February, following the urging of friends and relatives in the United States. The Lipszycs, who were conscientiously apolitical, were—unlike Kapustin—eventually able to return to Crimea. This has been cited by some within Chabad as proof of the superiority of their movement's policy of not making comments on political issues. See Sean Savage, "Chabad rabbi had front-row seat for unrest in Crimea," Jewish News Service, March 18, 2014, http://www.jns.org/latest-articles/2014/3/18/chabad-rabbi-had-front-row-seat-for-unrest-in-crimea#.WUpHfhOGN0s=; Batya Ungar-Sargon, "Fleeing Crimea for Crown Heights," *Tablet*, March 11, 2014, http://www.tabletmag.com/scroll/165742/fleeing-crimea-for-crown-heights.

55. "Rabbi in Crimea urges Jews to leave Ukraine, fears neo-Nazi attacks," YouTube video, 3:30. Posted by RT, March 15, 2014, https://www.youtube.com/watch?v=ZrzQqY-Up2g. The segment was broadcast twice, with slight differences in the introductions.

56. "'Pushed to leave': Packing moods among Ukraine's Jewish minority amidst far-right rise," Russia Today, March 15, 2014, https://www.rt.com/news/jews-jewish-ukraine-nationalist-106/. This article also claimed that Kapustin had found the message "death to the Jews" on the wall of his home. This was a total fabrication.

57. Sokol, Sam, "Butchering History but Not the Jews, the Case of Post-Revolutionary Ukraine," in *The ISGAP Papers: Antisemitism in Comparative Perspective*, vol. 3, ed. Charles Small (New York: ISGAP, 2018).

58. For an in-depth examination of the centrality of the myth of the Great Patriotic War in contemporary Russia, see Shaun Walker, *The Long Hangover: Putin's New Russia and the Ghosts of the Past* (New York: Oxford University Press, 2018).

59. Anton Shekhovtsov, *Russia and the Western Far Right: Tango Noir* (Abingdon: Routledge, 2018), 14-15.

60. Glenn Kates, "Russian TV Anchor Implies Jews Brought Holocaust On Themselves," RFE/RL, March 24, 2014, https://www

.rferl.org/a/russian-tv-anchor-accuses-jews-of-bringing-holocaust-on-themselves-/25307640.html.

61. Ibid.

62. David E. Fishman, "The real truth about those anti-Semitic flyers in Donetsk," *Jewish Daily Forward*, April 22, 2014, http://forward.com/opinion/world/196864/the-real-truth-about-those-anti-semitic-flyers-in-/?p=all.

     Fishman, a history professor at the Jewish Theological Seminary in New York, noted that the allegations contained in these programs were "picked up instantaneously in a pro-Russian separatist demonstration in Luhansk" in which a speaker roiled up the crowd by listing "major Ukrainian politicians, adding their alleged Jewish names to prove their true origin."

     At the time, he asserted that Kremlin propaganda aimed at portraying the new government as fascist and antisemitic had failed, leading to a shift in focus toward a domestic audience. That a shift occurred is undeniable, but subsequent events would prove that the two approaches were not mutually exclusive, as Russia continued to not only accuse Kyiv of xenophobia but also branched out into fabricating antisemitic incidents.

63. See http://help.rjc.ru/site.aspx?SECTIONID=85646&IID=2580752.

64. Stephen Ennis, "Russian Jews fear anti-Semitism amid Crimea fervour," BBC, March 28, 2014, http://www.bbc.com/news/world-europe-26786213.

65. See http://www.rjc.ru/rus/site.aspx?SECTIONID=91208&IID=25 40774. The so-called "doctors' plot" was an episode in which six prominent Jewish medical practitioners were falsely accused of seeking to assassinate senior communist leaders. These accusations were accompanied by an antisemitic campaign in the Soviet press and are believed to have been fabricated as a pretext for subsequent anti-Jewish violence. After Stalin's death all of the physicians were declared innocent and set free.

66. "Chief Russian rabbi slams Ukrainians Jews for criticizing Putin," Jewish Telegraphic Agency, March 26, 2014, http://www.jta.org/2014/03/26/news-opinion/world/chief-russian-rabbi-slams-Ukrainian-jews-for-criticizing-putin. Several days later, Zissels and other Ukrainians ran an open letter to Putin in the *International New York Times, Haaretz* and the *National Post*, asserting that the strongman had "confused Ukraine with Russia, where Jewish or-

ganizations have noticed growth in anti-Semitic tendencies last year." See "Ukrainian Jews slam Putin in full-page ad in *New York Times*," Jewish Telegraphic Agency, March 27, 2014, http://www.jta.org/2014/03/27/news-opinion/world/Ukrainian-jews-slam-putin-in-full-page-ad-in-new-york-times.

67. Letter from Berel Lazar to Efraim Zuroff, dated March 28, 2014, and provided to the author by its recipient.

68. Simon Wiesenthal Center, "2012 Top Ten Anti-Semitic/Anti-Israel Slurs," http://www.wiesenthal.com/atf/cf/%7B54d385e6-f1b9-4e9f-8e94-890c3e6dd277%7D/TT_2012_3.PDF.

69. Michal Margalit, "Donetsk leaflet: Jews must register or face deportation," Ynet, April 16, 2014, https://www.ynetnews.com/articles/0,7340,L-4510688,00.html.

70. See https://www.ushmm.org/information/press/press-releases/museum-statement-on-antisemitic-flyer-in-ukraine.

71. According to Dina Privalko, this estimate "represent[s] popular estimates of the Jewish population according to the Israeli Law of Return." See Darina Privalko, *Jewish Life in Ukraine: Achievements, Challenges and Priorities from the Collapse of Communism to 2013* (London: Institute for Jewish Policy Research, September 2014), http://archive.jpr.org.uk/object-ukr2. However, according to the 2001 Ukrainian census, there were only 8,800 Jews in the Donetsk region at the turn of the century. See http://2001.ukrcensus.gov.ua/eng/results/general/nationality/. As always, it is a difficult matter to estimate Jewish population figures in the former Soviet Union.

72. Sam Sokol, "Jews cast doubt on origin of anti-Semitic flyers in Donetsk," *Jerusalem Post*, April 18, 2014, http://www.jpost.com/Jewish-World/Jewish-News/Jews-cast-doubt-on-origin-of-anti-Semitic-flyers-in-Donetsk-349848.

73. Alec Luhn, "Antisemitic flyer 'by Donetsk People's Republic' in Ukraine a hoax," *Guardian*, April 18, 2014, https://www.theguardian.com/world/2014/apr/18/antisemitic-donetsk-peoples-republic-ukraine-hoax.

74. "In Donetsk, Nazi instructions were distributed to the Jews," Evreiskiy Kiev, April 16, 2014, http://evreiskiy.kiev.ua/v-donecke-razdali-nacistskuju-13077.html (in Russian).

75. David Blair, "Ukraine crisis: 'The last time someone wrote a text like that was under the Nazis,'" *Telegraph*, April 18, 2014, http://

www.telegraph.co.uk/news/worldnews/europe/ukraine/1077531
0/Ukraine-crisis-The-last-time-someone-wrote-a-text-like-that-
was-under-the-Nazis.html.

76. "Ukrainian Prime Minister Yatsenyuk: Who Knows Where Putin
Will Go Next," NBC News, April 19, 2014, https://www.nbcnews
.com/storyline/ukraine-crisis/Ukrainian-prime-minister-yatsen
yuk-who-knows-where-putin-will-go-n84856.

77. David Fishman, "The real truth about those anti-semitic flyers in
Donetsk," *Jewish Daily Forward*, April 22, 2014, http://forward.com/
opinion/world/196864/the-real-truth-about-those-anti-semitic-
flyers-in/.

78. Ibid.

79. See http://eajc.org/page16/news44509.html; Mikhail Ryabov, "In
Sevastopol the monument to the victims of the Holocaust was
desecrated again," *Sevastopolskaya Gazeta*, April 22, 2014, http://
sevastopol.press/2014/04/22/v-sevastopole-opjat-oskvernili-pam
jatnik-zhertvam-holokosta/ (in Russian).

80. "'Go back to Kiev, fascists!': Outraged locals chase off Ukrainian
troops," Russia Today, May 3, 2014, https://www.rt.com/news/
156628-kramatorsk-residents-Ukrainian-military/. It is telling that
the use of such language was quickly adopted by those seeking to
imitate the separatists, such as in the case of the ersatz flyers.

81. Alec Luhn, "East Ukraine protesters joined by miners on the
barricades," *Guardian*, April 13, 2014, https://www.theguardian
.com/world/2014/apr/12/east-ukraine-protesters-miners-donetsk-
russia.

82. Alastair Macdonald and Pavel Polityuk, "Ukraine government
pledges Russian language rights," Reuters, April 18, 2014, http://
www.reuters.com/article/us-ukraine-crisis-constitution/ukraine-
government-pledges-russian-language-rights-idUSBREA3H0GC
20140418.

83. Piotr Zalewski, "Russian Separatism Gains Ground in Eastern
Ukraine," *Time*, March 19, 2014, http://time.com/30636/russian-
separatism-gains-ground-in-eastern-ukraine/.

84. Office of the United Nations High Commissioner for Human
Rights, *Report on the Human Rights Situation in Ukraine*, June 15,
2014, https://www.ohchr.org/Documents/Countries/UA/HRMMU
Report15June2014.pdf.

85. Sam Sokol, "Odessa Jewish Community Mulls Emergency Evacuation," *Jerusalem Post*, May 5, 2014, http://www.jpost.com/International/Odessa-Jewish-community-mulls-emergency-evacuation-351334.

86. See "Odessa Jews prepared for evacuation from the city," Interfax, May 5, 2014, http://www.interfax.ru/world/374862 (in Russian); "Buses and armed guards: Odessa Jews ready for mass evacuation," Russia Today, May 5, 2014, https://www.rt.com/news/156792-odessa-jews-evacuation-plans/; Elena Chinkova, "Did the Jews decide to flee Odessa," *Komsomolskaya Pravda*, May 6, 2014, https://www.kp.ru/daily/26227/3110660/ (in Russian); "Odessa Jewish community prepares for evacuation from the city," Vesti, May 5, 2014, http://www.vesti.ru/doc.html?id=1549369# (in Russian); "Jerusalem Post: Are Jews running from Odessa," Pravda, May 5, 2014, https://www.pravda.ru/news/world/formerussr/ukraine/05-05-2014/1206721-jews-0/ (in Russian).

87. See "Odessa is again waiting for the pogroms," UralPress, May 5, 2014, http://uralpress.ru/news/2014/05/05/odessa-vnov-v-ozhidanii-evreyskih-pogromov (in Russian), no longer available online.

88. See http://www.chabad.odessa.ua/templates/blog/post.asp?aid=1658934&postid=45550&p=1.

89. "Leaders of Odessa's Jewish community deny evacuation plans," Jewish Telegraphic Agency, May 7, 2014, https://www.jta.org/2014/05/07/news-opinion/world/leaders-of-odessas-jewish-community-deny-evacuation-plans.

90. Glenn Kates, "Reports Of Plans To Evacuate Odesa's Jewish Community Appear To Miss Mark," RFE/RL, May 12, 2014, https://www.rferl.org/a/reports-of-plans-to-evacuate-odesas-jewish-community-appear-to-miss-mark/25382281.html.

91. Sam Sokol, "Jewish leaders dispute reports of Odessa evacuation," *Jerusalem Post*, May 8, 2014, http://www.jpost.com/Jewish-World/Jewish-Features/Russian-Jewish-Congress-disputes-report-of-Odessa-evacuation-351603.

92. Luhansk would likewise declare itself an independent people's republic a month later.

93. "In Donetsk, Odessa, Kharkiv and Luhansk, the separatists staged rallies," Ukrainian Pravda, March 30, 2014, https://www.pravda.com.ua/news/2014/03/30/7020775/ (in Ukrainian).

94. "Rally in Luhansk: Zionists seized power in Ukraine," Evreiskiy Kiev, April 1, 2014, http://evreiskiy.kiev.ua/miting-v-luganske-vlast-v-ukraine-12969.html (in Russian).

95. Chana Gopin, "'My City Is Being Shelled': Chabad Emissary to Lugansk, Ukraine, Relates Her Story," Chabad.org, September 3, 2014, http://www.chabad.org/news/article_cdo/aid/2689252/jew ish/My-City-Is-Being-Shelled-Chabad-Emissary-to-Lugansk-Ukr aine-Relates-Her-Story.htm.

96. Gabriela Baczynska, "Kiev pins hopes on oligarch in battle against eastern separatists," Reuters, May 23, 2014, https://www.reuters .com/article/us-ukraine-crisis-oligarch/kiev-pins-hopes-on-oligarch-in-battle-against-eastern-separatists-idUSBREA4M0OU20140523.

97. In late April, photoshopped images of Kolomoisky wearing a tee shirt adorned with a mashup of the UPA logo and a menorah began showing up on Facebook. The image was accompanied by the Ukrainian portmanteau Zhidbanderovets, or Jewish-Banderite, a satirical phrase intended to make fun of the idea that Jewish supporters of the new government were collaborating with anti-semites. See Talia Lavin and Cnaan Liphshiz, "A satirical neologism becomes a weapon in the fight over Ukrainian Jewry," Jewish Telegraphic Agency, April 25, 2014, https://www.jta.org/2014/04/25/news-opinion/world/a-neologism-used-as-a-weapon-in-the-fight-over-Ukrainian-jewry.

98. Gopin described what happened as follows: "There was a Jew from Kyiv who wanted to pay for our security. He wanted to give us money. He had money and sent us his representative. A private individual. So he sent us his man to check the building and see where to put security. The guard was there when suddenly someone showed up and wanted to inspect the building and he thought they had arrived to replace him and so he immediately ran to inform the separatists, to the Russians, that another guard is arriving here from Kolomoisky and from Jews in Kyiv. ... So he arranged the whole thing."

99. "Ukrainian oligarch puts $1 million bounty on opponent's head—audio recording," Voice of Russia, May 15, 2014, https://sputnik news.com/voiceofrussia/news/2014_05_15/Ukrainian-oligarch-puts-1-million-bounty-on-opponents-head-audio-recording-9493/.

100. Alan Cullison, "Ukraine's Secret Weapon: Feisty Oligarch Ihor Kolomoisky," *Wall Street Journal*, June 27, 2014, https://www.wsj

.com/articles/ukraines-secret-weapon-feisty-oligarch-ihor-kolo moisky-1403886665.

101. "Mariupol separatists killed future priest from Carpathian region," *Segodnya*, March 13, 2014, https://www.segodnya.ua/regions/lvov/ mariupolskie-separatisty-ubili-budushchego-svyashchennika-iz- prikarpatya-519902.html (in Russian).

102. See http://cxid.info/iudei-luganskoy-oblasti-trebuut-ot-kolomoy skogo-nikogda-ne-govorit-ot-imeni-evreyskogo-naroda-n114305. Rabbi Gopin confirmed that this is the accurate text of his letter.

103. "Jews preparing to evacuate Ukraine," WorldNetDaily, May 4, 2014, http://www.wnd.com/2014/05/jews-preparing-to-evacuate- ukraine/.

104. That isn't to say that there wasn't a significant increase in *aliya* (immigration to Israel) during the beginning of 2014. However, the exaggerated level of preparation for flight described by Bleich is incompatible with both the published immigration statistics and (as we shall later see) the testimonies of the vast majority of immigrants and IDPs interviewed for this book, especially those from the Donbas. According to the Jewish Agency, *aliya* from the Kyiv region between January and November 2014 was 87 percent higher than in the same period the year before. The largest increase, predictably, came from the Donetsk and Luhansk regions, which experienced a 1,001 percent increase during this period. In May 2014 alone, 531 Ukrainians from all regions immigrated to Israel, up from 137 in January. Thereafter, *aliya* rates dipped and re- bounded several times, falling to 441 by November before spiking to 1,013 in December. In total, some 5,917 Jews made *aliya* from Ukraine in 2014. These calculations are based on a briefing pre- pared by the Jewish Agency's Unit for Russian-Speaking Jewry on December 9, 2014, as well as a graph presented by unit director Roman Polonsky at the Jewish Agency's Board of Governors (BoG) meeting in Tel Aviv in October 2015. The final total for 2014 was taken from another update document prepared by Polonsky's unit, which may be found at https://fedweb-assets.s3 .amazonaws.com/fed-2/2/Crisis-in-Ukraine_JAN%25209%252C %25202015-3p.pdf. During the BoG meeting, Polonsky described Ukrainian *aliya* as reminiscent of the "temperature of a very sick man." He pointed out that the numbers spiked and dropped ac- cording to the state of the conflict. "It drops when there is hope

for a cease-fire and there are sharp increases when this collapses." Sam Sokol, "At Jewish Agency Board Meeting, Future of Aliyah Very Much on the Mind," *Jerusalem Post*, October 25, 2014, http://www.jpost.com/Diaspora/At-Jewish-Agency-board-meeting-future-of-aliyah-very-much-on-the-mind-430027.

105. JTA and Sam Sokol, "Ukrainian Jews form defense force to combat anti-Semitic attacks," *Jerusalem Post*, May 8, 2014, http://www.jpost.com/Jewish-World/Jewish-News/Ukrainian-Jews-form-defense-force-to-combat-anti-Semitic-attacks-351701.

106. Cnaan Liphshiz, "Odessa's Jews lay low as violence engulfs their oasis of calm," Jewish Telegraphic Agency, May 12, 2014, https://www.jta.org/2014/05/12/news-opinion/world/odessas-jews-lay-low-as-violence-engulfs-their-oasis-of-calm. Graffiti blaming the Jews was subsequently found among the ruins of the Trade Union Building, while attendees at a pro-Russian protest in the city were reported to have carried signs carrying the same message. "Inscriptions on the walls: Jews are blamed for the Odessa tragedy," Evreiskiy Kiev, May 19, 2014, http://evreiskiy.kiev.ua/nadpisi-na-stenakh-v-odesskojj-tragedii-13257.html (in Russian).

107. In Russian, the phrase literally means pre-war photographs.

108. Rabbi Menachem Mendel Schneerson (1902-1994), the seventh Grand Rabbi of the Chabad-Lubavitch sect, was well known for sending Hasidic families around the world to establish communities and institutions and promote religious observance among non-practicing Jews. After his death, he was hailed as the messiah by some streams within the overall the Chabad movement.

109. "Dozens reported killed in eastern Ukraine fighting," Associated Press, May 27, 2014, http://www.dailymail.co.uk/wires/ap/article-2640295/Dozens-reported-killed-eastern-Ukraine-fighting.html.

110. The myriad cultural, economic, linguistic, and familial connections between Kharkiv and Russia did not necessarily translate into overwhelming support for separatism. One reporter originally from the city noted that, after visiting, he believed that "the majority of the people in the city of Kharkiv are absolutely against joining Russia anytime soon." See "Three more Ukrainian cities are vulnerable to a Russian takeover," PRI, April 7, 2014, https://www.pri.org/stories/2014-04-07/three-more-Ukrainian-cities-are-vulnerable-russian-takeover.

111. See Olga Rudenko, "Kharkiv settles down, while pro-Russian separatists still hold buildings in Luhansk, Donetsk," *Kyiv Post*, April 8, 2014, https://www.kyivpost.com/article/content/war-against-ukraine/kharkiv-settles-down-while-pro-russian-separatists-still-hold-buildings-in-luhansk-donetsk-342517.html.

     In April, Kernes was shot while exercising in a local park. The city's rabbi prayed for the mayor, whom he described as "a good friend of the Jewish community." There was little to no suspicion among local Jews that the attack had anything to do with his religious affiliation. (He was subsequently airlifted to Israel for further treatment.) In fact, the attack was more likely the result of either Kernes's underworld connections or his wavering loyalties. (Oliver Carroll, "Why Ukraine's Separatist Movement Failed in Kharkiv," *New Republic*, June 23, 2014, https://newrepublic.com/article/118301/kharkivs-kernes-returns-different-city-after-being-shot.) The Mayor initially exhibited separatist leanings and, after Yanukovich's ouster, had temporarily fled the country. After returning he was placed under house arrest and recanted, coming out in support of the revolution and expressing vehement opposition to secessionism. ("Court places Kernes under night-time house arrest," InterFax Ukraine, March 14, 2014, http://en.interfax.com.ua/news/general/195935.html.) Given that he was widely believed to have sent Titushky to Kyiv during the Maidan before switching sides, it is not unreasonable to assume that he had made enemies on both sides of the political divide. (Daryna Shevchenko, "Kharkiv's Kernes justifies his 180-degree political turn by saying he was 'prisoner' of Yanukovych system," *Kyiv Post*, March 6, 2014, https://www.kyivpost.com/article/content/ukraine-politics/kharkivs-kernes-justifies-his-180-degree-political-turn-by-saying-he-was-prisoner-of-yanukovych-system-338568.html.)

112. Full size replicas of 770, as it is popularly known, can be found in cities around the world, including Jerusalem, Kfar Chabad, Sao Paulo, and elsewhere. Among Chabadniks, its likeness is also used to adorn charity boxes, phylactery bags, and other Judaica items.

113. Sam Sokol, "In Kharkov, life continues as usual but Jews are wary," *Jerusalem Post*, May 29, 2014, http://www.jpost.com/Jewish-World/Jewish-Features/In-Kharkov-life-continues-as-usual-but-Jews-are-wary-354714.

114. Udi Segal, "The Foreign Ministry versus the Jewish Agency," Mako, May 28, 2014, https://www.mako.co.il/news-military/israel/Article-35986311a844641004.htm?sCh=31750a2610f26110&pId=237936823 (in Hebrew).

115. "Jewish Agency accused of leaking Ukraine evacuation plans," Jewish Telegraphic Agency, May 29, 2014, https://www.jta.org/2014/05/29/news-opinion/israel-middle-east/plans-to-evacuate-Ukrainian-jews-leaked-to-media-foreign-ministry-charges.

116. On May 27, the Jewish Agency issued a press release describing how it "rescue[d a] group of immigrants from Donetsk." In the release, chairman Natan Sharansky stated that "Jewish Agency representatives in Ukraine continue to be active in all areas and are prepared for any eventuality, as shown by this latest event in my own city of birth, Donetsk. Due to the current situation in the country, we have significantly expanded our activities, assisting those who wish to immigrate to Israel, bringing young people to experience life in Israel on a variety of Jewish Agency programs, providing Hebrew classes, and so on." He also stated that during the first four months of the year, *aliya* had increased by 142 percent over the same period the previous year. This was picked up by local media, which dutifully reported it. See "Sohnut stepped up the export of Jews from the Donbas," Vesti, May 28, 2014, https://web.archive.org/web/20140531040428/http://vesti.ua/donbass/53940-sohnut-aktiviziroval-vyvoz-evreev-iz-donbassa (in Russian).

117. See Sam Sokol, "From Kiev to Donetsk," *Jerusalem Post*, June 19, 2014, http://www.jpost.com/Magazine/Features/From-Kiev-to-Donetsk-Covering-Ukraines-journey-from-protests-to-civil-war-359881; Sam Sokol, "Donetsk's 11,000 Jews live in fear of rising violence," *Jerusalem Post*, May 30, 2014, http://www.jpost.com/Jewish-World/Jewish-News/Donetsks-11000-Jews-live-in-fear-of-rising-violence-354862.

118. "Ukrainian businessman Rabinovich decided to run for president," Lenta, March 25, 2014, https://lenta.ru/news/2014/03/25/rabinovich/ (in Russian).

119. Cnaan Liphshiz, "For Ukrainian Jews, far-right's electoral defeat is proof that Putin lied," Jewish Telegraphic Agency, June 2, 2014, https://www.jta.org/2014/06/02/news-opinion/world/for-Ukrainian-jews-far-rights-electoral-defeat-is-proof-that-putin-lied.

120. Likhachev recorded 23 such incidents over the course of the year within both Ukrainian and separatist-held territory. According to his figures, incidents of vandalism had held steady at nine annually since 2011, having fallen from a peak of 21 in 2006. Sam Sokol, "Report: Anti-semitic vandalism spiked in Ukraine in 2014," *Jerusalem Post*, May 10, 2015, http://www.jpost.com/Diaspora/Report-Anti-Semitic-vandalism-spiked-in-Ukraine-in-2014-402631.

121. "Report: armed men threatened to burn down Ukrainian rabbi's home," Jewish Telegraphic Agency, June 2, 2014, https://www.jta.org/2014/06/02/news-opinion/world/report-armed-men-threaten-to-burn-down-Ukrainian-rabbis-home. Later that month, Oleksandr Feldman claimed to have been accosted in an antisemitic incident. However, a video of the altercation (http://youtu.be/El Al6_ijgF8) showed that no antisemitic epithets had been uttered.

122. Zvika Gronich, "Uman: Antisemitic assault in Mikveh," Kikar Ha-Shabbat, June 26, 2014, https://tinyurl.com/y6ux7zux (in Hebrew).

123. See http://www.unhcr.org/53ad57099.html.

124. Alec Luhn, "Donetsk becomes a ghost town as fearful residents flee conflict," *Guardian*, July 6, 2014, https://www.theguardian.com/world/2014/jul/06/ukraine-crisis-donetsk.

125. "Berlin simplifies immigration procedures for Jews from Ukraine," Interfax-Ukraine, July 1, 2014, https://www.kyivpost.com/article/content/ukraine-politics/berlin-simplifies-immigration-procedures-for-jews-from-ukraine-354181.html.

126. Another, smaller camp would subsequently be established in the city of Shpola in September. It is of lesser importance as it only played a minor role in the Jewish migration from the Donbas. See Amie Ferris-Rotman, "The Scattering of Ukraine's Jews," *Atlantic*, September 21, 2014, https://www.theatlantic.com/international/archive/2014/09/ukraine-jewish-community-israel/380515/.

127. Sam Sokol, "Donetsk Jewish community struggles to hold together under fire," *Jerusalem Post*, July 27, 2014, http://www.jpost.com/Jewish-World/Jewish-Features/Donetsk-Jewish-community-struggles-to-hold-together-under-fire-369090.

128. Cnaan Liphshiz, "At Crimean Holocaust event, a chance to burnish Russia's image as defender of minorities," Jewish Telegraphic Agency, July 14, 2014, https://www.jta.org/2014/07/14/arts-entertainment/at-high-profile-crimean-holocaust-event-a-chance-to-burnish-russias-image-as-defender-of-minorities.

129. See http://en.kremlin.ru/events/president/news/46180.

130. Moscow's claim to be acting in the interests of local minorities is suspect in light of its suppression of the local Crimean Tatar population. See https://www.hrw.org/news/2016/03/18/ukraine-fear-repression-crimea.

131. Sam Sokol, "Israel's chief rabbis deny claims they'll take part in controversial Holocaust memorial in Crimea," *Jerusalem Post*, July 7, 2014, http://www.jpost.com/Jewish-World/Jewish-Features/Israels-chief-rabbis-deny-claims-theyll-take-part-in-controversial-Holocaust-memorial-in-Crimea-361723.

132. The initial invitation listed Lau and made no mention of Yosef. After this author asked why Lau was listed, given that his office stated he was not participating, an updated list was sent containing Yosef's name. The Israeli foreign ministry likewise stated that there had been no effort to arrange the rabbis' participation through regular diplomatic channels.

133. Part of that assistance was a promise that Russia would provide the funding for the completion of a local synagogue/community center in Sevastopol and that the Federation of Jewish Communities of Russia would likewise construct a new Jewish center in Simferopol. See Avi Hofmann, "Crimean Foray," *Jerusalem Report*, August 25, 2014, http://www.jpost.com/Jerusalem-Report/Crimean-foray-372238; and Andrey Melnikov, "Anticipation of the 'Jewish wars' in the Crimea," *Nezavisimaya Gazeta*, August 6, 2014, http://www.ng.ru/ng_religii/2014-08-06/4_jews.html (in Russian).

134. See http://www.djc.com.ua/news/view/new/?id=11797&lang=ru (in Russian).

135. Dmitry Mezentsev, "Alexander Dugin: 'Ukraine in the hands of homosexuals and Jewish oligarchs,'" Krymskaya Pravda, May 28, 2014, http://c-pravda.ru/newspapers/2014/05/29/aleksandr-dugin-ukraina-v-rukakh-gomoseksualistov-i-evrejjskikh-oligarkhov (in Russian), no longer available online (emphasis mine).

136. In the video, the Hasidic Jews entered before their security detail. I have uploaded a copy of the video on YouTube for those unable to access Gendin's Facebook page. See "Russian rabbis entering the Ner Tamid synagogue in Simferopol," YouTube video, 10:20. Posted by Samuel Sokol, November 14, 2017, https://www.youtube.com/watch?v=MKRqouTDDNA&feature=youtu.be.

137. See https://www.facebook.com/gendin.anatoliy/videos/vb.10000 0351973467/789539867734405/?type=2&theater.

138. Gendin also complained bitterly about the Dnipropetrovsk Jewish community. He blamed Ihor Kolomoisky, the community's financial backer, of stealing nearly 40,000 hryvnia of his community's money that had been deposited in Privatbank, of which he was a major shareholder. Gendin criticized Dnipropetrovsk's orthodox chief rabbi rabbi of failing to condemn Kolomoisky and accused him of collecting aid through the synagogue for "soldiers of the National Guard who are engaged in the murder and robbery of their fellow citizens." He offered no proof to back up his assertion. Owners of accounts throughout Crimea made similar accusations against Privatbank during the post-annexation banking crisis. See Steve Stecklow, Elizabeth Piper, and Oleksandr Akymenko, "Special Report: Crimean savers ask: Where's our money?," Reuters, November 20, 2014, https://www.reuters.com/ article/us-ukraine-crisis-banks-specialreport/special-report-crimean-savers-ask-wheres-our-money-idUSKCN0J40FJ20141120.

139. "Russia vs. Ukraine, Chabad vs. Reform," Jewish Telegraphic Agency, July 14, 2014, http://www.timesofisrael.com/russia-vs-ukraine-chabad-vs-reform/.

140. Dovid Margolin, "In Chaos of Ukraine, Dnepropetrovsk Again Stands as a Beacon of Refuge," Chabad.org, October 7, 2014, http://www.chabad.org/news/article_cdo/aid/2725375/jewish/In-Chaos-of-Ukraine-Dnepropetrovsk-Again-Stands-as-a-Beacon-of-Refuge.htm.

141. Sam Sokol, "Unable to flee, elderly Jews remain behind in eastern Ukraine," *Jerusalem Post*, September 19, 2014, http://www.jpost .com/Diaspora/Unable-to-flee-elderly-Jews-remain-behind-in-eastern-Ukraine-375806.

142. Briefing paper prepared by the Jewish Agency's Unit for Russian-Speaking Jewry on December 9, 2014.

143. I had asked multiple colleagues who had reported on the European migrant crisis about the tee shirts. Not one could recall seeing any other organization present refugees in its care to reporters in such a fashion. The omnipresent branding wasn't surprising, given Eckstein's penchant for self-promotion. The 66-year-old rabbi's clean-shaven visage was well known from the Fellowship's American television commercials, and for many tourists landing

in Tel Aviv, their first sight in Israel was Eckstein's face beaming from advertisements along the course of the jetway as they made their way off their planes.

In late 2014, Eckstein, a longtime donor, ceased supporting the Jewish Agency after the organization turned down a list of 22 demands that would "create wide publicity buzz" for the Fellowship. Judy Maltz, "Jewish Agency Loses Key Christian Funder Over PR Demands," *Haaretz*, October 26, 2014, https://www.haaretz.com/jewish/.premium-1.622398.

These tensions led to the Fellowship establishing its own *aliya* organization to compete with the Agency which in turn resulted in a public spat between the two organizations. Sam Sokol, "Jewish Agency, IFCJ spar over Ukrainian immigration," *Jerusalem Post*, March 30, 2014, http://www.jpost.com/Diaspora/Jewish-Agency-IFCJ-spar-over-Ukrainian-immigration-395544.

144. Sam Sokol, "In Zhytomyr, Jewish refugees find both safety and uncertainty," *Jerusalem Post*, August 6, 2014, http://www.jpost.com/Jewish-World/Jewish-Features/In-Zhytomyr-Jewish-refugees-find-both-safety-and-uncertainty-370247.

145. See "Jewish mother and daughter killed in Ukraine shelling," Jewish Telegraphic Agency, July 20, 2014, https://www.jta.org/2014/07/20/news-opinion/world/two-Ukrainian-jews-killed-in-shelling-in-lugansk and https://web.archive.org/web/20140722162816/http://jewishlugansk.com:80/news/?id=860#.Wg29ULD1XSw.

146. Gopin elaborated on these rescue efforts during a subsequent interview with *Israel HaYom*. "A Jewish woman rented an apartment in a nearby town and contacted smugglers from all sorts of organizations, Christian missionaries, who finished the task. It reminded me a lot of a military operation," he told the Israeli daily. "In the last three weeks, approximately 80 Jews were smuggled out. I don't understand how people manage to survive there for over a month, when they are living just on bread and vegetables that are smuggled in there." "Fleeing the inferno," *Israel HaYom*, September 12, 2014, http://www.israelhayom.com/2017/07/20/fleeing-the-inferno/.

147. Sam Sokol, "Fleeing unrest, Ukrainian Jews arrive in Israel," *Jerusalem Post*, September 22, 2014, http://www.jpost.com/Diaspora/Fleeing-unrest-Ukrainian-Jews-arrive-in-Israel-376065.

148. Sam Sokol, "Sharansky predicts further growth in Ukrainian aliyah," *Jerusalem Post*, September 29, 2014, http://www.jpost .com/Diaspora/Sharansky-predicts-further-growth-in-Ukrainian-aliyah-376599.

149. Sam Sokol, "At Jewish Agency Board Meeting, Future of Aliyah Very Much on the Mind," *Jerusalem Post*, October 25, 2014, http://www.jpost.com/Diaspora/At-Jewish-Agency-board-meeting-future-of-aliyah-very-much-on-the-mind-430027.

150. By August 22, there were approximately 20,000 IDPs living in "dire conditions" in or near Mariupol, according to the United Nations Office for the Coordination of Humanitarian Affairs. In a contemporaneous report, the agency reported that these people were "sleep[ing] in tents, cars or decrepit summer camp facilities which have been unused for years, and lack the most basic services, such as access to water." See OCHA Ukraine Situation Report no. 8, Kyiv, August 2014, https://www.humanitarianresponse.info/ sites/www.humanitarianresponse.info/files/documents/files/OCHA %20Ukraine%20Situation%20Report%2022%20August%202014 _1.pdf.

151. See https://web.archive.org/web/20140721232043/http://www.mer .dn.ua/news_echo.php?id_news=9832.

152. See https://web.archive.org/web/20140721232040/http://www.mer .dn.ua/news_echo.php?id_news=9829.

153. See Charles Miranda, "Donetsk train station under fire with reports that Ukrainian army is attacking rebel stronghold," news.com.au, July 22, 2014, http://www.news.com.au/travel/travel-updates/inci dents/donetsk-train-station-under-fire-with-reports-that-Ukrain ian-army-is-attacking-rebel-stronghold/news-story/2e7a912c24d e44078fe886a8c14ddee7.

154. The Lubavitcher Rebbe had a custom of handing out dollar bills during public receptions at 770. These bills were supposed to be given to charity but Hasidim would often keep the bills and instead donate money that had not been handled by the Rebbe. These bills are treasured by Chabad Hasidim. Vishedski described the letters and dollars as items which were "very, very precious to me that I wanted to keep with me at all times."

155. See http://www.jewishvirtuallibrary.org/donetsk.

156. Ukraine lost much of its Jewish population during the "great migration" of the late 1980s-early 1990s. For a detailed breakdown

of post-Soviet migration patterns, see http://www.yivoency
clopedia.org/article.aspx/Population_and_Migration/Migration
_since_World_War_I#id0epybi. According to Ukrainian census
data, the "nucleus" (those with two Jewish parents) of the Jewish
community of Ukraine stood at 120,525 in 2002, down from
487,300 in 1989. By 2010, the "core" Jewish community numbered
some 71,500 people, according to Hebrew University demo-
grapher Sergio Della Pergola. In addition to emigration, Ukrainian Jewry also contracted due to extremely high levels of intermarriage and low birthrates. See Darina Privalko, *Jewish Life in
Ukraine: Achievements, Challenges and Priorities from the Collapse of Communism to 2013* (London: Institute for Jewish Policy
Research. September 2014), http://archive.jpr.org.uk/object-ukr2.

157. Dovid Margolin, "Prominent Member of Jewish Community Shot
and Killed in Donetsk, Ukraine," Chabad.org, September 4, 2014,
http://www.chabad.org/news/article_cdo/aid/2690382/jewish/
Prominent-Member-of-Jewish-Community-Shot-and-Killed-in-
Donetsk-Ukraine.htm.

158. See http://eajc.org/page34/news47426.html.

159. Dovid Margolin, "Mariupol Jewish Community Sits Tight as Tanks
From Russia Roll Into Ukraine," Chabad.org, August 27, 2014,
http://www.chabad.org/news/article_cdo/aid/2683242/jewish/Ma
riupol-Jewish-Community-Sits-Tight-as-Tanks-From-Russia-Roll-
Into-Ukraine.htm.

160. For a day-by-day description of the Battle for Mariupol, read
Noland Peterson, "Lighting and thunder: diary of the siege of
Mariupol," *Newsweek*, September 10, 2016, http://www.newsweek
.com/lightning-and-thunder-diary-siege-mariupol-495901.

161. Ibid.

162. Sam Sokol, "Fearing rebels, Donetsk's Jews flee Mariupol," *Jerusalem Post*, September 10, 2014, http://www.jpost.com/printarticle
.aspx?id=374913.

163. Sam Sokol, "Displaced Jews in Ukraine are once again in harms
way," *Jerusalem Post*, September 1, 2014, http://www.jpost.com/
printarticle.aspx?id=373047#.

164. Parts of this chapter are based on my feature article "The forgotten
Jews," which was published in the *Jerusalem Post* Magazine on
October 2, 2014. It has been expanded and supplemented with

additional material, including numerous first person interviews, for this book.

165. In all, the Jewish Agency only employed four emissaries, each with around fifteen staffers, in all of Ukraine, according to Nabitovsky.

166. "These are people who are in a cage from the trauma that they went through, and we said that we need to maybe try to find for them something to keep them busy. And we said if they are already arriving on the way to Israel, it is important and correct to learn Hebrew," Nabitovsky explained.

167. For a further description of the conditions Larissa described, see "Donetsk separatists impose martial law, night curfew," *Kyiv Post*, July 16, 2014, https://www.kyivpost.com/article/content/ukraine-politics/donetsk-separatists-impose-martial-law-night-curfew-356288.html; Charles Recknagel and Merhat Sharipzhan, "Donetsk Separatists Dig In For Street Fighting," RFE/RL, July 17, 2014, https://www.rferl.org/a/ukraine-donetsk-separatists-dig-in/25460807.html.

168. See David Blair, "Beaten and threatened: the 'Donetsk People's Republic' turns on city's priests," *Telegraph*, June 18, 2014, http://www.telegraph.co.uk/news/worldnews/europe/ukraine/10880652/Beaten-and-threatened-the-Donetsk-Peoples-Republic-turns-on-citys-priests.html.

169. See Christopher Miller, "Hundreds of People Have Disappeared in Eastern Ukraine," Mashable, June 30, 2014, http://mashable.com/2014/06/30/hundreds-kidnapped-eastern-ukraine/#_.9OBwcapmqq.

170. *You Don't Exist: Arbitrary Detentions, Enforced Disappearances, and Torture in Eastern Ukraine* (London: Amnesty International, July 2016), https://www.amnesty.org/en/documents/eur50/4455/2016/en/.

171. See https://www.hrw.org/news/2014/09/04/ukraine-rebels-subject-civilians-forced-labor.

172. See http://www.yadvashem.org/untoldstories/database/index.asp?cid=283.

173. See http://www.jewishvirtuallibrary.org/dnepropetrovsk.

174. See Sam Sokol, "19 weddings and a refugee crisis," *Jerusalem Post*, September 15, 2014, http://www.jpost.com/printarticle.aspx?id=375358.

175. See Shimon Briman, "Josef Zissels: A Ukrainian Jewry Is Being Created," Ukrainian Jewish Encounter, March 6, 2017, https://Ukrainianjewishencounter.org/en/josef-zissels-Ukrainian-jewry-created/.

176. See Babylonian Talmud, Tractate Shavuot 39a: *"Kol Yisrael Arevim Ze Laze."* This concept is generally understood to provide the philosophical-legal underpinnings of a Talmudic obligation of Jewish solidarity and is frequently invoked to mobilize Jews to assist their less fortunate brethren, both locally and across the global Diaspora.

177. See Sam Sokol, "Ukraine's chief rabbi to 'Post': We've lost most local donors," *Jerusalem Post*, March 14, 2014, http://www.jpost.com/printarticle.aspx?id=345354.

178. Cnaan Liphshiz, "Ukraine fiscal crisis leads to major setback for homegrown Jewish philanthropy," Jewish Telegraphic Agency, July 29, 2015, https://www.jta.org/2015/07/29/news-opinion/world/ukraine-fiscal-crisis-leads-to-major-setback-for-homegrown-jewish-philanthropy.

179. See World Bank, "Ukraine: Economic Update," April 29, 2015, http://www.worldbank.org/content/dam/Worldbank/document/eca/ukraine/ua-macro-april-2015-en.pdf.

180. These groups included the IFCJ, JDC, World Jewish Relief and the Combined Jewish Philanthropies of Boston.

181. See Sam Sokol, "Unable to flee, elderly Jews remain behind in eastern Ukraine," *Jerusalem Post*, September 19, 2014, http://www.jpost.com/printarticle.aspx?id=375806.

182. This section incorporates material from my article "Here we stand and here we stay," *Jerusalem Post*, September 18, 2014, http://www.jpost.com/printarticle.aspx?id=375667, as well as previously unpublished segments of interviews conducted during the course of reporting that story.

183. The local orthodox community and the Hesed each provided a different tally of Donetsk Jews who stayed in the city. It is possible that this discrepancy was caused by the Hesed tracking people who arrived on their own and were not in contact with Chabad.

184. See https://www.bellingcat.com/tag/mh17/.

185. This number conflates refugees and IDPs and is based on a United Nations funding appeal. See http://www.emro.who.int/syr/syria-news/response-plan-2015.html.

186. This sentiment echoed statements I had heard in many other interviews, and while immigration to Israel was up (sharply) many locals still expressed an extreme reluctance to countenance leaving their country.

187. See Anton Shekhovtsov, "Patriot of Ukraine and Maidan," The Interpreter, January 9, 2015, http://www.interpretermag.com/a-comment-on-the-involvement-of-the-patriot-of-ukraine-in-the-Ukrainian-revolution/.

188. Tom Parfitt, "Ukraine crisis: the neo-Nazi brigade fighting pro-Russian separatists," *Telegraph*, August 11, 2014, http://www.telegraph.co.uk/news/worldnews/europe/ukraine/11025137/Ukraine-crisis-the-neo-Nazi-brigade-fighting-pro-Russian-separatists.html. See also Shaun Walker, "Azov fighters are Ukraine's greatest weapon and may be its greatest threat," *Guardian*, September 10, 2014, https://www.theguardian.com/world/2014/sep/10/azov-far-right-fighters-ukraine-neo-nazis. Likhachev has asserted that, despite its members harsh rhetoric, not everybody in the battalion was a neo-Nazi and that for many people the only option for fighting against the separatists was to join volunteer units headed to the front, regardless of their ideological orientation. Zissels has asserted (see https://nv.ua/publications/odin-iz-samyh-vliyatelnyh-otechestvennyh-evreev-stavit-neuteshitelnyy-diagnoz-ukraine-4 6467.html) that a number of Jews fought in Azov, although given his previous claims regarding Jewish members of the Heavenly Hundred, this assertion is suspect. Natan Chazin claimed to have served briefly with Azov, but this has been difficult to verify. This affiliation has been been reported by several news outlets (see https://112.ua/statji/ierusalimskiy-manevr-ukrainy-i-ego-celi-426 747.html and https://www.theparisreview.org/blog/2017/02/28/letter-from-kiev/), but Chazin's general lack of credibility (which will be discussed in a subsequent note) makes it difficult to accept at face value. Nolan Peterson, writing for the Daily Signal, reported that there were Jews in the unit (http://dailysignal.com/2015/08/10/meet-the-former-neo-nazi-spokesman-who-now-fights-for-freedom-in-ukraine/), but it is instructive that not one correspondent who wrote about or embedded with Azov has identified any Jewish members by name or written a dedicated piece about their experience, even though for most journalists such a story would be incredibly attractive. It is certainly possible that he did

serve in Azov. When asked for proof, Chazin initially responded with profanity but subsequently pointed me to a Radio Svoboda video of him participating in the funeral of a battalion member killed in Mariupol. See "A warfighter of the Interior Ministry's special task unit Azov was fatally shot in the back by terrorists—the Azov Battalion deputy leader," YouTube video, 3:10. Posted by Radio Svoboda Ukraine, May 12, 2014, https://www.youtube.com/watch?v=1x0XKtoi6-4 (in Ukrainian).

189. Aleksandar Vasovic, "Frontline city in east Ukraine imposes tough new security measures," Reuters, September 10, 2014, https://www.yahoo.com/news/frontline-city-east-ukraine-imposes-tough-security-measures-144318865.html.

190. Sam Sokol, "Fleeing unrest, Ukrainian Jews arrive in Israel," *Jerusalem Post*, September 22, 2014, http://www.jpost.com/print article.aspx?id=376065.

191. For a Hasidic explanation of the pilgrimage, see https://www.breslev.co.il/html/rebbe_nachmans_gravesite.aspx?id=21&language=english.

192. Cnaan Liphshiz, "As Uman pilgrimage grows, the devout invent new customs," Jewish Telegraphic Agency, October 15, 2013, https://www.jta.org/2013/10/15/news-opinion/world/as-uman-pilgrimage-turns-mainstream-a-hard-core-invents-new-customs.

193. See Cnaan Liphshiz, "What happens in Uman stays in Uman," Jewish Telegraphic Agency, September 12, 2012, http://www.timesofisrael.com/what-happens-in-uman-stays-in-uman/; "Jewish pilgrims in Ukraine trigger brawl by shooting local with BB gun," Jewish Telegraphic Agency, June 16, 2016, https://www.timesofisrael.com/jewish-pilgrims-in-ukraine-trigger-brawl-by-shooting-local-with-bb-gun/; "Chief Ukrainian rabbi: Remove 'provocative' cross," Jewish Telegraphic Agency, August 22, 2013, https://www.timesofisrael.com/chief-Ukrainian-rabbi-remove-provocative-cross/; Itamar Eichner, "2 Breslov Hasidim lightly hurt in grenade explosion in Uman," Ynetnews, September 21, 2017, https://www.ynetnews.com/articles/0,7340,L-5019420,00.html; "Ukrainian nationalists destroy Hasidic tent city at rabbi's grave in Uman," Jewish Telegraphic Agency, September 9, 2015, https://www.timesofisrael.com/Ukrainian-nationalists-destroy-hasidic-tent-city-at-rabbis-grave-in-uman/; Sam Sokol, "I Thought There Was Going to Be a Pogrom," *Mishpacha*, December 28, 2016, http://www.mish

pacha.com/Browse/Article/7002/I-Thought-There-Was-Going-to-Be-a-Pogrom.

194. "Ten Hasidic pilgrims guilty of disorderly conduct in Uman deported from Ukraine to Israel," Interfax-Ukraine, September 13, 2010, http://en.interfax.com.ua/news/general/48186.html; Marcy Oster," Jewish Telegraphic Agency, September 26, 2010, https://www.jta.org/2010/09/26/news-opinion/world/israeli-chasid-killed-in-uman; Ben Hartman, "Israeli in custody after stabbing Ukrainian man in Uman," *Jerusalem Post*, September 11, 2010, http://www.jpost.com/Jewish-World/Jewish-News/Israeli-in-custody-for-stabbing-Ukrainian-man-in-Uman.

195. Sam Sokol, "Despite war, Breslov hasidim plan on making Ukraine pilgrimage," *Jerusalem Post*, September 18, 2014, http://www.jpost.com/Magazine/Despite-war-Breslov-Hassidim-plan-on-making-Ukraine-pilgrimage-375702.

196. See Shimon Ifergen, "Hasidic Pilgrims and Ukrainian Sex Workers: Prayer and Pleasure in Uman," *Haaretz*, July 5, 2015, https://www.haaretz.com/jewish/.premium-prayer-and-pleasure-in-uman-1.5375280.

197. Sam Sokol, "In Ukraine, Jews mark vastly different new years," *Jerusalem Post*, September 29, 2014, http://www.jpost.com/printarticle.aspx?id=376544.

198. "Vandals attack Jews," *Jewish Observer*, http://jew-observer.com/antisemitizm/vandaly-atakuyut-evreev/ (in Russian). Several days after this incident, at a ceremony marking the 73rd anniversary of the Babi Yar massacre, President Poroshenko made assurances that Ukraine would never allow fascism to take root. See Sam Sokol, "Reports of anti-Semitism in Odessa highlights use of Jews in wartime propaganda," *Jerusalem Post*, October 12, 2014, http://www.jpost.com/printarticle.aspx?id=378664. Kyiv Mayor Vitali Klitschko also responded, calling for additional security for Jewish institutions. See Sam Sokol, "Ukrainian official: Jews 'among the best protectors of our country,'" *Jerusalem Post*, October 2, 2014, http://www.jpost.com/printarticle.aspx?id=377940.

199. Ibid.

200. The vandalism against Babi Yar would continue and become a regular occurrence. See Sam Sokol, "Babi Yar as a Symbol of Holocaust Distortion in Post-Maidan Ukraine," *Israel Journal of Foreign Affairs* (2017), doi:10.1080/23739770.2017.1315694.

201. See "Hasidim in Uman raise money for anti-terrorist operation forces," YouTube video, 3:45. Posted by Breaking news ICTV, September 11, 2014, https://www.youtube.com/watch?time_con tinue=24&v=SE0_IxYf_uM. The phrase "Slava Ukrainy," accompanied by a "fascist-style hand salute," was used by members of the OUN(b) and the UPA. It was traditionally met with a response of "Heroiam slava" (glory to the heroes). See Ivan Katchanovski, "The Politics of World War II in Contemporary Ukraine," *Journal of Slavic Military Studies* 27, no. 2 (2014): 210-233, doi:10.1080/13 518046.2013.844493; Per Anders Rudling, "Memories of 'Holodomor' and National Socialism in Ukrainian Political Culture," in *Rekonstruktion des Nationalmythos? Frankreich, Deutschland und die Ukraine im Vergleich*, ed. Yves Bizeul (Göttingen: Vandenhoeck & Ruprecht Unipress, 2013), 227-258, doi:10.14220/978 3737001816.227.

202. Sam Sokol, "Ukrainian official: Jews 'among the best protectors of our country,'" *Jerusalem Post*, October 2, 2014, http://www.jpost .com/printarticle.aspx?id=377940.

203. David E. Fishman, "Moscow Tear Gas Attack Shows Rise of Anti-Semitism in Putin Era," *Jewish Daily Forward*, October 12, 2014, https://forward.com/news/207171/moscow-tear-gas-attack-shows-rise-of-anti-semitism/.

204. Ibid.

CHAPTER FOUR

1. Nikolay Koposov, *Memory Laws, Memory Wars: The Politics of the Past in Europe and Russia* (Cambridge; Cambridge University Press, 2018), 280.

2. Serhii Plokhy, *The Gates of Europe: A History of Ukraine* (New York: Basic Books, 2015), 189-190.

3. See http://www.yadvashem.org/untoldstories/database/index.asp? cid=292.

4. David Patrikarakos, *War in 140 Characters: How Social Media is Reshaping Conflict in the Twenty-First Century* (New York: Basic Books, 2017), 146. I noted earlier that Russian propaganda was intended to delegitimize Kyiv while at the same time rallying domestic support for Putin's agenda. Patrikarakos described another

aim of Kremlin propaganda, namely stirring up sympathy for Russian intervention among the residents of eastern Ukraine. "The people I spoke to did not articulate complaints so much as repeat mantras about fascist juntas and the ubiquity of Pravy Sektor terrorists, mantras that existed only on Russian TV and the Internet—that is to say, in the Kremlin's imagination," he wrote. "The influence of domestic Russian-language channels on elderly eastern Ukrainians and of the articles and memes on VKontakte among the youth I met was almost total." Ibid., 159. On a number of occasions, Jewish communal representatives told me that they believed that sympathy for Russia was more prevalent among the elderly, who grew up under the Soviet system.

5. "Right Sector radicals terrorize Jewish community of Odessa," Pravda, October 7, 2014, http://www.pravdareport.com/news/hot spots/07-10-2014/128737-right_sector_odessa_jews-0/.

6. "Jewish community of Odessa wants to disperse 'Right Sector,'" *Izvestia*, October 1, 2014, https://iz.ru/news/577432 (in Russian).

7. Chabad of Odessa issued a statement on its website asserting that Maiman was "not only not a leader of the community, but does not even belong to it. Mikhail Maiman does not appear in any of the community databases, and, it seems, does not exist at all." See http://www.chabad.odessa.ua/templates/blog/post_cdo/aid/1658 934/postid/49169.

8. Sam Sokol, "Reports of anti-Semitism in Odessa highlights use of Jews in wartime propaganda," *Jerusalem Post*, October 12, 2014, http://www.jpost.com/printarticle.aspx?id=378664.

9. In fact, Chief Rabbi Bleich seemed rather calm about the incident. Asked about the firebomb and the graffiti, the rabbi, who had blamed several antisemitic incidents over the past year on Russian provocateurs, said that "it doesn't feel very frightening" at all. Eduard Dolinsky, a figure usually much more outspoken about issues of antisemitism than other Ukrainian Jews, expressed a similar sentiment, stating that while the attack was alarming, "anti-Semitism is not a danger." However, given his track record, it is hard to believe that Dolinsky would pull his punches on anti-semitism for any government figure. Sam Sokol, "Ukrainian official: Jews 'among the best protectors of our country,'" *Jerusalem Post*, October 2, 2014, http://www.jpost.com/printarticle.aspx?id= 377940.

10. Sam Sokol, "Ukrainian official: Jews 'among the best protectors of our country,'" *Jerusalem Post*, October 2, 2014, http://www.jpost.com/printarticle.aspx?id=377940.

11. Sam Sokol, "Report: Anti-Semitic vandalism spiked in Ukraine in 2014," *Jerusalem Post*, May 10, 2015, http://www.jpost.com/printarticle.aspx?id=402631.

12. See Sam Sokol, "Babi Yar Holocaust site vandalized for sixth time this year," *Jerusalem Post*, September 16, 2015, http://www.jpost.com/printarticle.aspx?id=416306 and http://khpg.org/en/index.php?id=1442244524&w=babi+yar.

13. Sam Sokol, "Ukrainian Jews demand protection for Holocaust sites," *Jerusalem Post*, September 24, 2015, http://www.jpost.com/printarticle.aspx?id=419037.

14. See https://www.academia.edu/35921427/Yatsenyuk_letter_to_Robert_Singer_on_Babyn_Yar_vandalism_2015. See also Sam Sokol, "Ukrainian PM: attacks on Babi Yar are meant to 'destabilize' us," *Jerusalem Post*, September 30, 2015, http://www.jpost.com/printarticle.aspx?id=419443.

15. Borislav Bereza, "'Anti-semitism' in Ukraine: Standing ovation in Moscow," Obozrevatel, December 26, 2017, https://www.obozrevatel.com/society/antisemitizm-v-ukraine-v-moskve-aplodiruyut-stoya/amp.htm?__twitter_impression=true (in Russian). It is instructive that Yatsenyuk's letter after the Babi Yar vandalism was significantly different from his response to the Donetsk flyer incident, when he called for Ukraine's security services to find the "bastards and to bring them to justice." Erik Wasson, "Ukraine PM: Find anti-Jewish 'bastards,'" *The Hill*, http://thehill.com/policy/international/203928-ukraine-pm-orders-troops-to-find-anti-jewish-bastards?amp.

16. In the Kantor Center's annual antisemitism report for 2014, researcher Irena Cantorovich discussed the idea of "provocative antisemitism," which she defined as "antisemitic incidents in which the motive behind them can be either pure antisemitism or an attempt to prove that the other side in the Russian-Ukrainian conflict is antisemitic or at least is not able to protect the Jews. 'Provocative antisemitism' was most probably behind attacks against Jews in Kiev in January, February, and March; distribution of leaflets, allegedly by pro-Russian separatists calling Donetsk Jews to register in April; desecration of Jewish institutions in

Odessa in May; etc." See Dina Porat, ed., *Antisemitism Worldwide 2014* (Tel Aviv: Tel Aviv University Kantor Center for the Study of Contemporary European Jewry, 2015), http://www.kantorcenter .tau.ac.il/sites/default/files/Doch2014-2.pdf.

17. Oskar Górzyński, "Russia's Covert Campaign to Inflame East Europe," *The Daily Beast*, March 2, 2018, https://www.thedaily beast.com/russias-covert-campaign-inflaming-east-europe.

18. See Valery Chepurko and Victoria Makarenko, "The Torpedo grouping, whose arrest was reported by Avakov, is even involved in organ trafficking," *KP*, October 3, 2017, https://kp.ua/incidents/ 588278-hruppyrovka-torpedy-o-zaderzhanyy-kotoroi-soobschyl- avakov-zameshana-dazhe-v-torhovle-orhanamy (in Russian); Valery Chepurko, "Avakovsky terrorists arrested as ordinary hooligans," *KP*, October 5, 2017, https://kp.ua/incidents/588603-avakovskykh- terrorystov-arestovaly-kak-obychnykh-khulyhanov (in Russian).

19. Sam Sokol, "Russia: Ukraine concealing crimes against Jews and other minorities," *Jerusalem Post*, November 10, 2014, http://www .pressreader.com/israel/jerusalem-post/20141110/281685433132245. Responding to Piskunov, the Vaad's Josef Zissels countered that it was "quite probable that over half of the antisemitic incidents of the recent year are provocations, committed to support and en- rich with facts the powerful propaganda campaign of the former Ukrainian and current Russian government against the democratic, pro-European movement in Ukraine."

Piskunov emailed me regularly with information and sup- posed corrections. This included the Russian Foreign Ministry's *White Book on Violations of Human Rights and the Rule of Law in Ukraine* and links to material that reflected badly on Ukraine. After one article in which I referred to Russia as a party to the Donbas war, he asserted that my use of the phrase "Ukrainian-Russian conflict" actually "contradicts international law, in particular, UN Security Council resolution 2202."

20. Nikolay Koposov, *Memory Laws, Memory Wars: The Politics of the Past in Europe and Russia* (Cambridge: Cambridge University Press, 2018), 178-179.

21. Shaun Walker, Leonid Ragozin, and Matthew Weaver, "Putin likens Ukraine's forces to Nazis and threatens standoff in the Arc- tic," *Guardian*, August 29, 2014, https://www.theguardian.com/ world/2014/aug/29/putin-ukraine-forces-nazis-arctic.

22. In an interview less than a year before the Euromaidan, RT editor-in-chief Margarita Simonyan stated explicitly that the network was the sort of "information weapon" that had been lacking during the 2008 Georgian war and was as necessary as a Ministry of Defense. See "Not going to pretend that I'm objective," Lenta.ru, March 7, 2013, http://archive.is/RzLyk#selection-485.0-488.0 (in Russian). This interview was cited by the Atlantic Council's Digital Forensic Research Lab, which asserted that "at critical moments, RT's support for Russian government positions has become even more explicit, adopting almost identical language to Kremlin statements. This is the most overt form of propaganda, literally propagating the government's messages in the very same words in which they are given." See "Question That: RT's Military Mission," Medium, January 7, 2018, https://medium.com/dfrlab/question-that-rts-military-mission-4c4bd9f72c88.

23. Lawrence Alexander and Aric Toler, "Pro-Russian Web Network Digs Up the Dirt on Kremlin Critics," Global Voices, August 10, 2015, https://globalvoices.org/2015/08/10/pro-russian-web-network-digs-up-the-dirt-on-kremlin-critics/#.

24. Andrei Soshnikov, "Inside a pro-Russia propaganda machine in Ukraine," BBC, November 13, 2017, http://www.bbc.com/news/blogs-trending-41915295. As we will later see, the leadership of both the DNR and the LNR have also publicly endorsed such claims.

25. "Russian Jews Push Back at Campaign Against Ukraine Oligarch," Jewish Telegraphic Agency, November 12, 2014, https://forward.com/news/breaking-news/209085/russian-jews-push-back-at-campaign-against-ukraine/.

26. Ibid.

27. Sam Sokol, "Demand for Jewish condemnation elicits limited backlash in Turkey," *Jerusalem Post*, August 31, 2014, http://www.jpost.com/Diaspora/Demand-for-Jewish-condemnation-elicits-limited-backlash-in-Turkey-372998.

28. Twitter conversation, December 2017.

29. Sam Sokol, "Election results buoy Ukrainian Jews," *Jerusalem Post*, October 27, 2014, http://www.jpost.com/printarticle.aspx?id=379969.

30. Ibid.

31. "Rada elects new Speaker," Ukrainska Pravda, November 27, 2014, https://www.pravda.com.ua/news/2014/11/27/7045630/ (in

Ukrainian). In response to Groysman's appointment, Jewish leaders stated that they did not believe that it had any great significance for their communities, characterizing the development as "just another proof that Ukraine is a normal multicultural society." However, one local stated that "whether the current fragile balance between Ukrainian Jews and ultra-right nationalists remains depends on a great variety of factors that are difficult to predict at the moment, from actual results of the economic policy of the new Ukrainian government and their impact on general well-being of the Ukrainian population to cessation of hostility from the side of the Eastern neighbor." See Sam Sokol, "Choice of Jew as Ukrainian parliament speaker won't have direct impact on community," *Jerusalem Post*, November 30, 2014, http://www.jpost.com/printarticle.aspx?id=383252.

32. "Svoboda party members in Ukrainian government resign—Deputy Premier Sych," Interfax-Ukraine, November 12, 2014, http://en.interfax.com.ua/news/general/234059.html.

33. Anton Shekhovtsov, "Ukraine's Parliamentary Elections and the Far Right," The Interpreter, October 26, 2014, http://www.interpretermag.com/ukraines-parliamentary-elections-and-the-far-right/.

34. Biletsky ran as an independent but later joined the newly formed Ukrop party of Jewish oligarch Hennadiy Korban. See "The Ministry of Justice registered the party of Kolomoisky," *Korrespondent*, June 18, 2015, https://ua.korrespondent.net/ukraine/3529272-minuist-zareiestruvav-partiui-kolomoiskoho (in Ukrainian).

35. Sam Sokol, "Ukrainian legislator toasts Adolf Hitler," *Jerusalem Post*, December 27, 2015, http://www.jpost.com/printarticle.aspx?id=438561.

36. "Ukraine Votes On Oct. 26 To Elect New Parliament," *Kyiv Post*, October 24, 2014, https://www.kyivpost.com/article/content/oct-26-parliamentary-election/ukraine-votes-on-oct-26-to-elect-new-parliament-369193.html.

37. See Anton Shekhovtsov, "Ukraine's Parliamentary Elections and the Far Right," The Interpreter, October 26, 2014, http://www.interpretermag.com/ukraines-parliamentary-elections-and-the-far-right/; Sam Sokol, "Kiev regional police head accused of neo-Nazi ties," *Jerusalem Post*, November 12, 2014, http://www.jpost.com/printarticle.aspx?id=381559.

38. See http://www.europarl.europa.eu/meetdocs/2014_2019/docu ments/d-ru/dv/12_dru_20141126_/12_dru_20141126_en.pdf. Lavrov's statement was somewhat ironic in light of the role of members of Hungary's far-right and antisemitic Jobbik party as monitors in the local (and illegal) elections held in the Russian-backed DNR and LNR only weeks earlier. See Csaba Tóth, "Pro-Russian Jobbik 'election observers' banned from Ukraine," Budapest Beacon, November 4, 2014, https://budapestbeacon.com/pro-russian-jobbik-election-observers-banned-ukraine/ and https://jobbik .com/jobbik_respects_results_donetsk_and_lugansk_elections.

39. See http://global100.adl.org/#map/eeurope; Sam Sokol and Maya Shwayder, "Poll: One quarter of adults worldwide 'deeply infected' with anti-Semitism," *Jerusalem Post*, May 13, 2014, http://www .jpost.com/printarticle.aspx?id=352154.

40. See Jesse Singal, "The ADL's Flawed Anti-Semitism Survey," The Cut, May 14, 2014, https://www.thecut.com/2014/05/adls-flawed-anti-semitism-survey.html.

41. Ivan Katchanovski, "Terrorists or national heroes? Politics and perceptions of the OUN and the UPA in Ukraine," *Communist and Post-Communist Studies* 48, nos. 2-3 (2015), http://dx.doi.org/ 10.1016/j.postcomstud.2015.06.006.

42. Ibid.

43. See http://ratingpro.org/en/research/discrimination-in-ukraine .html and http://ratinggroup.ua/research/ukraine/rasprostrane nie_diskriminaciy_v_ukraine.html. Fifty-six percent of respondents were neutral and a full 18 percent would approve of such a match.

44. "Tolerance of the Ukrainian Population," Kyiv International Institute of Sociology, November 16, 2010, http://www.kiis.com .ua/?lang=ukr&cat=reports&id=279&t=10&page=4.

45. I have purposefully refrained from using Vitaliy Nachmanovych's 2017 study "The Jewish Question in Ukraine: The Attitude of the Population" (in Ukrainian) (http://www.kiis.com.ua/materials/ articles/Evreyske_pitannya.pdf) as a source on this issue due to the author's close working relationship with Volodymyr Viatrovych and the UINM. Nachmanovych was also responsible for the erection of a sign in memory of Ivan Rohach, the editor of an antisemitic OUN(m) newspaper, at Babi Yar. See Natalia Swan, "Volodymyr Viatrovych: The ones who are preventing the

demounting of Shchors are to blame for the damage against it," Channel 24, May 4, 2017, https://24tv.ua/volodimir_vyatrovich_u_poshkodzhenni_shhorsa_vinni_ti_hto_zavazhaye_yogo_dem ontazhu_n813365; Sam Sokol, "Ukraine has only just begun its journey to the truth," *Jewish Chronicle*, October 6, 2016, https://www.thejc.com/news/world/ukraine-has-only-just-begun-its-jour ney-to-the-truth-1.53768. A study on attitudes toward minorities in Eastern Europe conducted by the Pew Research Center in 2015-2016 found that five percent of Ukrainians, the lowest number in the region, "would not accept Jews as fellow citizens." See http://www.pewresearch.org/fact-tank/2018/03/28/most-poles-accept-jews-as-fellow-citizens-and-neighbors-but-a-minority-do-not/. However, Katchanovski has asserted that the numbers in the Pew survey "lack reliability" and that "the percentages of those who did not accept Jews as citizens/residents of Ukraine are several times lower in this Pew survey compared to the annual surveys conducted by the Kyiv International Institute of Sociology." See https://www.facebook.com/photo.php?fbid=1955557641140779 &set=a.117187214977840.13788.100000596862745&type=3&thea ter. Michael Colborne, a journalist with a background in statistics and antisemitism, likewise questioned the survey, casting doubts on the way in which Pew structured its questions. See https://michaelcolborne.com/2018/03/29/on-the-use-and-abuse-of-statis tics-instrumentalizing-minorities-edition/.

46. Sam Sokol, "Ukrainian general calls for destruction of Jews," *Jewish Chronicle*, May 11, 2017, https://www.thejc.com/news/world/Ukrainian-general-calls-for-destruction-of-jews-1.438400.

47. Vladislav Davidzon, "Ukrainian Politician Nadia Savchenko Questions 'Jewish Yoke' Over Country," *Tablet*, March 28, 2017, http://www.tabletmag.com/scroll/228365/Ukrainian-politician-nadia-savchenko-questions-jewish-yoke-over-country.

48. "Hanging Jews amused the Ukrainian party," Coordination Forum for Countering Anti-Semitism, April 24, 2017, https://tinyurl.com/y95e95ls (in Russian).

49. "Saakashvili dismissed his press secretary for anti-Semitic statement against Poroshenko," MK.ru, September 19, 2017, http://www.mk.ru/politics/2017/09/19/saakashvili-otstranil-svoego-press sekretarya-za-antisemitskoe-vyskazyvanie-protiv-poroshenko.html (in Russian).

50. Sam Sokol, "Backlash over Ukrainian president's award for anti-semite," *Jewish Chronicle*, February 2, 2017, https://www.thejc.com/news/world/backlash-over-Ukrainian-president-s-award-for-anti semite-1.431900.

51. See http://www.vesti.ru/videos/show/vid/645287/cid/1/#.

52. Sam Sokol, "Ukrainian rights group blasts Russia for faking anti-Semitic news," *Jerusalem Post*, June 10, 2015, http://www.jpost .com/printarticle.aspx?id=405608.

53. Emphasis mine. I have uploaded a copy of the letter, which was republished on a number of websites, at https://www.academia .edu/35984441/Margolin_letter_regarding_Ukraine.

54. For more background on Eskin, see Shay Fogelman, "We Won," *Haaretz*, November 5, 2010, https://www.haaretz.com/1.5135481.

55. "A significant number of Ukrainian governors or local activists, for example, sincerely or out of common cowardice, from stupidity or from common meanness, says that 'Bandera did not kill Jews.' Proceeding from what I personally repeated many times: when and if there will be such a path, then I will hang at least Kolomoisky and Josef Zissels in Dnipropetrovsk in front of the 'Golden Rose' synagogue…." See https://govoritmoskva.ru/inter views/514/; Sam Sokol, "Hang Ukrainian Jewish leaders says former Russian Jewish Congress president," *Jerusalem Post*, March 12, 2015, http://www.jpost.com/printarticle.aspx?id=393774.

56. Matthew Luxmoore, "Putin's No-Spin Zone," *Foreign Policy*, December 28, 2015, http://foreignpolicy.com/2015/12/28/putins-no-spin-zone-russian-political-talk-shows-television/.

57. Sam Sokol, "Chief Rabbi asserts Ukrainian Jews will not run away if war breaks out with Russia," *Jerusalem Post*, March 5, 2014, http://www.jpost.com/Jewish-World/Jewish-News/Chief-rabbi-asserts-Ukrainian-Jews-will-not-run-away-if-war-breaks-out-with-Russia-344434.

58. "'Want to retaliate for my son? Finish the war'—mother of the deceased 'cyborg,'" LB.ua, May 14, 2015, https://lb.ua/society/2015/05/14/304946_hochete_pomstitis_mogo_sina.html (in Ukrainian). See also Sam Sokol, "Jewish soldier found dead in snow in eastern Ukraine," *Jerusalem Post*, February 21, 2015, http://www .jpost.com/printarticle.aspx?id=391749.

59. See Dmytro Gorshkov, "The unorthodox path of a Jewish man in the 'new' Ukraine," *Times of Israel*, January 24, 2016, http://www

.timesofisrael.com/the-unorthodox-path-of-a-jewish-man-in-the-new-ukraine/.

60. Sam Sokol, "'Civic obligation' to defend Ukraine, says hassid," *Jerusalem Post*, December 18, 2014, http://www.jpost.com/print article.aspx?id=385013.

61. Cherkassky's story changed somewhat in the telling. Initially, when I first interviewed him in late 2014, he told me through a translator that he was wounded at the Donetsk airport. However, in a subsequent interview almost two years later, he admitted that while he took part in "very hard fights" near the airport, he was never actually one of the cyborgs.

62. Cnaan Liphshiz, "Ukrainian Jewish fighter touted as 'hero, symbol of resistance' to Russia," Jewish Telegraphic Agency, November 24, 2014, https://www.jta.org/2014/11/24/news-opinion/world/ Ukrainian-jewish-fighter-touted-as-hero-symbol-of-resistance-to-russia.

In an interview with *Lechaim*, Filatov stated that he had intentionally recruited Israelis to train local fighters. "These are my friends, they are citizens of Israel … and are patriots of Ukraine. At the time of the Maidan, because of the danger, we had to emigrate to Israel, and I met with the Israelis who served in the IDF, who wanted to help us. They have high motivation, but there are also families, and I pay them out of my own pocket." Edward Doks, "Alex: 'I will stay for as long as my help is needed,'" *Lechaim*, October 12, 2014, https://lechaim.ru/events/aleks-ya-ostanus-na-stolko-na-skolko-budet-nuzhna-moya-pomosht/.

Filatov, who is not Jewish, fled to Israel for a short period during the revolution. See Svitlana Tuchynska, "More Ukrainians fleeing political strife at home," *Kyiv Post*, February 7, 2014, https://www.kyivpost.com/article/content/ukraine-politics/more-Ukrainians-fleeing-political-strife-at-home-336406.html.

63. Sam Sokol, "Muslims, Jews—we fight Russia as one, says Ukraine's battle-hardened Chasid," *Jewish Chronicle*, October 27, 2016, https://www.thejc.com/news/world/muslims-jews-we-%EF %AC%81ght-russia-as-one-says-ukraine-s-battle-hardened-chasid-1.54311.

It is unclear if there would have been enough soldiers to fill out such a unit. According to Pavel Khazan, one of the leaders of the Dnipropetrovsk Maidan and the head of the Foundation for

Defense NGO, several members of the local Jewish community aside from Cherkassky had joined the Ukrainian army. See Sam Sokol, "Israeli captured in combat in Ukraine freed in prisoner exchange," *Jerusalem Post*, September 21, 2014, http://www.jpost .com/printarticle.aspx?id=375966.

Ukrainian media did report that a Jewish unit existed under Yarosh's command. However, the report, which was based on a video posted by a nationalist blogger, lacked credibility. See "A new synagogue was opened in the volunteer battalion of Yarosh," *Korrespondent*, September 19, 2016, https://korrespondent.net/ ukraine/3746968-v-dobrobate-yarosha-otkryly-pervuui-synahohu (in Russian).

64. Cherkassky's comments on Russia were made in response to a query as to whether he saw himself as a tool of Ukrainian propaganda. Following Cherkassky's answer, his translator interjected, stating that he did not think that he "even thinks about that possibility."

65. For more information on the role of civilians in provisioning the army, see David Patrikarakos, *War in 140 Characters: How Social Media is Reshaping Conflict in the Twenty-First Century* (New York: Basic Books, 2017), ch. 4.

66. For Khazan and the NDF's descriptions of their work, see http://helpua.info/eng/?p=2185, http://helpua.info/eng/?p=2730 and https://www.facebook.com/pavlo.khazan/posts/1020512457 1072175?pnref=story.

67. He kept a flag with a combined trident/Jewish star symbol on his office wall that bore the legend "together until the end" in Hebrew and Ukrainian and would sometimes wear a Zhidbanderovets sweatshirt he had received as a gag gift from his sister.

68. This estimate does not include Russian "volunteers" sent by the Kremlin. See "The Foreign Fighters Battling for Ukraine," *Medium*, November 14, 2016, https://medium.com/@DFRLab/the-foreign-fighters-battling-for-ukraine-c314e3c3e6e2. See also Alexander Clapp, "Why American Right-Wingers Are Going to War in Ukraine," Vice News, June 20, 2016, https://www.vice .com/en_us/article/exk4dj/nationalist-interest-v23n4; "Some 20 Swedes fighting in Ukraine: source," Radio Sweden, August 3, 2014, http://sverigesradio.se/sida/artikel.aspx?programid=2054& artikel=5928895; Dina Newman, "Ukraine conflict: 'White power'

warrior from Sweden," BBC, July 16, 2014, http://www.bbc.com/news/world-europe-28329329; and Sam Sokol, "French mayor pledges to prevent gathering of Ukrainian 'neo-Nazi' militia," *Jerusalem Post*, January 16, 2016, http://www.jpost.com/printarticle.aspx?id=441441.

69. Edward Doks, "Alexander Kofman: "I am sincerely afraid for my fellow Jews," *Lechaim*, December 10, 2014, http://old.lechaim.ru/2999 (in Russian). See also Sam Sokol, "Dozens of Israelis fighting in Ukraine, rebel leader claims," *Jerusalem Post*, December 19, 2014, http://www.jpost.com/printarticle.aspx?id=385170.

70. Novorossiya is the Russian imperial designation for the regions now comprising southeastern Ukraine.

71. See http://maki.org.il/he/wp-content/uploads/2015/08/G31_2015.pdf.

72. Sam Sokol, "Israeli communist joins Ukrainian rebels to fight 'fascists and neo-Nazis,'" *Jerusalem Post*, August 20, 2015, http://www.jpost.com/printarticle.aspx?id=412785.

73. Sam Sokol, "Israeli captured in combat in Ukraine freed in prisoner exchange," *Jerusalem Post*, September 21, 2014, http://www.jpost.com/printarticle.aspx?id=375966.

74. Chazin was an Odessa native who immigrated to Israel before returning to Ukraine and working as a kosher certification supervisor prior to the outbreak of the revolution. He led a small unit of men during the defense of the Maidan. Fond of giving interviews while dressed in paramilitary garb and a small kippa in OUN red and black, Chazin had initially stated that he had led around forty fighters, several of them Israeli. Like many fabulists, his stories grew in the telling, and when he was interviewed for this book he told me that three hundred men had followed him. He also told reporters that he had served in the Israeli army's elite Shualei Shimshon unit. An investigation by Israel's Russian-language news site IzRus, however, discovered that he had only served in the IDF for a month and a half. That was in 1996, several years before the formation of Shualei Shimshon. In an interview for this book, Chief Rabbi Bleich called Chazin's story a "farce," adding that "someone may have spoken to him about helping the synagogue, they may have pretended he was doing it but it was nothing serious. … All he did in the Israeli army was [serve as a] kosher supervisor. He had a dishonorable discharge."

Asked about Chazin, Azman stated that he had offered to protect his synagogue in case of trouble and left it at that, seemingly indicating that he did not play a large role in defending the community. Tzvi Arieli, a former Israeli soldier who would soon go on to form an actual Jewish defense unit in Kyiv, said that the two had fallen out over the latter's falsification of his military service. "Claiming it was a Jewish unit is an exaggeration, as far as I know," Arieli said of Chazin's small band. "I know there were a few Israelis. At least one or two. Not with him though. He greatly exaggerated all or some of his stories." See Cnaan Liphshiz, "In Kiev, an Israeli army vet led a street-fighting unit," Jewish Telegraphic Agency, February 28, 2014, http://www.jta.org/2014/02/28/news-opinion/world/in-kiev-an-israeli-militia-commander-fights-in-the-streets-and-saves-lives; Alexander Kogan, "IzRus portal got to the bottom of the military past of the 'Israeli officer of Euromaidan,'" IzRus, March 27, 2014, http://izrus.co.il/diasporaIL/article/2014-03-27/24020.html (in Russian).

75. Patrick Tucker, "In Ukraine, Tomorrow's Drone War Is Alive Today," Defense One, March 9, 2015, http://www.defenseone.com/technology/2015/03/ukraine-tomorrows-drone-war-alive-today/107085/.

76. Shimon Briman, "How a Religious Jew Aids the Ukrainian Army," Ukrainian Jewish Encounter, December 19, 2016, https://Ukrainianjewishencounter.org/en/religious-jew-aids-Ukrainian-army/.

77. See "Expert: Israeli-made drone shot down over Donbas 'points to Russian involvement in conflict,'" UNIAN, May 8, 2015, https://www.unian.info/war/1076058-expert-israeli-made-drone-shot-down-over-donbas-points-to-russian-involvement-in-conflict.html; Yaakov Lappin, "Report: Moscow purchased 10 Israeli drones," *Jerusalem Post*, September 8, 2015, http://www.jpost.com/printarticle.aspx?id=415575.

78. Sam Sokol, "In Israel, aiding both sides of the Ukrainian conflict," *Jerusalem Post*, November 6, 2014, http://www.jpost.com/Metro/n-Israel-aiding-both-sides-of-the-Ukrainian-conflict-380969. He took a different tack when speaking at the Ukraine Crisis Media Center in October 2014, stating that a "pro-Ukrainian Peace March in Tel Aviv gathered 500 supporters, while the pro-Russian counter protest drew only 15 people." See http://uacrisis.org/10788-izrailskie-volontery.

79. Sam Sokol, "Looking to create a Jewish defense force in eastern Ukraine," *Jerusalem Post*, December 28, 2014, http://www.jpost .com/printarticle.aspx?id=385981.

80. During a trip to Mariupol in March 2015, a representative of the local Chabad community informed me of Arieli's role as an instructor, but I did not visit him at his nearby base, instead going on patrol with soldiers of the Dnipro Battalion in the nearby village of Chermalyk. For more information on Arieli, see "Training course for National Guard light infantry brigade according to NATO procedure to start tomorrow," Censor.net, February 14, 2016, https://en.censor.net.ua/news/374216/training_course_for_ national_guard_light_infantry_brigade_according_to_nato_pro cedure_to_start_tomorrow; "Modern Western-model infantry brigade created in National Guard—Patriot Training Center," Censor.net, November 6, 2015, https://en.censor.net.ua/photo_ news/359492/modern_westernmodel_infantry_brigade_created_ in_national_guard_patriot_training_center_photos.

81. See "Ukrainian 'Foreign legion': foreign volunteers and their reasons to fight in Donbas on Ukrainian side," UAposition, May 31, 2017, http://uaposition.com/latest-news/Ukrainian-foreign- legion-foreign-volunteers-reasons-fight-donbas-Ukrainian-side/.

82. "Abuses and War Crimes by the Aidar Volunteer Battalion in the North Luhansk Region," Amnesty International, September 8, 2014, https://www.amnesty.org/en/documents/EUR50/040/2014/ en/. The battalion had another Jewish connection. It was partially funded by Ihor Kolomoisky. See Damien Sharkov, "Ukrainian nationalist volunteers committing 'ISIS-style' war crimes," *Newsweek*, September 10, 2014, http://www.newsweek.com/evidence- war-crimes-committed-Ukrainian-nationalist-volunteers-grows- 269604. See also Allison Quin, "Governor of Luhansk region accuses Aidar of terrorizing the region," *Kyiv Post*, April 1, 2015, https://www.kyivpost.com/article/content/war-against-ukraine/ governor-of-luhansk-region-accuses-aidar-of-terrorizing-the-region- 385054.html.

83. Edward Doks, "In front of the cameras: the Golani who fought Putin," Ynet, December 14, 2014, https://www.ynet.co.il/articles/ 0,7340,L-4602136,00.html (in Hebrew).

84. In *The Nation*, Lev Golinkin wrote that "in addition to stymieing the Ukraine peace process and resolution of EU-Russia sanctions,

the far right has flouted the rule of law, fostered instability, and undermined basic democratic institutions within Ukraine. Gangs tied to the Azov, Aidar, Right Sector, and Tornado battalions have had gun battles with police, intimidated court proceedings, over-turned local elections, torched media buildings, attacked undesir-able Soviet monuments, violently threatened journalists, and overtly spoken of overthrowing the government." Lev Golinkin, "The Ukrainian Far Right—and the Danger It Poses," *The Nation*, December 5, 2016, https://www.thenation.com/article/the-Ukrain ian-far-right-and-the-danger-it-poses/.

See also Elizabeth Piper and Sergiy Karazy, "Special Report: Ukraine struggles to control maverick battalions," Reuters, July 29, 2015, https://www.reuters.com/article/us-ukraine-crisis-bat talions-special-rep/special-report-ukraine-struggles-to-control-maverick-battalions-idUSKCN0Q30YT20150729; Vera Mironova and Ekaterina Sergatskova, "How Ukraine Reined In Its Militias," *Foreign Affairs*, August 1, 2017, https://www.foreignaffairs.com/articles/ukraine/2017-08-01/how-ukraine-reined-its-militias.

85. During the interwar years, OUN was involved in a series of attacks that killed more than sixty people in Poland. Leading fig-ures in the organization, such as Stepan Bandera, Mykola Lebed, and Roman Shukhevych, were convicted for acts that meet the dictionary definition of terrorism. Both Bandera and Lebed re-ceived the death sentence for their part in the 1931 assassination of Polish Interior Minister Bronisław Pieracki. See Grzegorz Rossoliński-Liebe, *Stepan Bandera: The Life and Afterlife of a Ukrainian Nationalist: Fascism, Genocide, and Cult* (Stuttgart: Ibidem Verlag, 2014).

86. Jan Gross, *Neighbors: The Destruction of the Jewish Community of Jedwabne, Poland* (New York: Penguin Books, 2002), 95.

87. Interview with Volodymyr Viatrovych on February 3, 2016.

88. See http://rada.gov.ua/en/news/News/News/87088.html.

89. Bill 728-VII: On Amendments to Article 297 of the Criminal Code of Ukraine concerning liability for the desecration or de-struction of monuments built in memory of those who fought against Nazism during the Second World War—Soviet soldiers-liberators, [the] partisan movement, [the] underground, victims of Nazi persecution, as well as international warriors and peace-keepers. See http://zakon4.rada.gov.ua/laws/show/728-18.

90. "The public denial or justification of the crimes of fascism against humanity committed during the Second World War, in particular the crimes committed by the Waffen-SS, its subordinate structures, those who fought against the anti-Hitler coalition and collaborated with fascist occupiers, as well as propaganda of neo-Nazi ideology and the manufacture and (or) distribution of materials that justify the crimes of the fascists and their supporters, shall be punishable by a fine of five hundred to one thousand non-taxable minimum incomes, or restraint of liberty for a term up to two years, or imprisonment for the same term." Bill 729-VII: On Amendments to the Criminal Code of Ukraine regarding liability for the denial or justification of the crimes of fascism. See https://web.archive.org/web/20140201160239/http://zakon0.rada.gov.ua/laws/show/729-18.

91. See Sam Sokol, "Ukrainian Jews seek to rehabilitate Holocaust era priest," *Jerusalem Post*, November 19, 2014, https://www.jpost.com/printarticle.aspx?id=382280.

92. For an in-depth treatment of Sheptytsky's views on the OUN and the Jews, see John-Paul Himka, "Metropolitan Andrey Sheptytsky and the Holocaust," *Polin: Studies in Polish Jewry* 26 (2014).

93. "Thou Shalt Not Kill," November 21, 1942, https://training.ehri-project.eu/sites/training.ehri-project.eu/files/EHRI_Ua_D03_Sheptyts%27kyi_Nov_1942_0.pdf.

94. John-Paul Himka, "Metropolitan Andrey Sheptytsky and the Holocaust," *Polin: Studies in Polish Jewry* 26 (2014).

95. Ibid.

96. Ibid.

97. For a description of the 14th Waffen SS Grenadier Division, known popularly as the Waffen-SS Galizien, and its role in war crimes, including the Huta Pieniacka massacre, see Per Anders Rudling, "'They Defended Ukraine': The 14. Waffen-Grenadier-Division der SS (Galizische Nr. 1) Revisited," *Journal of Slavic Military Studies* 25, no. 3 (2012): 329-368. Ironically, Rudling, citing Himka, posits that "keeping young Galicians out of the UPA appears to have been one of the reasons why Sheptyts'kyi endorsed the Waffen-SS Galizien."

98. See Sam Sokol, "Russian-Ukrainian spat over anti-Semitism reaches the UN," *Jerusalem Post*, November 25, 2014, http://www.jpost.com/printarticle.aspx?id=382811.

99. For the full text of the declaration, see http://www.praguedeclara
tion.eu/.

100. Dovid Katz, "Is Eastern European 'Double Genocide' Revisionism
Reaching Museums?," *Dapim: Studies on the Holocaust* (2016),
https://doi.org/10.1080/23256249.2016.1242043.

101. Ibid. As we will soon see, within half a year of the passage of
Russia's Nazism resolution, Ukraine would pass a series of bills
known collectively as the Decommunization Laws, which would
begin the process of rehabilitating anti-communist Ukrainian nationalists who had fought alongside the Nazis. Adherence to the
tenets of Double Genocide theory had both the advantage of dele-
gitimizing the Russians and at the same time helping to excuse
Ukrainian collaboration, allowing for an inversion in which
Ukrainians who committed war crimes were the real victims and
creating a precedent for contemporary Ukrainian narratives of
victimization.

102. Ibid.

103. Per Anders Rudling, "Memories of 'Holodomor' and National
Socialism in Ukrainian Political Culture," in *Rekonstruktion Des
Nationalmythos? Frankreich, Deutschland und die Ukraine im
Vergleich*, ed. Yves Bizeul (Göttingen: Vandenhoeck & Ruprecht
Unipress, 2013), 227-258, doi:10.14220/9783737001816.227.

104. Ibid.

105. "Ukraine remembers victims of Holodomor (1932-1933),"
UNIAN, November 25, 2017, https://www.unian.info/society/226
2574-ukraine-remembers-victims-of-holodomor-1932-1933.html.

106. See Lahav Harkov, "Bill to remember 'Ukrainian Genocide' under
Stalin treads tricky ground," *Jerusalem Post*, February 6, 2018,
https://www.jpost.com/printarticle.aspx?id=540847; and Timothy
Snyder, *Bloodlands: Europe between Hitler and Stalin* (New York:
Basic Books, 2010).

107. John-Paul Himka, "How Many Perished in the Famine and Why
Does It Matter," Brama, February 2, 2008, http://www.brama
.com/news/press/2008/02/080202himka_famine.html.

108. See http://www.president.gov.ua/en/news/prezident-ne-viznavati-
golodomor-tak-samo-amoralno-yak-i-zap-44702. The Jewish community has been far from monolithic in its approach to this issue.
Two years earlier, the Simon Wiesenthal Center's Efraim Zuroff
had slammed a bill drafted and proposed by Jewish MP Olek-

sandr Feldman, which defined the Holodomor and the Holocaust as the "genocide of the Ukrainian people" and the "genocide of the Jewish people" respectively. Defending the legislation, Eduard Dolinsky explained that the juxtaposition of the two tragedies was intended to "ease the path for the law's adoption" in a country where "officials have juxtaposed the Holocaust and Holodomor in various forums." See Sam Sokol, "Wiesenthal Center slams Ukrainian Holocaust bill," *Jerusalem Post*, July 10, 2015, https://www.jpost.com/printarticle.aspx?id=408575.

109. See http://www.demokratiezentrum.org/fileadmin/media/img/Gedenktage/GO_5.3_Yehuda_Bauer.pdf.

110. This anecdote was originally published in Sam Sokol, "At Auschwitz a call to remember includes a call to preserve," *Jerusalem Post*, January 28, 2015, https://www.jpost.com/printarticle.aspx?id=389294.

111. "Protest against Putin attending Auschwitz liberation ceremony," Radio Poland, September 5, 2014, http://thenews.pl/1/10/Artykul/170416,Protest-against-Putin-attending-Auschwitz-liberation-ceremony.

112. Sam Sokol, "Czech Jews protest invitation of Putin to Holocaust memorial," *Jerusalem Post*, December 21, 2014, https://www.jpost.com/printarticle.aspx?id=385333.

113. Christian Lowe, "Exclusive: Ukraine tensions keep Putin away from Auschwitz anniversary," Reuters, January 12, 2015, https://www.reuters.com/article/us-auschwitz-anniversary-putin/exclusive-ukraine-tensions-keep-putin-away-from-auschwitz-anniversary-idUSKBN0KL1U620150112.

114. Sam Sokol, "Ukraine tensions keep Putin away from Auschwitz anniversary," *Jerusalem Post*, January 13, 2015, https://www.jpost.com/printarticle.aspx?id=387564.

115. President Bronisław Komorowski subsequently walked back Schetyna's remarks. See "Komorowski defends Russian role in Auschwitz liberation," Radio Poland, January 23, 2015, http://www.thenews.pl/1/2/Artykul/194540,Komorowski-defends-Russian-role-in-Auschwitz-liberation.

116. Glenn Kates, "Auschwitz Ceremony Lays Bare Russian Tension With Europe," RFE/RL, January 23, 2015, https://www.rferl.org/a/auschwitz-ukraine-liberators-russia-tensions/26810197.html.

117. This was not a one-time occurrence. For instance, four years later, in its official International Holocaust Remembrance Day statement (http://mfa.gov.ua/ua/press-center/news/62661-27-sichnya-svit-vshanovuje-pamjaty-zhertv-golokostu), the Ukrainian Ministry of Foreign Affairs wrote that "the memory of the victims of the Nazi terror in Ukraine in the Second World War, which is 1.5 million Jews and more than 4 million Ukrainians and representatives of other nationalities, is holy in our country." There was nothing in the statement differentiating between Holocaust victims from other casualties of the war, as if the Holocaust must be paid lip service but is not really considered special. This kind of rhetoric is, ironically, a continuation of Soviet propaganda which described Holocaust victims as Soviet victims of Nazism and fascism. Prior to Ukrainian independence, it was the stated policy of the Soviet state to eschew and even eradicate any separate mention of the Jewish victims of the [Babi Yar massacre], a policy carried on by the nation's post-Soviet leadership, which has put into effect a policy of "minimization." See Aleksandr Burakovskiy, "Holocaust Remembrance in Ukraine: Memorialization of the Jewish Tragedy at Babi Yar," *Nationalities Papers* 39, no. 3 (2011): 371-389, doi:10.1080/00905992.2011.565316. See also Sam Sokol, "Babi Yar as a Symbol of Holocaust Distortion in Post-Maidan Ukraine," *Israel Journal of Foreign Affairs* (2017), doi:10.1080/23739770.2017.1315694. In his own official statements on Facebook and Twitter on International Holocaust Remembrance Day 2018, Poroshenko also neglected to mention Jews (see https://www.facebook.com/petroporoshenko/posts/1192821480852242 and https://twitter.com/poroshenko/status/957131607609135105), as did his Jewish prime minister, Volodymyr Groysman (see https://twitter.com/VGroysman/status/957154754282614784).

118. See http://mfa.gov.ua/en/press-center/news/32497-richnicya-visvolennya-osvencimu-svit-maje-pamjatati-uroki-minulogo-i-nedopustiti-povtorennya-tragichnih-podij-u-syogodenni--glava-derzhavi, emphasis mine.

119. See http://en.kremlin.ru/events/president/news/47529.

120. Bill #2538-1: "On the Legal Status and Honoring the Memory of Fighters for Ukraine's Independence in the Twentieth Century," http://www.memory.gov.ua/laws/law-ukraine-legal-status-and-honoring-memory-fighters-ukraines-independence-twentieth-

century. See also http://w1.c1.rada.gov.ua/pls/radan_gs09/ns_go
los?g_id=1421.

121. Bill #2540: "On Access to Archives of Repressive Agencies of Totalitarian Communist Regime of 1917-1991," http://www.memory
.gov.ua/laws/law-ukraine-access-archives-repressive-agencies-
totalitarian-communist-regime-1917-1991.

122. Bill #2539: "On Perpetuation of the Victory over Nazism in
World War II of 1939-1945," http://www.memory.gov.ua/laws/
law-ukraine-perpetuation-victory-over-nazism-world-war-ii-1939-
1945.

123. Bill #2558: "On the Condemnation of the Communist and National
Socialist (Nazi) Regimes, and Prohibition of Propaganda of Their
Symbols," http://www.memory.gov.ua/laws/law-ukraine-condem
nation-communist-and-national-socialist-nazi-regimes-and-pro
hibition-propagan.

124. See Nikolay Koposov, *Memory Laws, Memory Wars: The Politics
of the Past in Europe and Russia* (Cambridge; Cambridge University Press, 2018). One of the lawmakers behind the Radical Party's
proposals was Yuriy Shukhevych, the son of UPA wartime leader
Roman Shukhevych.

125. For an example of this phenomenon, see Olga Perekrest, "An
exhibition about the SS Division Halychyna was opened in L'viv,"
Zaxid.net, April 19, 2018, https://zaxid.net/bilya_loda_vidkrili_
vistavku_pro_diviziyu_ss_galichina_n1454624 (in Ukrainian).

126. See "The symbolism of the SS division 'Galichina' does not fall
under the law banning propaganda of communism and Nazism—
Viatrovych," Strana, May 18, 2017, https://strana.ua/news/71386-
simvolika-divizii-ss-galichina-ne-yavlyaetsya-nacistskoj-vyatro
vich.html (in Russian).

127. For further analysis, see Sergey Movchan, "Why is Ukraine Afraid
of the Internet, But Not Afraid of the SS," Krytyka Polityczna,
June 29, 2017, http://politicalcritique.org/cee/ukraine/2017/mov
chan-ukraine-decommunisation-history-symbols-totalitarianism/.

128. Tarik Cyril Amar, "A Certain Spirit of the Laws: Ukraine's
Nationalist 'Decommunization' Laws of Spring 2015—Shielding
Perpetrators and Excluding Victims from the Universe of Obligation," forthcoming. This view is bolstered by Viatrovych's own
words. In an interview for this book, the Ukrainian historian stated explicitly that, with the new law, the Soviet and Nazi "regimes

are announced to be criminal" and "equal in their methods" but that the "wide set of symbols which are to be banned in Ukraine" was composed of "mostly Soviet symbols" because "thank God, Nazi symbols have not been used in Ukraine for many years already."

129. Per Anders Rudling, "Memories of 'Holodomor' and National Socialism in Ukrainian Political Culture," in *Rekonstruktion Des Nationalmythos? Frankreich, Deutschland und die Ukraine im Vergleich*, ed. Yves Bizeul (Göttingen: Vandenhoeck & Ruprecht Unipress, 2013), 227-258, doi:10.14220/9783737001816.227.

130. "The potential consequences of both these laws are disturbing. Not only would it be a crime to question the legitimacy of an organization (UPA) that slaughtered tens of thousands of Poles in one of the most heinous acts of ethnic cleansing in the history of Ukraine, but also it would exempt from criticism the OUN, one of the most extreme political groups in Western Ukraine between the wars, and one which collaborated with Nazi Germany at the outset of the Soviet invasion in 1941. It also took part in anti-Jewish pogroms in Ukraine and, in the case of the Melnyk faction, remained allied with the occupation regime throughout the war." "Open Letter from Scholars and Experts on Ukraine Re. the So-Called 'Anti-Communist Law,'" *Krytyka*, April 2015, https://krytyka.com/en/articles/open-letter-scholars-and-experts-ukraine-re-so-called-anti-communist-law#footnote1_42zgrk1.

131. See https://www.ushmm.org/information/press/press-releases/statement-on-Ukrainian-legislation-on-historical-research-and-debate.

132. See https://www.osce.org/fom/158581.

133. Sam Sokol, "Ukrainian parliament recognizes militia that collaborated with Nazis," *Jerusalem Post*, April 13, 2015, https://www.jpost.com/printarticle.aspx?id=396848.

134. For a more in-depth treatment of this issue, see Sam Sokol, "The Tension between Historical Memory and Realpolitik in Israel's Foreign Policy," *Israel Journal of Foreign Affairs* (2019), doi.org/10.1080/23739770.2018.1560563.

135. Per Anders Rudling, "The Return of the Ukrainian Far Right: The Case of VO Svoboda," in *Analyzing Fascist Discourse: European Fascism in Talk and Text*, ed. Ruth Wodak and John E. Richardson (London and New York: Routledge, 2013).

136. Per Anders Rudling, "The OUN, the UPA and the Holocaust: A Study in the Manufacturing of Historical Myths," Carl Beck Papers in Russian and East European Studies, no. 2107 (2011), doi:10.5195/cbp.2011.164.

137. Victor Yushchenko, "Ukraine and Israel: A Dialogue in the Name of the Future." *Israel Journal of Foreign Affairs* 2, no. 1 (2008): 111-118, doi:10.1080/23739770.2008.11446300.

138. Josh Cohen, "The Historian Whitewashing Ukraine's Past," *Foreign Policy*, May 2, 2016, http://foreignpolicy.com/2016/05/02/the-historian-whitewashing-ukraines-past-volodymyr-viatrovych/. For a contemporaneous description of Yushchenkoism, see Ofri Ilany, "Kiev Names Street After Mass-murderer of Jews," *Haaretz*, July 13, 2009, https://www.haaretz.com/1.5076317.

139. Clifford J. Levy, "'Hero of Ukraine' Prize to Wartime Partisan Leader Is Revoked," *New York Times*, January 12, 2011, https://www.nytimes.com/2011/01/13/world/europe/13ukraine.html.

140. John-Paul Himka, "Collaboration and/or Resistance: The OUN and UPA during the War," paper prepared for the Ukrainian Jewish Encounter Shared Narrative Series: Conference on Issues Relating to World War II, Potsdam, June 27-30, 2011.

141. See "Jews in Ukraine were a minority in the minority—Viatrovych," *Gazeta*, May 29, 2015, https://gazeta.ua/articles/history/_evreyi-v-ukrayini-buli-menshinoyu-v-menshini-vyatrovich/629131 (in Ukrainian).

142. Jared McBride, "Ukraine's Invented a 'Jewish-Ukrainian Nationalist' to Whitewash Its Nazi-era Past," *Haaretz*, November 9, 2017, https://www.haaretz.com/opinion/ukraine-nationalists-are-using-a-jew-to-whitewash-their-nazi-era-past-1.5464194.

143. John-Paul Himka, "The Ukrainian Insurgent Army and the Holocaust," paper prepared for the 41st National Convention of the American Association for the Advancement of Slavic Studies, Boston, November 12-15, 2009.

144. Per Anders Rudling, "The Cult of Roman Shukhevych in Ukraine: Myth Making with Complications," *Fascism* 5, no. 1 (2016): 26-65, doi:10.1163/22116257-00501003.

145. Delphine Bechtel, "The 1941 Pogroms as Represented in Western Ukrainian Historiography and Memorial Culture," in *The Holocaust in Ukraine: New Sources and Perspectives* (Washington D.C., United States: United States Holocaust Memorial Museum, 2013), 1-15.

146. "Shukhevych's involvement in the murder of Jews will be checked again," *Korrespondent*, March 7, 2008, https://ua.korrespondent .net/ukraine/397069-prichetnist-shuhevicha-do-vbivstva-evreyiv-pereviryat-shche-raz (in Ukrainian).

147. See http://www.yadvashem.org/press-release/19-march-2008-09-06.html.

148. Interview with Volodymyr Viatrovych, February 3, 2016. Some minor grammatical changes have been made for the sake of clarity.

149. For a brief summary of the massacres, see Andrii Portnov, "Clash of victimhoods: the Volhynia Massacre in Polish and Ukrainian memory," Open Democracy Russia, November 16, 2016, https:// www.opendemocracy.net/od-russia/andrii-portnov/clash-of-victim hood-1943-volhynian-massacre-in-polish-and-Ukrainian-culture.

150. See Vladimir Matveyev, "Jewish group objects to 'Great Famine' case," Jewish Telegraphic Agency, June 15, 2009, https://www.jta .org/2009/06/15/news-opinion/world/jewish-group-objects-to-great-famine-case; "List blames Jews for Ukrainian famine," Jewish Telegraphic Agency, July 27, 2008, https://www.jta.org/2008/07/27/news-opinion/list-blames-jews-for-Ukrainian-famine.

151. See Myroslav Shkandrij, *Ukrainian Nationalism: Politics, Ideology, and Literature, 1929-1956* (New Haven, Yale University Press, 2015), 54-55; John-Paul Himka, "The Lviv Pogrom of 1941: The Germans, Ukrainian Nationalists, and the Carnival Crowd," *Canadian Slavonic Papers* 53, nos. 2-4 (2011): 209-243, doi:10.1080/00085006.2011.11092673.

152. For a brief description of the phenomenon, see Joanna Beata Michlic, *Poland's Threatening Other: The Image of the Jew from 1880 to the Present* (Lincoln, University of Nebraska Press, 2006), 89.

153. See Per Anders Rudling, "Bogdan Musial and the Question of Jewish Responsibility for the Pogroms in Lviv in the Summer of 1941," *East European Jewish Affairs* 35, no. 1 (2005): 69-89, doi: 10.1080/13501670500191819.

154. Eduard Dolinsky, "What Ukraine's Jews Fear," *New York Times*, April 11, 2017, https://www.nytimes.com/2017/04/11/opinion/what-ukraines-jews-fear.html.

155. See https://www.facebook.com/volodymyr.viatrovych/posts/1020 8893176026157.

156. See https://www.facebook.com/eduard.dolinsky/posts/148489144 4876252.

157. "Decommunization reform: 25 districts and 987 populated areas in Ukraine renamed in 2016," Ukrinform, December 27, 2016, https://www.ukrinform.net/rubric-society/2147127-decommuni zation-reform-25-districts-and-987-populated-areas-in-ukraine-renamed-in-2016.html.

158. "Ukrainian City Naming Street in Honor of Waffen-SS Hauptsturmführer," Defending History, October 7, 2017, http://defend inghistory.com/Ukrainian-city-naming-street-in-honor-of-waffen-ss-hauptsturmfuhrer/90373; "Kiev renames major street to honor Russian Nazi collaborator," *Times of Israel*, July 7, 2016, https://www.timesofisrael.com/kiev-renames-major-street-to-honor-rus sian-nazi-collaborator/; "Kyiv's General Vatutin Avenue renamed Roman Shukhevych Avenue," *Kyiv Post*, June 1, 2017, https://www.kyivpost.com/ukraine-politics/kyivs-general-vatutin-avenue-renamed-roman-shukhevych-avenue.html.

159. Dovid Margolin, "Ukrainian City Renames Street in Honor of the Rebbe," Chabad.org, June 24, 2016, https://www.chabad.org/news/article_cdo/aid/3366452/jewish/Ukrainian-City-Renames-Street-in-Honor-of-the-Rebbe.htm; Sam Sokol, "Ukrainian city to rename streets after Jewish leader, and anti-Semite," *Jerusalem Post*, December 14, 2015, https://www.jpost.com/printarticle.aspx ?id=437292.

160. A copy of this letter was sent to journalists by Eduard Dolinsky. Signatories included representatives of the Jewish Confederation of Ukraine, Jewish Forum of Ukraine, Kiev Jewish Religious community, Ukrainian Jewish Committee, Union of Jewish Religious Organizations of Ukraine, Ukrainian Association of Jews—former prisoners of Ghetto and Nazi concentration camps, and others. Emphasis mine.

161. See https://www.facebook.com/permalink.php?story_fbid=48379 1415305209&id=388184211532597. Azman later told this author that he had Sheptytsky in mind when making this statement.

162. "In Ukraine, they will hold an information campaign on the UPA fight against Nazi occupiers," *Novoe Vremya*, February 8, 2017, https://nv.ua/ukr/ukraine/events/v-ukrajini-provedut-informatsij nu-kampaniju-pro-borotbu-upa-proti-natsistskih-okupantiv-614 319.html (in Ukrainian).

163. See https://web.archive.org/web/20170216195423/http://www. memory.gov.ua/page/ukrainska-povstanska-armiya; "The 'UPA—

the response of the unconquered people' exhibition opens in all regions of Ukraine," Istorychna Pravda, March 7, 2018, http://www.istpravda.com.ua/short/2018/03/7/152181/ (in Ukrainian). Other efforts, both official and unofficial, included the UINM's development of an UPA board game targeted at young people and the publication of a graphic novel (produced by Svoboda politicians) whose entire print run was sent to the east. See https://www.facebook.com/uinp.gov.ua/posts/1030868503734450; "The comic book about UPA last battle was published in Ternopil," Doba.te.ua, May 27, 2017, https://doba.te.ua/post/34741 (in Ukrainian). Viatrovych's efforts to reach out to Ukrainian youth began long before the Maidan. See Per Anders Rudling, "The Return of the Ukrainian Far Right: The Case of VO Svoboda," in *Analyzing Fascist Discourse: European Fascism in Talk and Text*, ed. Ruth Wodak and John E. Richardson (London and New York: Routledge, 2013).

164. See http://uacrisis.org/42802-volodimir-v-yatrovich.

165. See http://www.memory.gov.ua/news/do-dnya-pamyati-i-primi rennya-ukraina-zgaduvatime-svii-vnesok-v-peremogu-nad-agre sorom and https://www.facebook.com/photo.php?fbid=80848464 5982189&set=a.335339763296682.1073741845.10000461983612 9&type=3. Poroshenko also equated the UPA and the Red Army, tweeting "Glory to the veterans of the Red Army and partisan movement! Glory to the UPA soldiers and all participants in the national liberation struggle!" See https://twitter.com/poroshenko/status/861539430947069953.

166. "10 myths about the Ukrainian Insurgent Army (UPA). Myth #5: Ukrainian nationalists were massively killing Jews during World War II, especially in Lviv and in Babyn Yar," Ukraine Crisis Media Center, July 20, 2017, http://uacrisis.org/58749-upa-myth-5-jews. See also http://www.memory.gov.ua/news/10-mifiv-pro-upa-ukrain ski-natsionalisti-masovo-vinishchuvali-evreiv-pid-chas-viini-oso blivo-u-.

167. See http://www.president.gov.ua/en/news/mayemo-znati-j-pamya tati-pro-usih-hto-muzhno-boroniv-ridnu-z-47286; http://www.president.gov.ua/en/news/pamyatayemo-vse-velichne-i-ne-zabu vayemo-pro-vazhki-storinki-43954; "Feats of UPA heroes inspire current Ukrainian defenders—Poroshenko," Ukrinform, October 14, 2017, https://www.ukrinform.net/rubric-society/2324702-feats-

of-upa-heroes-inspire-current-Ukrainian-defenders-poroshenko
.html.

168. This "objective information" was to be disseminated through "mass media," "educational events," and "civic initiatives," which would focus on the UPA as "part of the pan-European movement resistance to the Nazis and their allies." See Josh Cohen, "Remembering the Holocaust in Ukraine," *National Interest*, February 3, 2018, http://nationalinterest.org/feature/remembering-the-holocaust-ukraine-24344 and https://www.academia.edu/351656 46/UPA_Poroshenko.pdf. In L'viv, long the center of right-wing Ukrainian nationalism, examples of these kinds of initiatives include a festival aptly titled Shukhevychfest and an art competition for teenagers in which participants were instructed to submit drawings related to the SS Galizien Division. See "Ukraine city to hold festival in honor of Nazi collaborator whose troops killed Jews," Jewish Telegraphic Agency, June 28, 2017, https://www.jta .org/2017/06/28/news-opinion/world/ukraine-city-to-hold-festi val-in-honor-of-nazi-collaborator-whose-troops-killed-jews; "In Lviv a competition was held among teenagers for the best picture of the division SS 'Galichina,'" Strana, April 24, 2018, https://strana .ua/news/137598-vo-lvove-provodjat-denezhnyj-konkurs-na-luch shij-risunok-divizii-ss-halichina.html (in Russian). During the course of the Shukhevych festival, which was held on the anniversary of the L'viv Pogrom of 1941, antisemitic graffiti was found scrawled on a local building. See https://www.facebook.com/eduard .dolinsky/posts/1574671069231622.

169. Ibid.

170. Paul Robert Magocsi and Yohanan Petrovsky-Shtern, *Jews and Ukrainians: A Millennium of Co-existence* (University of Toronto Press, 2016), 55.

171. S.A. Smith, *Russia in Revolution: An Empire in Crisis 1890-1928* (Oxford, Oxford University Press, 2017), 188; Serhii Plokhy, *The Gates of Europe: A History of Ukraine* (New York, Basic Books, 2015), 222.

172. Ibid., 223-224.

173. Sue Surkes, "Statue of nationalist blamed for pogroms against Jews is unveiled in Ukraine," *Times of Israel*, October 16, 2017, https://www.timesofisrael.com/statue-of-nationalist-blamed-for-pogroms-against-jews-unveiled-in-ukraine/.

174. Cnaan Liphshiz, "Ukraine honors nationalist whose troops killed 50,000 Jews," Jewish Telegraphic Agency, May 31, 2016, https://www.timesofisrael.com/ukraine-honors-nationalist-whose-troops-killed-50000-jews/; Vladislav Davidzon, "Ukrainians Ask: Was Their Hero an Anti-Semite? And Should His Statue Be Removed?," *Tablet*, October 27, 2017, http://www.tabletmag.com/scroll/248091/Ukrainians-ask-was-their-hero-an-anti-semite-and-should-his-statue-be-removed; Sue Surkes, "Ukrainian nationalist to Jews: 'Get used to our rules' or be punished," *Times of Israel*, October 23, 2017, https://www.timesofisrael.com/Ukrainian-nationalist-to-jews-get-used-to-our-rules-or-be-punished/.

175. See https://www.facebook.com/eduard.dolinsky/posts/1447203158645081; Sam Sokol, "Row after Ukrainian Jewish leader Josef Zissels 'defends' Nazi collaborators," *Jewish Chronicle*, May 25, 2018, https://www.thejc.com/news/world/row-after-Ukrainian-jewish-leader-josef-zissels-defends-nazi-collaborators-1.464583.

176. Sam Sokol "Ukrainians erect monument to 'national heroes' who killed Uman's Jews in 18th century," *Jerusalem Post*, November 30, 2015, https://www.jpost.com/printarticle.aspx?id=435884.

177. For further details, see http://www.jewishvirtuallibrary.org/chmielnicki-khmelnitski-bogdan-x00b0.

178. For a deeper treatment of this issue, see Oleksandra Iwaniuk, "Ukrainian-Polish Relations in the Context of the Memory War: A Game of Lose-Lose," Kennan Institute-Focus Ukraine, October 13, 2017, http://www.kennan-focusukraine.org/Ukrainian-polish-relations-in-the-context-of-the-memory-war-a-game-of-lose-lose/.

179. Jan Grabowski, "The Holocaust and Poland's 'History Policy,'" *Israel Journal of Foreign Affairs* 10, no. 3 (2016): 481-486. In his essay, Grabowski quotes Justice Minister Zbigniew Ziobro, who positioned PiS history policy as an effort "to better defend the good name of the Polish nation."

180. See Ofer Aderet, "Historian May Face Charges in Poland for Writing That Poles Killed Jews in World War II," *Haaretz*, Oct 30, 2016, https://www.haaretz.com/world-news/europe/.premium-historian-may-face-charges-for-writing-that-poles-killed-jews-in-wwii-1.5454793; Larry Cohler-Esses, "The Holocaust Activist Who's Warning Poland—About Danger Posed By Jews," *Jewish Daily Forward*, November 5, 2017, https://forward.com/news/

world/386714/the-holocaust-activist-whos-warning-poland-about-danger-posed-by-jews/.

181. Sam Sokol, "Polish historian says he was forced to switch jobs because of his Holocaust research," *Jewish Chronicle*, April 5, 2018, https://www.thejc.com/news/world/polish-historian-says-he-was-forced-to-switch-jobs-because-of-his-holocaust-research-1.461937.

182. "Ukrainian and Polish Institutes of national memory decided to create a joint commission of historians to study the Volyn tragedy," Radio Poland, May 19, 2015, https://tinyurl.com/yasm2pq2 (in Russian); "Poland's Parliament Declares Volyn Massacres 'Genocide,' Ukraine Laments Move," RFE/RL, July 22, 2016, https://www.rferl.org/a/poland-parliament-declares-volyn-massacres-/27874252.html.

183. "Kaczynski—Poroshenko: You will not enter the EU with Bandera," *Korrespondent*, February 6, 2017, https://korrespondent.net/world/worldabus/3811069-kachynskyi-poroshenko-v-es-s-banderoi-ne-voidete (in Russian). See also "Kyiv-Warsaw relations depend on Ukraine's stance toward UPA—Kaczynski," UNIAN, January 30, 2017, https://www.unian.info/politics/1749537-kyiv-warsaw-relations-depend-on-ukraines-stance-toward-upa-kaczynski.html.

184. This statement came around the same time that Viatrovych was banned from entering Poland. "Ukrainian official banned from entering Poland: report," Radio Poland, November 10, 2017, http://www.thenews.pl/1/10/Artykul/334427,Ukrainian-official-banned-from-entering-Poland-report.

185. For the full text of Poland's controversial Holocaust legislation, see https://www.timesofisrael.com/full-text-of-polands-controversial-holocaust-legislation/.

186. This section is primarily based on Sam Sokol, "Babi Yar as a Symbol of Holocaust Distortion in Post-Maidan Ukraine," *Israel Journal of Foreign Affairs* 11, no. 1 (2017): 35-46, doi:10.1080/23739770.2017.1315694, as well as a series of articles on Babi Yar and memory that I wrote for the *Jerusalem Post* and the *Jewish Chronicle*.

187. See http://www.yadvashem.org/education/educational-materials/learning-environment/babi-yar/historical-background3.html.

188. See http://www.yadvashem.org/education/educational-materials/learning-environment/babi-yar/historical-background3.html.

189. Aleksandr Burakovskiy, "Holocaust Remembrance in Ukraine: Memorialization of the Jewish Tragedy at Babi Yar," *Nationalities Papers* 39, no. 3 (2011): 371-389, doi:10.1080/00905992.2011.565316.

190. There were also fleeting periods of greater openness and recognition of the Jewish nature of the tragedy when commemorations mentioning the ethnicity of the victims were permitted, such as during the 25th anniversary in 1966; however, the complexities of Soviet memorialization policy are beyond the scope of the present chapter.

191. I am, of necessity, simplifying an extremely complex issue and would recommend anyone interested in the issue to read Burakovskiy's paper, which is cited several times throughout this chapter. Examples of memorialization during the Soviet period include Yevgeny Yevtushenko's poem "Babi Yar" and Dimitri Shostakovich's stirring 13th Symphony, in which that poem was set to music. It would also be appropriate to mention Ivan Dzyuba. This Ukrainian dissident spoke at an unofficial Babi Yar commemoration ceremony in 1966 on the dangers of silence, which he called "the accomplice of lies and captivity."

192. See https://Ukrainianjewishencounter.org/en/news/speech-of-the-president-of-ukraine-in-the-israeli-knesset/.

193. The organizers of the contest included Ukrainian Jewish Encounter, the Ukrainian Institute of National Memory, the National Organizing Committee on the preparation and holding of events in connection with 75th anniversary of the Babyn Yar tragedy (operating under the auspices of the President's Office), and the Public Committee for the Commemoration of the Victims of Babyn Yar. A screenshot of the original language can be found at https://www.academia.edu/36869534/Babi_Yar_competition_screenshot.

194. Sam Sokol, "Ukraine backtracks on Babi Yar plans amid accusations of Holocaust revisionism," *Jerusalem Post*, February 8, 2016, https://www.jpost.com/printarticle.aspx?id=444268. In response to the controversy, UJE co-director Adrian Karatnycky stated that the initial intent of the contest had been to make the park in which Babi Yar is located a "more respectful place and a more

dignified place of memory" and that when his organization became aware of the language used it made the rounds of governmental and civil society partners in Ukraine to emphasize that the wording was unacceptable. "There should be no equivocation," he said. "It must be understood that the Holocaust was a unique historical event intended to wipe out an entire ethno-cultural people, and [that] it's intent was global." According to Karatnycky, the problematic original text had been written by Jewish-Ukrainian historian Vitaliy Nachmanovych. The amended text acknowledged Babi Yar as "a symbol of the Holocaust" and "Nazi Germany's ambition to destroy all Jews throughout the world [as] a unique atrocity in human history." See http://konkurs.kby.kiev.ua/en/.

195. See http://www.president.gov.ua/en/news/vistup-prezidenta-petra-poroshenka-na-zhalobnij-ceremoniyi-z-38337, emphasis mine.

196. In 1940, the OUN broke into two factions, one lead by Stepan Bandera, representing the younger, more radical wing of the movement, and the other, led by Andriy Melnykm, representing the older, more conservative wing. An image of the text of the sign can be found at https://twitter.com/SamuelSokol/status/7816 52152511070208. According to Viatrovych, the exhibition was developed by Vitaliy Nachmanovych. Natalia Swan, "Volodymyr Viatrovych: The ones who are preventing the dismantling of Shchors are to blame for the damage against it," Channel 24, May 4, 2017, https://24tv.ua/volodimir_vyatrovich_u_poshkodzhenni _shhorsa_vinni_ti_hto_zavazhaye_yogo_demontazhu_n813365.

197. See *Ukrainske Slovo* (Kyiv), no. 26, October 9, 1941, https://tiny url.com/y8xrjnth. I have used a translation from Yad Vashem that can be found at http://www.yadvashem.org/education/educational-materials/learning-environment/babi-yar/historical-background 3.html. It is important to note that the term *zhyd*, which is translated here as Yid, was the normal term that western Ukrainians of Rohach's generation would have used to refer to Jews. It did not necessarily have an antisemitic connotation. However, given the context of the statement in which the word was used, it is absolutely clear that it was being used in a pejorative sense here.

198. Sam Sokol, "Ukraine has only just begun its journey to the truth," *Jewish Chronicle*, October 6, 2016, https://www.thejc.com/news/world/ukraine-has-only-just-begun-its-journey-to-the-truth-1.53 768.

199. See http://mfa.gov.il/MFA/PressRoom/2016/Pages/President-Riv lin-addresses-Ukrainian-Parliament-session-27-September-2016 .aspx.

200. See https://www.facebook.com/volodymyr.viatrovych/posts/1020 7314368196948. See also https://www.facebook.com/volodymyr .viatrovych/posts/10207318795667632 and https://www.facebook .com/volodymyr.viatrovych/posts/10207331796792652. Given what the Decommunization Laws said about denigrating nationalist movements and sharing Soviet propaganda, Viatrovych was essentially accusing a foreign head of state of criminal activity.

201. Benjamin Cohen, "Israel's President Confronts Ukrainians With Their Past," *Foreign Policy*, September 30, 2016, http://foreign policy.com/2016/09/30/israels-president-confronts-Ukrainians-with-their-past/. Chervak has also argued that the OUN's wartime actions were justified because they "brought Poles to their senses" and has called for the arrest of anyone who opposes his campaign to rehabilitate Ukrainian nationalists such as Petliura. See https:// www.academia.edu/36887507/Bohdan_Chervak_FB_commen_ts.

202. Aleksandr Burakovskiy, "Holocaust Remembrance in Ukraine: Memorialization of the Jewish Tragedy at Babi Yar," *Nationalities Papers* 39, no. 3 (2011): 371-389, doi:10.1080/00905992.2011.565 316.

203. Bohdan Chervak, "Babi Yar: The War of the monuments continues?," Ukrainska Pravda, August 11, 2017, https://www.pravda .com.ua/columns/2017/08/11/7151687/ (in Ukrainian). The OUN issued a statement opposing the project in the relaunched *Ukrainske Slovo*, http://ukrslovo-litavry.org.ua/attachments/article/470/ %D0%A3%D0%A1%D0%9B_2018%20%D0%A7.2%20%D0%B B%D1%8E%D1%82%D0%B8%D0%B9.pdf.

204. "Museum 'Babi Yar.' Open letter of warning from Ukrainian historians," Istorychna Pravda, March 28, 2017, http://www.ist pravda.com.ua/articles/2017/03/28/149652/ (in Ukrainian).

205. Josef Zissels, "Babi Yar Memorial Center for the Holocaust—a paternalistic project," Istorychna Pravda, July 13, 2017, http://www .istpravda.com.ua/articles/2017/07/13/150044/ (in Ukrainian).

206. Izabella Tabarovsky, "Is Ukraine's Holocaust Memorial at Babi Yar in Trouble?," *Tablet*, January 24, 2018, https://www.tabletmag.com/ jewish-news-and-politics/253736/holocaust-memorial-babi-yar.

207. See http://www.president.gov.ua/documents/3312017-22866.

208. Sam Sokol, "Anxiety over far-right role in Ukraine's plans to mark Babi Yar anniversary," *Jewish Chronicle*, February 25, 2018, https://www.thejc.com/news/world/anxiety-over-far-right-involvement-in-ukraine-s-plans-to-commemorate-babi-yar-bohdan-chervak-1.459389.

CHAPTER FIVE

1. Sam Sokol, "Ukrainian president to 'Post': We do not allow Russia to affect our ties with Israel," *Jerusalem Post*, December 23, 2015, https://www.jpost.com/printarticle.aspx?id=438130.
2. See https://mfa.gov.ua/ua/press-center/news/46968-shhodo-priz nachennya-specialynogo-predstavnika-ministra-zakordonnih-sprav-ukrajini-z-pitany-zapobigannya-i-protidiji-projavam-anti-semitizmu-rasizmu-i-ksenofobiji.
3. Sam Sokol, "Kiev to appoint special envoy to combat anti-Semitism," *Jerusalem Post*, January 25, 2016, https://www.jpost.com/printarticle.aspx?id=388814.
4. Sam Sokol, "Ukraine's leader in the fight against Jew-hate bends Holocaust history," *Jewish Chronicle*, March 9, 2017, https://www.thejc.com/news/news-features/ukraine-s-leader-in-the-%EF%AC%81ght-against-jew-hate-bends-holocaust-history-1.434037.
5. Most Ukrainian Jews seemed to have little awareness of Zakharchuk. Dolinsky and Azman stated that they were unfamiliar with him, while Zissels and Arkadiy Monastirsky of the Jewish Fund of Ukraine stated that, while they had both met the official, neither recalled any significant outcomes from their talks. Zakharchuk also seemed generally unfamiliar with antisemitism in his country, stating—based on what he said were police sources—that there had only been four cases of vandalism at Babi Yar in 2015 and one in 2016. He also defended the decision to erect a statue of OUN member Olena Teliha at Babi Yar. A noted poetess and nationalist, Teliha, who died at the hands of the Germans and went on to become a national icon, was a colleague of Ivan Rohach, working alongside him as an editor at the deeply antisemitic collaborationist newspaper *Ukrainske Slovo*. For more information on Teliha, see Myroslav Shkandrij, *Ukrainian Nationalism: Politics, Ideology, and Literature, 1929-1956* (New Haven: Yale University Press, 2015), 175-190. For more on the erection of the

statue, see "A monument to the poetess Olena Teliha was opened in Kyiv," Radio Svoboda, February 25, 2017, https://www.radio svoboda.org/a/news/28332116.html (in Ukrainian). Zakharchuk justified the statue's presence by asserting that Teliha and other editors of *Ukrainske Slovo* were murdered by the Nazis because they had "helped some Jews to avoid to be victims of the Nazi regime." Ukrainian claims about Teliha were also picked up by the US Embassy in Kyiv, which presented her as one of the "women who inspire Ukraine." "US embassy in Kiev criticized for praising Ukrainian nationalist," Jewish Telegraphic Agency, March 29, 2017, https://www.jta.org/2017/03/29/news-opinion/world/us-embassy-in-kiev-criticized-for-praising-for-Ukrainian-nationalist.

6. It must be noted, however, that the announcement of his assumption of his position, despite most likely being intended for the purpose of external consumption, was made exclusively in Ukrainian on the foreign ministry's website and that journalists covering Ukrainian Jewry such as myself were not sent any press releases about him. Prior to my interview with Zakharchuk, I had been promised an interview with Prime Minister Groysman during a planned upcoming trip to Israel. The embassy stopped responding to emails regarding Groysman following the publication of the resultant article, and the promised meeting never materialized.

7. Prior to the revolution, President Yanukovych was reported to have engaged in similar activities, allegedly using American political fixer Paul Manafort to spread rumors that rival Yulia Tymoshenko and her supporters were "supporting anti-Semitism." See "Manafort and 'senior Israeli' spread anti-Semitism story to boost Ukraine leader," *Times of Israel*, September 14, 2018, https://www.timesofisrael.com/manafort-senior-israeli-spread-anti-semitism-story-to-hurt-ukraine-politician/.

8. Sam Sokol, "Reports of death of Jewish leader in Ukraine greatly exaggerated," *Jerusalem Post*, January 22, 2015, https://www.jpost.com/printarticle.aspx?id=388632.

9. Unlike the Kellerman case, however, there appeared to be a grain of truth in the Ukrainian reports. According to local rabbi Shalom Gopin, the separatists, thinking it was abandoned, did attempt to seize the building but were persuaded to leave without violence. See Dovid Margolin, "Lugansk Jewish Community: School Building Not Confiscated During Passover," Chabad.org, April 14, 2015,

https://www.chabad.org/news/article_cdo/aid/2917370/jewish/
Lugansk-Jewish-Community-School-Building-Not-Confiscated-
During-Passover.htm.

10. See Sam Sokol, "Separatist leader says 'miserable Jews' running Ukraine," *Jerusalem Post*, February 3, 2015, https://www.jpost.com/printarticle.aspx?id=389883; "Ukraine run by 'miserable' Jews: rebel chief," AFP, February 2, 2015, https://www.yahoo.com/news/ukraine-run-miserable-jews-rebel-chief-202600090.html.

11. Sam Sokol, "Top rebel leader accuses Jews of masterminding Ukrainian revolution," *Jerusalem Post*, June 22, 2015, https://www.jpost.com/printarticle.aspx?id=406729.

12. Sam Sokol, "OSCE denies rebel claim it will attend Donetsk conference on fascism and anti-Semitism," *Jerusalem Post*, November 8, 2015, https://www.jpost.com/printarticle.aspx?id=432407; "Anti-Israel fake on DNR TV," Channel 9, November 4, 2015, http://9tv.co.il/news/2015/11/04/216417.html.

13. "Pro-Russian TV channel in Ukraine said to combat 'zombie Zionists,'" Jewish Telegraphic Agency, April 22, 2014, https://www.jpost.com/printarticle.aspx?id=350076.

14. Afanasy Mammadov, "Alexander Kofman: 'I am against any fascism, including Jewish,'" *Lechaim*, September 16, 2015, https://lechaim.ru/events/6118-2/ (in Russian).

15. See http://mid-dnr.su/en/pages/news/anons-091115-sostoitsya-kruglyj-stol-priurochennyj-k-mezhdunarodnomu-dnyu-protiv-fashizma-0549/.

16. See http://mid-dnr.su/en/pages/news/kruglyj-stol-priurochennyj-k-mezhdunarodnomu-dnyu-protiv-fashizma-0556/.

17. Sam Sokol, "Ukrainian president to 'Post': We do not allow Russia to affect our ties with Israel," *Jerusalem Post*, December 23, 2015, https://www.jpost.com/printarticle.aspx?id=438130.

18. See https://www.knesset.gov.il/spokesman/eng/PR_eng.asp?PRID=11839.

19. See https://www.facebook.com/photo.php?fbid=10153914847231414&set=a.10150221290791414.348974.542996413&type=3&theater.

20. Sam Sokol, "Crimean Jews angry after Poroshenko says Russia instigating anti-Semitism," *Jerusalem Post*, December 27, 2015, https://www.jpost.com/printarticle.aspx?id=438513.

21. For example, Zissels was part of a committee of representatives of Ukrainian minority groups convened under the auspices of the Ministry of Culture that issued a scathing denunciation of Dolinsky for allegedly disseminating "false and speculative information about the allegedly high level of antisemitism in Ukraine." See http://mincult.kmu.gov.ua/control/publish/article?art_id=245 376501.

22. Will Stewart, "'Blood oozed through the soil at grave sites. You could see the pits move, some of them were still alive': The secrets of Ukraine's shameful 'Holocaust of Bullets' killing centre where 1.6 million Jews were executed," *Daily Mail*, August 24, 2015, http://www.dailymail.co.uk/news/article-3205754/Blood-oozed-soil-grave-sites-pits-alive-secrets-Ukraine-s-shameful-Holocaust-Bullets-killing-centre-1-6million-Jews-executed.html.

23. Efraim Zuroff of the Simon Wiesenthal Center explicitly accused Zissels of distorting history in order to "find favor in the eyes of the Ukrainian government." Zissels accused the *Daily Mail* of fabricating his quotes, a claim undercut by similar statements he subsequently made. See Sam Sokol, "Ukrainian Jewish leader accuses 'Daily Mail' of fabricating Holocaust revisionism quote," *Jerusalem Post*, August 27, 2015, https://www.jpost.com/printarticle.aspx?id=413494.

24. Olga Dukhnich, "Human rights activist Josef Zissels made a disappointing diagnosis for Ukraine," *Novoe Vremya*, May 1, 2015, https://nv.ua/publications/odin-iz-samyh-vliyatelnyh-otechest vennyh-evreev-stavit-neuteshitelnyy-diagnoz-ukraine-46467.html (in Russian).

25. See https://web.archive.org/web/20140707150801/http://www.eajc-moscow.info/?p=358 and "Jewish group cuts funding for Kiev office over criticism of Putin," Jewish Telegraphic Agency, July 3, 2014, https://www.jta.org/2014/07/03/news-opinion/world/jewish-group-cuts-funding-for-kiev-office-over-criticism-of-putin.

26. Cnaan Liphshiz, "Ukraine's honoring of war criminals leaves its Jews uneasy—and divided," Jewish Telegraphic Agency, August 16, 2016, https://www.jta.org/2016/08/16/news-opinion/world/ukraines-honoring-of-war-criminals-leaves-its-jews-uneasy-and-divided.

27. "Ukraine honors nationalists whose troops butchered Jews," Jewish Telegraphic Agency, May 31, 2016, https://www.jta.org/

2016/05/31/news-opinion/world/Ukrainian-authorities-honor-nationalists-whose-troops-butchered-jews.

28. See "Josef Zissels on the Ukrainian Insurgent Army," YouTube video, 0:33. Posted by Samuel Sokol, July 1, 2018, https://www.youtube.com/watch?v=1x3l8NXfmwU&feature=youtu.be; "Josef Zissels on Ukrainian police," YouTube video, 2:46. Posted by Samuel Sokol, July 1, 2018, https://www.youtube.com/watch?v=SSDkFUGBIh4&feature=youtu.be. In one talk touching on the Volhynian massacres, Zissels questioned the presence of Poles in the region, causing Dolinsky to accuse him of implying that the Poles were somehow deserving of their fate. See https://www.facebook.com/eduard.dolinsky/videos/1809076939124366.

29. See https://www.facebook.com/josef.zissels/posts/1917063028303818.

30. "Everything is unimportant, except the fact that they are Ukrainians and that they are heroes of Ukraine, who died in its honor while fighting against evil and injustice," he wrote. "But the propaganda makers in Kremlin's pay, as well as those who listen to them and who are too rooted in their stereotypes to open their eyes and see the truth for themselves, are still continuing their ritual howling about 'antisemitic Bandera followers taking power—the descendants of those who killed the Jews at Babiy Yar!'" Vyacheslav Likhachev, "The Jewish Division of Ukraine's Heaven's Hundred," Euro-Asian Jewish Congress, March 11, 2014, http://eajc.org/page34/news43797.html.

31. Ilya Grigoryev, "Jews of the Heavenly Hundred," *Jewish Observer*, no. 04/256, April 2014, http://jew-observer.com/tochka-zreniya/evrei-nebesnoj-sotni (in Russian).

32. Paul Berger, "Three Jews Among Those Killed in Ukraine Uprising," *Jewish Daily Forward*, March 18, 2014, http://forward.com/news/world/194722/three-jews-among-those-killed-in-ukraine-uprising/.

33. In an interview with the *Times of Israel*, David Benish of World ORT—the organization that funded Scherbanyuk's son's school—indicated that Scherbanyuk was Jewish. However, when contacted by this author, Benish indicated that he did not remember anything about that specific case and subsequently forwarded me a statement from Mrs. Ludviga Tsurkan, the principal of the ORT school in Chernivtsi, in which she admitted that Alexander Scher-

banyuk would not be considered Jewish according to the traditional definition.

34. Meylakh Sheykhet, a local Jewish activist in L'viv, told a similar story, informing me that he had spoken to Yosif Karpin, the head of the Drogobych community, who stated that Shiling was not Jewish.

35. When questioned regarding the challenges to his heroic narrative, Likhachev retorted (contradicting his own prior statements) that only one of the three had been affiliated with organized religion and that "to speak about 'communities' as a way to be a Jew in post-Soviet context means gaps in understanding of the situation." And while it is true that many Jews are largely disconnected from formal communal life in Ukraine, Likhachev's defense didn't seem especially credible, especially since he declined to provide contact information for anyone who could corroborate his claims.

36. See Dina Porat, ed., *Antisemitism Worldwide 2015* (Tel Aviv: Tel Aviv University Kantor Center for the Study of Contemporary European Jewry, 2016), http://kantorcenter.tau.ac.il/sites/default/files/Report%202015%20with%20graphs.pdf; Dina Porat, ed., *Antisemitism Worldwide 2016* (Tel Aviv: Tel Aviv University Kantor Center for the Study of Contemporary European Jewry, 2017), http://www.kantorcenter.tau.ac.il/sites/default/files/Doch_full_2016_230417.pdf.

37. That many incidents would go unreported is unsurprising. As Cantorovich wrote, many incidents occurred "without any adequate response from the authorities and law enforcement agencies." Ukraine's failure to address the issue of antisemitism in a serious way likely deterred some victims from coming forward. It is important to note that according to a 2015 report by the European Union's Fundamental Rights Agency (FRA), "few EU member states operate official data collection mechanisms that record antisemitic incidents in any great detail," a failing that "limits the ability of policy makers" to come to grips with rising Judeophobia. See Sam Sokol, "'Gross under-reporting' of anti-Semitism plagues Europe, says EU agency," *Jerusalem Post*, September 30, 2015, https://www.jpost.com/printarticle.aspx?id=419500.

38. "Chabad rabbi beaten in Ukraine dies of injuries 6 months after attack," Jewish Telegraphic Agency, April 16, 2017, https://www

.jta.org/2017/04/16/news-opinion/world/chabad-rabbi-beaten-in-ukraine-dies-of-injuries-6-months-after-attack.

39. Sam Sokol, "I Thought There Was Going to Be a Pogrom," *Mishpacha*, December 28, 2016, http://www.mishpacha.com/Browse/Article/7002/I-Thought-There-Was-Going-to-Be-a-Pogrom.

40. "Uman, synagogue and antisemitism: pogrom, pig head and swastika," RIA Novosti Ukraine, December 22, 2016, https://rian.com.ua/analytics/20161222/1019898287.html (in Russian); "Finding those responsible for the attack on the synagogue in Uman is a matter of honor for law enforcement, Groysman points out," Interfax Ukraine, December 21, 2016, https://interfax.com.ua/news/general/392252.html (in Russian).

41. "The attackers of the tomb of Rebbe Nachman did not arouse guard's suspicion," Radio Svoboda, December 22, 2016, https://www.radiosvoboda.org/a/28190593.html (in Ukrainian); "'Real Ukrainians are not involved in this'—Lutsenko on the desecration of the tomb of Rebbe Nachman in Uman," Censor.net, December 21, 2016, https://censor.net.ua/video_news/420426/nasto yaschie_ukraintsy_k_etomu_ne_prichastny_lutsenko_ob_oskver nenii_mogily_tsadika_nahmana_v_umani (in Russian).

42. See https://www.facebook.com/borislav.bereza/posts/166718725 9974040.

43. Christopher Miller, "Police Break Silence After Video Shows Far-Right Attack On Kyiv Roma," RFE/RL, April 26, 2018, https://www.rferl.org/a/ukraine-police-break-silence-after-video-shows-far-right-attack-on-kyiv-roma/29194216.html. Under Avakov, far-right groups such as C14 have been allowed to patrol Ukrainian streets, and there has been an uptick in attacks against the LGBT community and the Roma minority. See Josh Cohen, "Commentary: Ukraine's neo-Nazi problem," Reuters, March 20, 2018, https://www.reuters.com/article/us-cohen-ukraine-commen tary/commentary-ukraines-neo-nazi-problem-idUSKBN1GV2TY; Marc Bennetts, "Ukraine's National Militia: 'We're not neo-Nazis, we just want to make our country better,'" *Guardian*, March 13, 2018, https://www.theguardian.com/world/2018/mar/13/ukraine-far-right-national-militia-takes-law-into-own-hands-neo-nazi-links. See also http://khpg.org/en/index.php?id=1517275970.

44. See http://khpg.org/en/index.php?id=1479165299.

45. See http://khpg.org/en/index.php?id=1415367345. The credibility of any investigation undertaken by officers under Troyan's command can be considered automatically compromised, both because of his previous affiliations and because of his outspoken denial of political extremism in Ukraine. In an interview with the *Kyiv Post*, Troyan practically denied the existence of the far right, claiming "we don't have skinheads." Ian Bateson, "Former Azov Battalion leader works to clean up Kyiv regional police, his image," *Kyiv Post*, December 3, 2014, https://www.kyivpost.com/article/content/reform-watch/former-azov-battalion-leader-works-to-clean-up-kyiv-regional-police-his-image-373927.html.

46. See Eilish Hart, "Ukraine's Police Reform: What's Really Going On?," Hromadske International, November 16, 2017, https://en.hromadske.ua/posts/ukraines-police-reform-whats-really-going-on.

47. See Office of the United Nations High Commissioner for Human Rights, *Report on the Human Rights Situation in Ukraine*, November 2017, https://www.ohchr.org/Documents/Countries/UA/UA Report20th_EN.pdf; Amnesty International, *"You Don't Exist": Arbitrary Detentions, Enforced Disappearances, and Torture in Eastern Ukraine*, July 21, 2016, https://www.amnesty.org/en/documents/eur50/4455/2016/en/. Ukrainian law enforcement's credibility was further eroded in mid-2018 when Ukrainian authorities faked the death of journalist Arkady Babchenko. For more information about that case, see https://cpj.org/blog/2018/05/the-many-questions-about-arkady-babchenkos-staged-.php.

48. "Ukraine bans Russian media outlets, websites," Committee to Protect Journalists, May 17, 2017, https://cpj.org/2017/05/ukraine-bans-russian-media-outlets-websites.php.

49. Sam Sokol, "Journalists blast Ukraine for blacklisting Israelis," *Jerusalem Post*, September 18, 2015, https://www.jpost.com/printarticle.aspx?id=416524. While the vast majority of journalists on the list were legitimate newsmen, it is worth noting that among the banned Israelis were Max Lurie of cursorinfo.co.il, who was reported to have served as an election observer in the occupied Donbas, and Avigdor Eskin, a Russian-Israeli propagandist and a close collaborator of Russian hyper-militarist philosopher Aleksandr Dugin.

50. See http://comin.kmu.gov.ua/control/uk/publish/article?art_id=121879&cat_id=117238.

51. Coilin O'Connor and Andy Heil, "Historian Beevor 'Astonished' At Ukraine Ban On Best-Selling 'Stalingrad,'" RFE/RL, January 17, 2018, https://www.rferl.org/a/beevor-historian-ukraine-ban-stalingrad/28980932.html.

CHAPTER SIX

1. Sam Sokol, "Still Homeless in Ukraine," *Jerusalem Post*, March 23, 2015, https://www.jpost.com/Diaspora/Reporters-Notebook-Still-homeless-in-Ukraine-394774.

2. Sam Sokol, "Reporter's notebook: Ukraine rabbi tries to hold a dispersed community together," *Jerusalem Post*, November 19, 2014, https://www.jpost.com/printarticle.aspx?id=382209.

3. Office of the United Nations High Commissioner for Human Rights, *Report on the Human Rights Situation in Ukraine*, December 2014, https://www.ohchr.org/Documents/Countries/UA/OHCHR_eighth_report_on_Ukraine.pdf.

4. International Crisis Group, *Eastern Ukraine: A Dangerous Winter*, Europe Report no. 235, December 18, 2014, https://www.crisisgroup.org/europe-central-asia/eastern-europe/ukraine/eastern-ukraine-dangerous-winter.

5. Sam Sokol, "Sharansky: 2014 'a year of record-breaking aliya,'" *Jerusalem Post*, December 31, 2014, https://www.jpost.com/printarticle.aspx?id=386279.

6. See https://www.facebook.com/djc.dn.ua/posts/402306853276883. Aid was also distributed at the Luhansk synagogue. See "Hundreds of Ukrainian Jews receive aid packages at Lugansk synagogue," Jewish Telegraphic Agency, December 4, 2014, https://www.jta.org/2014/12/04/news-opinion/world/hundreds-of-Ukrainian-jews-receive-aid-packages-in-lugansks-synagogue.

7. Dovid Margolin, "With Russian Tanks in Ukraine and Winter Approaching, Jews Try to Subsist," eJewishPhilanthropy, November 16, 2014, http://ejewishphilanthropy.com/with-russian-tanks-in-ukraine-and-winter-approaching-jews-try-to-subsist/.

8. Sam Sokol, "Once Ukraine's kosher food basket, Donetsk now reliant on food packages," *Jerusalem Post*, June 1, 2015, https://www.jpost.com/printarticle.aspx?id=404740. See also Margarita Ormotsadze and Shimon Briman, "Kosher Ukraine: How to overcome the deficit," Forbes Ukraine, April 24, 2015, http://forbes.net

.ua/lifestyle/1392946-koshernaya-ukraina-kak-preodolet-deficit (in Russian).

9. Sam Sokol, "Ukraine conflict raises religious issue for Russian Jews," *Jerusalem Post*, November 4, 2014, https://www.jpost.com/printarticle.aspx?id=380768.

10. Sam Sokol, "Israel to provide aid to displaced Ukrainian Jews," *Jerusalem Post*, October 30, 2014, https://www.jpost.com/print article.aspx?id=380374.

11. Sam Sokol, "Diaspora Ministry official calls for expanded aid to Ukraine Jews," *Jerusalem Post*, January 19, 2015, https://www.jpost.com/printarticle.aspx?id=388190.

12. Sam Sokol, "Exclusive: Diaspora Ministry renews grant for Ukrainian Jews," *Jerusalem Post*, May 13, 2015, https://www.jpost.com/printarticle.aspx?id=403005.

13. Sam Sokol, "Ukraine's Jews praise easing of Israeli immigration policy," *Jerusalem Post*, December 12, 2014, https://www.jpost.com/printarticle.aspx?id=384439.

14. Earlier in 2014, the Israelis had also approved a measure providing escapees from high-risk areas with a NIS 15,000 grant over and above the standard absorption basket.

15. While it originally stated that "every Jew has the right to come to this country as an oleh," the Law was amended in 1970 to allow for the immigration of "a child and a grandchild of a Jew, the spouse of a Jew, the spouse of a child of a Jew and the spouse of a grandchild of a Jew, except for a person who has been a Jew and has voluntarily changed his religion." See the Law of Return 5710 (1950), https://www.knesset.gov.il/laws/special/eng/return.htm. In a backgrounder on its website, the Jewish Agency explained that the expanded terminology "not only ensured that families would not be broken apart, but also promised a safe haven in Israel for non-Jews subject to persecution because of their Jewish roots." See http://www.jewishagency.org/first-steps/program/5131.

16. Sam Sokol, "Tzohar opens center for verification of Jewish identity in eastern Ukraine," *Jerusalem Post*, July 5, 2015, https://www.jpost.com/printarticle.aspx?id=408084.

17. Sam Sokol, "Jewish Agency seeks to streamline Ukraine efforts as immigrants deal with war traumas," *Jerusalem Post*, June 26, 2015, https://www.jpost.com/printarticle.aspx?id=407210.

18. The Jewish Agency runs a network of absorption centers in Israel in which new immigrants are provided with free or heavily subsidized lodgings as they learn Hebrew and prepare to enter the workforce.

19. Sam Sokol, "Chief Rabbi calls on separatists to cease fighting as Ukrainian Jewish center hit by rockets," *Jerusalem Post*, February 10, 2015, https://www.jpost.com/printarticle.aspx?id=390615.

20. Daniel Schearf, "Russia-Backed Rebels Blamed for Deadly Rocket Attack," VOA News, February 10, 2015, https://www.voanews.com/a/2637702.html.

21. Sam Sokol, "Jewish woman killed in Ukraine; rocket hits near synagogue," *Jerusalem Post*, February 11, 2015, https://www.jpost.com/printarticle.aspx?id=390675.

22. See Irina Rudenko, "Three buses with immigrants collected and taken out of the ATO area in just an hour," *KP*, February 12, 2015, https://m.kp.ua/kiev/life/490381-try-avtobusa-s-pereselent samy-sobraly-y-vyvezly-yz-zony-ato-vseho-za-chas.

23. Sam Sokol, "Reporter's Notebook: Still homeless in Ukraine," *Jerusalem Post*, March 23, 2015, https://www.jpost.com/printarticle.aspx?id=394774.

24. Sam Sokol, "Savings of Ukrainian Jewish refugees from Donetsk stolen in Kiev," *Jerusalem Post*, February 23, 2015, https://www.jpost.com/printarticle.aspx?id=391913.

25. Sam Sokol, "Expanding its reach into Ukrainian aliya, IFCJ ups its aid to war-torn country's Jews," *Jerusalem Post*, March 24, 2015, https://www.jpost.com/printarticle.aspx?id=394871. For more on the conflict between the Jewish Agency and the IFCJ, see Sam Sokol, "Jewish Agency, IFCJ spar over Ukrainian immigration," *Jerusalem Post*, March 30, 2015, https://www.jpost.com/printarticle.aspx?id=395544.

26. Sam Sokol, "Reporter's Notebook: For Ukrainian communities outside the war zone, life must continue," *Jerusalem Post*, March 24, 2015, https://www.jpost.com/printarticle.aspx?id=394956.

27. Sam Sokol, "Reporter's Notebook: In Mariupol, a war only minutes away," *Jerusalem Post*, March 26, 2015, https://www.jpost.com/printarticle.aspx?id=395133.

28. See Sam Sokol, "Prominent Ukrainian Jewish politician arrested in security raid," *Jerusalem Post*, November 1, 2015, https://www.jpost.com/printarticle.aspx?id=431729; Olga Rudenko and Isobel

Koshiw, "Head of UKROP party detained on kidnapping suspicions; his allies outraged," *Kyiv Post*, October 31, 2015, https://www.kyivpost.com/article/content/ukraine-politics/ukrop-party-claims-its-head-korban-detained-by-sbu-401057.html.

29. Sam Sokol, "Ukrainian Jews call for government to free imprisoned politician," *Jerusalem Post*, January 4, 2016, https://www.jpost.com/printarticle.aspx?id=439290.

30. Sam Sokol, "Jewish politician on trial in Ukraine invokes blood libel," *Jerusalem Post*, January 7, 2016, https://www.jpost.com/printarticle.aspx?id=440685.

31. Sam Sokol, "Jewish charities strive to prepare for Passover amid war-torn Ukraine," *Jerusalem Post*, April 1, 2015, https://www.jpost.com/printarticle.aspx?id=395766.

32. Dovid Margolin, "Lugansk Jewish Community: School Building Not Confiscated During Passover," Chabad.org, April 14, 2015, https://www.chabad.org/news/article_cdo/aid/2917370/jewish/Lugansk-Jewish-Community-School-Building-Not-Confiscated-During-Passover.htm.

33. It is important to note that for a variety of factors, such as not counting people who obtained citizenship once in Israel, the Jewish Agency's immigration statistics are usually slightly different than those of the Ministry of Immigrant Absorption.

34. These statistics were provided by the Jewish Agency and Ministry of Immigrant Absorption at the request of the author.

35. By the end of 2017, the JDC had added more than 6,500 people to its aid rolls, many of them "working families with children facing job loss and financial strain." The figures quoted here were provided by the JDC in response to an inquiry by the author.

36. Figures provided by the Jewish Agency in response to an inquiry by the author. Despite the exodus from Donetsk, a member of the rump community that remained in the Donetsk People's Republic told the Russian-Jewish publication *Lechaim* that, as of December 2017, there were 3,000-5,000 Jews left in the city. "On the Sabbath, as before, 80-100 people come to the synagogue, and often these are the same people that came 3-5 years ago." See Simon Charny, "David Yusimov: 'The same Jews come to the synagogue of Donetsk as before,'" *Lechaim*, December 13, 2017, https://lechaim.ru/events/v-donetskuyu-sinagogu-prihodyat-te-zhe-evrei-

chto-i-ranshe/?fbclid=IwAR3OUwYHNzFwSSUAk9D0IesTsLWo
9qUknZdHttqokt9oWAHa0eaauvl4nKs (in Russian).

37. Sam Sokol, "Jewish refugees in Ukraine start building 'shtetl'—
     Tevye's modern-day Anatevka," *Jerusalem Post*, July 21, 2015,
     https://www.jpost.com/printarticle.aspx?id=409655.

38. Sam Sokol, "For Kiev's Jewish refugees, little thought about
     tomorrow," *Jerusalem Post*, February 7, 2016, https://www.jpost.
     com/printarticle.aspx?id=444084.

CHAPTER SEVEN

1.   This chapter is adapted from my coverage of the aftermath of the
     Ukrainian refugee crisis for the *Times of Israel*. See Sam Sokol,
     "Displaced by a brutal war, Ukraine's Jews start life anew," *Times
     of Israel*, January 26, 2020, https://www.timesofisrael.com/dis
     placed-by-a-brutal-war-ukraines-jews-start-life-anew/.

2.   Simona Weinglass, "Inside Anatevka, the curious Chabad hamlet
     in Ukraine where Giuliani is 'mayor,'" *Times of Israel*, January 31,
     2020, https://www.timesofisrael.com/inside-anatevka-the-curious-
     chabad-hamlet-in-ukraine-where-giuliani-is-mayor/.

3.   Stephanie Baker and Daryna Krasnolutska, "Rudy Giuliani Has
     Curious Links to a Jewish Village in Ukraine," *Bloomberg*, Novem-
     ber 27, 2019, https://www.bloomberg.com/news/articles/2019-11-
     27/rudy-giuliani-has-curious-links-to-a-jewish-village-in-ukraine.

4.   This section is adapted from Sam Sokol and Cnaan Liphshiz,
     "One of Ukraine's chief rabbis endorses siege of US Capitol by
     Trump supporters," *Jewish Telegraphic Agency*, January 6, 2021,
     https://www.jta.org/2021/01/06/global/one-of-ukraines-chief-rab
     bis-endorses-siege-of-us-capitol-by-trump-supporters and Sam
     Sokol and Anna Myroniuk, "Why is Rudy Giuliani close with this
     Hasidic Ukrainian rabbi," *Jewish Telegraphic Agency*, October 28,
     2019, https://www.jta.org/2019/10/28/global/why-is-rudy-giuliani-
     close-with-this-hasidic-ukrainian-rabbi.

5.   Rudy W. Giuliani (@RudyGiuliani), "Having a great conversation
     with the Chief Rabbi of Kiev, Moshe Azman. A truly wise man,"
     Twitter, May 21, 2019, 7:33 p.m., https://twitter.com/RudyGiuliani/
     status/1130874226620141568?s=20&t=qD5ZcFFEul6fvkQ2wjDDaw.

6.   Aubrey Belford and Veronika Melkozerova, "Meet the Florida Duo
     Helping Giuliani Investigate for Trump in Ukraine," Organized

Crime and Corruption Reporting Project, July 22, 2019, https://www.occrp.org/en/investigations/meet-the-florida-duo-helping-giuliani-dig-dirt-for-trump-in-ukraine.

7. Azman would later go on to endorse the January 6 Capitol insurrection in a Facebook post which he subsequently deleted. See Sam Sokol and Cnaan Liphshiz, "One of Ukraine's chief rabbis endorses siege of US Capitol by Trump supporters," *Jewish Telegraphic Agency*, January 6, 2021, https://www.jta.org/2021/01/06/global/one-of-ukraines-chief-rabbis-endorses-siege-of-us-capitol-by-trump-supporters.

8. This section is adapted from Sam Sokol, "Ukrainian Jews find both refuge, exile in Israel," *Kyiv Post*, May 9, 2019, https://www.kyivpost.com/business/ukrainian-jews-find-both-refuge-exile-in-israel.html.

9. See Sam Sokol, "Why most recent immigrants to Israel aren't considered Jewish," *Jewish Telegraphic Agency*, January 3, 2019, https://www.jta.org/2019/01/03/israel/why-most-recent-immigrants-to-israel-arent-considered-jewish.

10. Christopher Miller, "In Ukraine, Ultranationalist Militia Strikes Fear in Some Quarters," RFE/RL, January 30, 2018, https://www.rferl.org/a/ukraine-azov-right-wing-militia-to-patrol-kyiv/29008036.html.

11. Ibid.

12. "Amnesty Says Attack on Gay Event in Kyiv Shows Police Inaction," RFE/RL, May 11, 2018, https://www.rferl.org/a/attack-on-lgbti-event-in-kyiv-highlights-police-inaction-says-watchdog/29221677.html.

13. Tim Hume, "Ukrainian cops have ignored far-right attacks on Roma. Now they've turned deadly," *Vice News*, June 26, 2018, https://news.vice.com/en_us/article/a3amnb/ukraine-police-roma-nationalist-attacks.

14. "Far-Right Group C14 Wins Funding from Ukrainian Government," *Hromadske International*, June 14, 2018, https://en.hromadske.ua/posts/far-right-group-c14-wins-funding-from-ukrainian-government.

15. See "Guard at Ukrainian synagogue fends off ax-wielding attacker," *Times of Israel*, July 28, 2020, https://www.timesofisrael.com/guard-at-ukrainian-synagogue-fends-off-ax-wielding-attacker and Sam Sokol, "Someone Shot at a Synagogue in Ukraine, but

the Community Tried to Keep It Quiet," *Haaretz*, June 2, 2021, https://www.haaretz.com/world-news/europe/.premium-some one-shot-at-a-synagogue-in-ukraine-but-the-community-tried-to-keep-it-quiet-1.9869234.

16. See Michael Colborne, "Silence won't make the Ukrainian far right go away," *New Statesman*, February 22, 2022, https://www.newstatesman.com/international-content/2022/02/silence-wont-make-the-ukrainian-far-right-go-away.

17. Sam Sokol, "Analysis: Choice of Jewish PM undercuts long-held accusations of state anti-Semitism in Ukraine," *Jerusalem Post*, April 5, 2016, https://www.jpost.com/printarticle.aspx?id=450262.

18. See Sam Sokol, "With two Jews in the country's top jobs, what is next for Ukraine?," *Jewish Chronicle*, April 24, 2019, https://www.thejc.com/lets-talk/all/with-two-jews-in-the-countrys-top-jobs-what-is-next-for-ukraine-1.483338 and Sam Sokol, "Ukraine's next president could be Jewish—and it is not an issue," *Jewish Chronicle*, April 4, 2019, https://www.thejc.com/news/world/ukraines-next-president-could-be-jewish-and-it-is-not-an-issue-1.482565. Note that Russian Security Council Deputy Chairman and former President Dmitry Medvedev called Zelensky "a man with certain ethnic roots" who "gave up his identity" and "began to fervently serve the most rabid nationalist forces of Ukraine," comparing his presidency to "a crazy situation when representatives of the Jewish intelligentsia in Nazi Germany would ask for service in the SS for ideological reasons." See "Почему бессмысленны контакты с нынешним украинским руководством," *Kommersant*, November 10, 2021, https://www.kommersant.ru/doc/5028300.

19. See Sam Sokol, "In row over Holocaust history, Israel and Poland issue joint critique of Ukraine," *Times of Israel*, January 2, 2020, https://www.timesofisrael.com/in-row-over-holocaust-history-israel-and-poland-issue-joint-critique-of-ukraine and Sam Sokol, "Jerusalem issues rare critique of Ukraine's glorification of Holocaust deniers," *Times of Israel*, January 13, 2020, https://www.timesofisrael.com/jerusalem-issues-rare-critique-of-ukraines-glorification-of-holocaust-deniers/.

20. Sam Sokol, "Ukrainian PM, minister attended neo-Nazi concert in Kyiv," *Times of Israel*, October 27, 2019, https://www.timesofisrael.com/ukrainian-pm-minister-attended-neo-nazi-concert-in-kyiv.

21. Fabrice Deprez (@fabrice_deprez), "Volodymyr Viatrovych, head of the nationalist 'Ukrainian Institute of National Memory' reacts gracefully to Zelensky's victory with a picture of Germans doing the Nazi salute and the comment 'the majority isn't a proof of righteousness.'" Twitter, April 22, 2019, 8:33 a.m., https://twitter.com/fabrice_deprez/status/1120198826315350018?s=20&t=XRwOLcZrMMU6cTAAlj7Msw.

22. Sam Sokol, "Ukraine fires historian criticized for rehabilitating wartime nationalists," *Jewish Chronicle*, September 19, 2019, https://www.thejc.com/news/world/ukraine-fires-historian-criticised-for-rehabilitating-wartime-nationalists-1.488880.

23. "Що чекає УІНП? Бліц із кандидатами на посаду голови. ЕКСКЛЮЗИВ," *Istorychna Pravda*, November 20, 2019, https://www.istpravda.com.ua/columns/2019/11/20/156576 and Sam Sokol, "Ukraine to revise its war history—again," *Jewish Chronicle*, December 11, 2019, https://www.thejc.com/lets-talk/all/ukraine-to-revise-its-war-history-again-1.494280.

24. Sam Sokol, "Ukraine's new memory czar tones down glorification of war criminals," *Times of Israel*, June 23, 2020, https://www.timesofisrael.com/ukraines-new-memory-czar-tones-down-glorification-of-war-criminals/.

25. Sam Sokol, "Ukrainian Official Changes Tune on 'Unacceptable' March Honoring SS Unit," *Haaretz*, May 4, 2021, https://www.haaretz.com/world-news/europe/.premium-ukrainian-official-changes-tune-on-unacceptable-march-honoring-ss-unit-1.9772739.

26. Sam Sokol, "Ukrainian Parliament Accepts Resignation of Minister Seen as Far-right Patron," *Haaretz*, July 15, 2021, https://www.haaretz.com/world-news/europe/.premium-ukrainian-parliament-accepts-resignation-of-minister-seen-as-far-right-patron-1.10002868.

27. Sam Sokol, "For Ukraine's Far Right, War With Russia Can Be an Opportunity," *Haaretz*, February 19, 2022, https://www.haaretz.com/world-news/europe/for-ukraine-s-far-right-war-with-russia-can-be-an-opportunity-1.10618564.

CHAPTER EIGHT

1. Sam Sokol, "Ukrainian Jews Prepare for Worst, Pray for Best and Vow to Stay," *Haaretz*, February 14, 2022, https://www.haaretz.

com/world-news/europe/.premium.HIGHLIGHT-ukrainian-jews-prepare-for-worst-pray-for-best-and-vow-to-stay-1.10611283.

2. "Transcript: Vladimir Putin's Televised Address on Ukraine," *Bloomberg*, February 24, 2022, https://www.bloomberg.com/news/articles/2022-02-24/full-transcript-vladimir-putin-s-televised-address-to-russia-on-ukraine-feb-24.

3. Eva Hartog, "In Moscow, Russians watch a show of Western aggression," *Politico*, February 23, 2022, https://www.politico.eu/article/moscow-russians-watch-show-western-aggression/.

4. Sam Sokol, "Ukrainian Jews Angry and Appalled at Putin's 'Denazification' Claim," *Haaretz*, February 24, 2022, https://www.haaretz.com/world-news/.premium-ukrainian-jews-angry-and-appalled-at-putin-s-denazification-claim-1.10632913.

5. One communal leader told me two days before the invasion that he was more concerned about the possibility that Russia would stage antisemitic provocations than about a ground incursion. See Sam Sokol and Nastya Shub, "Eastern Ukraine's Jews Brace for Food Shortages and Antisemitic Provocations," *Haaretz*, February 22, 2022 https://www.haaretz.com/world-news/europe/.premium-eastern-ukraine-s-jews-brace-for-food-shortages-and-antisemitic-provocations-1.10628147.

6. Sam Sokol, "Kremlin Fires Back at Yad Vashem: We'll Show You Mass Graves in East Ukraine," *Haaretz*, March 2, 2022, https://www.haaretz.com/israel-news/.premium.HIGHLIGHT-kremlin-fires-back-at-yad-vashem-we-ll-show-you-mass-graves-in-east-ukraine-1.10647038.

7. Sam Sokol, "Ukrainian Jews Angry and Appalled at Putin's 'Denazification' Claim," *Haaretz*, February 24, 2022, https://www.haaretz.com/world-news/.premium-ukrainian-jews-angry-and-appalled-at-putin-s-denazification-claim-1.10632913.

8. Ibid.

9. Ishay Coen (@ishaycoen), "Morning prayers and explosions. Commemoration of Rabbi Nachman of Breslov in Uman, this morning" (in Hebrew), Twitter, February 24, 2022, 7:59 a.m., https://twitter.com/ishaycoen/status/1496726551026675714?s=20&t=8MAmFBJZW6aRaR4rNW0t4g and Sam Sokol (@SamuelSokol), "Jews pray in Kharkiv as the sounds of battle echo through the synagogue," Twitter, 25 February 25, 2022, 10:43 a.m., https://twitter.com/SamuelSokol/status/1497130234931470350?s=20&t=o13bV4PyZsWdNYaAjM4Pbg.

10. Sam Sokol, "Moldovan Jewish Community Mobilizes to Help Evacuate Ukrainian Jews," *Haaretz*, February 24, 2022, https://www.haaretz.com/world-news/europe/.premium-moldovan-jewish-community-mobilizes-to-help-evacuate-ukrainian-jews-1.10632225.

11. Sam Sokol, "Jews Begin Evacuating from Ukraine's Odessa as Russia Attacks, Israel Pledges Aid," *Haaretz*, February 24, 2022, https://www.haaretz.com/world-news/europe/.premium-jews-begin-evacuating-from-ukraine-s-odessa-as-russia-attacks-israel-pledges-aid-1.10633499. See also Sam Sokol (@SamuelSokol), "A spokesman for the Jewish community in Moldova says that hundreds of Jewish refugees from Ukraine have already arrived since the start of the invasion early Thursday morning," Twitter, 25 February 25, 2022, 10:14 a.m., https://twitter.com/SamuelSokol/status/1497122858014760975?s=20&t=0MAzoFDgtM0MQINHo_njRQ.

12. Sam Sokol, "Still Reeling from Last War with Russia, Ukrainian Jews Are Staying in Place for Now," *Haaretz*, January 20, 2022, https://www.haaretz.com/world-news/europe/.premium-still-reeling-from-last-war-with-russia-ukrainian-jews-are-staying-in-place-for-now-1.10554319.

13. Sam Sokol, "Ukrainian Jews Prepare for Worst, Pray for Best and Vow to Stay," *Haaretz*, February 14, 2022, https://www.haaretz.com/world-news/europe/.premium.HIGHLIGHT-ukrainian-jews-prepare-for-worst-pray-for-best-and-vow-to-stay-1.10611283.

14. Sam Sokol, "At Babi Yar, Top Ukrainian Rabbi Urges Putin Not to Invade," *Haaretz*, January 27, 2022, https://www.haaretz.com/jewish/.premium-at-site-of-babi-yar-massacre-top-ukrainian-rabbi-urges-putin-not-to-invade-1.10571154 and Sam Sokol and Nastya Shub, "Eastern Ukraine's Jews Brace for Food Shortages and Antisemitic Provocations," *Haaretz*, February 22, 2022, https://www.haaretz.com/world-news/europe/.premium-eastern-ukraine-s-jews-brace-for-food-shortages-and-antisemitic-provocations-1.10628147. See also Sam Sokol (@SamuelSokol), "Rabbi Azman of Kyiv holds a havdalah ceremony to end the sabbath at his Anatevka compound outside Kyiv. He has invited any members of the community who can get out to join him there," Twitter, February 26, 2022, 9:34 p.m., https://twitter.com/SamuelSokol/status/1497656434036666368?s=20&t=wRKnQIKclpf5-uHgq9QOyA.

15. Judy Maltz, "Jewish Agency 'Flooded' with Requests from Jews in Ukraine," *Haaretz*, February 24, 2022, https://www.haaretz.com/israel-news/.premium-jewish-agency-flooded-with-requests-from-jews-in-ukraine-desperate-to-get-out-1.10632804.

16. Sam Sokol (@SamuelSokol), "He prefaces his remarks by saying הדרן עלך, an Aramaic phrase which means 'we will return to you,' to promise that the community will return to Odessa. הדרן עלך is best known as a phrase used to celebrate the completion of the study of Talmudic tractates," Twitter, February 26, 2022, 9:47 p.m., https://twitter.com/SamuelSokol/status/1497659721104465926?s=20&t=hE9yZoH4O94BzHw0GI-6-w.

17. Sam Sokol, "'History Repeating,' Zelenskyy Says after Russian Strike on Holocaust Massacre Site in Kyiv," *Haaretz*, March 1, 2022, https://www.haaretz.com/world-news/europe/.premium-russia-strikes-kyiv-tv-tower-site-of-babi-yar-massacre-1.10644774.

18. Sam Sokol, "Russian Strikes Destroy Centers of Jewish Life in Kharkiv As Community Members Flee," *Haaretz*, March 3, 2022, https://www.haaretz.com/world-news/europe/.premium-russian-strikes-destroy-centers-of-jewish-life-in-kharkiv-as-community-members-flee-1.10649500.

19. Ibid.

20. Sam Sokol, "Kharkiv Jewish Community Mourns Member Killed While Fighting for Ukraine," *Haaretz*, March 16, 2022, https://www.haaretz.com/world-news/.premium-kharkiv-jewish-community-mourns-member-killed-while-fighting-for-ukraine-1.10678734.

21. Marcus Yam and Laura King, "In Ukraine, a Holocaust survivor killed by a Russian missile is buried in haste," *Los Angeles Times*, March 24, 2022, https://www.latimes.com/world-nation/story/2022-03-24/a-youth-blighted-by-war-robbed-of-life-in-old-age-96-year-old-holocaust-survivor-is-laid-to-rest?_amp=true.

22. Sam Sokol, "96-year-old Holocaust Survivor Reportedly Killed in Kharkiv Airstrike," *Haaretz*, March 21, 2022, https://www.haaretz.com/world-news/europe/96-year-old-holocaust-survivor-reportedly-killed-in-kharkiv-airstrike-1.10688521.

23. Sam Sokol, "Yad Vashem Condemns Russian Strike on Ukrainian Holocaust Memorial," *Haaretz*, March 26, 2022, https://www.haaretz.com/world-news/europe/.premium-russian-strike-damages-holocaust-memorial-in-ukraine-s-kharkiv-1.10700207.

24. Sam Sokol and Anastasia Shub, "Russian Chief Rabbi, Seen as Putin Ally, Calls for End to Ukraine War," *Haaretz*, March 2, 2022, https://www.haaretz.com/world-news/europe/.premium-ukraine-s-chief-rabbi-condemns-russian-jews-for-silence-on-invasion-1.10646894.

25. Sam Sokol, "Russia Pressures Jewish Leaders to Support Putin's Ukraine War," *Haaretz*, March 24, 2022, https://www.haaretz.com/world-news/europe/.premium.HIGHLIGHT-russia-pressures-jewish-leaders-to-support-putin-s-ukraine-war-1.10696049.

26. UNHCR, the UN Refugee Agency (@Refugees), "11 days. 1.7 million people. This is now the fastest growing refugee crisis in Europe since World War II. In the coming days, millions more lives will be uprooted, unless there is an immediate end to this senseless conflict," Twitter, March 7, 2022, 3:15 p.m., https://twitter.com/Refugees/status/1500822336672608262?s=20&t=-gnW93pWlX2h7bp0iC1wkw.

27. Sam Sokol, "Jewish Agency Gearing Up for Massive Wave of Ukraine Aliyah Amid Russia Fighting," *Haaretz*, March 2, 2022, https://www.haaretz.com/israel-news/.premium-jewish-agency-gearing-up-for-massive-wave-of-ukraine-aliyah-1.10647572.

28. Summary of press briefing from Lviv by Karolina Lindholm Billing, UNHCR Representative to Ukraine, March 25, 2022, https://www.unhcr.org/news/briefing/2022/3/623da5894/month-since-start-war-quarter-ukraines-population-displaced.html.

29. Sam Sokol (@SamuelSokol), "From GPO: Prime Minister Naftali Bennett and Aliyah and Integration Minister [...] Pnina Tamano Shete [sic] have appointed Meir Spiegler as Director of the National Task Force on the Integration of Aliyah from Ukraine, Russia and the countries of the CIS," Twitter, March 7, 2022, 10:06 p.m., https://twitter.com/SamuelSokol/status/1500925863843536904?s=20&t=3E6931-n6qfuMxfAIF-xYw.

30. Sam Sokol, "'From Here We Can Do a Lot More': Kyiv Chief Rabbi Lands in Israel to Lobby for Ukraine Aid," *Haaretz*, March 3, 2022, https://www.haaretz.com/israel-news/.premium-from-here-we-can-do-a-lot-more-kyiv-chief-rabbi-lands-in-israel-to-lobby-for-aid-1.10650949.

A Note on Jewish Identity

Over the course of the first phase of the conflict described in this book (2014-2018), more than 30,000 refugees fled Ukraine for Israel. Although most of those who arrived in the Jewish state during the first great migration from the Soviet Union in the 1990s were considered Jewish according to both official Soviet taxonomies and the Orthodox interpretation of Halacha (Jewish religious law), the majority of recent immigrants (olim in Hebrew) have been classified by the Israeli Interior Ministry as "having no religion."* While they are descended from Jews and were thus eligible for Israeli citizenship, they are not considered Jewish according to Orthodox religious standards and are thus unable to marry through the state Rabbinical system. Nevertheless, for the purposes of this book, I have referred to anyone eligible for Israeli citizenship as Jewish, choosing to sidestep the political and religious debates raging both in Israel and the Diaspora. The contentious religious status of many of those who fled Ukraine over the past several years may help explain

---

*   See Sam Sokol, "Why most new immigrants to Israel aren't considered Jewish," *Times of Israel*, January 4, 2019, https://www.timesofisrael.com/why-most-new-immigrants-to-israel-arent-considered-jewish/. For a more in-depth treatment of the issue, see Vladimir Khanin, *Joining the Jewish Collective: Formalizing the Jewish Status of Repatriates from the Former Soviet Union in the Post Communist Era* (Jerusalem: Israel Ministry of Aliyah and Immigrant Absorption, May 2014).

discrepancies between available Ukrainian Jewish demographic data and immigration records that may perplex readers. That being said, nearly every member of the Ukrainian Jewish community mentioned in this book is Jewish both according to all relevant standards.

About the Author

Sam Sokol is a reporter for *Haaretz*, Israel's oldest and most venerated newspaper, and a Research Fellow at the Institute for Global Antisemitism and Policy (ISGAP). He was previously a correspondent at the *Jerusalem Post* and has reported for the Jewish Telegraphic Agency, the Israel Broadcasting Authority, and the *Times of Israel*. He lives in Bet Shemesh with his wife Chava and seven children.

He tweets at @samuelsokol.

www.ingramcontent.com/pod-product-compliance
Lightning Source LLC
LaVergne TN
LVHW090922060325
805171LV00001B/18